RAIL 99 FAIR

California Calls You

California State Railroad Museum & Foundation

For ten days–June 18-27, 1999–one of the largest and most elaborate railroad festivals in the world will take place in Old Sacramento, California: *Railfair '99*. Visiting locomotives and railroad cars, train rides, live entertainment and performances, unique and colorful exhibits, children's activities, and living history demonstrations will make this an event for the whole family. Join us as the California State Railroad Museum celebrates the many ways railroads have helped transform California from a distant, mythical land into one of the most diverse and productive regions on earth.

Railfair '99 will tell the story of 170 years of growth, progress, and westward expansion. It will celebrate the many ways in which railroads have shaped our lives, our economy, and our culture. It will use the railroad–its workers, equipment, music, experiences, and heritage–as a way to understand who we are as a people and what is so special about the Golden State. As with past Railfairs at the California State Railroad Museum–in both 1981 and 1991–this is a celebration that history and technology enthusiasts everywhere won't want to miss! Mark your calendars now, and make plans soon: *California Calls You* to *Railfair '99*!

Biggest News Since the Gold Rush

Railfair '99 Hotline (916) 445-6645 or visit our website at www.csrmf.org

Advance Tickets available at the Sacramento Community Center Box Office 916-264-5181 or all Bass Tickets locations (outside California, call 800-225-BASS)

Membership information and Railfair News subscriptions call 916-322-8485 or visit our website at www.csrmf.org

For assistance with travel/hotel arrangements, call the Sacramento Convention & Visitors Bureau 916-264-7777

111 " I " Street • Sacramento, California 95814

CALIFORNIA STATE
RAILROAD
MUSEUM
FOUNDATION

CALIFORNIA STATE PARKS

cali5ornia
SESQUICENTENNIAL

 JUNE 18 - 27, 1999 • OLD SACRAMENTO, CALIFORNIA

RAILROAD ARTWORK

Color prints of WaterColor and Ink originals by Harvey Hoover, Railroad and Museum Artist. The style is the 1930's and 1940's orange crate label in bright colors and includes an information box for the important railroad information. Available in 36 Railroad theme designs. Limited number of originals available.

PRINT SIZING PRICES

6" by 8" print with 8" by 10" Mat . . . . $15 ppd . . . . . .Oak Framed $30 S&H $6.95
10" by 12" print with 14" by 16" Mat . . . . . . $20 ppd . . . . . .Oak Framed $40 S&H $6.95
12" by 14" print with 16" by 18" Mat . . . . . . $25 ppd . . . . . .Oak Framed $50 S&H $6.95
18" by 22" print with 22" by 26" Mat . . . . . . $30 ppd . . . . . .Oak Framed $60 S&H $6.95
20" by 24" print with 24" by 28" Mat . . . . . . $35 ppd . . . . . .Oak Framed $70 S&H $6.95

T-SHIRT PRINTS

Youth Size S-M-L . . . .$12 + $3.95 S&H
Adult S-M-L-XL . . . .$14 + $3.95 S&H
Adult 2XL . . . .$16 + $3.95 S&H
Adult 3XL . . . .$17.50 + $3.95 S&H

Full Color Brochure $3.00 ppd
Email:hhoover@lemoorernet.com

CHECKS-MONEY ORDERS-VISA-MASTERCARD-AMERICAN EXPRESS
Credit card order, include card number and expiration date

ANNE HOOVER ENTERPRISES
Phone 209-924-8634 • Fax 209-924-1868
368 Riviera Dr., Lemoore, CA 93245-9020
www.hooverstudios.com

Empire State Railway Museum's 34th Annual

Guide to Tourist Railroads and Museums

1999 Edition

KALMBACH
BOOKS

Copyright © 1999 Empire State Railway Museum, Inc., P.O. Box 455, Phoenicia, NY 12464. All Rights Reserved. Printed in the United States of America.

Cover Design: Kristi Ludwig   ISSN: 0081-542X

To the Museums and Tourist Railroads

Listings: We would like to consider for inclusion every tourist railroad, trolley operation, railroad museum, live-steam railroad, and toy train exhibit in the United States and Canada that is open to the public and has regular hours and about which reliable information is available. If you know of an operation that is not included in the book, please send information to the address below.

2000 Directory: To be published in February 2000. A packet that includes all pertinent information needed for inclusion in the 2000 Guide will be mailed to all organizations listed in this book. New listings are welcomed. For information, please write to:
    Editor—Guide to Tourist Railroads and Museums
    Books Division
    Kalmbach Publishing Co.
    P.O. Box 1612
    Waukesha, WI 53187–1612

Advertising: Advertising space for the 2000 Guide must be reserved by November 5, 1999. Please contact Deborah Simon at 1-800-558-1544, extension 654.

Publisher's Cataloging in Publication
(Prepared by Quality Books, Inc.)

Empire State Railway Museum's 34th annual guide to tourist railroads and museums.
    —34th ed
    p. cm.
    Guide to tourist railroads and museums
    Includes index.
    ISBN: 0-89024-404-9

    1. Railroad museums—United States—Directories. 2. Railroad museums—Canada—Directories. I. Empire State Railway Museum. II. Title: Guide to tourist railroads and museums

TF6.U5E67 1999   625.1'0074'7
                           QBI98-1058

Contents

Advertising Contents

TOURIST RAILROADS

TRAVEL

VIDEO

WHOLESALERS

Great Smoky Mountains Railway

ALL ABOARD

THE New 20TH CENTURY LIMITED

NEW YORK-16 hours-CHICAGO

NEW YORK CENTRAL SYSTEM

Preserving Yesterday For Tomorrow

NATIONAL·RAILROAD MUSEUM

Green Bay, Wisconsin

From the Fastest   *...To the Largest*

Eisenhower Train   Big Boy Engine

1999 SPECIAL EVENTS*

For brochure
or more
information,
write or call:

**National
Railroad Museum**

2285 S. Broadway
Green Bay, WI 54304
Telephone:
(920) 437-7623
www.nationalrrmuseum.org

* All events are subject to change

ANTIQUE AUTO SHOW ~ May 22

RAILFEST WEEKEND ~ June 24 & 27
(WITH THOMAS THE TANK ENGINE)

A DAY OUT WITH THOMAS
September 11 & 12

**TERROR ON THE FOX
HAUNTED HOUSE AND TRAIN**
During October 1999

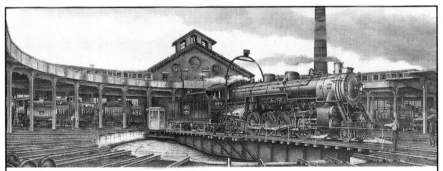

HISTORIC RAILROAD SHOPS

Georgia's State Railroad Museum -- The oldest and most complete Antebellum railroad manufacturing and repair facility still in existence in the U.S. Collection highlights southern industrial technology. Included are the massive Roundhouse, Operating Turntable, and the 125-foot Smokestack. Also, an HO scale layout of Savannah, shaft and belt driven machinery exhibit, and the oldest portable steam engine in the U.S.

Open daily from 10 am - 4 pm. Blacksmithing every Thursday.

For information on tours and private parties:

601 West Harris Street	**Phone: (912) 651-6823**
Savannah, GA 31401	**Fax: (912) 651-3691**

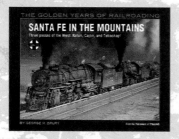

McCLOUD RAILWAY OPEN-AIR TRAIN RIDES

Bring the whole family for a delightful, inexpensive, excursion trip featuring either diesel locomotives or historic steam locomotive No.25. Try our new "double deck" car for incomparable views of unspoiled northern California.

Hear the "clickety clack" as your trains winds its way around the base of Mt. Shasta. Open Air Excursion Trains depart McCloud, California, late April through September 30th, with trips Wednesday through Saturday in mid-summer. Call for schedule details.

ALL ABOARD! SHASTA SUNSET DINNER TRAIN

A nostalgic train ride through spectacular scenery in the shadow of Mt. Shasta featuring elegant four-course dining aboard restored vintage rail cars. A memorable evening riding the rails into yesterday!

Experience true luxury in our 1916-vintage rail cars amid surroundings of mahogany and brass. Shasta Sunset Dinner Train departs McCloud, California, weekends April through December, Wednesday through Saturday in mid-summer. Reservations are required.

McCLOUD

To reach McCloud from I-5, take the McCloud/Reno exit and travel ten miles east turning left on Columbero Drive. Follow Columbero into town turning right after the railroad tracks.

For schedules & reservations call the

Shasta Sunset Excursions
P.O.Box 1199 McCloud, CA 96057
(800) 733-2141 (530) 964-2142

A-14

Once upon a time......

*A*merica was served by trains of classic design.

*T*oday, they are largely only memories.

*E*xcept, at the museums in this directory where hard work and dedication of a few have preserved important examples from the glory days of railroading.

Visit them. Ride their trains. Patronize their efforts.

*A*nd, for action programs of the glory days of railroading look for our videos in their gift shops for we're just as dedicated to preservation of the imagery of the classic trains as the museums are to their collections.

For new releases see our ads in leading railroad magazines
Download our catalog on the internet at http://www.rrhistorical.com/hrv

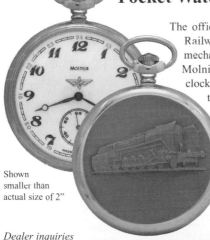

Leadership in Creative Railroading

TRAIN, Inc., the Tourist Railway Association, Inc. was formed in 1972 to foster the development and operation of tourist railways and museums. Membership is open to all railway museums, tourist railroads, excursion operators, private car owners, railroad publishers, industry suppliers and other interested persons and organizations. **TRAIN, Inc.** is the only trade association created to represent the broad spectrum of what is called "creative railroading".

Our members included in the Guide to Tourist Railroads and Museums may be identified by the **TRAIN** logo on their listing page. Members receive our quarterly magazine, **TrainLine**, which contains articles on creative railroading and railroad preservation. Our annual convention provides educational seminars, speakers of national import, updates on federal regulations along with product and supplier displays.

TRAIN, Inc. is a leader on issues such as insurance, safety and legislation affecting the operation and display of vintage and historic railway equipment. **TRAIN, Inc.** serves as a voice for the total industry and keeps members informed on laws , regulations and actions that affect us all.

For More Information Contact:

Tourist Railway Association, INc.

P.O. Box 1022
Madison, WI 53701-1022
1-800-67TRAIN
(608) 273-3470
FAX (608) 271-4339
Email address: office@train.org
Visit our website at *http://www.train.org*

Subscribe to TrainLine, the quarterly magazine of railroad preservation and tourist railroads. Send $15 and your address to the above address.

Passage to the Past.

The weather is always beautiful for a steam train ride.

Take a seven-mile, 50-minute round trip on a former Chicago & North Western branch line built in 1903, and experience small town America in simpler times.

Smell the coal smoke and listen to the lonesome whistle against the wind.

Depart on a train from a restored 1894 C&NW depot. Then visit the museum with its nationally acclaimed, restored, turn-of-the-century wooden passenger and freight cars. North Freedom is near Baraboo and Wisconsin Dells in the heart of one of America's favorite tourist destination areas.

Mid-Continent Railway always welcomes members and volunteers. Call 608-522-4261, or write P.O. Box 358, North Freedom, WI 53951, for brochure and schedule materials; or member and volunteer information.

MidContinent Railway

"Gifts for Railroad Buffs"

E & M Specialty Co. *established 1964*

ATTENTION GIFT SHOP BUYERS
Increase your selection - Increase your sales

Large selection of costume Jewelry - Men's Ties, Hickory stripe Aprons & Hot pads - Adult Puzzles Engineer Hats in adjustable sizes - Metal signs Wall clocks & Alarm clocks - Stationary Items Keychains - Suncatchers. Children's Toys and Books including Thomas the Tank Engine Merchandise. We also offer over 75 assortments of Die Cast Cars & Trucks.

NEW Address! P.O. Box 3766   Sparks, NV 89432
1 800/701-5464 • FAX 702/356-9117

See our display at the Seattle & San Francisco gift shows   Member **TRAINS**

A-21

Stone Consulting & Design, Inc.

Serving Shortlines, Tourist Railroads, Trolley & Transit Systems, Rail Foundations and Museums

Planning & Studies
- ⊗ Rail Freight Development & Planning
- ⊗ Feasibility Studies
- ⊗ Marketing, Ridership, & Financial Analysis
- ⊗ Museum & Station Facilities

Design & Engineering Services
- ⊗ Licensed for Engineering Services in __ states
- ⊗ Canadian Services provided through Northwest Theil Rail Consultants, Ltd.
- ⊗ Design/Build Capabilities
- ⊗ Project Management & Inspection
- ⊗ Track Inspection
- ⊗ Full CAD Capabilities

Operations
- ⊗ Shortline and Regional Rail Analysis
- ⊗ For-Profit Operator Selection
- ⊗ Ridership and Capacity Studies

Liaison
- ⊗ Professional Rail Consultant for Community & Industrial Groups
- ⊗ Class-1 Railroad Issues

Grantsmanship
- ⊗ ISTEA Grant Preparation & Assistance
- ⊗ Economic Development Grants & Foundation Fundings
- ⊗ Historic Register Nominations

Harvey H. Stone, President - registered as a Professional Engineer in over 25 states
Randall D. Gustafson, Gary E. Landrio, Paul A. Jannotti
327 Pennsylvania Avenue West, P.O. Box 306, Warren, PA 16365 (814) 726-9870
e-mail: scdemail@stoneconsulting.com   Visit our web page at www.stoneconsulting.com!

1999 RAILROAD TOURS

** SAN DIEGO & ARIZONA EASTERN SPECTACULAR - April 10
Charter train in Baja, California

** SAN DIEGO & ARIZONA EASTERN RAILFAN DAY - April 17
Charter train in Baja, California

** SACRAMENTO RIVER & RAIL STEAM SPECTACULAR - April 24
Charter steam on the Yolo Shortline & Sacramento River boat cruise

** WISCONSIN & SOUTHERN RAIL CRUISE - May 1-2
Charter on the Wisconsin & Southern Railroad Madison to Prairie du Chien and return

** NORTH AMERICAN RAILFAN SPECTACULAR - May 15-30
Railfanning in British Columbia - Alberta - Washington & Oregon

** CARIBOO STEAM SPECIAL - May 22-24
Charter steam on the British Columbia Railway North Vancouver to Lollooet and return using ex-CP 3716, a 2-8-0

** STEAM IN THE ANDES - July 10-18
7 charters in Ecuador

** GREAT PERUVIAN RAIL ADVENTURE - August 14-28
9 charter trains including charter steamship on Lake Titicaca

** WHITE PASS & YUKON SPECTACULAR - September 16-19
4 charters on the White Pass & Yukon Railroad

** NEW ENGLAND FALL COLORS SPECTACULAR - September 17-19
4 charters in New Hampshire during the fall colors

** CUMBRES & TOLTEC FALL COLORS SPECTACULAR - September 27-28
Charter freight and doubleheader in Colorado & New Mexico

** REDWOOD STEAM SPECTACULAR - October 3
Charter steam on the California Western Railroad out of Fort Bragg through the Redwoods

**McCLOUD RAILFAN DAY - October 17
Charter steam photo freight on the McCloud Railroad

** THE OLD PATAGONIAN EXPRESS ADVENTURE - October 23 - November 6
6 charters in Chile & Argentina including the famous "Old Patagonian Express"

** MEXICAN & COPPER CANYON RAIL ADVENTURE - November 13-21
All by private charter train from Mexicali including the last operating FT diesel, workshop visits, photo run-bys and sightseeing

Please call for our 1999 all-color brochure

P.O. Box 1997 • Portola, California 96122 USA
(530) 836-1745   FAX (530) 836-1748
1-800-359-4870 Toll Free in USA
http://www.trainsunltdtours.com

TRAINS UNLIMITED, TOURS

A-25

Empire State Railway Centennial

The Empire State Railway Museum proudly presents the
CENTENNIAL CELEBRATION
of our home
THE PHOENICIA STATION

"Gateway to the Catskills"

Phoenicia Station, December 1899. John Ham Collection

Now on the National Register of historic places, the Phoenicia station is well preserved and restored to its original condition. Come join us on weekends and holidays during the summer and see photographic and memorabilia exhibits depicting the station's 100-year history and the railroad lore of the beautiful Catskill Mountains.

For times and location, see our listing in this issue of the *Guide to Tourist Railroads and Museums* (see page 270).

We will see you this summer.

Members of E.S.R.M.
Lonnie Gale, Curator

Original Ulster & Delaware Station, Phoenicia, New York, March 1896. John Ham Collection

The railroad came to Phoenicia, New York, in 1870 and rapidly transformed this sleepy Catskill Mountain town into a bustling center of regional commerce. In neighboring Greene County, large resort hotels were springing up everywhere, and rail transportation to this area became a necessity. In 1881 the Ulster & Delaware Railroad built a 36-inch narrow gauge line, the Stony Clove & Catskill Mountain Railroad, from Phoenicia to Hunter in Greene County, beginning a rail era that mushroomed over the next thirty years.

The original station at Phoenicia was built in the early 1870s on a curve ¼ mile west of the current station. It was of adequate size to serve for years, but it was on a poor alignment, and when the narrow gauge line was standardized in 1899, the curve into the old station was just too tight for the larger, standard gauge trains. In 1899 a new station was built and the old one was torn down.

Three trains meet at Phoenicia, July 1930. John Ham Collection

With the coming of the new station and the ever-increasing number of trains, this busy junction at Phoenicia became known as "The Gateway to the Catskills." Traffic increased until in 1913 over 650,000 passengers traveled the old Ulster & Delaware. The Phoenicia station served as the main junction point between westbound trains for Oneonta and those of the Stony Clove Branch, both coming and going, for years. When the New York Central took the line over in 1932, things were no longer the same. The Stony Clove Branch was abandoned in 1940 and Phoenicia's importance diminished. In 1954 all passenger service ended, leaving the old U&D line as freight only.

The railroad sold the station to private owners who kept it in reasonably good shape until it was purchased by the Empire State Railway Museum in 1985. Since that time, the station has been restored to its original condition and is now open to the public on summer weekends and holidays.

Years of Catskill Mountain history will be on display at this old station, and you can enjoy it with us this summer when you visit our 100-year-old station at Phoenicia. See you there!

John M. Ham
Ulster & Delaware Railroad Historian

Empire State Railway Museum's 34th Annual

Guide to Tourist
Railroads and Museums

To the Reader

In 1966, railroad enthusiasts Marvin Cohen and Steve Bogen produced, and the Empire State Railway Museum published, the first *Steam Passenger Service Directory* (now titled *Empire State Railway Museum's Guide to Tourist Railroads and Museums*). At that time, tourist railroading was in its infancy, and the book featured 62 tourist railroads and steam excursion operations. Four years later, in 1970, the Museum and *Directory* sponsored a tourist railroad conference, and the Tourist Railroad Association, Inc. (TRAIN), was founded.

The tourist railroad industry has flourished over the past three decades, with local groups of rail enthusiasts and preservationists banding together to return to service locomotives and rolling stock that have sat dormant and neglected for too many years. The mission of these organizations includes educating and entertaining the general public. That's where the Empire State Railway Museum and this book fit in. Through the foresight and perseverance of the Museum, this book continues to be published so that rail enthusiasts, as well as those who are only casually interested in trains, can become aware of the hundreds of wonderful tourist railroads and railroad attractions available for them to enjoy and learn from. Kalmbach Publishing Co. is pleased and proud to be able to produce this book on behalf of the Empire State Railway Museum.

Guest Coupons: The reduced-rate coupons provided by many operations in this edition of the *Guide to Tourist Railroads and Museums* will be honored by the museums. Be sure to present them when purchasing tickets.

Brochures: Many operations offer brochures and/or timetables. Please see the symbol sections in the listings for those operations that provide brochures.

Every effort has been made to ensure the accuracy of the contents. However, we depend on the information supplied by each operation. Internet addresses, business office locations, and phone and Fax numbers are subject to change. We cannot assume responsibility for errors, omissions, or fare and schedule changes. Be sure to write or phone ahead to confirm hours and prices.

Symbols

♿	Handicapped accessible	🏛	National Register of Historic Places
P	Parking	✉	Brochure available; send SASE
🚌	Bus/RV parking	M	Memberships available
✳	Gift, book, or museum shop	**arm**	Association of Railway Museums, member
☕	Refreshments	**TRAIN**	Tourist Railway Association, Inc., member
🍴	Restaurant	🚄	Amtrak service to nearby city
👤	Dinner train/dining car	VIA	VIA service to nearby city
📷	Guided tours	MasterCard	Credit cards accepted
⛱	Picnic area	VISA	
🚂	Excursions		
🎨	Arts and crafts		

HUNTSVILLE DEPOT

Description: Built in 1860, the three-story structure is the only surviving antebellum passenger depot in Alabama and one of few in the U.S. It features guided tours of the three-story structure plus a model railroad with 15 trains running simultaneously on four different levels. Andy, the robotic ticket agent, and his friends tell visitors about life in the depot. The Phantoms of the depot exhibit includes graffiti written on the walls by Civil War prisoners and others that were housed in the depot during its history. Steam engines, rail cars, and other land transportation equipment are available for inspection. Tours of historic downtown on an air-conditioned trolley with stops and pickups at other attractions also.

Schedule: Monday through Saturday, 9 a.m. to 5 p.m.

Admission/Fare: Depot–adults $6.00; seniors $5.00; students 4-18 $3.50. Trolley–adults $2.00; seniors and children $1.00.

Special Events: Families First Depot, third Saturday in August. Call to confirm.

Nearby Attractions/Accommodations: EarlyWorks–a hands-on museum, Alabama Constitution Village.

Location/Directions: I-565 east, exit 19-Washington/Jefferson Street exit, right to Monroe Street, right to Church Street, depot on right.

Site Address: 320 Church Street, Huntsville, AL
Mailing Address: 404 Madison Street, Huntsville, AL 35801
Telephone: (256) 564-8100
Fax: (256) 564-8151
Internet: www.earlyworks.com

NORTH ALABAMA
RAILROAD MUSEUM, INC.
Train ride, museum
Standard gauge

NORTH ALABAMA RAILROAD MUSEUM, INC.

Description: Headquartered in the Chase Depot, the smallest union station in the country, the focus is on telling the history of the railroads in North Alabama and South Central Tennessee. The story is told through old photographs, maps, an A/V presentation, and a walk through display train. Ride 1¼ hours on museum's Mercury & Chase Railroad, which follows the route of Nashville, Chattanooga & St. Louis Railway's 1887 Huntsville branch.

Schedule: Museum–April through October: Wednesdays and Saturdays, 9:30 a.m. to 2 p.m. Train–Dates vary; contact for information.

Admission/Fare: Grounds and depot free; donations welcome. Train–adults $8.00; children under 12 $4.00.

Locomotive/Rolling Stock: Alco S2; 1926 boxcab; 26 pieces passenger and freight equipment; maintenance of way equipment; three motor cars.

Special Events: North Alabama Railroad History Festival, April 17-18; Goblin Special, October 30; Santa Train Special, December 4-5.

Nearby Attractions/Accommodations: Alabama Space and Rocket Center (home of Space Camp), The Huntsville Depot Museum, Twickenham Historic District, Dogwood Manor Bed & Breakfast.

Location/Directions: From east end I-565 in Huntsville, continue east on U.S. 72 for 2 miles, take left on Moores Mill Road for one mile, cross second railroad track, left on Chase Road for ½ mile to museum on left.

      M

Radio frequency: 452.325 & 457.325

Site Address: 694 Chase Road, Chase Community, Huntsville, AL
Mailing Address: PO Box 4163, Huntsville, AL 35815-4163
Telephone: (256) 851-6276 (voice on Wed. and Sat., otherwise recording)
Fax: (256) 895-0222
E-mail: fredrrman@aol.com
Internet: www.suncompsvc.com/narm/

ALASKA RAILROAD
Train ride
Standard gauge

ALASKA RAILROAD

Description: The Alaska Railroad, established in 1914 with railroad equipment used in the construction of the Panama Canal, provides passenger service between Anchorage and Seward and between Anchorage, Denali National Park, and Fairbanks. Scenic rides on 469 miles of mainline track through state and national parks offer passengers an opportunity to view wildlife such as bear, moose, beavers, and birds. Spectacular mountain terrain and optional tours are also available at stops along the way. Potter Section House State Historic Park, 10 miles south of Anchorage, features rail cars depicting the history of the Alaska Railroad. Small gift shops.

Schedule: Year round with limited service from mid-September to mid-May. Call or write for information.

Admission/Fare: Call or write for information.

Locomotive/Rolling Stock: Four rail diesel cars; 48 locomotives of various types; three Vista-Dome cars; seven coaches; six new coaches constructed in 1990; five diners/food-service cars.

Special Events: Call or write for information.

Site Address: 411 W. 1st Ave., Anchorage, AK
Mailing Address: PO Box 107500, Anchorage, AK 99510
Telephone: (907) 265-2494 and (800) 544-0552
E-mail: reservations@akrr.com
Internet: www.akrr.com

WHITE PASS & YUKON ROUTE
Train ride
36" gauge

DEDMAN'S PHOTO

Description: Built in 1898 to supply the Klondike Gold Rush, the White Pass Railroad is one of the most spectacular mountain railroads in the world. An International Historic Civil Engineering Landmark, the WP&YR offers round trip excursions from Skagway to the White Pass Summit, Lake Bennett, and through rail/bus connections to Whitehorse, Yukon.

Schedule: May 15 through September 20: daily. Summit Excursion–depart Skagway 8:30 a.m. and 1 p.m., 3-hour round trip and Lake Bennett Adventure 8 a.m. (8-hour round trip). Through service north-bound–depart Skagway 12:40 p.m. (train); arr. Fraser, B.C., 2 p.m. (change to bus); arr. Whitehorse, Yukon, 6 p.m. Through service south-bound–depart Whitehorse, Yukon, 8:15 a.m. (bus); arr. Fraser, B.C., 10:20 a.m. (change to train); arr. Skagway, Alaska, 12 p.m. Steam Train–June through August: second and fourth Saturday, departs at 8 a.m.

Admission/Fare: Summit Excursion–adults $78.00; children $39.00. Through service–adults $95.00; children $47.50. Bennett steam train–adults $156.00; children $78.00. Bennett diesel train–adults $128; children $64.00. Reservations recommended.

Locomotive/Rolling Stock: 1947 Baldwin no. 73 2-8-2; more.

Special Events: Centennial Ceremony at Lake Bennett, BC, July 10.

Nearby Attractions/Accommodations: Klondike Gold Rush National Park.

Radio frequency: 160.325

Site Address: 2nd and Spring Street, Skagway, AK
Mailing Address: PO Box 435, Skagway, AK 99840
Telephone: (907) 983-2217 and (800) 343-7373
Fax: (907) 983-2734
E-mail: info@whitepass.net
Internet: www.whitepassrailroad.com

MUSEUM OF ALASKA
TRANSPORTATION & INDUSTRY
Museum
Standard gauge

PATRICK DURAND

Description: Alaska Railroad locomotives and 26 items of rolling stock. Also, aircraft, boats, automobiles, heavy equipment, and other varieties of transport important in Alaska's history.

Schedule: Museum–May 1 through September 30: open daily, 9 a.m. to 6 p.m.; October 1 through April 30: Tuesday through Saturday, 9 a.m. to 5 p.m.

Admission/Fare: Adults $5.00; seniors and students $4.00; children under age 8 are free; family rate $12.00.

Locomotive/Rolling Stock: Alaska Railroad RS1 no. 1000; Chitina auto railer; EMD F7A no. 1500; USAF Baldwins nos. 1841 and 1842; GM Center Cab Diesel, Pullman McCord, U.S. Bureau of Mines Safety Car.

Special Events: Blast From the Past, July 3. Great Alaska Antique Power Show, August 21-22.

Nearby Attractions/Accommodations: Alaska Live Steamers 1.5" scale railroad is next door. Train ride, $1.00 each, operates the third Saturday of the month May through September; also holiday weekends and other weekends depending on weather.

Location/Directions: Follow signs at mile 47 of Parks Highway, north of Wasilla. Museum is ¾ mile west of highway, next to airport.

Site Address: 3800 W. Neuser Drive off Mile 47, Parks Highway, Wasilla, AK
Mailing Address: PO Box 870646, Wasilla, AK 99687
Telephone: (907) 376-1211
Fax: (907) 376-3082
E-mail: mati@mtaonline.com
Internet: www.alaska.net/~rmorris/mati1.htm

Arizona, Clarkdale

VERDE CANYON RAILROAD, LC
Train ride
Standard gauge

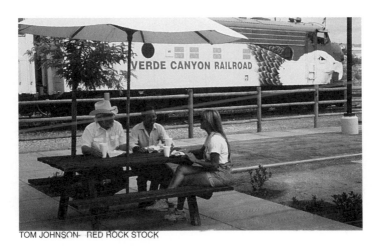

TOM JOHNSON- RED ROCK STOCK

Description: The Verde Canyon Railroad offers a panoramic rail experience into Arizona's other grand canyon, accessible only by rail. The flora, fauna, and rugged high desert rock faces are distinctive to this geological mecca. The train rolls past looming crimson cliffs, near ancient Indian ruins and passes through a 680-foot man-made tunnel.

Schedule: Year round: Tuesdays through Sundays, depart at 1 p.m.; summers at 9 a.m. March, April, May, October, November: add Mondays. March, April, October, November: Saturdays, double trains depart 9 a.m. and 2:30 p.m.

Admission/Fare: Train–adult coach $35.95; senior coach $32.95; children under 12 coach $20.95. All first class $54.95. Mini-museum/depot are free.

Locomotive/Rolling Stock: FP7 engines nos. 1510 and 1512 pull five Pullman Standards and two Budd Stainless Steel which access five flatcars converted to open-air viewing cars with canopies.

Special Events: Starlight Trains, June through October. "Throw Mama on the Train," Mother's Day. Firecracker Barbecue, July 4. Early Bird New Year's Eve Party, December 31.

Nearby Attractions/Accommodations: Room and ride packages with Sedona & Verde Valley motels, Tuzigoot National Monument, historic Jerome.

Location/Directions: I-17 exit 260 to Cottonwood, 89A to Clarkdale.

Flagstaff

Site Address: 300 N. Broadway, Clarkdale, AZ
Mailing Address: 300 N. Broadway, Clarkdale, AZ 86324
Telephone: (800) 293-7245
Fax: (520) 639-1653
E-mail: verdecanyonrr@cybertrails.com
Internet: www.verdecanyonrr.com

ARIZONA TRAIN DEPOT

Description: Store carrying most gauges and specializing in G scale, having the largest display of G scale in Arizona. Overhead train running as well as three on the layout.

Schedule: Year round: Mondays, Tuesdays, Thursdays, Fridays, 10 a.m. to 5 p.m.; Wednesdays, 1 to 8 p.m.; Saturdays 10 a.m. to 3 p.m. Closed Sundays.

Admission/Fare: Free to anyone with enthusiasm and a smile.

Locomotive/Rolling Stock: LGB, Lionel, Aristocraft, U.S.A., Athearn, Bachmann, Model Power, Lifelike, Mikes Train House, Mantua.

Nearby Attractions/Accommodations: Desert Breeze Railroad Park, Chandler Railroad Museum, McCormick Ranch Railroad Park, Grand Canyon Railroad, Verde Canyon Railroad, Sabino Railroad.

Location/Directions: Highway 60 to Mesa, Mesa Drive exit north to McKellips, east to Horne, right on Horne and an immediate right into mall.

Site Address: 755 E. McKellips Road (southwest corner), Mesa, AR
Mailing Address: 755 E. McKellips Road, Mesa, AR 85203
Telephone: (602) 833-9486
Fax: (602) 834-4644

MC CORMICK-STILLMAN
RAILROAD PARK
Train ride, museum, display, layout

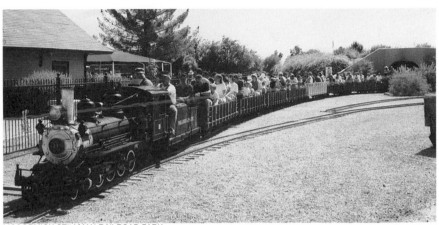

MCCORMICK-STILLMAN RAILROAD PARK

Description: A 30-acre theme park with train rides, carousel rides, railroad museum, retail shops, picnic area, two playgrounds, snack stop and model railroad displays.

Schedule: Year round: daily 10 a.m. to sunset.

Admission/Fare: $1.00 per person for train or carousel rides.

Locomotive/Rolling Stock: 5-inch scale locomotives. Steam–2-8-2, 4-6-0, 2-6-2. Diesel–GP-7, SW-1; 20 various cars.

Special Events: Railfair, October 10-11. Holiday Lights, December 18-January 3 (no December 24, 25, 31). Exclusively Little, March 7. Free summer concert series, May, June.

Nearby Attractions/Accommodations: Shopping, resorts, restaurants.

Location/Directions: Southeast corner of Scottsdale Road and Indian Bend Road.

Site Address: 7301 E. Indian Bend Road, Scottsdale, AZ
Mailing Address: 7301 E. Indian Bend Road, Scottsdale, AZ 85250
Telephone: (602) 994-2312
Fax: (602) 994-7001

OLD PUEBLO TROLLEY

Description: Operating trolleys through historic business and residential areas.

Schedule: Year round: Fridays, 6 to 10 p.m.; Saturdays, 12 p.m. to 12 a.m.; Sundays 12 to 6 p.m.

Admission/Fare: Adults $1.00; children $ .50; special fares on Sundays. Local holidays and other special events operate with lower fares.

Locomotive/Rolling Stock: Historic trolleys in operation and undergoing restoration; historic buses under restoration.

Nearby Attractions/Accommodations: Hotels, bed & breakfasts, numerous restaurants, shopping.

Location/Directions: Car barn at 4th Avenue and 8th Street.

Site Address: 360 E. 8th Street, Tucson, AZ
Mailing Address: PO Box 1373, Tucson, AZ 85702
Telephone: (520) 791-1802 and (520) 791-0225
Fax: (520) 791-4964
Internet: www.azstarnet.com/~bnoon/opthome.html

GRAND CANYON RAILWAY
Train ride, museum, display
Standard gauge

JEFF KIDA

Description: Grand Canyon Railway combines the nostalgia of train travel and the wonder of the Old West, creating a unique journey to Grand Canyon National Park. Departing from a historic depot in Williams, Arizona, the train meanders through uniquely beautiful terrain, arriving just steps from the canyon's rim.

Schedule: Year round: daily. Williams departure–9:30 a.m., arrives Grand Canyon National Park 11:45 a.m., departs Grand Canyon 3:15 p.m., returning to Williams at 5:30 p.m.

Admission/Fare: Adults $49.50; children under age 16 and under $24.95. Additional park entrance fee and tax. Upgrades available.

Locomotive/Rolling Stock: Steam: Nos. 18 and 20, 1910 Alco SC-4 2-8-0s; no. 29, 1906 Alco SC-3 2-8-0; no. 4960, 1923 Baldwin O1A 2-8-2 Diesel; no. 2134 GP7 Electro-Motive Division of GM Corporation; no. 6762, 6768, 6773, 6793 and B-unit 6871, 1959 Alco FPA-4.

Nearby Attractions/Accommodations: Kaibab National Forest, historic Williams, which has Route 66 running through the heart of town, golf course.

Location/Directions: I-40 exit 163 (Williams), Grand Canyon Blvd. ½ mile south to Williams depot.

Site Address: 235 N. Grand Canyon Blvd., Williams, AZ
Mailing Address: 123 N. San Francisco, Ste. 210, Flagstaff, AZ 86001
Telephone: (800) THE TRAIN (843-8724)
Fax: (520) 773-1610
Internet: www.thetrain.com

EUREKA SPRINGS &
NORTH ARKANSAS RAILWAY
Train ride
Standard gauge

EUREKA SPRINGS & NORTH ARKANSAS RAILWAY

Description: Five-mile round trip excursion trains. Diesel-pulled dining cars.

Schedule: Excursions 10 a.m.–4 p.m. Dining trains 12 and 5 p.m. daily. Closed Sundays, except Memorial Day, July 4th, and Labor Day weekends.

Admission/Fare: Excursion $8 adults, $4 children ages 4-10. Lunch $14.95, Dinner $23.95. All plus tax.

Locomotive/Rolling Stock: No. 1, 1906 Baldwin 2-6-0, former W.T. Carter; no. 201, 1906 Alco 2-6-0, former Moscow, Camden & San Augustine; no. 226, 1927 Baldwin 2-8-2, former Dierks For. & Coal; six commuter cars, former Rock Island; no. 4742, 1942 EMD SW1.

Location/Directions: Highway 23 north to the city limits. Site is located in northwest Arkansas, a short distance from the Missouri border.

Site Address: 299 N. Main, Eureka Springs, AR
Mailing Address: PO Box 310, Eureka Springs, AR 72632
Telephone: (501) 253-9623
Fax: (501) 253-6406

Description: Unique tourist lodging romantically secluded, nestled in the countryside.

Schedule: Year round: daily. Closed January 1 to February 14.

Admission/Fare: $95.00 per night.

Locomotive/Rolling Stock: Two Burlington cabooses.

Nearby Attractions/Accommodations: Eureka Springs.

Location/Directions: Two miles north on Highway 23 after crossing over the highway bridge on the upper gravel road.

Site Address: Highway 23N, Eureka Springs, AR
Mailing Address: 1473 CR 222, Eureka Springs, AR
Telephone: (501) 253-7143 and (888) 878-7246

WHITE RIVER SCENIC RAILWAY
Train ride
Standard gauge

WHITE RIVER SCENIC RAILROAD, INC.

Description: Enjoy breathtaking vistas, historical sights and engineering landmarks accessible by no other form of transportation. Recapture the romance and nostalgia of an era lost to our modern times and the scenery of the ancient Ozark mountains. Multiple routes and boarding locations to choose from.

Schedule: April through November: Wednesday through Sunday, two trips daily. Call for departure times, reservations, and winter schedule. Available for birthdays, reunions, meetings, or any special occasion.

Admission/Fare: Adults $23.50, first class $30, seniors $22.50; children 4-12 $17.50.

Locomotive/Rolling Stock: Alco RSX-4 (MRS-1) 1953, 1600 hp; one coach; two table cars; one power car; one platform lounge.

Nearby Attractions/Accommodations: Bull Shoals Lake, White River, Ozark Folk Center State Park, Blanchard Springs Caverns.

Location/Directions: Please call for directions to our various boarding locations.

Mailing Address: PO Box 40, Cotter, AR 72626
Telephone: (870) 435-6000 and (800) 305-6527
Fax: (870) 435-2062
E-mail: wrsr@southshore.com
Internet: www.trainfun.com

FORT SMITH TROLLEY MUSEUM
Museum

BRADLEY MARTIN

Description: Birney trolley on ½-mile track.

Schedule: May through October: Mondays through Saturdays 10 a.m. to 5 p.m.; Sundays 1 to 5 p.m. November through April: Saturdays 10 a.m. to 5 p.m.; Sundays 1 to 5 p.m.

Admission/Fare: Adults $1.00; children $ .50.

Locomotive/Rolling Stock: Birney 1926 American Car Co.

⑤ Ⓟ 🚌 🎁 🏛 M arm

Site Address: 100 S. 4th Street, Fort Smith, AR
Mailing Address: 100 S. 4th Street, Fort Smith, AR 72901
Telephone: (501) 783-0205
Fax: (501) 782-0649
E-mail: bmartin@ipa.net

FRISCO DEPOT MUSEUM
Museum
Standard gauge

CHARLES ELLIS

Description: Beautifully restored Victorian depot built in 1885. Operated by the Frisco Railroad 1901 to 1968. Static displays, audio-visual programs, historical figures. Guided interpretive tours available with advance notice.

Schedule: Year round beginning April 1: Wednesdays through Sundays, 9 a.m. to 5 p.m.

Admission/Fare: Adults $2.25; children $1.25; age 5 and under are free. Season passes available.

Locomotive/Rolling Stock: Frisco caboose SL-SF no. 1176.

Special Events: Big Boxcar Bazaar Sale & Exhibit held in conjunction with Old Soldiers Reunion, early August. Call for dates and information.

Nearby Attractions/Accommodations: Mammoth Spring State Park, Mammoth Spring Federal Fish Hatchery, camping, canoeing, trout fishing on Spring River, museums, antique stores in nearby Mammoth Spring and Hardy.

Location/Directions: Located in Mammoth Spring State Park on Highway 63. Twenty seven miles south of West Plains, Missouri, and 16 miles north of Hardy, Arkansas.

Radio frequency:
160.35000

Site Address: Hwy. 63, Mammoth Spring, AR
Mailing Address: Frisco Depot Museum, Mammoth Spring State Park, PO Box 36, Mammoth Spring, AR 72554
Telephone: (860) 625-7364, ext. 14
E-mail: mammoth@mail.oci-i.com

BARRY ROBINSON

Description: Located in the 1.5-acre former Cotton Belt erecting and machine shop. It contains the last two SSW steam locomotives and other railroad equipment and artifacts.

Schedule: Year round: Mondays through Saturdays, 9 a.m. to 3 p.m. Closed during periods of extremely cold weather.

Admission/Fare: Free; donations appreciated.

Locomotive/Rolling Stock: SSW 4-8-4 no. 819; SSW 2-6-0 no. 336; GP 30; SSW relief crane and outfit train; cabooses; passenger cars; snow plow.

Special Events: Annual Model Train Show and Sale, April. Mainline steam excursions with SSW 819.

Nearby Attractions/Accommodations: Jefferson County Museum in Old Union Station; Band Museum; Arkansas Entertainment Hall of Fame.

Location/Directions: Highway 65, Port Road exit.

♿ P 🚌 ✳ 📷 🎋 🚂 ✉ M 🚃

Site Address: 1700 Port Road, Pine Bluff, AR
Mailing Address: PO Box 2044, Pine Bluff, AR 71613
Telephone: (870) 535-8819

ARKANSAS & MISSOURI RAILROAD
Train ride
Standard gauge

ARKANSAS & MISSOURI RAILROAD

Description: Visitors can choose either a 134-mile round trip journey from Springdale or a 70-mile round trip journey from Van Buren. Both rides cross the Boston range of the Ozark Mountains.

Schedule: April through September, early November: Wednesdays and Saturdays. October: Tuesdays, Wednesdays, Fridays and Saturdays. Springdale–8 a.m. to 4 p.m. Van Buren–10:30 a.m. to 1:15 p.m.

Admission/Fare: April through September, November: Springdale $25.00; Van Buren $17.00; Saturdays add $5.00; October add $10.00.

Locomotive/Rolling Stock: 1899 B&M combine no. 102; 1917 DL&W (Pullman) coach no. 104; 1925 CNJ (Harlen & Hollingsworth) coaches no. 105 and 106.; all Alco.

Special Events: Please write or call for information.

Nearby Attractions/Accommodations: Numerous hotels in Springdale and Fayetteville, historic district in Van Buren. Devil's Den State Park near Winslow.

Location/Directions: U.S. 71 exit 52. Arkansas route 412 east to U.S. 71B. Route 71B north to Emma Street. East on Emma to tracks.

Site Address: 306 E. Emma Street, Springdale, AR
Mailing Address: 306 E. Emma Street, Springdale, AR 72764
Telephone: (501) 751-8600 and (800) 687-8600
Fax: (501) 751-2225

DESCANSO, ALPINE & PACIFIC RAILWAY

Train ride
24" gauge

WEBB PHOTOGRAPHY

Description: Passengers ride an industrial 2-foot-gauge railway to yester-year among 100-year-old Engelman oaks in San Diego County's foothills. The train leaves Shade Depot and makes a ½-mile round trip, climbing the 6½-percent grade to High Pass/Lookout and crossing a spectacular 100-foot-long wooden trestle, giving passengers magnificent views of the surrounding area. At Shade Depot and Freight Shed is a display of railroad artifacts, including those of the DA&P. Mail service with mailer's postmark permit cancelling is available.

Schedule: June through August: Sundays, 1 to 3 p.m., every half hour. September through May: intermittent Sunday operation. Rides and tours may be scheduled at other times with advance notice; please call to arrange.

Admission/Fare: Free.

Locomotive/Rolling Stock: No. 2, 1935 2½-ton Brookville, SN 2003, powered by original McCormick-Deering 22½-horsepower P-12 gasoline engine, former Carthage (Missouri) Crushed Limestone Company.

Location/Directions: Thirty miles east of San Diego. I-8 exit Tavern Road, travel south on Tavern 1.9 miles, turn right on South Grade Road and travel .6 mile, turn left onto Alpine Heights Road; the DA&P is the fifth driveway on the right.

Site Address: 1266 Alpine Heights Road, Alpine, CA
Mailing Address: 1266 Alpine Heights Road, Alpine, CA 91901
Telephone: (619) 445-4781

GOLDEN GATE LIVE STEAMERS, INC.

Train ride

2½", 3¼", 4¾", 7½" gauges

BILL STAUFFER

Description: Operating live steam club since 1936. GGLS is the oldest live steam club in the U.S.

Schedule: Year round: Sundays, weather permitting.

Admission/Fare: Donations appreciated.

Locomotive/Rolling Stock: Two steam locomotives 1½" gauge plus various club members' locomotives.

Special Events: Spring Meet, May 8-9. Fall Meet, October 9-10.

Nearby Attractions/Accommodations: Redwood Valley Railway 15" gauge next door.

Location/Directions: Tilden Park, East Oakland Hills.

Site Address: Berkeley, CA
Mailing Address: 130 Pereira Avenue, Tracy, CA 95367
Telephone: (510) 486-0623

REDWOOD VALLEY RAILWAY CORP.
Train ride
15" gauge

REDWOOD VALLEY RAILWAY

Description: A 1¼-mile, 12-minute ride through redwoods, laurels, and the scenic wilds of Tilden Park, passing through a tunnel, over a trestle, up and down grades, and around many curves. The operation re-creates an old-time narrow-gauge atmosphere with authentically designed loco- motives, wooden cars, realistic trackwork, and scale buildings.

Schedule: Year round: weekends and holidays, 11 a.m. to 6 p.m., weather permitting (no trains after dark). Weekdays, Easter and summer vaca- tions, 12 to 5 p.m. Closed Thanksgiving Day, Christmas Day.

Admission/Fare: Single-ride ticket $1.50, five-ride ticket $6.00, under age two ride free.

Locomotive/Rolling Stock: 0-4-0 no. 2, "Juniper," internal-combustion switcher; 2-4-2 no. 4, "Laurel"; 4-4-0 no. 5, "Fern"; 4-6-0 no. 11, "Sequoia"; freight-type cars with wood bodies, truss rods, and archbar trucks; Denver & Rio Grande Western-style eight-wheel caboose; nine four-wheel work "Jimmies"; weed-spray car; tie-inserter car; ballast-reg- ulator car; push car.

Location/Directions: Tilden Regional Park.

P   TRAIN

Site Address: Berkeley, CA
Mailing Address: 2950 Magnolia Street, Berkeley, CA 94705
Telephone: (510) 548-6100
Fax: (510) 841-3609
Internet: members.aol.com/rvrytrain/index.html

LAWS RAILROAD MUSEUM AND HISTORICAL SITE
Museum
Narrow gauge

LAWS RAILROAD MUSEUM & HISTORICAL SITE

Description: Original 1883 depot and agent's house, including over 20 other historic buildings with exhibits, and 11 acres of mining, farming, and railroad equipment. Located on the original location of the Carson-Colorado and later the Southern Pacific site.

Schedule: Year round: daily, 10 a.m. to 4 p.m. except Thanksgiving and Christmas.

Admission/Fare: Donations appreciated, suggested $2 per person.

Locomotive/Rolling Stock: 1909 Baldwin engine; no. 9 tender, cars, and caboose. Brill self-powered car.

Special Events: Pioneer Skills Day, call for information.

Location/Directions: From Bishop follow Highway 6 north 4.5 miles, then turn right on Silver Canyon Road. Look for signs.

        M

Site Address: Silver Canyon Road, Bishop, CA
Mailing Address: Box 363, Bishop, CA 93515
Telephone: (760) 873-5950
Internet: www.the sierraweb.com/bishop/laws

California, Buena Park

KNOTT'S BERRY FARM
Train ride
Narrow gauge

KNOTT'S BERRY FARM

Description: The Ghost Town & Calico Railway (GT&C) is America's only narrow-gauge passenger train operating on a daily, year round basis. America's first theme park and the newest member of the Cedar Fair family of amusement parks and resorts nationwide, Knott's Berry Farm is 165 wild rides, live shows and attractions designed for real family fun and adventure.

Schedule: Year round: Summer and seasonal periods, Mondays through Thursdays and Sundays 9 a.m. to 11 p.m., weekends till midnight. Remainder of year: Mondays through Fridays 10 a.m. to 6 p.m., Saturdays till 10 p.m., Sundays till 7 p.m.

Admission/Fare: Train fares are included with regular Knott's Berry Farm admission.

Locomotive/Rolling Stock: No. 41 "Red Cliff" Rio Grand Southern; no. 40 "Green River" Denver & Rio Grande and Denver & Rio Grande Western; railway coaches; special cars; Galloping Goose gasoline-driven railway car former Rio Grande Southern; more.

Location/Directions: Located 10 minutes from Disneyland in Buena Park, Orange County. Call or view website for detailed directions.

Site Address: 8039 Beach Blvd., Buena Park, CA
Mailing Address: 8039 Beach Blvd., Buena Park, CA 90620
Telephone: (714) 220-5200
Fax: (714) 220-5124
E-mail: pr@knotts.com
Internet: www.knotts.com

RAILROAD PARK RESORT
Dinner train, display
Standard gauge

RAILROAD PARK

Description: A 28-room caboose motel and restaurant, dinner house in refurbished train cars. RV park and campground on premises.

Schedule: Year round.

Admission/Fare: Room–$70 to $75 per night. Dinner average $15 per person.

Locomotive/Rolling Stock: Willamette Shay; snow plow, flanger; cabooses; speeders.

Special Events: Dunsmuir City Winter Rail Fare, February 14.

Nearby Attractions/Accommodations: Golfing, skiing, camping, hiking, lakes, fishing, boating and state park.

Location/Directions: I-5, Railroad Park exit. Forty miles north of Redding, just south of city of Dunsmuir.

Site Address: 100 Railrod Park Road, Dunsmuir, CA
Mailing Address: 100 Railrod Park Road, Dunsmuir, CA 96025
Telephone: (530) 235-4440
Fax: (530) 235-4470
E-mail: rrp@rrpark.com
Internet: www.rrpark.com

California, Eureka

MICHAEL KELLOGG

Description: Fort Humbolt's State Historic Park includes a logging museum. The exhibit emphasizes historic steam logging equipment used in redwood logging. Several artifacts have been restored to operating condition and are demonstrated on occasion by the Northern Counties Logging Interpretive Association. Two small steam locomotives provide short rides on a recently reconfigured right-of-way once a month during the summer. Cab rides are given to members.

Schedule: Museum–year round: daily, 9 a.m. to 5 p.m. Steam trains and equipment–April 24, 25, May 15, June 19, July 17, August 21, September 18, 11 a.m. to 4 p.m.

Admission/Fare: Museum–free. Train–adults $1.00; children $ .50

Locomotive/Rolling Stock: No. 1 "Gypsy" 1892 Marshutz & Cantrell, 12-ton 0-4-0, former Bear Harbor Lumber Co.; no. 1 "Falk" 1884 Marshutz & Cantrell, 9-ton 0-4-0, former Elk River Mill and Lumber Co.; loaded log car no. 40; riding car no. 10; more.

Special Events: Dolbeer Steam Donkey Days, April 24-25; demonstration of steam locomotives at various special events. Training for members interested in operating equipment, Spring.

Location/Directions: Off Highway 101 at the southern end of Eureka, opposite Bayshore Mall.

Site Address: 3431 Fort Avenue, Eureka, CA
Mailing Address: 3431 Fort Avenue, Eureka, CA 95503
Telephone: (707) 445-6567

California, Felton   ROARING CAMP &
                                   BIG TREES RAILROAD
                                        Train ride
                                       Narrow gauge

ROARING CAMP & BIG TREES RAILROAD

Description: Antique steam locomotives taking passengers on a 6.5-mile round trip through the redwoods of Santa Cruz County. Situated in the recreated townsite of an old time logging camp complete with 1880s general store, operating saw mill and chuckwagon barbecue.

Schedule: April through October, daily with additional departures during the summer. November through March, weekends.

Admission/Fare: Adults $13.75; children 3-12 $9.50.

Locomotive/Rolling Stock: No. 1 1912 Lima 2-truck Shay, former Coal Processing Corp; no. 2 1899 2-truck Heisler, former West Side Lumber; more.

Special Events: Civil War Re-enactment, Memorial weekend. Frog Jump and Race, July 4. Handcar races, July. Labor Day Roundup. October Harvest Fare, Thanksgiving Mountain Man Rendezvous. Pioneer Christmas, December.

Nearby Attractions/Accommodations: Winchester Mystery House, Mystery Spot, Marine World, Monterey Bay Aquarium, Santa Cruz Beach and Boardwalk, Paramount's Great America, Red and White Fleet, Pier 39.

Location/Directions: Off State Highway 17/880 to Santa Cruz, Mt. Hermon exit, 3.5 miles to left on Graham Hill Road, ½ mile to Roaring Camp.

*Coupon available, see coupon section.

Site Address: Graham Hill Road and Roaring Camp Road, Felton, CA
Mailing Address: PO Box G-1, Felton, CA 95018
Telephone: (831) 335-4484
Fax: (831) 335-3509
E-mail: RCamp448@aol.com
Internet: www.roaringcamprr.com

SANTA CRUZ, BIG TREES & PACIFIC RAILWAY
Train ride
Standard gauge

SANTA CRUZ, BIG TREES & PACIFIC RAILWAY.

Description: Our Santa Cruz, Big Trees & Pacific Railway carries passengers from Roaring Camp, through Henry Cowell Redwood State Park, then proceeds down the spectacular San Lorenzo River Canyon. After leaving the forest, this turn-of-the-century passenger train rolls sedately through a beautiful "gingerbread" residential section of downtown Santa Cruz. The train then stops in front of the Carousel at the Beach/Boardwalk in Santa Cruz.

Schedule: May, September, October: weekends. June, July, August: daily.

Admission/Fare: Adults $15.00; children 3-12 $11.00.

Locomotive/Rolling Stock: Nos. 2600 & 2641, CF7 1500-horsepower diesels, former Santa Fe; no. 20, 50-ton center-cab Whitcomb; three 1900-era wooden passenger coaches; two 1920s-era steel coaches; seven open-air cars; restored 1895 caboose, former Lake Superior & Ishpeming.

Special Events: Handcar races and motorcar rallies, July.

Location/Directions: Six miles inland from Santa Cruz on Graham Hill Road.

Site Address: Graham Hill Road, Felton, CA
Mailing Address: PO Box G-1, Felton, CA 95018
Telephone: (831) 335-4484
Fax: (831) 335-3509
Internet: www.furryfriends.org/roaringcamp/roaring1.htm

FILLMORE & WESTERN RAILWAY
Train ride, dinner train
Standard gauge

FILLMORE & WESTERN RAILWAY

Description: This railway offers rides through the citrus groves on a former Southern Pacific branch line. The trains have appeared in over 150 Hollywood films, television series and commercials. Many specialty train rides such as dinner trains, BBQ trains, senior trains, school trains, summer camp trains, wine tasting trains, wedding trains and more.

Schedule: Year round: weekends. Selected weekdays. Closed Christmas Day and Easter.

Admission/Fare: Daytime: adults $15.00; seniors $12.00; children 12 and under $6.00. Call for evening prices.

Locomotive/Rolling Stock: 1906 Baldwin steam locomotive no. 51; 1949 F7 engines nos. 100 and 101; more.

Special Events: Rail Festival, March. Orange Festival, May. Fourth of July, July. Pumpkinliner, October weekends. Christmas tree and Santa Claus train, weekends in December.

Nearby Attractions/Accommodations: Antique stores, museum, Magic Mountain Amusement Park, restaurants, hotels.

Location/Directions: On State Highway 126, midway between Los Angeles and Santa Barbara.

Site Address: 250 Central Avenue, Fillmore, CA
Mailing Address: PO Box 960, Fillmore, CA 93016
Telephone: (805) 524-2546 and (800) 773 TRAIN (773-8724)
Fax: (805) 524-1838
E-mail: fwry@earthlink.net
Internet: www.fwry.com

California, Fish Camp

**YOSEMITE MOUNTAIN-
SUGAR PINE RAILROAD**
Train ride
36" gauge

JOSEPH T. BISPO

Description: A museum housed in an 1856 log cabin displays railroad artifacts, antique Yosemite photos, and many relics of sawmill life. Steam
donkey engine and assorted rolling stock on display. The YM-SP operates a narrated, four-mile, 45-minute round trip over the restored line of
the Madera Sugar Pine Lumber Company. Track runs through the scenic
Sierra Nevada at an elevation of 5,000 feet, winds down a 4-percent
grade into Lewis Creek Canyon, passes Horseshoe Curve, crosses Cold
Spring Crossing, and stops at Lewis Creep Loop.

Schedule· Railcars: April through October: daily. Steam train: May 10
through September: daily. Late April, early May and October: weekends.

Admission/Fare: Railcars: adults $7.00; children 3-12 $4.00. Steam train:
adults $11.00; children 3-12 $6.00.

Locomotive/Rolling Stock: 1928 Lima 3-truck Shay, no. 10; 1913 Lima 3-
truck Shay, no. 15; logging cars; covered and open converted flatcars;
wedge snowplow, oil tank car, refrigerator cars, parts car, and more.

Special Events: Gold panning, outdoor concerts, Moonlight Special with steak
barbecue and music every Saturday night in summer; reservations advised.

Nearby Attractions/Accommodations: Location/Directions: Operating
in the Sierra National Forest, 4 miles south of Yosemite National Park
on Highway 41.

Site Address: 56001 Yosemite Highway 41, Fish Camp, CA
Mailing Address: 56001 Yosemite Highway 41, Fish Camp, CA 93623
Telephone: (559) 683-7273
Internet: www.ymsprr.com

California, Folsom
(Folsom City Zoo)

**FOLSOM VALLEY RAILWAY
DIV. OF GOLDEN SPIKE ENTERPRISES**
Train ride
12" Narrow gauge

TERRY GOLD

Description: A ¾-mile ride through a 50-acre city park features vintage wooden freight cars drawn by a ⅓-scale coal burning locomotive representative of late nineteenth century steam motive power.

Schedule: February through November: Tuesdays through Fridays, 11 a.m. to 2 p.m.; weekends and holidays, 11 a.m. to 5 p.m. December through January: weekends and school holidays., 11 a.m. to 4 p.m. All are weather permitting.

Admission/Fare: $1 per person.

Locomotive/Rolling Stock: 1950 Ottaway old-time wooder; truss rod-style freight car; cattle car; hopper car; five open gondola cars; bobber caboose.

Special Events: Train will operate all day until 10 p.m., week of July 4.

Nearby Attractions/Accommodations: Folsom City Zoo.

Location/Directions: Folsom is 25 miles east of Sacramento off U.S. 50.

Site Address: Folsom City Zoo, 50 Natoma Street, Folsom, CA
Mailing Address: 121 Dunstable Way, Folsom, CA 95630
Telephone: (916) 983-1873
Fax: (916) 983-1873 call first
E-mail: goldtown@juno or goldtown@jps.net
Internet: www.bylinusa.com/goldtown/

California, Fort Bragg-Willits

CALIFORNIA WESTERN RAILROAD
THE SKUNK TRAIN
Train ride, dinner train
Standard gauge

GARY RICHARDS

Description: Located on the Pacific Ocean in Fort Bragg. Come ride the Skunk Train where the redwoods meet the river.

Schedule: Year round: varies, please call or write for information.

Admission/Fare: Full day–adults $35.00; children 5-11 $18.00. Half day or one way–adults $27.00; children $14.00.

Locomotive/Rolling Stock: 1924 Baldwin 2-8-2 no. 45; 1924 Baldwin 2-6-2 no. 14; 1955 EMD GP9 nos. 64, 65; 1955 Alco RS11 no. 62; 1956 EMD GP9 nos. 66, 67; 1925 M100; 1935 M300; coaches nos. 655, 656, 657, 658, 696, 697, 698, 699, 700, 701.

Nearby Attractions/Accommodations: Roots of Motive Power, historic logging museum and railroad equipment, Fort Bragg, lodging, dining.

Location/Directions: Highway 1 and Laurel Street in Fort Bragg or Highway 101 and Commercial Street in Willits.

*Coupon available, see coupon section.

Radio frequency: 160.650

Site Address: Fort Bragg and Willits, CA
Mailing Address: PO Box 907, Fort Bragg, CA 95437
Telephone: (800) 77-SKUNK and (707) 964-6371
Fax: (707) 964-6754
E-mail: skunk@mcn.org
Internet: www.skunktrain.com

California, Fremont

NILES DEPOT MUSEUM
Museum, display, layout
HO and N

NILES DEPOT MUSEUM

Description: Historic 1904 Southern Pacific depot. Museum on mail floor along with N scale layout. HO scale layout in basement. Western Pacific wide vision caboose also open.

Schedule: Year round: first and third Sundays of each month, 10 a.m. to 4 p.m.

Admission/Fare: Donations appreciated.

Locomotive/Rolling Stock: Western Pacific wide vision caboose no. 467.

Nearby Attractions/Accommodations: Niles Canyon Railroad.

Location/Directions: In Fremont between Niles Canyon Road and Nursery Blvd.

        M Fremont (Centerville)

Site Address: 37997 Mission Blvd, Fremont, CA
Mailing Address: PO Box 2716, Fremont, CA 94536
Telephone: (510) 797-4449
E-mail: pnyhun@aol.com
Internet: nilesdepot.railfan.net

SOCIETY FOR THE PRESERVATION
OF CARTER RAILROAD RESOURCES
Train ride
36" gauge

RICH HILL

Description: This group is dedicated to acquiring and restoring railroad cars constructed by Carter Brothers of Newark, California in the late 1800s. The society currently has seven Carter cars and three other cars. The cars are restored using appropriate hand tools, following the techniques used in the original construction. The 1½-mile ride is powered by a draft horse, making this the only regularly scheduled horse-drawn railroad in the U.S.

Schedule: April through October: Thursdays and Fridays, 10:30 a.m. to 3 p.m. and weekends, 10:30 a.m. to 4 p.m.

Admission/Fare: Park admission–adults $5.00; seniors $4.00; children 4-17 $3.50; special events more. Prices subject to change, please call for information.

Locomotive/Rolling Stock: "Tucker" and "Jiggs" 1989 Belgians, 0-2-2-0T hay burners; 1940 Whitcomb no. 2 14-ton, former ASARCO; 1922 Plymouth DL 7-ton, former Old Mission Cement Company.

Nearby Attractions/Accommodations: The museum is located in the Ardenwood Historic Farm, which demonstrates life on a farm at the turn of the century. It consists of a historic farmhouse, blacksmith shop, farmyard, and operating Best steam tractor

Location/Directions: Fifteen miles south of Oakland at the intersection of I-880 and Highway 84.

          atm

Site Address: 34600 Ardenwood Blvd., Fremont, CA
Mailing Address: SPCRR, PO Box 783, Newark, CA 94560
Telephone: (408) 370-3555
E-mail: rkhill@worldnet.att.net

SOUTH COAST RAILROAD MUSEUM
Museum
Standard gauge

DAVID HIETER

Description: The centerpiece is the historic Goleta Depot, a victorian styled Southern Pacific country station. The museum features refurnished rooms and station grounds, and a variety of informative displays, including a 300-square-foot HO scale model railroad exhibit. Other attractions include miniature train and handcar rides, Gandy Dancer Theater, picnic grounds, and a museum store and gift shop.

Schedule: Museum–Wednesdays through Sundays, 1 to 4 p.m. Miniature train–Wednesdays and Fridays, 2 to 3:40 p.m.; weekends, 1 to 3:45 p.m. Handcar–third Saturday of each month, 1 to 3:45 p.m.

Admission/Fare: Museum–donations appreciated. Handcar–free. Miniature train–$1.00.

Locomotive/Rolling Stock: 1960s Southern Pacific bay window caboose no. 4023.

Special Events: Depot Day, September 26, 11 a.m. to 4 p.m.

Location/Directions: Goleta is seven miles west of Santa Barbara, U.S. 101 north exit Los Carneros Road.

Site Address: 300 N. Los Carneros Road, Goleta, CA
Mailing Address: 300 N. Los Carneros Road, Goleta, CA 93117-1502
Telephone: (805) 964-3540
Fax: (805) 964-3549
E-mail: scrm@silcom.com
Internet: www.silcom.com/~scrm/

California, Jamestown

TED BENSON

Description: Operated by the California State Railroad Museum, Railtown State Historical Park is one of Hollywood's most popular feature film and television locations. The Historic Sierra Railroad Shops at Railtown 1897 have been in continuous operation as a steam locomotive maintenance facility for over a century.

Schedule: Park–year round: daily, 9:30 a.m. to 4:30 p.m. Trains–April through October: weekends, 11 a.m. to 3 p.m. on the hour. November: Saturdays only. Closed Thanksgiving, Christmas, New Year's.

Admission/Fare: Roundhouse tour–adults $2.00; youth 6-12 $1.00. Train–adults $6.00; youth $3.00; age five and under are free.

Locomotive/Rolling Stock: 1922 no. 2 Shay; 1891 no. 3 Rogers 4-6-0; no. 5 combine; no. 6 coach.

Special Events: School Daze, Living History programs, holiday specials.

Nearby Attractions/Accommodations: Jamestown, Gateway to the Mother Lode country, is located 2 blocks west of Railtown 1897. The thriving gold rush towns of Sonora and Columbia State Historical Park are within a 15-minute drive and beautiful Yosemite National Park is approximately a 1.5-hour drive.

Location/Directions: Located at 5th Avenue & Reservoir Road, five blocks off Highway 49/108.

Site Address: 5th Avenue and Reservoir Road, Jamestown, CA
Mailing Address: PO Box 1250, Jamestown, CA 95327
Telephone: (209) 984-3953
Fax: (209) 984-4936
E-mail: railtown@sonnet.com
Internet: www.csrmf.org

LOMITA RAILROAD MUSEUM
Museum
Standard gauge

LOMITA RAILROAD MUSEUM

Description: This museum is a replica of the Boston & Maine station at Wakefield, Massachusetts. On display are lanterns of the steam era, chinaware and silverware of the period, scale model live steam engines, spikes, tie date nails, insulators, prints, photographs, clocks, and more.

Schedule: Year round: Wednesdays through Sundays, 10 a.m. to 5 p.m. Closed Thanksgiving and Christmas.

Admission/Fare: Adults $1.00; children under age 12 $ .50.

Locomotive/Rolling Stock: 1902 Baldwin 2-6-0 (Mogul) no. 1765 with a whale-back tender, former Southern Pacific; 1910 yellow caboose, UP OWR&N; 1913 UP boxcar; 1923 oil tank car, Union Oil Co.; Santa Fe red caboose.

Special Events: Call or write for details.

Nearby Attractions/Accommodations: So. Bay Botanical Gardens, Torrance, Cabrillo Museum, San Pedro, Banning House and Drum Barracks, Wilmington.

Location/Directions: Take 110 (Harbor) Freeway South to Pacific Coast Highway off ramp. Turn right going west to Narbonne Avenue. Turn right going east one block. Parking lot on 250th Street.

*Coupon available, see coupon section.

        M

Site Address: 250th and Woodward Avenue, Lomita, CA
Mailing Address: 2137 W. 250th Street, Lomita, CA 90717
Telephone: (310) 326-6255
Fax: (310) 325-4024
Internet: www.lomita-rr.org

ELDORADO EXPRESS RAILROAD
Train ride
18" gauge

ELDORADO EXPRESS RAILROAD

Description: Experience a scenic one-mile round trip through the park while viewing a 150-year-old lake that features paddle boats.

Schedule: Year round: Wednesdays through Fridays, 10:30 a.m. to 4 p.m. Weekends, 10:30 a.m. to 5 p.m.

Admission/Fare: Adults $1.75; children $1.25. Parking: autos $3.00 weekdays and $5.00 weekends and holidays; buses $10.00.

Locomotive/Rolling Stock: Gas-powered locomotive 4-6-2, former live steamer; tender; three open-air passenger cars.

Special Events: Birthday parties, anniversaries.

Nearby Attractions/Accommodations: Queen Mary, Long Beach, Knotts Berry Farm, Eldorado Park, featuring pony rides, boat rides, archery, golf, nature center.

Location/Directions: South on 605 Freeway, exit Spring. Eldorado Regional Park in Long Beach.

Site Address: 605 Freeway and Spring Streets
Mailing Address: 4943 Lincoln Avenue, Cypress, CA 90630
Telephone: (562) 496-4228

CRYSTAL SPRINGS & CAHUENGA VALLEY RAILROAD

Train ride
Standard gauge

ED SIKORA

Description: The first section of a planned demonstration railroad through Griffith Park. A diesel locomotive pulls caboose train on available track at the Travel Town Museum.

Schedule: First Sunday of every month, 10 a.m. to 4 p.m.

Admission/Fare: Donations appreciated.

Locomotive/Rolling Stock: EMD model 40, CS&CV no. 1; California Western Railroad RS12; St&SSF caboose no. 999110; SP caboose no. 4049.

Nearby Attractions/Accommodations: Griffith Park, Griffith Observatory, LA Zoo, Autry Museum of Western Heritage, Universal, Warner Brothers, and NBC studios.

Location/Directions: Ventura Freeway exit 134 (Forest Lawn Drive) located at Griffith Park and Zoo Drive in the Travel Town Museum.

Site Address: 5200 Zoo Drive, Los Angeles, CA
Mailing Address: 3900 W. Chevy Chase Drive, Los Angeles, CA 90039
Telephone: (323) 662-5874 and (213) 485-5520
Fax: (818) 247-4740
Internet: www.ci.la.ca.us/dept/RAP/grifmet/tt/index.htm *or*
www.scsra.org/~scsra

CITY OF LOS ANGELES, RECREATION AND PARKS DEPT.

Description: One of the oldest displays of pre-World War II passenger cars and steam locomotives in the United State, concentrating on railroads in the west, specifically California.

Schedule: Year round: weekdays 10 a.m. to 4 p.m., weekends 10 a.m. to 5 p.m.

Admission/Fare: Museum–free. Scale train ride–adults $1.75; children age 12 and under $1.25.

Locomotive/Rolling Stock: No. 1, 1864 Norris-Lancaster 4-4-0, former Stockton Terminal & Eastern; no. 664, 1899 Baldwin 2-8-0, former Santa Fe; no. 3025, 1904 Alco 4-4-2, former Southern Pacific; no. 1544, 1902 steeple-cab electric, former Pacific Electric; 1955 Baldwin RS-12, former McCloud River no. 33, later California Western No. 56, "The Little Nugget," 1937 club-dorm no. 701 from the Union Pacific Streamliner *City of Los Angeles,* and sleeping cars "Rose Bowl" (1937) and "Hunters Points" (1940), both originally on *City of San Francisco;* others.

Special Events: Pullman car tours, third Sunday of every month.

Nearby Attractions/Accommodations: Griffith Park, Griffith Observatory, LA Zoo, Autry Museum of Western Heritage, Universal, Warner Brothers, and NBC studios.

Location/Directions: Ventura Freeway exit 134 (Forest Lawn Drive), located at Griffith Park and Zoo Drives.

Site Address: 5200 Zoo Drive, Los Angeles, CA
Mailing Address: 3900 W. Chevy Chase Drive, Los Angeles, CA 90039
Telephone: (323) 662-5874 and (213) 485-5520
Fax: (818) 247-4740
Internet: www.ci.la.ca.us/dept/RAP/grifmet/tt/index.htm

BILLY JONES WILDCAT RAILROAD
Train ride
18" gauge

BILLY JONES WILDCAT RAILROAD

Description: A one-mile, 8-minute loop through a park featuring a 40-foot wooden trestle, a 2 percent grade and a hand operated turntable. The railroad crosses Los Gatos Creek on an 86-foot long bridge. The railroad is a 1/3 scale operation. A 1910 Savage carousel is in operation.

Schedule: Train: March 15 through start of school summer vacation and September 6 through October 31, weekends 10:30 a.m. to 4:30 p.m. Start of school vacation through September 5, daily 10:30 a.m. to 4:30 p.m. November 1 through March 14, weekends 11 a.m. to 3 p.m. Call or write for carousel dates.

Admission/Fare: Train and carousel $1.00; handicapped and children under age 2 are free.

Locomotive/Rolling Stock: 1905 Johnson Machine Works 2-6-2 no. 2; 1915 MacDermott San Francisco Overfair Railway; more.

Location/Directions: Oak Meadow Park, 1 block west of State Highway 17, enter on Blossom Hill Road.

Site Address: Blossom Hill Road, Los Gatos, CA
Mailing Address: PO Box 234, Los Gatos, CA 95031
Telephone: (408) 395-RIDE

SHASTA SUNSET DINNER TRAIN
Dinner train
Standard gauge

MCCLOUD RAILWAY COMPANY

Description: Four-course gourmet meal served in elegantly restored 1920 era dining cars. Three-hour ride with meal. Our new No. 18 steam engine is a McCloud River engine and it will run this year for the first time in over 30 years.

Schedule: April through December: 6 p.m.

Admission/Fare: Adults $70.00. Beer and wine available.

Locomotive/Rolling Stock: No. 25 steam engine; nos. 36, 37, 38, 39 diesel; no. 18 steam engine; 1916 IC coaches furnished in mahogany and antique brass.

Location/Directions: I-5 to Mt. Shasta, California (60 miles north of Redding, California, and 90 miles south of Medford, Oregon), then 10 miles east on Highway 89 South. In McCloud trains load on Main Street across from the post office, bank, and McCloud Hotel.

Site Address: McCloud, CA
Mailing Address: PO Box 1199, McCloud, CA 96057
Telephone: (916) 964-2142
Fax: (916)964-2250
E-mail: shastatrains@hotmail.com
Internet: www.metrain.com

NAPA VALLEY WINE TRAIN
Train ride, dinner train
Standard gauge

NAPA VALLEY WINE TRAIN

Description: Gourmet dining excursion aboard lavishly restored 1915 Pullman dining and lounge cars while gently gliding past picturesque vineyards of Napa Valley.

Schedule: Year round: daily for brunch, lunch, dinner.

Admission/Fare: $27.50 to $99.00 per person.

Locomotive/Rolling Stock: Four 1951 Alco diesel engines; eight 1915 Pullman dining and lounge cars; one 1952 Pullman standard dome car.

Special Events: Operate over 88 special food and wine events plus holidays.

Nearby Attractions/Accommodations: San Francisco.

Location/Directions: Off First and McKinstry Streets on the east side of downtown Napa. Use Highways 29 or 121 to enter Napa.

Site Address: 1275 McKinstry Street, Napa, CA
Mailing Address: 1275 McKinstry Street, Napa, CA 94559
Telephone: (707) 253-2111 and (800) 427-4124
E-mail: reservations@winetrain.com
Internet: www.winetrain.com

SAN DIEGO HISTORICAL SOCIETY

Description: This 1882 Santa Fe Transcontinental Terminus Depot was the first west coast depot and the last one remaining. It has been restored to its original condition and is now open as a museum representing the Santa Fe and the local San Diego Electric Railway Trolley Company.

Schedule: Year round: weekends 12 to 4 p.m.

Admission/Fare: $2.00; children under age 12 $ .50.

Locomotive/Rolling Stock: National City and Otay car no. 1 (NC&O no. 1).

Nearby Attractions/Accommodations: San Diego and attractions.

Location/Directions: Five miles south of San Diego on Highway 5 to 24th Street. Right at the light, two blocks to Harrison, depot is on the corner.

 M arm

Site Address: 922 West 23rd Street, National City, CA
Mailing Address: 922 West 23rd Street, National City, CA 91950
Telephone: (619) 474-4400
E-mail: NCD@trainweb.com
Internet: trainweb.com/sandiegorail/sdera/ncd.html

NEVADA COUNTY TRACTION COMPANY
Train ride, museum, display

NEVADA COUNTY TRACTION COMPANY

Description: We offer a 3-mile round trip talking tour 1½ hours with a transfer 3-foot to 2-foot rail. Points of interest, authentic Chinese cemetery, Mohawk Mine, visit rolling stock belonging to Nevada County Historical Society from 1888 to 1917.

Schedule: Year round weather permitting: daily departures at 10 a.m., 2 p.m. and 4 p.m. June through September, add Saturdays 6 p.m. October Pumpkin Hunt–weekdays 10 a.m. to 4 p.m., hourly departures, Fridays and Saturdays 12, 2, 4, 6 and 7 p.m. departures.

Admission/Fare: Adults $6.00; children ages 2-12 $3.00 (except October). Pumpkin Hunt $8.00.

Special Events: Pumpkin Hunt and Haunted Forest By Rail, October.

Nearby Attractions/Accommodations: Northern Queen Inn, National Hotel, Trolley Junction restaurant, Empire Mine, historical Nevada City, state parks, Yuba River.

Location/Directions: From Sacramento east on Highway 80 to Highway 49, north at Auburn to Nevada City. Sacramento Street to Railroad Avenue, travel ¼ mile. Located at Northern Queen Inn, upper parking lot.

Site Address: 402 Rail Road Avenue, Nevada City, CA
Mailing Address: 402 Rail Road Avenue, Nevada City, CA 95959
Telephone: (530) 265-0896
Fax: (530) 265-3720
Internet: www.northernqueeninn.com

HERITAGE JUNCTION HISTORIC PARK
Museum, display
Standard gauge

HERITAGE JUNCTION HISTORIC PARK

Description: Restored Saugus train station with museum on local history. Mogul 1629 steam locomotive and a narrow gauge engine, both undergoing restoration.

Schedule: Year round: weekend 1 to 4 p.m.

Admission/Fare: Free.

Locomotive/Rolling Stock: Caboose and tank car on loan; see above.

Nearby Attractions/Accommodations: William S. Hart Park next door.

Location/Directions: State Route 14 (Antelope Valley Freeway) exit San Fernando Road turning west, past Pine Street, east of park.

Site Address: San Fernando Road, Newhall, CA
Mailing Address: PO Box 221925, Newhall, CA 91322
Telephone: (805) 254-1275
E-mail: miss.music@scvnet.com
Internet: www.scvnet.com/scuhs

California, Orange

IRVINE PARK RAILROAD
Train ride
24" gauge

JOHN FORD

Description: Irvine Park Railroad is located on 500 acres in Irvine Regional Park, the oldest county park in the state of California. The train departs from an old fashioned depot, where railroad folk songs fill the air. The locomotive will make a scenic one-mile journey around the park during which riders can view two lakes complete with waterfalls and fountains, a grove of oak trees, and the Orange County Zoo. The ride is narrated by the engineer and lasts approximately 12 minutes.

Schedule: Winter–daily, 10 a.m. to 4 p.m. Summer–daily, 10 a.m. to 6 p.m. Closed Thanksgiving and Christmas.

Admission/Fare: $2.00; children under age one are free. School group rates available.

Special Events: Christmas train two weeks prior to Christmas.

Nearby Attractions/Accommodations: Bicycle and paddleboat rentals.

Locomotive/Rolling Stock: A ⅓ scale replica of the 1863 C.P. Huntington; four coaches.

Location/Directions: From State Highway 55 take the Chapman Avenue exit and drive east to Jamboree Road. Turn left into the park entrance.

Site Address: 1 Irvine Park Road, Orange, CA
Mailing Address: 1 Irvine Park Road, Orange, CA 92669
Telephone: (714) 997-3968
Fax: (714) 997-0459

California, Orland

ORLAND, NEWVILLE &
PACIFIC RAILROAD
Train ride
15" gauge

ONP RAILROAD

Description: The ON&P is an all-volunteer railroad operating in the Glenn County Fairgrounds. A 1-mile ride takes visitors past the original Orland Southern Pacific depot, the picnic site, and the demonstration orchard, then through a tunnel and along Heritage Trail. The train is normally pulled by a magnificent 5/12-scale live-steam model of the North Pacific Coast's 1875 Baldwin narrow-gauge locomotive "Sonoma." The picnic grounds at Deadowl Station are open whenever the train is running. Former Orland Southern Pacific depot, 1918 Southern Pacific 2-8-0 no. 2852, caboose, schoolhouse, blacksmith shop, print shop, 1920s gas station, miscellaneous steam machinery, old farm equipment. Livestock is also exhibited at fair time, during May and October.

Schedule: April 11-12, 18-19, 25-26, May 2-3, 9-10, 23-24, 30-31, June 14, July 4, August 29-31, September 5-6, 12-13, 19-20, 26-27, October 3-4, 10-11.

Admission/Fare: $1.00; under age two are free.

Locomotive/Rolling Stock: No. 12 replica of 1876 Baldwin 4-4-0; no. 2 4-4-0 amusement park type; four open gondolas; covered car.

Special Events: Glenn County Fair, May 13-17. Harvest Festival, October 17-18. Spook Train, October 31.

Location/Directions: Glenn County Fairgrounds. Orland is 100 miles north of Sacramento on I-5.

Site Address: 221 E. Yolo Street, Orland, CA
Mailing Address: 221 E. Yolo Street, Orland, CA 95963
Telephone: (530) 865-1168 and (916) 865-9747
Fax: (530) 865-1197

ORANGE EMPIRE RAILWAY MUSEUM
Train ride
Standard, 36", and 42" gauge

JIM WALKER, JR.

Description: More than 200 streetcars, interurbans, locomotives (electric, diesel, and steam), passenger and freight cars, work cars, and cabooses. Trains run on 1.5-mile right-of-way, streetcars on 0.7-mile loop within museum.

Schedule: Demonstration railroad–year round: weekends and some holidays, 11 a.m. to 5 p.m. Museum grounds–daily: 9 a.m. to 5 p.m. Closed Thanksgiving and Christmas.

Admission/Fare: Free admission. All day ride pass–adults $7.00; children 5-11 $5.00; under age 5 are free. Special events have additional fees.

Locomotive/Rolling Stock: VC Ry 2 Prairie; GF 2 Mogul; UP 2564 Mikado; SP 1474 S4; SP 3100 U25B; UP 942 E8A; and more.

Special Events: Rail Festival, April and October. Railroadiana Swap Meets, spring and fall. Pumpkin Trains, October. Santa's Christmas Trains, December. Trains to March Field Air Museum, May and November.

Nearby Attractions/Accommodations: Perris Valley Skydiving Center, Perris Auto Speedway, Lake Perris Recreation Area, March Field Air Museum, Temecula Wineries; Best Western Perris Inn, Mission Inn in Riverside.

Location/Directions: I-215, exit west onto 4th Street/Route 74, left on "A" Street to museum.

Site Address: 2201 South "A" Street, Perris, CA
Mailing Address: PO Box 548, Perris, CA 92572-0548
Telephone: (909) 657-2605 and (909) 943-3020
Fax: (909) 943-2676
E-mail: oerm@juno.com
Internet: www.oerm.mus.ca.us

PORTOLA RAILROAD MUSEUM
Museum
Standard gauge

PORTOLA RAILROAD MUSEUM

Description: A one-mile ride around a balloon turning track through pine forest. On display are more than 70 freight cars representing nearly every car type of the Western Pacific Railroad; several passenger cars; other rolling stock; railroad artifacts in the diesel shop building.

Schedule: Museum–March through mid-December 10 a.m. to 5 p.m. Train–Memorial Day through Sunday after Labor Day: weekends, 11 a.m. to 4 p.m. Grounds open in winter weather permitting.

Admission/Fare: Call or write for information.

Locomotive/Rolling Stock: Two steam, 1 electric and 40 diesels of all types including 13 former Western Pacific, 6 former Southern Pacific and 3 former Union Pacific. Manufacturers represented: Alco, Baldwin, Electro-Motive, Fairbanks-Morse, General Electric, Ingersol-Rand and Plymouth. Steam locomotives are former UP 737, an 1887 4-4-0 and former SP 1215, a 1913 0-6-0.

Special Events: Feather River Railroad Days, August 22-23. Railfan Photographers Day, September 19.

Location/Directions: From state route 70, travel one mile south on county road A-15 (Gulling) across the river and through town. Follow signs to the museum.

Site Address: 700 Western Pacific Way, Portola, CA
Mailing Address: PO Box 608, Portola, CA 96122-0608
Telephone: (530) 832-4131
Fax: (530) 832-1854
E-mail: 76043.741@compuserve.com
Internet: wprr.railfan.net/ or www.oz.net/~samh/frrs/

POWAY-MIDLAND RAILROAD
Train ride
Standard gauge

POWAY-MIDLAND RAILROAD

Description: Located in Old Poway Park, a place for folks to come and enjoy the old west. See restored historic buildings and antique train and rolling stock.

Schedule: Year round: Saturdays 10 a.m. to 4 p.m., Sundays 11 a.m. to 2 p.m. No operation second Sunday of each month.

Admission/Fare: Locomotive–$2.00; Trolley–$1.50; Speeder–$1.00. Children under age 12 are $ .50.

Locomotive/Rolling Stock: 1907 Baldwin 0-4-0 no. 3; 1894 Los Angeles Railway yellow car no. 17; 1950 Fairmont speeder no. 38; four 1880s ore cars; replica of 1907 passenger car.

Special Events: Fourth of July. Christmas in the Park, second Saturday in December.

Nearby Attractions/Accommodations: San Diego.

Location/Directions: From Los Angeles–S-5 to East 78, to South 15, exit Camino del Norte, east to light at Midland Road, turn right, travel south half mile to park.

          M

Site Address: 14134 Midland Road, Poway, CA
Mailing Address: PO Box 1244, Poway, CA 92074-1244
Telephone: (619) 486-4063
Fax: (619) 513-0745
E-mail: marycross@juno.com

CALIFORNIA STATE RAILROAD MUSEUM

Description: One of the finest interpretive railroad museums in North America, CSRM's 11 acre facilities in Old Sacramento include the 100,000 square feet museum of railroad history, a reconstructed 1870s Central Pacific passenger station, and an extensive library and archive.

Schedule: Year round: daily, 10 a.m to 5 p.m. Closed Thanksgiving, Christmas, New Year's Day.

Admission/Fare: Adults $6.00; youth 6-12 $3.00; children under age 6 free.

Locomotive/Rolling Stock: More than 30 meticulously restored locomotives and cars on display dating from the 1860s to present. Favorites are Pullman-style sleeper; streamlined dining car; 1870s Victorian coaches and a railway post office.

Special Events: Railfair '99, June 18-27 (one of the largest and most elaborate railroad festivals in the world). Harvest Haunt and Goosebump Express, October weekends. Train Time for Santa, Thanksgiving weekend and December.

Nearby Attractions/Accommodations: Old Sacramento (California's largest concentration of restored 19th century commercial structures), state capitol, Sutter's Fort, Crocker Art Museum, dining, shopping, and lodging.

Location/Directions: In Old Sacramento, adjacent to I-5 exit "J" Street.

           M

  Radio frequencies: 160.335 and 160.440

Site Address: Corner of 2nd and "I" Streets, Old Sacramento, CA
Mailing Address: 111 "I" Street, Sacramento, CA 95814
Telephone: (916) 445-6645
Fax: (916) 327-5655
E-mail: csrmf@csrmf.org (general) and csrmlibrary@csrmf.org (library/archives)
Internet: www.csrmf.org

California, Sacramento　　**CALIFORNIA STATE RAILROAD MUSEUM**
SACRAMENTO SOUTHERN RAILROAD
Train ride, dinner train
Standard gauge

CALIFORNIA STATE RAILROAD MUSEUM

Description: Sacramento Southern is the excursion railroad of the California State Railroad Museum. Built as a subsidiary of the Southern Pacific at the turn of the century, the museum trains have been in regular service since 1984. A 6-mile, 40-minute round trip takes passengers along the Sacramento River aboard vintage 1920s coaches and open-air excursion cars.

Schedule: Steam–April through September: weekends, 10 a.m. to 5 p.m., departures hourly behind steam locomotives. Brunch trains–Sundays. Dinner trains–Fridays and Saturdays.

Admission/Fare: Adults $6.00; youth 6-12 $3.00; children under age 6 free.

Locomotive/Rolling Stock: No. 10 1942 Porter 0-6-0T, former Granite Rock Company; no. 4466, 1920 Lima 0-6-0, former Union Pacific; more.

Railfair '99, June 18-27 (one of the largest and most elaborate railroad festivals in the world). Harvest Haunt and Goosebump Express, October weekends. Train Time for Santa, Thanksgiving weekend and December.

Nearby Attractions/Accommodations: Old Sacramento (California's largest concentration of restored 19th century commercial structures), state capitol, Sutter's Fort, Crocker Art Museum, dining, shopping, and lodging.

Location/Directions: Northern terminus is the reconstructed Central Pacific Railroad Freight Depot at Front and "K" Streets in Old Sacramento.

Radio frequencies: 160.335 and 160.440

Site Address: Front and "K" Streets, Sacramento, CA
Mailing Address: 111 "I" Street, Sacramento, CA 95814
Telephone: (916) 445-6645
Fax: (916) 327-5655
E-mail: csrmf@csrmf.org
Internet: www.csrmf.org

California, San Diego

SAN DIEGO MODEL
RAILROAD MUSEUM
Museum, display, layout
N, HO, O, 3-rail, G gauge

T. J. WEGMANN

Description: Largest model railroad museum in North America operating scale model trains and layouts of southwest. Interactive toy train exhibits for children and party/meeting facilities with kitchenette.

Schedule: Year round: Tuesdays through Fridays 11 a.m. to 4 p.m., weekends 11 a.m. to 5 p.m.

Admission/Fare: Adults $3.00; seniors/students/military w/ID $2.50; children under age 15 are free.

Special Events: Christmas on the Prado, first weekend in December. Tri-annual Swap Meet. Movie Night Bar-B-Q.

Nearby Attractions/Accommodations: San Diego Zoo, Balboa Park, 12 museums, 3 theaters.

Location/Directions: Off I-5 or California route 163. Take Park Blvd. to Space Theater Way; museum is located in the Casa de Balboa Building in Balboa Park.

*Coupon available, see coupon section.

Site Address: Balboa Park, 1649 El Prado, San Diego, CA
Mailing Address: 1649 El Prado, San Diego, CA 92101
Telephone: (619) 696-0199
Fax: (619) 696-0239
E-mail: SDModRailM@aol.com

55

SAN DIEGO RAILROAD MUSEUM
Museum
Standard gauge

BILL SCHNEIDER

Description: Over 80 pieces of rail equipment on display and regularly scheduled train trips featuring trips to Mexico.

Schedule: Year round: weekends and some holidays.

Admission/Fare: Adults $10.00; children 6-12 $3.00; ages 5 and under are free.

Locomotive/Rolling Stock: No. 2353 4-6-0 Baldwin steam; 1950s vintage diesels; variety of cars.

Special Events: Ticket to Tecate rail trips, Starlight Express, Dinner Train, Wine Train.

Nearby Attractions/Accommodations: Viejas Indian Casino, Stone Store Museum.

Location/Directions: Highway 94 and Campo in east San Diego County.

M arm
TRAIN   MasterCard   VISA

Site Address: Highway 94 & Campo, San Diego, CA
Mailing Address: 1050 Kettner Blvd., San Diego, CA 92101
Telephone: (619) 595-3030 and (888) 228-9246
Fax: (619) 595-3034
Internet: www.sdrm.com

California, San Francisco

GOLDEN GATE RAILROAD MUSEUM
Railway museum
Standard gauge

GOLDEN GATE RAILROAD MUSEUM

Description: Dedicated to the preservation of vintage steam and diesel locomotives and passenger equipment. Owns and operates many locomotives related to the Bay Area railroads.

Schedule: Year round: weekends, 10 a.m. to 4 p.m. Call to confirm.

Admission/Fare: Donations appreciated.

Locomotive/Rolling Stock: SP Baldwin P8 4-6-2 no. 2472; SF Belt Railway Alcos nos. 25 and 49; SF Belt Railway no. 4 0-6-0; SP nos. 3194 and 4450; assorted suburban commute coaches; daylight cars.

Special Events: Railroad Retirees Reunion, last weekend in June. Garlic Train to Gilroy Garlic Festival, last weekend in July. Rent-A-Locomotive Program (learn to run steam and diesel locomotives), by appointment.

Nearby Attractions/Accommodations: San Francisco Zoo with restored steam train, cable cars, many parks and other attractions.

Location/Directions: Highway 101 to Cesar Chavez Street (Army Street) to Evans Avenue to Hunters Point Shipyard, Building 809. Need vehicle registration, proof of insurance and picture ID for admission to shipyard.

Site Address: Bldg. 809, Hunter's Point Naval Shipyard, San Francisco, CA
Mailing Address: PO Box 881686, San Francisco, CA 94188-1686
Telephone: (415) 822-8728 or (650) 363-2472
Fax: (415) 822-8739
E-mail: info@ggrm.org
Internet: www.ggrm.org

SAN FRANCISCO CABLE CAR MUSEUM

Description: This museum, located in the historic San Francisco cable car barn and powerhouse, allows visitors to view the actual cable winding machinery as well as the path of the cable entering the building and leaving under the street. Included in the displays are three antique cable cars, a Sutter street dummy and trailer, and the first cable car built in 1873. Historic information gives visitors a peek at the cable cars' glorious past. Also on display is a photo narration of the 1981-84 reconstruction effort, as well as various mechanical devices, such as grips, track, trucks, cable, and brake mechanisms, with corresponding explanations.

Schedule: April through September: daily 10 a.m. to 6 p.m. October through March: daily 10 a.m. to 5 p.m. Closed Thanksgiving, Christmas, New Years.

Admission/Fare: Donations appreciated.

Locomotive/Rolling Stock: 1873 Clay Street Hill RR no. 8.

Location/Directions: Corner of Mason and Washington Streets.

    arm

Site Address: 1201 Mason Street, San Francisco, CA
Mailing Address: 1201 Mason Street, San Francisco, CA 94108
Telephone: (415) 474-1887

SAN FRANCISCO MUNICIPAL RAILWAY
Cable car ride
Standard gauge

SAN FRANCISCO MUNICIPAL RAILWAY

Description: The F MARKET is a regular Municipal Railway line, operating between the Transbay Terminal at 1st and Mission Streets and Castro and Market Streets via Market Street. Most service is with rehabilitated ex-Philadelphia PCC cars painted to represent U.S. cities where PCCs served. Occasionally, a car from the historic fleet takes the place of a PCC. Visit the cable barn, powerhouse and museum at Washington and Mason Streets. From a balcony in the museum visitors can see machinery that moves the cables beneath San Francisco's streets.

Schedule: Ride–year round: daily, 6 a.m. to 12:45 a.m. Frequent service all day and evening. Museum–April through September: 10 a.m. to 5 p.m. October through March: 10 a.m. to 6 p.m.

Admission/Fare: $2.00; seniors and disabled discount fare $1.00 after 9 p.m. and before 7 a.m. Call for more details.

Locomotive/Rolling Stock: Twenty-eight single-ended Powell cars and 12 double-ended California cars.

Nearby Attractions/Accommodations: San Francisco.

Location/Directions: The F operates on Market Street, the central thoroughfare. Stop in at the volunteers' site at Market & Duboce (near the new U.S. Mint).

Site Address: Ride–Along Market Street, San Francisco, CA
Site Address: Museum–1201 Mason Street, San Francisco, CA
Mailing Address: 949 Presidio Avenue, Room 238, San Francisco, CA 94115
Telephone: (415) 923-6162 (railway) and (415) 474-1887 (museum)

**CALIFORNIA TROLLEY AND
RAILROAD CORPORATION**
Display
Standard gauge

KEN MIDDLEBROOK

Description: The non-profit CTRC is developing a railroad museum which will include several relocated railroad structures. Visitors can watch the extensive restoration of steam locomotive no. 2479. A nearby bay window caboose displays the organization's activities and current museum development.

Schedule: Year round: Saturdays 9 a.m. to 4 p.m. and by appointment.

Admission/Fare: Donations appreciated.

Locomotive/Rolling Stock: 119234 Baldwin 4-6-2; Southern Pacific no. 2479; 1941 65-ton diesel; Kaiser cement no. 0002; two passenger cars; two cabooses.

Nearby Attractions/Accommodations: Kelley Park, Children's Discovery Museum, Tech Museum.

Location/Directions: Santa Clara County Fairgrounds, Tully Road, two miles west of US Highway 101.

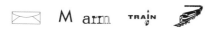
M arm TRAIN

Site Address: 344 Tulley Road, San Jose, CA
Mailing Address: PO Box 403, San Jose, CA 95009
Telephone: (408) 985-2479
Internet: www.ctrc.org

SAN JOSE HISTORICAL MUSEUM
Trolley ride

SAN JOSE HISTORICAL MUSEUM

Description: The trolley barn, in partnership with the California Train and Railroad Corporation, operates at the San Jose Historical Museum. The museum is a 25-acre complex with 27 historic and reconstructed buildings highlighting the history and culture of San Jose and Santa Clara County. The trolley barn offers visitors the opportunity to ride historic trolleys and observe restoration of historic vehicles in progress.

Schedule: Year round: Tuesdays through Sundays 12 to 5 p.m. Closed Thanksgiving, Christmas and New Year's Day.

Admission/Fare: Adults $6.00; seniors $5.00; youth $4.00; age 5 and under are free.

Locomotive/Rolling Stock: Operational trolley car no. 168, former Porto Portugal no. 154; no. 129, former Sacramento no. 35; Birney car no. 143, former Fresno no 68; San Francisco horse car no. 7.

Special Events: Chinese Summer Festival, Portuguese Festa, museum buildings are decorated during the month of December.

Nearby Attractions/Accommodations: Downtown San Jose offers many cultural and sporting activities.

Location/Directions: Located in southernmost part of Kelley Park, which is a short distance from Highways 280, 680 and 101.

Site Address: 1650 Senter Road, San Jose, CA
Mailing Address: 1650 Senter Road, San Jose, CA 95112
Telephone: (408) 287-2290 (museum) and (408) 293-2276 (trolley barn)
Fax: (408) 287-2291
Internet: www.Serve.com/SJHISTORY

California, Santa Clara

PARAMOUNT'S GREAT AMERICA
Train ride
Narrow gauge

PARAMOUNT'S GREAT AMERICA

Description: Paramount's Great America's Scenic Railway takes guests on a leisurely paced journey around the perimeter of the park, past Top Gun, Vortex and The Demon coasters. The train has stops at Hometown Square and County Fair.

Schedule: June 3 through August 29: daily 10 a.m. March 20 through May 30 and September 4 through October 17: weekends only. April 2 through April 11: limited schedule, call for information.

Admission/Fare: Ride is free with park admission.

Locomotive/Rolling Stock: Custom Fabricators (Johnson City, Tennessee) 190 hp at 2500 rpm Detroit diesel; six coaches.

Special Events: Many throughout the season.

Nearby Attractions/Accommodations: Park has many exciting rides and attractions.

Location/Directions: Fifty miles south of San Francisco and six miles north of San Jose between Highways 101 and 237 in Santa Clara.

Site Address: Great America Parkway, Santa Clara, CA
Mailing Address: PO Box 1776, Santa Clara, CA 95052
Telephone: (408) 988-1776
Fax: (408) 986-5863
Internet: www.pgathrills.com

TRAIN TOWN

Description: Train Town is a 10-acre railroad park filled with thousands of trees, animals, lakes, bridges, tunnels, waterfalls, and historic replica structures. Fifteen-inch-gauge live-steam locomotives and diesel replicas pull long passenger trains through the park. Railroad shops and a complete miniature town, built to the same ¼ scale as the railroad. Full-sized rail equipment includes Santa Fe caboose no. 999648; Union Pacific caboose no. 25155; and Southern Pacific's first steel caboose, no. 11.

Schedule: June 1 through September 30: daily. Year round: Fridays through Sundays. 10:30 a.m. to 5 p.m. Closed Christmas and Thanksgiving.

Admission/Fare: Adults $3.50; seniors and children 16 months to 16 $2.50.

Locomotive/Rolling Stock: Replica of no. 5212, 1937 Alco J-1a 4-6-4, former New York Central; no. 1, 1960 Winton Engineering 2-6-0; SW 1200, 1992 custom locomotive; no. 401, 1975 gas-electric motor car.

Location/Directions: Sonoma is in wine country, less than an hour north of San Francisco. Train Town is on Broadway (Highway 12), one mile south of the Sonoma Town Square.

*Coupon available, see coupon section.

Site Address: 20264 Broadway, Highway 12, Sonoma, CA
Mailing Address: PO Box 656, Sonoma, CA 95476
Telephone: (707) 996-2559
Fax: (707) 966-6344
Internet: www.traintown.com

WESTERN RAILWAY MUSEUM
Museum
Standard gauge

BART NADEAU

Description: An 8-mile interurban round trip over re-electrified Sacramento Northern Railway interurban in rural Solano County. Additional electrification in progress, to open in 1999 and 2000.

Schedule: Year round: weekends 11 a.m. to 5 p.m. July 4 through Labor Day: Wednesdays through Sundays 11 a.m. to 5 p.m.

Admission/Fare: Adults $6.00; seniors $5.00; children age 12 and under $3.00; families (2 adults, 3 children) $18.00.

Locomotive/Rolling Stock: Wood interurbans–Peninsular Railway no. 52; Petaluma & Santa Rosa no. 63; Sacramento Northern no. 1005. Steel interurbans–Napa Valley no. 63; key units 182 and 187. Steel locos–CCT no. 7; SN nos. 652, 654; many streetcars; more.

Special Events: Wildflower Prairie Trains, April, May. Santa Trains, December.

Nearby Attractions/Accommodations: Marine World, Africa USA.

Location/Directions: On Highway 12. I-80, 12 miles from the Suisun/Rio Vista exit; or I-5, 23 miles from the Rio Vista/Fairfield exit.

     M arm TRAIN

Site Address: 5848 State Highway 12, Suisun City, CA
Mailing Address: 5848 State Highway 12, Suisun City, CA 94585
Telephone: (707) 374-2978
Fax: (707) 374-6742
Internet: www.wrm.org

NILES CANYON RAILWAY
Train ride
Standard gauge

ALAN FRANK

Description: A 12-mile ride through scenic Niles Canyon over original transcontinental railroad route built in the 1860s.

Schedule: Year round: first and third Sunday of every month, 10 a.m. to 4 p.m.

Admission/Fare: Donation: adults $6.00; children 3-12 $3.00.

Locomotive/Rolling Stock: Ten steam locomotives; eight diesel locomotives; vintage rolling stock.

Special Events: Christmas trains, December; Wildflower excursions.

Nearby Attractions/Accommodations: Marine World, regional wilderness parks.

Location/Directions: One mile west of I-680 between Pleasanton and Freemont, California.

M   Radio frequency: 160.695

Site Address: Sunol Depot, Sunol, CA
Mailing Address: PO Box 2247, Niles Station, Fremont, CA 94536-0247
Telephone: (510) 862-9063
Fax: (510) 582-8840
E-mail: cliffow@aol.com
Internet: www.digisource.com/ncry/

SONORA SHORT LINE RAILWAY
Train ride
12" gauge

JAMES HOBACK

Description: Scenic ten-minute steam-powered train ride through a working apple ranch in the foothills of California's Sierra Nevada Mountains. Train is ⅓ full size, 12" gauge.

Display/Exhibits: Apple ranch has farm animals on display.

Schedule: Mid-February through Thanksgiving: weekends and holidays, 11 a.m. to 5 p.m.

Admission/Fare: $1.50 single ticket, $6.25 for a 5-ride ticket. Children under one year are free.

Locomotive/Rolling Stock: ⅓ scale: 4-4-0 steam locomotive, oil fired, 1910 era Baldwin narrow gauge styling; Plymouth, 1927, diesel powered (locomotives are 12 inch gauge); five Hurlbut-built excursion cars

Special Events: September through October, apple harvest season.

Location/Directions: Five miles east of Sonora, California.

      Riverbank

Site Address: Cover's Apple Ranch, 19200 Cherokee Road, Tuolumne, CA
Mailing Address: 19720 Tuolumne Road, North Tuolumne, CA 95379
Telephone: (209) 928-4689

California, Woodland

YOLO SHORTLINE
RAILROAD COMPANY
Train ride
Standard gauge

RICHARD JONES

Description: A 28-mile, two-hour round trip between Woodland and West Sacramento over former Sacramento Northern Interurban track. Crosses 8,000 foot Fremont Trestle and offers views of the Sacramento River and scenic Yolo County farmlands and wetlands. Also specials to Clarksburg.

Schedule: Mid-May through October: Sundays and holidays. Specials on selected Saturdays. Charters available year round.

Admission/Fare: Adults $13.00; seniors $11.00; children $8.00; children age 3 and under are free.

Locomotive/Rolling Stock: No. 1233, former Southern Pacific 0-6-0 switcher; nos. 131, 132, 133 GP-9 EMD diesels, former Southern Pacific.

Special Events: Great Train Robberies; BBQ trains; Beer & Salsa trains on selected Saturdays; Santa Train, December.

Nearby Attractions/Accommodations: Hayes Truck and Tractor Museum, Southern Pacific Depot (under restoration), Woodland Opera House.

Location/Directions: I-5, Main Street exit, one mile west to East Main and Thomas Streets. Twenty minutes from Sacramento.

Radio Frequency: 160.260

Site Address: East Main and Thomas, Woodland, CA
Mailing Address: 1965 East Main Street, Woodland, CA 95776
Telephone: (916) 666-9646 and (800) 942-6387
Fax: (916) 666-2919
E-mail: dmagaw@worldnet.att.net
Internet: http://www.ysrr.com

Colorado, Canon City

CANON CITY AND ROYAL GORGE SCENIC RAILWAY AND MUSEUM
Train ride
Standard gauge

DAVE ROPCHAN

Description: Experience the grandeur of traveling by train through the spectacular Royal Gorge on the Royal Gorge route. The train operates alongside the Arkansas River from Canon City, traveling over the famous "Hanging Bridge" where the canyon rim towers 1000 feet above.

Schedule: Mid-May through mid-October: three departures daily.

Admission/Fare: Adults $24.50; children $16.50 round trip.

Locomotive/Rolling Stock: FC&NW EMD F7A nos. 402, 403; VIA Rail CC&F passenger car nos. 3225, 5497, 5541, 5562, 5580, 5586, Club car 650.

Nearby Attractions/Accommodations: Royal Gorge bridge, rafting, horseback riding, fishing, camping.

Location/Directions: Located one mile off Highway 50, Royal Gorge Road, eight miles west of Canon City, 35 miles from Colorado Springs.

Site Address: 330 Royal Gorge Blvd., Canon City, CO
Mailing Address: PO Box 859, Georgetown, CO 80444
Telephone: (888) RAILS-4-U
Fax: (303) 569-2894
E-mail: markg@royalgorgeroute.com
Internet: www.royalgorgeroute.com

NPS PHOTO BY LISA LYNCH

Description: At Cimarron, 20 miles east of Montrose, a historic narrow gauge railroad exhibit with engine no. 278, its coal tender, a boxcar, and a caboose sit on a stone and steel trestle one mile into the Cimarron River Canyon. At the Cimarron Visitor Center, a cattle car, sheep car, outfit car, hoist car, livestock corral, and interpretive panels illustrate early mountain railroad operations of the Denver & Rio Grande.

Schedule: Year round.

Admission/Fare: Free.

Locomotive/Rolling Stock: 1882 Baldwin locomotive no. 278.

Nearby Attractions/Accommodations: Morrow Point Dam. Black Canyon, New Mexico has hiking, fishing, camping, biking, cross country skiing, snowshoeing. Cimarron has campgrounds, motels, and restaurants.

Location/Directions: Cimarron is 20 miles west of Montrose on U.S. highway 50. Exhibit can be seen from the highway. Follow Curecanti National Recreation Area signs.

Site Address: U.S. Highway 59, Cimarron, CO
Mailing Address: Curecanti NRA, 102 Elk Creek, Gunnison, CO 81230
Telephone: (970) 249-1915 ext. 23 and (970) 641-2337 ext. 205
Fax: (970) 240-5368
E-mail: cure_vis_mail@nps.gov
Internet: www.nps.gov/cure

Colorado, Colorado Springs

PIKE'S PEAK HISTORICAL STREET RAILWAY FOUNDATION, INC.

Ride
Standard gauge

PIKES PEAK HISTORICAL STREET RAILWAY FOUNDATION, INC.

Description: Interpretive center displaying street railway history with a strong emphasis on Colorado Springs street railway history. Also lecture on history and return of streetcars to Colorado Springs. Several trips over 500' test track. Operation and history of car explained during ride. Visit a working car house (former Rock Island Engine House) built in 1888. See cars under restoration. Guided tour of cars on hand and shop area.

Schedule: Saturday, 10:00 a.m.-4:00 p.m., year round except Thanksgiving, Christmas and New Year's week. Other times please write or call. Group tours, please call ahead for special showing.

Admission/Fare: Adults $2.00, children (12 and under) $1.00.

Locomotive/Rolling Stock: Nine Southeastern Pennsylvania Transportation Authority PCC's (Philadelphia) 1947; Los Angeles Railways PCC 1943; Colorado Springs double truck, 1901 Laclede Car Co.; Ft. Collins Municipal Railway, single truck, 1919 Birney, American Car Co.

Location/Directions: I-25, exit Fillmore Street east, south on Tremont Street, west on Polk Street. When forced to turn south, you will automatically be on Steel Drive. Site is located at the end of Steel Drive.

🚌 ✳ ☕ 📷 ✉ arm M

Site Address: 2333 Steel Drive, Colorado Springs, CO
Mailing Address: PO Box 544, Colorado Springs, CO 80901
Telephone: (719) 475-9508
Fax: (719) 475-2814

Colorado, Craig

MOFFAT COUNTY VISITORS CENTER
Museum

MOFFAT COUNTY VISITORS CENTER

Description: National registry site. Tours consist of a guided walk through an historic Pullman car owned by David Moffat, a Denver banker and President of Denver Northwest & Pacific Railroad. Car is stationary on location.

Schedule: May 15 through October. Other times by written request. Weather permitting.

Admission/Fare: Free.

Locomotive/Rolling Stock: Pullman car, Denver Northwest & Pacific (Moffat RR), private car "Marcia"; 1906 type A.

Special Events: Grand Olde West Days, Memorial Day weekend.

Nearby Attractions/Accommodations: Public park with swimming, water slide, wave pool, recreation complex and picnic area. Nearby motels, restaurants, golf.

Location/Directions: Corner of Washington Street and US Highway 40 west. Craig is located 180 miles west of Denver on US Highway 40 and State Highway 13.

Site Address: Washington Street, Craig, CO
Mailing Address: COC, 360 E. Victory Way, Craig, CO 81625
Telephone: (970) 824-5689
Fax: (970) 824-3046
E-mail: craigcoc@craig-chamber.com
Internet: www.craig-chamber.com

Colorado, Cripple Creek

CRIPPLE CREEK AND VICTOR NARROW GAUGE RAILROAD
Train ride
Narrow gauge

CRIPPLE CREEK NARROW GAUGE RAILROAD

Description: A 4-mile, 45-minute round trip over a portion of the old Midland Terminal Railroad. The train runs south out of Cripple Creek past the old MT wye, over a reconstructed trestle and past many historic mines to the deserted mining town of Anaconda.

Schedule: May through October: daily, 9:30 a.m. to 5:30 p.m., departing every 45 minutes.

Admission/Fare: Adults $7.50; seniors $6.75; children ages 3-12 $3.75; under age 3 are free.

Locomotive/Rolling Stock: No. 1 1902 Orenstein & Koppel 0-4-4-0; no. 2 1936 Henschel 0-4-0; no. 3 1927 Porter 0-4-0T; no. 13 1946 Bagnall 0-4-0T

Location/Directions: Trains leave from the former Midland Terminal Railroad Bull Hill Depot.

*Coupon available, see coupon section.

Site Address: Cripple Creek, CO
Mailing Address: PO Box 459, Cripple Creek, CO 80813
Telephone: (719) 689-2640

THE SKI TRAIN

Description: The Ski Train, a Colorado tradition since 1940, offers a 120-mile round trip from Denver's Union Station over the main line of the Rio Grande, passing through the famous Moffat Tunnel and stopping at West Portal, the location of Winter Park Resort.

Schedule: Call or write for information.

Admission/Fare: Call or write for information.

Locomotive/Rolling Stock: Varies.

Location/Directions: Train departs from Denver Union Station.

Site Address: Denver Union Station, Denver, CO
Mailing Address: 555 17th Street, Suite 2400, Denver, CO 80202
Telephone: (303) 296-4754

Colorado, Durango

DURANGO & SILVERTON NARROW-GAUGE RAILROAD
Train ride, museum
Narrow gauge

AMOS CORDOVA

Description: The Durango & Silverton was established in 1881 to transport miners to and from Silverton and to haul precious metals to smelters. Today, a coal-fired, steam-powered, narrow-gauge train travels through the wilderness of the two-million-acre San Juan National Forest, following the Animas River through breathtaking Rocky Mountain scenery. The 90-mile round trip, which originates at Durango, takes approximately nine hours, including a 2¼-hour layover at Silverton for lunch and sightseeing. A half-day winter trip to Cascade Canyon is also offered.

Schedule: Train–June 22 through August 13, 7:30 a.m. May 9 through October 31, 8:15 a.m. May 19 through October 11, 9 a.m. June 8 through August 20, 9:45 a.m. September 14 through September 27, 9:45 a.m. November 1 through November 28, 10 a.m. December 14 through May 7, 10 a.m., closed Christmas. Museum/Yard–daily, 7 a.m. to 7 p.m.

Admission/Fare: Round trip–adults $49.10; children ages 5-11 $24.65. Call or write for more detailed information.

Locomotive/Rolling Stock: Nos. 473, 476 and 478, 1923 Alco class K-28 2-8-2s; more.

Special Events: Narrow Gauge Days, May. Photographers Special, September.

Nearby Attractions/Accommodations: Many attractions, sports, lodging.

Location/Directions: Highways 160 and 550 to Durango, off College & Main.

Site Address: 479 Main Avenue, Durango, CO
Mailing Address: 479 Main Avenue, Durango, CO 81301
Telephone: (970) 247-2733
Fax: (970) 259-9349
Internet: durango.com/train

Colorado, Fort Collins   **FORT COLLINS MUNICIPAL RAILWAY**
                                                    Train ride
                                                 Standard gauge

AL KILMINSTER

Description: A 3-mile round trip from/to City Park through pleasant residential district on original trolley right-of-way on original 1919 City of Ft. Collins Birney safety car.

Schedule: May through September: weekends and holidays, noon to 5 p.m., weather permitting.

Admission/Fare: Adults $1.00; seniors $ .75; children $ .50

Locomotive/Rolling Stock: 1919 Birney safety car by American Car Co. of St. Louis, Missouri.

Special Events: Mother's Day, Father's Day, Fourth of July.

Nearby Attractions/Accommodations: Rocky Mtn. National Park in Denver, Poudre River, KOA campground.

Location/Directions: I-25 north to Colorado 14, Ft. Collins exit. Go west through Ft. Collins to Shields Street, north on Shields to W. Oak Street, west ½ mile to City Park loading area.

   M

Site Address: Carbarn, 1801 W. Mountain, Ft. Collins, CO
Mailing Address: PO Box 635, Ft. Collins, CO 80522
Telephone: (970) 224-5372 and (970) 482-8246

Colorado, Georgetown　　　**GEORGETOWN LOOP RAILROAD**
Train ride
36" gauge

RON RUHOFF

Description: A 6.5-mile, 70-minute round trip over the right-of-way of the former Colorado & Southern. The train travels through scenic, mountainous terrain and over the reconstructed Devil's Gate Viaduct, a spectacular 96-foot high curved trestle. The Georgetown Loop Railroad is a project of the Colorado Historical Society.

Schedule: Memorial Day weekend through first weekend in October: daily. Silver Plume (exit 226)–9:20 and 10:40 a.m., 12, 1:20, 2:40, and 4 p.m. Devil's Gate (exit 228)–10 and 11:20 a.m., 12:40, 2:00, and 3:20 p.m.

Admission/Fare: Train–adults $11.95; children $7.50; under age three ride free. Mine–adults $4.00; children $2.00. Charters and groups rates available. Tickets must be purchased at Old Georgetown Station, 1106 Rose, Georgetown.

Locomotive/Rolling Stock: No. 40, 1920 Baldwin 2-8-0 and no. 44, 1921 Baldwin 2-8-0, both former International Railways of Central America; Lima 3-truck Shay, nos. 4, 8, 12; more.

Nearby Attractions/Accommodations: Old Georgetown Station, Trails and Rails Mountain Bike Tours.

Location/Directions: I-70 exit 228 for Devil's Gate or exit 226 for Silver Plume. Tickets must be purchased at Old Georgetown Station, 1106 Rose, Georgetown.

 Radio frequency: 161.115

Site Address: 1106 Rose Street, Georgetown, CO
Mailing Address: PO Box 217, Georgetown, CO 80444
Telephone: (303) 569-2403 and (800) 691-4FUN
Fax: (303) 569-2873
E-mail: markg@gtownloop.com
Internet: www.gtownloop.com

Colorado, Golden

COLORADO RAILROAD MUSEUM
Museum
Standard gauge, 36" gauge

COLORADO RAILROAD MUSEUM

Description: The oldest and largest railroad museum in the Rocky Mountain area exhibits an extensive collection of Colorado railroad memorabilia and over 70 historic cars and locomotives, both standard and narrow gauge. It is the home of the Denver HO Model Railroad Club and the Denver Garden Railway Society. "Galloping Goose" motorcars operate on selected weekends.

Schedule: Museum–June through August, daily, 9 a.m. to 6 p.m.; September through May, 9 a.m. to 5 p.m. Train–call, fax, or write for schedule. HO Model Railroad–first Thursday of every month, 7:30 to 9:30 p.m. Richardson Railroad Research Library–Tuesdays through Saturdays 11 a.m. to 4 p.m., Thursdays to 9 p.m.

Admission/Fare: Adults $4.00; seniors $3.50; children under age 16 $2.00; families (parents and children under age 16) $9.50.

Locomotive/Rolling Stock: Three RGS "Galloping Geese" motorcars; Baldwin 1890 2-8-0 no. 683; Rio Grande Zephyr EMD F9s 5771 and 5762; Chicago Burlington & Quincy 4-8-4 no. 5629; Santa Fe Super Chief 1937 observation car Navajo; more.

Nearby Attractions/Accommodations: Coors Brewery, Buffalo Bill Museum, Colorado Rockies baseball.

Location/Directions: Twelve miles west of downtown Denver. I-70 west-bound exit 265 or eastbound exit 266 to West 44th Avenue.

Site Address: 17155 West 44th Avenue, Golden, CO
Mailing Address: PO Box 10, Golden, CO 80402
Telephone: (303) 279-4591 and (800) 365-6263
Fax: (303) 279-4229
E-mail: corrmus@aol.com
Internet: www.crrm.org

LEADVILLE, COLORADO & SOUTHERN RAILROAD
Train ride
Standard gauge

BARBARA MALLETTE, THE LEADVILLE PICTURE COMPANY

Description: The 22.5-mile, 2.5-hour train trip follows the headwaters of the Arkansas River to an elevation of 11,120 feet, over an old narrow-gauge roadbed converted to standard gauge in the 1940s. The train leaves from the restored 1894 railroad depot (formerly Colorado & Southern, built originally for the Denver, South Park & Pacific) in Leadville, the highest incorporated city in the United States. We offer enclosed, open and sun cars along with snacks, souvenirs and restrooms in the boxcars.

Schedule: May 23 through June 14, 1 p.m. June 15 through September 7, 10 a.m. and 2 p.m. September 8 through October 4, 1 p.m.

Admission/Fare: Adults $22.50; children 4-12 $12.50; age 3 and under are free. Group rates available for 20 or more.

Locomotive/Rolling Stock: 1955 EMD GP9 no. 1714, former Burlington Northern; EMD GP-9 no. 1918.

Nearby Attractions/Accommodations: National Mining Museum, Matchless Mine Leadville's historic mining district, Tabor Opera House, San Isabel National Forest.

Location/Directions: Located 25 miles south of I-70 on Highway 91, Copper Mountain exit. Travel south to Leadville, turn east on E. 7th Street to depot.

Site Address: 327 E. 7th Street, Leadville, CO
Mailing Address: Box 916, Leadville, CO 80461
Telephone: (719) 486-3936
Fax: (719) 486-0671
E-mail: info@leadville.train
Internet: www.leadville-train.com

LIMON HERITAGE MUSEUM AND RAILROAD PARK
Museum, layout

LIMON HERITAGE MUSEUM

Description: See the working N scale model of Limon's bustling 1940s rail yard. Touch the high plains agricultural history as you explore the sheepherder's wagon, vintage farm machinery, and Eclipse Windmill. Share the Colorado Outback ranching heritage as you view the Prairie Monument and walk back in time through the one-room schoolhouse, rail dining car and Native American teepee. Museum features railroad park.

Schedule: Museum–June through August: Mondays through Saturdays 1 to 8 p.m. Railroad park–year round.

Admission/Fare: Free, donations appreciated.

Locomotive/Rolling Stock: UP caboose no. 25670; 1935 Milwaukee Road branch line car; UP, former Rock Island snow plow 900016; Great Northern diner; former 1914 Pullman; former 1956 work train.

Special Events: Western Festival and Parade, second Saturday in June. Heritage Day, first Saturday in August.

Nearby Attractions/Accommodations: Colorado Springs, Pikes Peak, Denver, motels, camping.

Location/Directions: I-70 to downtown Limon, at light turn south for 1.5 blocks. Located opposite Town Hall in Old Limon Union in railyards.

     M

Site Address: 899 First Street, Limon, CO
Mailing Address: Box 341, Limon, CO 80828
Telephone: (719) 775-2373
Fax: (719) 775-9082

MANITOU & PIKE'S PEAK RAILWAY
Train ride
Standard gauge (cog)

MANITOU & PIKE'S PEAK RAILWAY

Description: The M&PP, the highest cog railway in the world, was established in 1889 and has been operating continuously since 1891; it celebrated its centennial of passenger operations in June 1991. A 3¼-hour round trip takes passengers to the summit of Pike's Peak (elevation 14,110 feet) from Manitou Springs (elevation 6,575 feet) and includes a 40-minute stop at the summit.

Schedule: Daily; May-mid June, September and October, 9:20 a.m. and 1:20 p.m.; mid June-August, every 80 minutes, 8:00 a.m.-5:20 p.m.

Admission/Fare: Adults $22.00; children 5-11 $10.50. July through August 15: adults $23.00; children $11.00.

Locomotive/Rolling Stock: Twin-unit diesel hydraulic railcars and single-unit diesel electric railcars.

Special Events: Occasional steam-up of former M&PP steam locomotive no. 4, built by Baldwin in 1896.

Location/Directions: Six miles west of Colorado Springs.

Radio frequency: 161.55 and 160.23

Site Address: 515 Ruxton Avenue, Manitou Springs, CO
Mailing Address: PO Box 351, Manitou Springs, CO 80829
Telephone: (719) 685-5401

Colorado, Morrison

TINY TOWN RAILROAD
Train ride
15" gauge

HAROLD AHNOLD

Description: Tiny Town Railroad, a ¼-scale live steam railroad, takes passengers from its full sized station on a one mile loop around Tiny Town. Started in 1915, Tiny Town is the oldest miniature town in the United States. It features more than 100 hand crafted, ⅙-sized structures laid out in the configuration of a real town, rural and mountain area.

Schedule: Memorial Day through Labor Day: daily. May, September, and October: weekends. 10 a.m. to 5 p.m. Train runs continuously.

Admission/Fare: Display–adults $2.50; children 3-12 $1.50; children under age three are free. Train–$1.00.

Locomotive/Rolling Stock: 1970 standard-gauge 4-6-2 "Occasional Rose" propane-fired; 1970 narrow-gauge 2-6-0 "Cinderbell" coal-fired; 1954 F-unit "Molly," gas-powered; 1952 A- and B-unit "Betsy" gas-powered. Open amusement park style cars, propane tank car and caboose.

Nearby Attractions/Accommodations: Red Rocks Park and Dinosaur Ridge.

Location/Directions: Approximately 30 minutes southwest of Denver, off Highway 285.

Site Address: 6249 S. Turkey Creek Road, Morrison, CO
Mailing Address: 6249 S. Turkey Creek Road, Morrison, CO 80465
Telephone: (303) 697-6829
Fax: (303) 674-4238

Colorado, Pueblo　　**PUEBLO LOCOMOTIVE & RAIL HISTORICAL SOCIETY INC., PUEBLO RAILWAY MUSEUM**
Museum
Standard and narrow gauge

RICHARD M. HOLMES

Description: Static displays, museum car and gift shop. Motor car or hi-rail rides on the old Pueblo Union Depot passenger tracks on selected weekends. Restoration work is ongoing on former ATSF steam locomotive no. 2912. Fantastic train watching on the BNSF and UP main, adjacent to the museum.

Schedule: Museum–Memorial Day through mid-October: weekends or by appointment. Static Displays–year round: daily. Hours are 9:30 a.m. to 4 p.m.

Admission/Fare: Free, donations appreciated.

Locomotive/Rolling Stock: ATSF Baldwin 4-8-4 Northern no. 2912; Colorado Fuel and Iron, GE 25-ton diesel no. 11; Colorado & Southern caboose no. 10538; Colorado & Wyoming locomotive simulator training car no. 100; Denver & Rio Grande Western caboose no. 01432; Southern Pacific bay window caboose nos. 4773, 4707; more.

Special Events: Open House, weekend following Memorial Day. Pueblo Railfest, October 2-3.

Nearby Attractions/Accommodations: Lake Pueblo State Park, Pueblo Weisbrod Aircraft Museum, Union Avenue Historic District.

Location/Directions: I-25, exit First Street. West to Union Avenue, south to B Street, right turn on B. Museum is located behind and to the west of the depot. Parking available behind the depot.

        M

Site Address: 200 W. B Street, Pueblo, CO
Mailing Address: PO Box 322, Pueblo, CO 81002
Telephone: (714) 544-3642
E-mail: plrhs@pueblorail.com
Internet: www.pueblorail.com

Connecticut, Danbury

DANBURY RAILWAY MUSEUM
Train ride, museum, displays
Standard gauge

BILL GUIDER

Description: Excursions over Metro-North commuter routes, or the seldom traveled Beacon branch (former New Haven Maybrook line), connecting with Hudson River cruises or other attractions. Displays consist of a locomotive, RDC's, FCD railbus, coaches, caboose, freight and maintenance of way cars in ex-New Haven yard. Exhibits in Danbury Union Station.

Schedule: January through March: Thursdays through Saturdays, 10 a.m. to 4 p.m.; Sundays, 12 to 4 p.m. April through December: Wednesdays through Saturdays, 10 a.m. to 4 p.m.; Sundays, 12 to 4 p.m. All other days open by appointment.

Admission/Fare: Adults $3.00; children 5-15 $2.00.

Locomotive/Rolling Stock: More than 40 pieces of rolling stock including RS-1, several RDCs and the Roger Williams, 2 observation cars, 5 coaches, 12 freight cars, cabooses, NYC E9 4096.

Special Events: Easter Bunny Trains, March 27. Spring Train Show, May 15-16. Fall Train Show, October 16-17. Holiday Express, December 4. Santa Trains, December 18.

Nearby Attractions/Accommodations: Several other rail attractions nearby.

Location/Directions: I-84 exit 5, right on Main Street, left on White Street.

Site Address: 120 White Street, Danbury, CT
Mailing Address: PO Box 90, Danbury, CT 06813
Telephone: (203) 778-8337
Fax: (203) 778-1836
E-mail: wguider@ibm.net
Internet: www.danbury.org/org/drm

SHORE LINE TROLLEY MUSEUM
Train ride, museum
Standard gauge

G. BOUCHER

Description: The Shore Line Trolley Museum operates the sole remaining segment of the historic 98-year-old Branford Electric Railway. The three mile round trip passes woods, salt marshes, and meadows along the scenic Connecticut shore.

Schedule: Memorial Day through Labor Day: daily. May, September, and October: weekends and holidays. April and November: Sundays. Hours 10:30 a.m. to 4:30 p.m. Cars depart every 30 minutes.

Admission/Fare: Unlimited rides and guided tours–adults $5.00; seniors $4.00; children 2-11 $2.00; under age two are free.

Locomotive/Rolling Stock: Connecticut Co. suburban no. 775; Montreal no. 2001; Johnstown no. 357; Brooklyn (NY) convertible no. 4573; 3rd Avenue no. 629.

Special Events: Santa Days, Thanksgiving to Christmas on weekends.

Nearby Attractions/Accommodations: Holiday Inn Express, East Haven. Yale University. Foxwoods Casino.

Location/Directions: I-95 exits 51 north or 52 south and follow signs.

Site Address: 17 River Street, East Haven, CT
Mailing Address: 17 River Street, East Haven, CT 06512-2519
Telephone: (203) 467-6927 and (203) 467-7635 group sales
E-mail: BERASLTM@aol.com
Internet: www.bera.org

CONNECTICUT TROLLEY MUSEUM
Museum
Standard gauge

SCOTT R. BECKER

Description: A 3-mile, 25-minute round trip through scenic woodlands on antique streetcars. Displays in Vicitor Center.

Schedule: April through Memorial Day and Labor Day through Thanksgiving: Saturdays, 10 a.m. to 5 p.m. and Sundays noon to 5 p.m.; Memorial Day through Labor Day, Mondays through Saturdays, 10 a.m. to 5 p.m. Sundays, noon to 5 p.m. Post Labor Day to Columbus Day: weekends noon to 5 p.m. Closed December 24-25.

Admission/Fare: Adults $6.00; seniors $5.00; children ages 5-12 $3.00; under age 5 are free. Group rates are available.

Trolleys: No. 840 open; four Montreal observation; 1850 open; 2600 closed; 2056 closed; more.

Special Events: Rails to the Darkside, last weekends in October, 6:30 to 10 p.m. Winterfest Light Display, Friday after Thanksgiving to December 31, Thursdays through Sundays 6 to 9 p.m. Call for more information.

Location/Directions: Between Hartford, Connecticut, and Springfield, Massachusetts. I-91, exit 45, ¾ mile east on Route 140.

Site Address: 58 North Road (Rt. 140), East Windsor, CT
Mailing Address: PO Box 360, East Windsor, CT 06088-0360
Telephone: (860) 627-6540
Fax: (860) 627-6510

Connecticut, Essex

ESSEX STEAM TRAIN AND RIVERBOAT RIDE

Description: A 2.5-hour excursion along the scenic banks of the Connecticut River on restored 1920s vintage cars. All trains except the last of the day connect with a riverboat cruise at Deep River. Dinner train available for private charters.

Schedule: May through October: daily. November through December: weekends for North Pole Express. Call or write for departure times.

Admission/Fare: Train and boat–adults $15.00; children 3-11 $7.50; under age three ride free. Train only–adults $10.00; children 3-11 $5.00.

Locomotive/Rolling Stock: No. 97, 1926 Alco 2-8-2, more.

Special Events: Presidents' Weekend Special, February. Easter Eggspress, April. Working on the Railroad Days, September. Hot Steamed Music Festival, June. Ghost Train, October. North Pole Express, November, December. Tuba Concert, December. Call or write for more information.

Nearby Attractions/Accommodations: Casinos, Mystic Aquarium.

Location/Directions: From shoreline, take exit 69 off I-95, travel north on state route 9 to exit 3. From Hartford take exit 22 off I-91, then travel south on state route 9 to exit 3. Valley Railroad is a half-mile west of route 9 on state route 154.

*Coupon available, see coupon section.

Site Address: Essex, CT
Mailing Address: PO Box 452, Essex, CT 06426
Telephone: (860) 767-0103
Fax: (860) 767-0104
Internet: www.valleyrr.com

Connecticut, Kent

CONNECTICUT ANTIQUE
MACHINERY ASSOCIATION, INC.
Museum
36" gauge

CONNECTICUT ANTIQUE MACHINERY

Description: A wide range of exhibits showing the development of the country's agricultural and industrial technology from the mid 1800s to the present, including a collection of large stationary steam engines in the Industrial Hall; a display of large gas-engines; a tractor and farm-implement display in the large tractor barn; and the reconstructed Cream Hill Agricultural School buildings, which housed an early agricultural school that was the forerunner of the University of Connecticut, and a large engine-pumping exhibit. A stretch of three-foot-gauge track is in operation during this group's popular Fall Festival.

Schedule: Memorial Day through Labor Day: weekends and by appointment.

Admission/Fare: Adults $4.00; children 5-12 $2.00; under age five are free.

Locomotive/Rolling Stock: No. 4 1908 Porter 2-8-0, former Argent Lumber Co.; no. 16 1921 Plymouth D1, former Hutton Brick Co.; no. 18 1917 Vulcan limited clearance 0-4-0T, former American Steel & Wire Co.; no. 111 caboose, former Tionesta Valley Railway; more.

Special Events: Spring Gas Up, first Sunday in May. Fall Festival, last full weekend in September.

Nearby Attractions/Accommodations: Sloane-Stanley Museum.

Location/Directions: One mile north of village on Route 7 adjacent to Housatonic Railroad.

Site Address: Kent, CT
Mailing Address: PO Box 1467, New Milford, CT 06776
Telephone: (860) 927-0050

NAUGATUCK RAILROAD
Train ride
Standard gauge

HOWARD PINCUS

Description: A 17.5-mile round trip over a former New Haven Railroad line, from the 1881 Thomaston Station along the scenic Naugatuck River and past 100-year old New England brass mills, on to the face of the Thomaston Dam. The original Naugatuck Railroad opened this route in 1849.

Schedule: May through October: Tuesdays, weekends and holidays. Call or write for information. Christmas trains operate in December

Admission/Fare: Adults $9.00; seniors and children 3-12, $8.00. Group rates and charters available.

Locomotive/Rolling Stock: New Haven RS-3 no. 529; New Haven U25B no. 2525; Naugatuck GP-9 no. 1732; Canadian National open window heavyweight coaches from 1920s.

Special Events: Occasional excursions over entire 19.6-mile route between Waterbury and Torrington. Also, engineer-for-an-hour program.

Nearby Attractions/Accommodations: Amusement parks, vineyards, state parks.

Location/Directions: In Waterville section of Waterbury, I-84, exit 20 to north on Route 8, exit 38 Thomaston.

Site Address: East Main Street, Thomaston, CT
Mailing Address: PO Box 400, Thomaston, CT 06787-0400
Telephone: (860) 273-RAIL
Fax: (203) 269-3364
E-mail: rrexc@snet.net
Internet: www.rmne.org

SMITHSONIAN INSTITUTION
NATIONAL MUSEUM OF AMERICAN HISTORY
Museum, display

SMITHSONIAN INSTITUTION

Description: The Smithsonian's Railroad Hall symbolizes the achievements of railroads and rail transit in the United States from the 1820s to about 1965. On display are original pieces of the "Stourbridge Lion" and the "Dewitt Clinton," a complete Winton 201-A engine from the *Pioneer Zephyr*, a series of ½-inch-scale models showing locomotive development from the earliest steam engine to present-day diesels, and many other exhibits. Information leaflet no. 455, available on request, describes the railroad exhibits. (Extensive research inquiries cannot be answered.)

Schedule: Year round: daily, 10 a.m. to 5:30 p.m. Closed Christmas and New Year's.

Admission/Fare: Free.

Locomotive/Rolling Stock: No. 1401, 1926 Alco 4-6-2, former Southern Railway; "John Bull" 1831 Stephenson 4-2-0, former Camden & Amboy Railroad. "No. 3" 1836 coach, former Camden & Amboy Railroad; "Jupiter," 1876 Baldwin narrow gauge 4-4-0.

   arm

Site Address: 14th Street and Constitution Avenue, Washington, D.C.
Mailing Address: National Museum of American History, Washington, D.C. 20560

QUEEN ANNE'S RAILROAD
Dinner train
Standard gauge

QARR

Description: The Queen Anne's Railroad travels through the southern Delaware countryside on the former Pennsylvania Railroad Lewes-Georgetown line. The passengers ride aboard the *Royal Zephyr* Dinner Train enjoying a full dinner reflecting the opulence of the 1940s. A live Murder Mystery or musical entertainment is provided to complete a pleasurable evening. A cash bar is on board. Luncheon trains and one-hour excursion trains may be scheduled.

Schedule: Dinner trains–April through November: Saturdays, 6 p.m. Special trains through December.

Admission/Fare: Call or write for information.

Locomotive/Rolling Stock: 1943 no. 3 Vulcan locomotive 0-6-0T, former U.S. Navy; 1959 Alco T-6 no. 19, former PRR; 1947 Pullman standard coaches, former New Haven; MP-54 coach, former PRR; coach, former New York Central; heavy combine, former Norfolk & Western baggage car.

Special Events: New Year's Eve, Valentine's Day, Halloween Ghost Train, Lunch with Santa Claus.

Nearby Attractions/Accommodations: Highway 1 to Highway 9 east.

*Coupon available, see coupon section.

Site Address: 730 Kings Highway, Lewes, DE
Mailing Address: 730 Kings Highway, Lewes, DE 19958
Telephone: (302) 644-1720 and (888) 456-TOOT
Fax: (302) 644-9212
E-mail: queenannes@dol.net
Internet: www.ridetherails.com

WILMINGTON & WESTERN RAILROAD
Train ride, dinner train
Standard gauge

MIKE CIOSEK

Description: A ten-mile, 1¼-hour round trip over a portion of former Baltimore & Ohio Landenberg Branch from Greenbank Station to Mt. Cuba. Occasional trips to Yorklyn and Hockessin are also offered.

Schedule: April through December: Saturdays and/or Sundays, one- and two-hour excursions along the Red Clay Valley. Call or write for timetable.

Admission/Fare: Varies, please call or write for information. Caboose rentals, group rates, and private charters are available.

Locomotive/Rolling Stock: Two SW-1 EMD switchers; 1909 Alco steam 4-4-0; 1907 Baldwin 0-6-0; 1910 Canadian Locomotive Co. 2-6-0; 1929 PRR railcar.

Special Events: Easter Bunny Special, Santa Claus Express, Dinner Murder Mystery Train.

Nearby Attractions/Accommodations: Longwood Gardens, Hagley Museum, Kalmar Nyckel, Winterthur Museum.

Location/Directions: I-95, exit 5, follow Route 141 north to Route 2 west, then follow Route 41 north. Greenbank Station is on Route 41 just north of Route 2, 4 miles southwest of Wilmington.

Radio frequency: 160.755

Site Address: 2201 Newport-Gap Pike, Route 41, Wilmington, DE
Mailing Address: PO Box 5787, Wilmington, DE 19808
Telephone: (302) 998-1930
Fax: (302) 998-7408

Delaware, Yorklyn

WEST CHESTER RAILROAD
Train ride, dinner train
Standard gauge

WEST CHESTER RAILROAD

Description: A 16-mile round trip from West Chester to Glen Mills. This line is the unused portion of SEPTA's R-3 Elwyn line, which is very scenic as it follows Chester Creek in western Delaware County through eastern Chester County.

Schedule: April, May, September through December: weekends. Charters available year round. Call for information on specials.

Admission/Fare: Adults $9.00; children 2-12 $5.00.

Locomotive/Rolling Stock: Loco-99 EMD GP-9 ex-B&O no. 6499; Loco 1803 is DRS-18U Alco former CP 1803; Reading Blue Liners coaches nos. 9114, 9124, 9117, 9107; baggage car former Pennsy B-60 7551; more.

Special Events: Monthly dinner trains. Easter Bunny Express. West Chester Restaurant Festival, third weekend in September. Pratt & Co. Fall Festival, fourth weekend in September. Fall Foliage, October. Holiday Express, November. Santa Express, November and December.

Nearby Attractions/Accommodations: Q.V.C., Valley Forge National Park, West Chester Restaurants, Chadds Ford, Brandywine Museum.

Location/Directions: Highway 202, exit Gay Street/West Chester. Follow Gay to Matlack turning left, one block to Market, left at railroad station, one block on right.

*Coupon available, see coupon section.

Radio frequency: 160.6050

Site Address: 230 E. Market Street, West Chester, PA
Mailing Address: PO Box 385, Yorklyn, DE 19736
Telephone: (610) 430-2233
Fax: (302) 995-5286

FORT MYERS HISTORICAL MUSEUM
Museum

FORT MYERS HISTORICAL MUSEUM

Description: An historical museum outlining the history of the Fort Myers area from pre-historic to present day; housed in an original ACL passenger depot with a 1929 private Pullman car as an outside exhibit.

Schedule: Year round: Tuesdays through Saturdays, 9 a.m. to 4 p.m.

Admission/Fare: Adults $4.00; children age 12 and under $2.00.

Locomotive/Rolling Stock: Pullman Standard Car & Manufacturing Co. 1929/30 Esperanza no. 6242

Nearby Attractions/Accommodations: Thomas A. Edison winter home, baseball spring training site for Boston Red Sox and Minnesota Twins, Sanibel Island, beaches.

Location/Directions: I-75, exit 23, drive 5 miles west to downtown Ft. Myers. Peck Street is one block south of Dr. Martin Luther King Jr. Blvd.

        M

Site Address: 2300 Peck Street, Ft. Myers, FL 33901
Mailing Address: 2300 Peck Street, Ft. Myers, FL 33901
Telephone: (941) 332-5955
Fax: (941) 332-6637

JEANNE HICKAM

Description: Historical exhibits featuring, but not limited to, railroads that operated in South Florida, historic locomotives, stations, and more.

Schedule: Year round: daily 10 a.m. to 6 p.m. Closed Christmas.

Admission/Fare: Free, donations appreciated.

Special Events: Open House when new major exhibits go on display.

Nearby Attractions/Accommodations: Spring training facilities for Red Sox and Twins. Edison and Ford winter estates. Many motels, hotels, campgrounds, and restaurants.

Location/Directions: Museum is in the Shell Factory complex on Tamiami Trail (Route 41), just north of Fort Myers.

       M

Site Address: 2787 N. Tamiami Trail, North Fort Myers, FL
Mailing Address: PO Box 7372, Fort Myers, FL 33911-7372
Telephone: (941) 997-2457
Fax: (941) 997-7673

**RAILROAD MUSEUM OF
SOUTH FLORIDA—TRAIN VILLAGE**
*Train ride
7½" gauge*

JEANNE HICKAM

Description: A 15-minute, 1⅛-mile ride in county park with tunnel, bridges, gardens, and miniature villages along the right-of-way.

Schedule: Year round: daily, Mondays through Fridays, 10 a.m. to 2 p.m. Saturdays and holidays, 10 a.m. to 4 p.m. Sundays 12 to 4 p.m. Closed Christmas.

Admission/Fare: $2.50; children under age 5, 50 cents. Park charges for parking–75 cents per hour with $3.00 maximum.

Locomotive/Rolling Stock: FP7A diesels nos. 1994, 1995, 1996; 7½" gauge 0-6-0 no. 143 gasoline w/steam sound; GP50 diesel with 3-5 riding cars; 1905 Baldwin 0-6-0 no. 143, former Atlantic Coast Line display (awaiting restoration).

Special Events. Easter Bunny Express–Good Friday, Saturday, Easter Sunday. Halloween Express and Holiday Express with night rides (extra fare). Call or write for information.

Nearby Attractions/Accommodations: Shell Factory, Edison and Ford winter estates, many motels, hotels, and campgrounds.

Location/Directions: Located in Lakes Park/Lee County Park, which is ⅛ mile west of route 41 (Cleveland Ave.) at the south end of Fort Myers.

*Coupon available, see coupon section.

        M

Site Address: 7330 Gladiolus Drive, Fort Myers, FL
Mailing Address: PO Box 7372, Fort Myers, FL 33911-7372
Telephone: (941) 997-2457
Fax: (941) 997-7673

Florida, Fort Myers

SEMINOLE GULF RAILWAY
Train ride, dinner museum
Standard gauge

SEMINOLE GULF RAILWAY

Description: Daytime excursion trains can be boarded at Colonial Station or at Bonita Springs for a 1½-hour round trip or for trips that include the scenic Caloosahatchee River bridge crossing. All dinner trains depart for a 3½-hour round trip from Colonial Station in Fort Myers. They stop during the trip on the Caloosahatchee Bridge for the scenic view or a sunset before continuing the ride north. Special holiday trains are popular, such as the Rail/Boat Christmas train to Punta Gorda featuring a tour by boat, viewing decorated homes and boats along the canals of Punta Gorda Isles.

Schedule: Excursion trains–year round: Wednesdays and weekends. Dinner train theater–Fridays and Saturdays, 6:30 p.m.; Sunday twilighter, 5:30 p.m.

Admission/Fare: Excursion train–adults $7.00 and up; children 3-12 $4.00 and up. Dinner train theater–$54.98; $39.98 Sunday twilighter.

Locomotive/Rolling Stock: Eight GP9s; three RDCs; four dining cars; Sanibel and Captiva, former CN; kitchen; more.

Special Events: Easter, Mother's Day, Father's Day, Thanksgiving, Christmas rail/boat dinner train, Christmas and New Year's Eve dinner trips.

Location/Directions: Excursion and dinner trains depart from Colonial Station near the Colonial Boulevard (SR 884) and Metro Parkway intersection in Fort Myers, three miles west of I-75 exit 22.

*Coupon available, see coupon section.

Site Address: Fort Myers, FL
Mailing Address: 4410 Centerpointe Drive, Fort Myers, FL 33916
Telephone: (941) 275-8487, (800) SEM-GULF, and (800) 736-4853
Fax: (941) 275-0581
E-mail: appelberg@semgulf.com
Internet: www.semgulf.com

GOLD COAST RAILROAD MUSEUM
Museum
Standard and narrow gauge

GOLD COAST RAILROAD EXHIBIT

Description: The Gold Coast Railroad Museum, a non-profit, volunteer organization, has been in existence for over 40 years. Located on approximately 60 acres, which formerly housed the N.A.S. Richmond base in World War II, the museum has over 30 pieces of rolling stock on display and hundreds of railroad memorabilia. Self-guided tours of railroad cars and engines dating from the 1920s to 1950s are available. Railroad artifacts are displayed in one of the baggage cars, while exhibits of N.A.S. Richmond and the early lumbering industry in South Florida, as well as several layouts of model railroads, including one that visitors can operate, are displayed in the buildings.

Schedule: Year round: Mondays through Fridays 11 a.m. to 3 p.m., weekends 11 a.m. to 4 p.m. Guided tours with appointment only.

Admission/Fare: Adults $5.00; children $3.00.

Locomotive/Rolling Stock: Nos. 113 and 153 Florida East Coast steam engines. Ferdinand Magellan, also known as U.S. Presidential Car no. 1, and the only Pullman car ever custom-built for the President of the U.S. The Silver Crescent built in 1948 for the *California Zephyr*.

Location/Directions: Florida Turnpike or U.S. 1 to SW 152nd Street, west to Metro Zoo entrance, take second right, following signs to Gold Coast Railroad Museum.

      M

Site Address: 12450 SW 152nd Street, Miami, FL
Mailing Address: 12450 SW 152nd Street, Miami, FL 33177
Telephone: (305) 253-0063
Fax: (305) 233-4641
Internet: www.elink.net/goldcoast

WEST FLORIDA RAILROAD MUSEUM

Description: Louisville & Nashville Depot was restored in 1992. It houses a telegraph office, exhibits and a gift/hobby shop. A former L&N bridge tender's house contains an HO model diorama and a Gallery of Railroad History. An L&N steel caboose and 4 former L&N passenger cars are also on display.

Schedule: Year round: weekends 10 a.m. to 4:30 p.m., and by appointment.

Admission/Fare: Adults $2.00; children $1.00.

Locomotive/Rolling Stock: Nos. 2715 and 2722 L&N diners; nos. 1652 and 1653 L&N dorm cars; no. 1148 L&N bay-window caboose; no. 1102 SL-SF caboose; no. 18050 L&N PS-1 boxcar.

Special Events: Depot Days Arts & Crafts Festival, first weekend in November.

Nearby Attractions/Accommodations: Near National Museum of Naval Aviation, N.A.S. Pensacola

Location/Directions: I-10, exit 8, north on 191 to Milton. South of Highway 90 on Canal Street to Henry Street.

Site Address: 206 Henry Street, Milton, FL
Mailing Address: 206 Henry Street, Milton, FL
Telephone: (904) 623-3645
Fax: (904) 623-0793

Florida, Mount Dora

MOUNT DORA, TAVARES & EUSTIS RAILROAD
Train ride
Standard gauge

DAVE MINER

Description: The Mount Dora Scenic Railway operates on the 11-mile Sorrento Branch of the Florida Central Railroad. The line was built in 1889 as the Sanford & Lake Eustis Railroad. It was merged into the "Plant System" and became the Atlantic Coast Line by 1902. The route travels through orange groves, rural Florida, and skirts around Lake Dora.

Schedule: Year round: daily, approximately six trips per day.

Admission/Fare: Adults $9.00; seniors $8.00; children 12 and under $5.00.

Locomotive/Rolling Stock: 1926 Edwards Railway Motor Car Company "Doodlebug" (steam operation planned for the future).

Special Events: Art festival, craft shows, bicycle festival, antique car meet, vintage boat festival, antique extravaganzas, and sailboat regatta.

Nearby Attractions/Accommodations: Walt Disney World, Universal Studios, historic downtown with antiquing, shopping, walking, dining, bed and breakfasts, inns, restaurants, lodging.

Location/Directions: Located 30 miles north of Orlando on U.S. highway 441.

Site Address: Pullman business car, 3rd and Alexander Streets, Mount Dora, FL.
Mailing Address: PO Box 641, Mount Dora, FL 32756
Telephone: (800) 625-4307
Fax: (352) 383-9360

Florida, Orlando

TRAINLAND EXPRESS
Train ride, museum
24" gauge

TRAINLAND EXPRESS

Description: One of the largest indoor G gauge train displays featuring interactive scavenger hunt and prize. Museum cabinets with trains from 1920s to present. Train ride lasts 20 minutes.

Schedule: Year round: daily, 10 a.m. to 9 p.m.. Sundays, 12 to 4 p.m.

Admission/Fare: Display, museum, ride–adults $8.95; seniors $7.95; children $5.95. Train only–adults $3.00; children $2.00.

Locomotive/Rolling Stock: No. 15 Mason Bogey replica; two excursion passenger cars.

Nearby Attractions/Accommodations: Disney World, Universal Studios, Sea World, numerous hotels and restaurants.

Location/Directions: I-4 exit 29 (Sand Lake Rd.), east one block to International Drive, turn south ½ mile to Goodings Plaza, on left next to Ripleys.

Site Address: 8255 International Drive, Orlando, FL
Mailing Address: 8255 International Drive, Orlando, FL 32819
Telephone: (407) 363-9002
Fax: (407) 363-0496
E-mail: wolcy@aol.com

THE HENRY MORRISON FLAGLER MUSEUM
Museum

THE HENRY MORRISON FLAGLER MUSEUM

Description: Whitehall, a 55-room Gilded Age estate, was the winter home of Henry M. Flagler, developer of the Florida East Coast Railway that linked the entire east coast of Florida. Visitors to the Flagler Museum experience life during America's Gilded Age through the eyes of one of its most important citizens, Henry Flagler. Flagler, with partners John D. Rockefeller and Samuel Andrews, founded Standard Oil. Displays and exhibits focus on the contributions Flagler made to the state of Florida by building the Florida East Coast Railway and developing tourism and agriculture as the state's major industries.

Schedule: Year round: Tuesdays through Saturdays, 10 a.m. to 5 p.m. Sundays noon to 5 p.m. Closed Thanksgiving, Christmas Day and New Year's Day.

Admission/Fare: Adults $7.00; children 6-12 $3.00. Free on Founders Day.

Locomotive/Rolling Stock: FEC car 91, Henry Flagler's private railcar, built in 1886.

Special Events: Founders Day, June 5. Holiday tours, December.

Nearby Attractions/Accommodations: Museums, zoo, Atlantic Ocean.

Location/Directions: I-95 to exit 52A (Okeechobee Blvd. E.).Travel 3 miles across Intracostal Waterway, left on Cocoanut Row. Museum is ¾ mile on left.

Site Address: One Whitehall Way, Palm Beach, FL
Mailing Address: PO Box 969, Palm Beach, FL 33480
Telephone: (561) 655-2833
Fax: (561) 655-2826
E-mail: flagler@emi.net
Internet: www.flagler.org

FLORIDA GULF COAST RAILROAD MUSEUM, INC.
Train ride, museum
Standard gauge

FLORIDA GULF COAST RAILROAD MUSEUM. INC.

Description: A 12-mile, one-hour-plus ride through rural Florida on passenger cars from the 1920s, 1940s and 1950s.

Schedule: January through April: Saturdays 11 a.m., 2 and 3 p.m.; Sundays 1 and 3 p.m. May through December: Saturdays 11 a.m. and 1 p.m.; Sundays 1 and 3 p.m.

Admission/Fare: Adults $8.00; children ages 3-11 $5.00.

Locomotive/Rolling Stock: GP7 no. 1835; R53 no. 1633; N&W caboose, Kentucky Club lounge; GA coach; Cape Torementire lounge.

Nearby Attractions/Accommodations: Gulf beaches, Busch Gardens.

Location/Directions: I-75 exit 45 (Moccasin Wallow Road, east to U.S. 301, south ¼ mile to 83rd Street, left to train.

*Coupon available, see coupon section.

P   ❋   ☕   🌲   🚂   atm   TRAIN   Tampa

Site Address: 83rd Street East, Parrish, FL
Mailing Address: PO Box 355, Parrish, FL 34219
Telephone: (813) 776-9656

CYPRESS GARDENS, INC.

Description: The world's foremost tropical showplace includes *Cypress Junction* where twenty high-speed model trains tour tiny replicas of U.S. landmarks—Miami, New Orleans, Mt. Rushmore—on 1,100 feet of track. New garden railway spanning 5000 square feet and 600 feet of track. Featured buildings include Florida capitol building, Edison and Hemingway homes, Church Street Depot and more.

Schedule: Year round: daily, 9:30 a.m. to 5:30 p.m. Extended hours during special seasons.

Admission/Fare: Entrance price to theme park: adults $30.95; seniors $26.30; youth 6-17 $20.95; under age 3 are free.

Locomotive/Rolling Stock: Santa Fe no. 3571; B&O or Chessie System BTO no. 3597; Seaboard System no. 6378; Lehigh Valley no. 211; Atlantic Coast Line C-O no. 47124.

Nearby Attractions/Accommodations: Bok Tower, Fantasy Flight and all Orlando attractions.

Location/Directions: I-4 to US 27 south to 540 west. Located in central Florida.

*Coupon available, see coupon section.

Site Address: 2641 S. Lake Summit, Winter Haven, FL
Mailing Address: PO Box 1, Cypress Gardens, FL 33884
Telephone: (941) 324-2111 and (800) 282-2123
Fax: (941) 324-7946
E-mail: robyn@cypressgardens.com
Internet: www.cypressgardens.com

Georgia, Duluth

SOUTHEASTERN RAILWAY MUSEUM
Train ride, display
Standard gauge

SOUTHEASTERN RAILWAY MUSEUM

Description: Visitors meet rail history "hands on" through the display of over 90 pieces of retired railway rolling stock, including a World War II troop kitchen, railway post office, the 1911 Pullman "Superb" used by President Warren Harding, a modern office car, vintage steam locomotives, restored wooden cabooses. Ride on ¾-mile loop track aboard vintage cabooses.

Schedule: April through November: Saturdays 9 a.m. to 5 p.m. Sundays, on third full weekend, 12 to 5 p.m. Train rides included with admission. Exhibits only–December through March: Saturdays, 9 a.m. to 5 p.m.

Admission/Fare: Adults $5.00; seniors and children 2-12 $3.00; under age 2 are free.

Locomotive/Rolling Stock: 1950 and 1941 HRT GE 44-ton nos. 2 and 5; 1943 Georgia Power Porter 0-6-0T no. 97; 1954 CRR caboose no. 1064; SOU caboose XC7871; SCL caboose no. 01077.

Location/Directions: I-85 NW of Atlanta to west on exit 40 (Pleasant Hill Rd.) for 3.5 miles to US 23 (Buford Highway). North ¼ mile to S. Old Peachtree Road, turn west to museum entrance.

Site Address: 3595 S. Old Peachtree Road, Duluth, GA
Mailing Address: PO Box 1267, Duluth, GA 30096
Telephone: (770) 476-2013
Fax: (770) 908-8322
E-mail: 71045.2202@compuserve.com
Internet: www.srmduluth.org

104

KENNESAW CIVIL WAR MUSEUM
Museum
Standard gauge

KENNESAW CIVIL WAR MUSEUM

Description: The Andrews Raid and the Great Locomotive Chase, one of the unusual episodes of the Civil War, has been much publicized over the years. The "General," now one of the most famous locomotives in American history, is enshrined in a museum within 100 yards of the spot where it was stolen on April 12, 1862. The old engine, still operable, last ran in 1962. The Kennesaw Civil War Museum was officially opened on April 12, 1972, 110 years after the historic seizure of the "General."

Schedule: April through September: Mondays through Saturdays, 9:30 a.m. to 5:30 p.m. and Sundays, 12 to 5:30 p.m. October through March: Monday through Saturdays, 10 a.m. to 4 p.m. and Sundays, 12 to 4 p.m.

Admission/Fare: Adults $3.00; seniors $2.50; children 7-15 $1.50; age 6 and under are free.

Locomotive/Rolling Stock: Rodgers Ketchum & Grosvenor 4-4-0 no. 3; Western & Atlantic "General."

Special Events: Big Shanty Festival, April. Kennesaw Antiques Fair, October. Tales From the Rails, Halloween.

Nearby Attractions/Accommodations: Kennesaw Mountain.

Location/Directions: I-75 north (from Atlanta) exit 118 (Wade Green Rd.), west 2.3 miles. Museum is on right.

*Coupon available, see coupon section.

Site Address: 2829 Cherokee Street, Kennesaw, GA
Mailing Address: 2829 Cherokee Street, Kennesaw, GA 30144
Telephone: (770) 427-2117 and (800) 742-6897
Fax: (770) 429-4559
E-mail: kcwm@juno.com
Internet: www.ngeorgia.com/history/kcwm.html

BLUE RIDGE SCENIC RAILWAY
Train ride
Standard gauge

MARTIN K. O'TOOLE

Description: A 26-mile round trip through Murphy Junction to McCaysville, Georgia on the old L&N Hook and Eye Division.

Schedule: April through mid-November: Fridays 3 p.m., Saturdays 9 a.m. and 2 p.m., Sundays 2 p.m.

Admission/Fare: Adults $19.95; seniors $17.95; children ages 4-12 $9.95; under age 3 are free.

Locomotive/Rolling Stock: GP7 no. 2097; GP20 no. 4125; coach 662; commissary car 206; coach 512; coach 972332; open air car 697.

Nearby Attractions/Accommodations: Tennessee Valley Railroad and Museum, Great Smoky Mountain Railroad.

Location/Directions: I-575 to Highway 515 to Blue Ridge. Approximately 1.5 hours due north of Atlanta.

Radio frequency: 160.56 / 154.60

Site Address: 241 Depot Street, Blue Ridge, GA
Mailing Address: 241 Depot Street, Blue Ridge, GA 30513
Telephone: (800) 934-1898
Fax: (706) 258-2756
Internet: www.brscenic.com

PAINTING BY T.J. SCYPINSKI

Description: Savannah's Historic Railroad Shops are an antebellum railroad manufacturing and repair facility. Construction of the site was begun in 1845 and 13 of the original structures are still standing. Included in these structures are the massive roundhouse and operating turntable, and the 125-foot smokestack. The Railroad Shops make up the oldest and most complete railroad repair and manufacturing facility still standing in the United States, and are a National Historic Landmark. The site, owned by the City of Savannah, was used for the filming of the motion picture "Glory" in 1988. On August 1, 1989, operation of the Railroad Shops was taken over by the Coastal Heritage Society. The goal of the site is to present a resource that protects its structures and its history, including artifacts and written history. The site is a multiple-use facility and therefore dedicates its mission to serving as wide a range of public and private use as possible. Permanent exhibits in five of the structures on the site. The Shops are open for self-guided tours.

Schedule: Self-guided tours daily, 10 a.m. to 4 p.m. Group tours and special daytime functions are available at the Shops as well as after-hours functions and dinner programs. Groups are welcomed to enjoy a variety of menus and historic programs. Please call for more information or reservations.

*Coupon available, see coupon section.

Site Address: 601 West Harris Street, Savannah, GA
Mailing Address: 601 West Harris Street, Savannah, GA 31402
Telephone: (912) 651-6823
Fax: (921) 651-3691

Georgia, Stone Mountain   **STONE MOUNTAIN SCENIC RAILROAD**
Train ride
Standard gauge

STONE MOUNTAIN SCENIC RR

Description: A 25-minute narrated trip around Stone Mountain, behind a diesel locomotive.

Schedule: September through May: 10 a.m. to 5:20 p.m. Memorial Day through Labor Day: 10 a.m. to 8 p.m. Extended weekend hours.

Admission/Fare: Adults $4.25; seniors $3.50; children 3-11 $3.20; discount for AAA and military.

Locomotive/Rolling Stock: Two FP7s; GP9; GP7; two Baldwin 4-4-0s; Vulcan 2-6-2 on display.

Special Events: Christmas Train, late November and December. Hayrides, October weekends. Call or write for information.

Nearby Attractions/Accommodations: Attractions within Stone Mountain Park: skylift, riverboat, auto museum, plantation, Confederate memorial carving, wildlife preserve, two hotels, 36-hole golf course.

Location/Directions: Site is 16 miles east of Atlanta off Stone Mountain freeway, U.S. 78, and into Stone Mountain Park.

Site Address: Stone Mountain Park, Stone Mountain, GA
Mailing Address: PO Box 778, Stone Mountain, GA 30086
Telephone: (770) 498-5616 and (770) 498-5615
Internet: www.stonemountainpark.org

HAWAIIAN RAILWAY SOCIETY
Train ride, museum, display
36" gauge

MARK D. BRUESHABER

Description: A 6½-mile, 90-minute ride along OR&L track from Ewa to Kahe
  Point where passengers can witness the surf crashing against the rocks.
  The train passes Barbers Point Naval Air Station, Ko'Olina Golf Course,
  and more. Fully narrated trip provides railroading history of the area.

Schedule: Every Sunday except major holidays. Weekdays by reservation.
  Weather permitting. Call for schedule.

Admission/Fare: Adults $8.00; seniors and children ages 2-12 $5.00; under
  age 2 are free.

Locomotive/Rolling Stock: Two Whitcomb diesel-electrics, nos. 302 and
  423; converted U.S. Army flatcars, parlor car no. 64.

Special Events: Halloween rides, Ewa Carnival. Call or write for information.

Nearby Attractions/Accommodations: Ihilani Resort; Ko'Olina Golf
  Course; Paradise Cover Luau.

Location/Directions: Freeway H-1, exit 5A, continue on 76 (Fort Weaver
  Road) south to Renton Road, right to Fleming Road.

 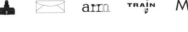 arm TRAIN M

Site Address: 91-1001 Renton Road, Ewa Town, HI
Mailing Address: PO Box 1208, Ewa Station, Ewa, HI 96706
Telephone: (808) 681-5461
Fax: (808) 681-4860
E-mail: hirailway@aolcom
Internet: http://members.aol.com/hawaiianrr/index.html

LAHAINA, KAANAPALI & PACIFIC RAILROAD
Train ride
36" gauge

LAHAINA, KAANAPALI & PACIFIC RAILROAD

Description: The "Sugar Cane Train" chugs its way through the colorful history and breath-taking scenes of Maui by bringing back memories, sounds, and experiences of turn-of-the-century sugar plantation life. The sugar trains of the past were used to transport sugar cane from the fields to the mills and were a popular means of transportation for sugar workers in the early 1900s. Passengers are taken on an entertaining and historical tour by one of our singing conductors. The train stations are designed to resemble turn-of-the-century boarding platforms and are a delightful glimpse at Hawaii's historical and cultural past.

Schedule: Year round: daily 8:55 a.m. to 4:50 p.m. Closed Thanksgiving, Christmas.

Admission/Fare: Round trip–adults $14.50, children $8.00. One-way–adults $10.50, children $6.00. Seniors, military, AAA discounts.

Locomotive/Rolling Stock: No. 1, "Anaka," 1943 Porter 2-4-0 and no. 3, "Myrtle," 1943 Porter 2-4-0, both former Carbon Limestone Co.; no. 45, "Oahu," 1959 Plymouth diesel, former Oahu Railway; nine 19th century King Kalakaua replica nostalgic coaches; two non-operational displays of Oahu 5 and Oahu 86 from Oahu Railway; more.

Nearby Attractions/Accommodations: Historic town of Lahaina, Maui and resort area of Kaanapali.

Location/Directions: Lahaina Station located near Pioneer Mill, turn off Highway 30 at Hinau Street, turn right at Limahana Street.

Site Address: 975 Limahana Place, Suite 203, Lahaina, Maui, HI
Mailing Address: 975 Limahana Place, Suite 203, Lahaina, Maui, HI 96761
Telephone: (800) 499-2307, (888) LKP-MAUI, and (808) 661-0089 (recording)
Fax: (808) 661-8389

SILVERWOOD THEME PARK

Description: A theme park with over 24 rides, shows and attractions.

Schedule: May and September: weekends 11 a.m. to 6 p.m. June through August: daily 11 a.m. to 8 p.m.

Admission/Fare: Ages 8-64 $21.99; ages 3-7 $13.99.

Locomotive/Rolling Stock: Eureka Northern 1915 H.K. Porter no. 7; Cumbras & Toltec Baldwin Locomotive Works 1928 no. 12.

Special Events: Memorial Day, July 4th, Labor Day celebrations.

Nearby Attractions/Accommodations: Farragut State Park, lakes, Spokane, Washington.

Location/Directions: On Highway 95.

Site Address: 26225 N. Highway 95, Athol, ID
Mailing Address: 26225 N. Highway 95, Athol, ID 83801
Telephone: (208) 683-3400
Fax: (208) 683-2268
E-mail: info@silverwood4fun.com
Internet: www.silverwood4fun.com

MONTANA ROCKIES RAIL TOURS
Train ride
Standard gauge

MONTANA ROCKIES RAIL TOURS

Description: Discover the Rocky Mountains by rail on the Montana Daylight. We offer panoramic dome viewing of 455 historic miles over the Northern Pacific route, Sandpoint, Idaho, to Livingston, Montana, in two days and nights. Motorcoach extension tours of Yellowstone, Grand Teton and Glacier Parks are also available.

Schedule: July 9 through September 12: Fridays, eastbound. Sundays: westbound.

Admission/Fare: From $429.00 per person, double.

Locomotive/Rolling Stock: Budd GN dome no. 9407; Pullman Milwaukee dome no. 800265; Budd NP dome no. 9410; SP 48 Budd coaches nos. 4001, 4013; AT&SF 48-seat Budd coaches nos. 4700, 4734.

Nearby Attractions/Accommodations: Lake Pend Oreille, Coeur d'Alene, Spokane River, golf, boat rentals, motorcoach extension tours of Yellowstone, Grand Teton and Glacier Parks.

Site Address: Keefler Junction, Kootenai Siding, Sandpoint, ID
Mailing Address: 1055 Baldy Park Avenue, Sandpoint, ID
Telephone: (208) 265-8618 and (800) 519-RAIL
Fax: (208) 265-8619
E-mail: mtrain@netw.com
Internet: www.keokee.com/railtour

NORTHERN PACIFIC DEPOT RAILROAD MUSEUM

Description: Railroad museum with nine room of exhibits, gift shop and book shop.

Schedule: April through October: daily 9 a.m. to 7 p.m.

Admission/Fare: Adults $2.00; seniors $1.50; children 6-16 $1.00; age 6 and under are free; families $6.00; tours $20.00; school groups $5.00.

Special Events: Depot Days, weekend after Mother's Day.

Nearby Attractions/Accommodations: Town of Wallace is on historical register, Silver Valley/Silver Country, Hiawatha Bike Trail, museums, ski resorts, Glacier National Park.

Location/Directions: I-90, exit 61 or 62. Northern Idaho.

*Coupon available, see coupon section.

Site Address: 219 6th Street, Wallace, ID
Mailing Address: PO Box 469, Wallace, ID 83873
Telephone: (208) 752-0111
Fax: (208) 753-9361

Illinois, Chicago

HISTORIC PULLMAN FOUNDATION
Museum, display

HISTORIC PULLMAN FOUNDATION

Description: The historic Pullman Foundation is a non-profit organization whose goals are preservation and education of the Pullman Historic District. The FPF operates the Hotel Florence Restaurant and Museum, c. 1881, and Pullman Visitor Center.

Schedule: Hotel Florence–Mondays through Fridays 11 a.m. to 2 p.m., Saturdays 10 a.m. to 2 p.m., Sunday Brunch 10 a.m. to 3 p.m. Visitor Center–Saturdays 11 a.m. to 2 p.m., Sundays 12 to 3 p.m. Guided Walking Tours–May through October, first Sunday 12:30 and 1:30 p.m.

Admission/Fare: Pullman Visitor Center: adults $3.00; students $2.00.

Special Events: Annual Pullman House Tour, second weekend in October. Quarterly Victorian Dinners at Hotel Florence.

Nearby Attractions/Accommodations: Downtown Chicago, Sandridge Nature Center, riverboat casinos.

Location/Directions: I-94 exit 66A (111th St.), travel west 4 blocks. Site is located 13 miles south of Chicago's Loop.

*Coupon available, see coupon section.

Site Address: 11111 S. Forrestville Avenue, Chicago, IL
Mailing Address: 11111 S. Forrestville Avenue, Chicago, IL 60628-4649
Telephone: (773) 785-3828
Fax: (773) 785-8182
E-mail: pullmanIL@aol.com

ALEX TREML

Description: The Museum of Science and Industry is one of the nation's preeminent centers for informal science and technology education. The model railroad exhibit was originally installed in 1941. The layout is approximately 3,000 square feet. Features include an O gauge track that is ⅟₄₈ the actual size, totaling 1,200 feet, in addition to 10,000 feet of switchboard wire, 350 relays, 5,500 trees, 150 telegraph poles, as well as a host of freight cars.

Schedule: Labor Day through Memorial Day: weekdays 9:30 a.m. to 4 p.m., weekends and holidays till 5:30 p.m. Memorial Day through Labor Day: daily 9:30 a.m. to 5:30 p.m. Closed Christmas.

Admission/Fare: Adults $7.00; seniors $6.00; children 3-11 $3.50; under age 3 are free. Free on Thursdays.

Locomotive/Rolling Stock: Engine 999 was the first vehicle to go over 100 mph. The *Pioneer Zephyr* was the first streamlined diesel-electric train.

Nearby Attractions/Accommodations: Hyde Park, University of Chicago, Shedd Aquarium, Field Museum, Planetarium, Art Institute, Navy Pier.

Location/Directions: Lake Shore Drive south to 57th Street.

Site Address: 57th Street and Lake Shore Drive, Chicago, IL
Mailing Address: 57th Street and Lake Shore Drive, Chicago, IL 60637
Telephone: (773) 684-1414
Fax: (773) 684-2907
Internet: www.msichicago.org

AMERICAN ORIENT EXPRESS
RAIL EXPEDITIONS
Train ride
Standard gauge

JACK PARSONS

Description: Travel through North America's most scenic regions aboard the American Orient Express. The train consists of 15 vintage carriages, which glisten with polished mahogany and brass. Relax in the comfort of a club car. Enjoy the thoughtful service of friendly porters. Savor superb cuisine at an elegant table with an ever-changing view.

Schedule: February through November.

Admission/Fare: Trips range from $1,890.00 to $4,990.00 per person including nights aboard the AOE, meals, excursions.

Locomotive/Rolling Stock: Two Amtrak locomotives.

Special Events: Family Departure to the Great Northwest, June 25 through July 1.

Site Address: Varies.
Mailing Address: 5100 Main Street, Suite 300, Downers Grove, IL 60515
Telephone: (888) 759-3944 and (630) 663-4550
Fax: (630) 663-1595

LITTLE TOOT RAILROAD COMPANY
Train ride, museum
15" gauge

LITTLE TOOT RAILROAD COMPANY

Description: A 1.25-mile, 20-minute ride through beautiful Charley Brown Memorial Park crossing three trestles, including a spectacular 150-foot-long wood trestle. The railroad was founded in 1959 by Gaylon F. Borders. Following his death in 1966 the train was sold and removed from the park. The train was purchased by a local railroad enthusiast and in 1999 it will reopen in its original location following a 32-year absence.

Schedule: May through October: Wednesdays through Fridays 11 a.m. to 9 p.m.; Saturdays 10 a.m. to 9 p.m.; Sundays 1 to 7 p.m. November 5 through January 1: daily 1 to 9 p.m.

Admission/Fare: $3.00.

Locomotive/Rolling Stock: Locomotives; coaches; flatcars; ballast cars; more.

Special Events: Grand Opening, May 15. Moonlight Dinner Trains, summer. Father's Day. Mother's Day. Throw Momma on the Train. Steam in the Park, June. Freedom Weekend, July 4. Pumpkin Trains, October. Christmas Trains, November and December.

Nearby Attractions/Accommodations: Camping, fishing, swimming, golf.

Location/Directions: Four miles west of downtown Flora on Old U.S. Route 50, Charley Brown Park.

Site Address: RR 2, Box 199B, Flora, IL
Mailing Address: RR 2, Box 199B, Flora, IL 62839
Telephone: (618) 662-6116
Fax: (618) 662-5036
Internet: www.littletootrailroad.com

SILVER CREEK & STEPHENSON RAILROAD
Train ride, display
Standard gauge

STEVE SNYDER

Description: The "Turn-of-the-Century" Silver Creek Depot is a tribute to an important part of our country's transportation history. On display are lanterns, locks and keys, whistles, sounders, tickets, couplers, and more, representing railroads from across the country. The 4-mile train trip travels through Illinois farmland and stands of virgin timber known as "Indian Gardens," crossing Yellow Creek on a 30-foot high cement and stone pier bridge.

Schedule: May 30-31; June 19-20; July 4, 23-25; September 6, 25-26; October 9-10, 23-24: 11 a.m. to 5 p.m.

Admission/Fare: Adults $4.00; children (under 12) $2.00.

Locomotive/Rolling Stock: 1912, 36-ton Heisler; 1941 bay-window caboose, former Chicago, Milwaukee, St. Paul & Pacific; 1889 wooden caboose with cupola, former Hannibal & St. Joseph, reported to be the oldest running caboose in Illinois; 1948 caboose, former Illinois Central Gulf; covered flatcar; 14-ton Brookville switch engine; 12-ton Plymouth switch engine; and work cars.

Location/Directions: Intersection of Walnut and Lamm Roads, ½ mile south of Stephenson County Fairgrounds.

        M

Site Address: 2954 W. Walnut Road, Freeport, IL
Mailing Address: PO Box 255, Freeport, IL 61032
Telephone: (800) 369-2955 and (815) 232-2306

GALESBURG RAILROAD MUSEUM

Description: As you visit the Galesburg Railroad Museum, you will experience railroading of the early 1900s. The Museum has restored an engine and three cars built in the 20s and 30s and maintains an extensive collection of railroad memorabilia.

Schedule: Memorial Day through Labor Day: daily except Mondays, 12 to 5 p.m. Group tours by appointment.

Admission/Fare: Adults $1.00; youth over age 12 $.50.

Locomotive/Rolling Stock: Steam engine CB&Q 300b Hudson 54; BCB&Q 2645 Pullman parlor car; CB&Q 1945 RPO baggage car; CB&Q 13501 caboose.

Special Events: Railroad Days city-wide celebration, last full weekend in June.

Nearby Attractions/Accommodations: Carl Sandburg birthsite, Knox College, site of Lincoln-Douglas debate, camping, amusement parks.

Location/Directions: I-74 exit 48, west to downtown Galesburg.

           M

Site Address: 423 Mulberry Street, Galesburg, IL
Mailing Address: PO Box 947, Galesburg, IL 61402-0947
Telephone: (309) 342-9400

UNION DEPOT RAILROAD MUSEUM
Museum

ALICE ZEMAN

Description: The restored 1940s station features an operating HO layout replica of downtown Mendota in the 1940s during its heyday as a railroad center with the Milwaukee, Illinois Central, and Burlington Railroads. Also see the old time telegraphy office, railroad memorabilia, and more.

Schedule: May through September: daily except Mondays and Tuesdays, 12 to 5 p.m. October through April: Saturdays and Sundays, 12 to 5 p.m.

Admission/Fare: $2.00; children under age 12 $1.00; members are free. Tours available.

Locomotive/Rolling Stock: Burlington O-1A Mikado-type locomotive 2-8-2 no. 4978; tender; Burlington waycar no. 14451.

Special Events: First annual Railroad Crossing Days Festival, June 19 and 20. Mendota Sweet Corn Festival, second week in August.

Nearby Attractions/Accommodations: Hume-Carnegie Historical Museum, Breaking the Prairie Agricultural Museum, restaurants, lodging, campgrounds.

Location/Directions: I-39/51 and route 34, approximately 100 miles west of Chicago, and 50 miles south of Rockford.

       M

Site Address: 783 Main Street, Mendota, IL
Mailing Address: PO Box 433, Mendota, IL 61342
Telephone: (815) 538-3800

MONTICELLO RAILWAY MUSEUM
Train ride, museum
Standard gauge

DAVID MARSHALL

Description: This museum, incorporated in 1966, offers a 50-minute round trip over former Illinois Central and Illinois Terminal trackage. Passengers board at the Illinois Central Depot at the museum or at the 1899 Wabash Depot in downtown Monticello. Displays of the following are on site: 1907 Baldwin 2-8-0, former Southern Railway no. 401; Shedd Aquarium's "Nautilus" (fish car); Nickel Plate RPO; Santa Fe Pullman "Pleasant Valley"; 1931 Alco 0-4-0 tank engine no. 1; 1944 Industrial Brownhoist; freight equipment; cabooses.

Schedule: May through October: weekends and holidays, 1, 2, 3, and 4 p.m. at museum site; 1:30, 2:30 and 3:30 p.m. in town. Charters, private cars, birthday caboose on request. Throttle times available.

Admission/Fare: Call or write for information.

Locomotive/Rolling Stock: No. 1, 1930 Alco 0-4-0, former Montezuma Gravel Co.; no. 191, 1916 Alco 0-6-0, former Republic Steel Corp.; no. 301, 1955 Alco RS-3, former Long Island Railroad; more.

Special Events: Photographer's Special, April. Railroad Days, September, more.

Nearby Attractions/Accommodations: Monticello's Millionaire Row, Amish.

Location/Directions: I-72 exit 166, Market Street. Site is located between Champaign and Decatur.

*Coupon available, see coupon section.

Champaign   **Radio frequency: 160.635**

Site Address: 993 Access Road, Monticello, IL
Mailing Address: PO Box 401, Monticello, IL 61856-0401
Telephone: (217) 762-9011 and (800) 952-3396
E-mail: mrm@prairienet.org
Internet: www.prairienet.org/mrm

RAYVILLE RAILROAD MUSEUM
(PIATT COUNTY MUSEUM)
Layout
HO gauge

RAYVILLE RAILROAD MUSEUM

Description: Enjoy a complete 10 x 36 foot HO layout with a town, circus, race track, coal mines, lakes, farms, picnic grounds and more. It is a beautiful hand built display crafted by the late Ray McIntyer.

Schedule: Weekends 1 to 3:30 p.m. Other times by appointment.

Admission/Fare: Adults $2.00; children $1.00.

Nearby Attractions/Accommodations: Railroad museum, train depot and rides, Best Western Motel, restaurants.

Location/Directions: Off I-72, Decatur/Champaign, half block west of court house. Twenty miles southwest of Champaign and 23 miles east of Decatur.

*Coupon available, see coupon section.

Site Address: 217 W. Washington, Monticello, IL
Mailing Address: Curator, 801 Tyler Ct., Monticello, IL 61856-2246
Telephone: (217) 762-2308

WHEELS O' TIME MUSEUM

Description: Steam locomotive with combo car, caboose, and switcher. Antique autos, fire trucks, clocks, tools, toys, farm equipment, and more.

Schedule: May through October: Wednesdays through Sundays and holidays, 12 to 5 p.m. and other times by appointment. Group tours available.

Admission/Fare: Adults $4.00; children $1.50. Group rates available.

Locomotive/Rolling Stock: Rock Island Pacific no. 886; Milwaukee Road combine no. 2716; TP&W caboose no. 508; Plymouth switcher.

Nearby Attractions/Accommodations: Wildlife Prairie Park, Lakeview Museum

Location/Directions: On Route 40, north of Peoria.

      M

Site Address: 11923 N. Knoxville, Dunlap, IL
Mailing Address: PO Box 9636, Peoria, IL 61612-9636
Telephone: (309) 243-9020 and (309) 691-3470
E-mail: wotmuseum@aol.com
Internet: members.aol.com/wotmuseum

DANVILLE JUNCTION CHAPTER, NRHS
Museum, layout

RICHARD M. SCHROEDER

Description: Displays show the history of former Chicago & Eastern Illinois and other area railroads. The Baggage Room contains an HO model railroad. The Depot Museum preserves the railroads' history in east Central Illinois and western Indiana in a former C&EI Railroad Depot.

Schedule: Memorial Day weekend through last Sunday in September: weekends, noon to 4 p.m. and by appointment.

Admission/Fare: Free. Donations are appreciated.

Nearby Attractions/Accommodations: Rossville Historical Society Museum, Mann's Chapel, Vermilion County Museum, 15 antique shops in downtown area.

Location/Directions: In Rossville, one block north on Illinois Route 1 to Benton Street, east three blocks to CSX transportation tracks.

    M

Site Address: East Benton Street, Rossville, IL
Mailing Address: PO Box 1013, Danville, IL 61834-1013
Telephone: (217) 748-6615
E-mail: djcnrhs@prairienet.org or rickshro@aol.com
Internet: http://www.prairienet.org/djc-nrhs/

FOX RIVER TROLLEY MUSEUM

Train ride, museum
Standard gauge

FRED LONNES

Description: Ride the historic 102-year-old remnant of an interurban rail-road aboard Chicago-area interurban and "el" equipment. Includes the oldest surviving American interurban, Chicago, Aurora & Elgin no. 20 (shown above).

Schedule: May 9 through November 7: Sundays and holidays, 11 a.m. to 5 p.m. June 19 through September 4, October 23 and 30: Saturdays. June 19-20, August 21-22: 11 a.m. to 8 p.m. November 6: 5 to 10 p.m.

Admission/Fare: Adults $2.50; seniors $2.00; children 3-11 $1.50; under age 3 are free. Second ride $.50 (exceptions noted).

Locomotive/Rolling Stock: Historic Chicago interurban and "el" equipment including CA&E no. 20; North Shore nos. 715 and 756; CTA 4451; CRT 5001; CSL S-202.

Special Events: Mother's Day; Spring Caboose Train Day, June 6; Family Fair, June 19-20; Red, White, Blue Dollar Day, July 4; Riverfest, August 21-22; Fall Foliage, October 3 and 10; Pumpkin Trolley, October 23, 24, 30; Haunted Trolley, October 31; Railfan Night, November 6.

Nearby Attractions/Accommodations: Grand Victoria Casino, Elgin; historic towns of St. Charles and Geneva; Blackhawk Forest Preserve.

Location/Directions: Illinois 31 south from I-90 or US 20, or north from I-88. Site is 3 blocks south of State Street stoplight in South Elgin.

Site Address: 365 S. LaFox Street (Illinois 31), South Elgin, IL
Mailing Address: PO Box 315, South Elgin, IL 60177-0315
Telephone: (847) 697-4676
E-mail: infor@foxtrolley.org
Internet: www.foxtrolley.org

ILLINOIS RAILWAY MUSEUM
Museum
Standard gauge

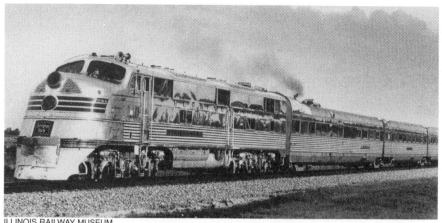

ILLINOIS RAILWAY MUSEUM

Description: I.R.M. is America's largest railroad museum with the most comprehensive collection in the nation. A collection of over 25 steam locomotives and more than 300 pieces of rail equipment of all types. The museum also has a C&NW depot built in 1851, a signal tower, and a restored Chicago "el" station. A 5-mile, 25-minute round trip over the reconstructed right-of-way of the former Elgin & Belvedere, featuring steam and/or diesel trains and electric interurban on weekends and streetcars on weekdays.

Schedule: May 25 through September 6: daily. April, May, September, and October: weekends.

Admission/Fare: Weekends: adults $8.00; children 5-11 $6.00. Weekdays: adults $6.00; children 5-11 $3.50. Maximum family admission $30.00. Higher fares for some special events.

Locomotive/Rolling Stock: No. 2903 Santa Fe 4-8-4; no. 2050 N&W 2-8-8-2; no. 9911A CB&Q EMC E5; no. 6930 UP DDA 40X; Electroliner; many more.

Special Events: Scout Day, May 15. Chicago Weekend, June 19-20. Trolley Pageant, July 4. Diesel Days, July 17-18. 9th Annual Vintage Transport Extravaganza, August 1. Railfan Weekend, September 4-6. Member's Weekend, September 25-26. Harvest Days Weekend, October 9-10.

Location/Directions: One mile east of Union off U.S. Route 20.

Site Address: 7000 Olson Road, Union, IL
Mailing Address: PO Box 427, Union, IL 60108
Telephone: (815) 923-4391 or (815) 923-4000 recorded message
Fax: (815) 923-2006
Internet: www.irm.org

Illinois, Union (McHenry County)

VALLEY VIEW
MODEL RAILROAD
Layout
HO gauge

VALLEY VIEW MODEL RAILROAD

Description: This display is modeled after the Chicago & North Western's Northwest line, with accurate track layouts of some of the towns modeled. Three to four trains operate simultaneously over the railroad, which has eight scale miles of track, 16 ever-changing trains, 250 buildings, 64 turnouts, 250 vehicles, 450 people, 84 operating signal lights, 250 pieces of rolling stock, and operating grade crossings with flashers and gates. Extra equipment is on static display in the gift shop.

Schedule: Memorial Day through Labor Day: Wednesdays, Saturdays, and Sundays.

Admission/Fare: Adults $4.00; seniors $3.50; children $2.00; age five and under are free.

Nearby Attractions/Accommodations: Illinois Railway Museum, Wild West Town, McHenry County Museum.

Location/Directions: Travel north ¾ mile on Olson Road to Highbridge.

*Coupon available, see coupon section.

Site Address: 17108 Highbridge Road, Union, IL
Mailing Address: 17108 Highbridge Road, Union, IL 60180
Telephone: (815) 923-4135

WHITEWATER VALLEY RAILROAD
Train ride
Standard gauge

MAURICE HENSLEY, WHITEWATER VALLEY RAILROAD

Description: This line offers a 32-mile, 5.5-hour round trip to Metamora, Indiana, a restored canal town featuring 100 shops and a working grist mill. A 2-hour stopover at Metamora gives passengers a chance to tour the town.

Schedule: June through September: weekends and holidays 12:01 p.m. May: Wednesdays through Sundays and holidays 10 a.m. October: Thursdays through Sundays and holidays 10 a.m.

Admission/Fare: Adults $12.00; children 2-12 $6.00; under age 2 are free. One-way and group rates available.

Locomotive/Rolling Stock: No. 6, 1907 Baldwin 0-6-0, former East Broad Top; no. 8, 1946 General Electric, former Muncie & Western; no. 11, 1924 Vulcan 0-4-0T; no. 100, 1919 Baldwin 2-6-2; no. 25, 1951 Lima SW7.5; no. 210, 1946 General Electric 70-ton; no. 709, 1950 Lima SW10; no. 2561, 1931 Plymouth 32-ton gas engine; no. 9339, 1948 Alco S1; no. 9376, 1950 Lima SW12, former Baltimore & Ohio.

Special Events: Metamora Canal Days, first weekend in October; Christmas Trains, November and December. Train-to-Dinner, first/third Fridays of each month May through October.

Nearby Attractions/Accommodations: Whitewater State Park, Brookville Lake, Mary Gray Bird Sanctuary.

*Coupon available, see coupon section.

       Radio Frequency: 160.650

Site Address: 300 S. Eastern Avenue, Connersville, IN
Mailing Address: PO Box 406, Connersville, IN 47331
Telephone: (765) 825-2054
Fax: (765) 825-4550
Internet: http://www.larryvaughn.com/WVRR

CORYDON SCENIC RAILROAD
Train ride
Standard gauge

RICHARD PEARSON

Description: A 1.5-hour, 16-mile ride over part of the 114-year-old Louisville, New Albany & Corydon Railroad from Corydon (the state's first capitol) to Corydon Junction. Air-conditioned trains with guides aboard to answer passengers' questions as the train travels along Big Indiana Creek into the southern Indiana woods and hills, crossing two major bridges and passing many sinkholes.

Schedule: May through October.

Admission/Fare: Adults $9.00; children $5.00.

Locomotive/Rolling Stock: Two 44-ton GE center cab diesels; two Alco 1000 horsepower RS1s.

Nearby Attractions/Accommodations: Bear Cave, first state capitol, Caesar's Gaming Boat.

Location/Directions: I-64, exit 105 to train station in downtown Corydon.

Site Address: 210 W. Walnut Street, Corydon, IN
Mailing Address: PO Box 10, Corydon, IN 47112
Telephone: (812) 738-8000
Fax: (812) 738-3101

NATIONAL NEW YORK CENTRAL
RAILROAD MUSEUM
Museum

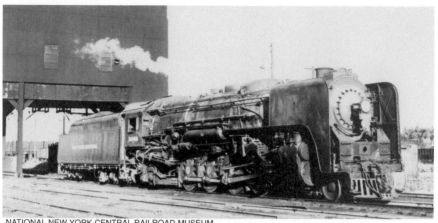

NATIONAL NEW YORK CENTRAL RAILROAD MUSEUM

Description: The museum traces the rich history of the New York Central and its impact on Elkhart and the nation. Extensive hands-on exhibits bring railroading alive!

Schedule: Year round: Tuesdays through Fridays, 10 a.m. to 2 p.m.; Saturdays 10 a.m. to 4 p.m.; Sundays 12 to 4 p.m. Closed Mondays and major holidays.

Admission/Fare: Adults $2.00; seniors and students 6-14 $1.00; children age five and under are free.

Locomotive/Rolling Stock: NYC 3001 L3a Mohawk Alco 1940; NYC 4085 E8 LaGrange 1951; PRR 4882 GG1; freight and passenger equipment.

Nearby Attractions/Accommodations: Northern Indiana Amish Country, Midwest Museum of American Art, S. Ray Miller Auto Museum, Ruthmere.

Location/Directions: Indiana Toll Road exit 92. Main Street in downtown Elkhart, next to the tracks.

Site Address: 721 S. Main Street, Elkhart, IN
Mailing Address: PO Box 1708, Elkhart, IN 46515
Telephone: (219) 294-3001
Fax: (219) 295-9434
E-mail: artscul@elkhartindiana.org
Internet: www.nycrrmuseum.railfan.net

FORT WAYNE RAILROAD
HISTORICAL SOCIETY
Train ride, museum
Standard gauge

TOM NITZA

Description: The FWRHS is America's most successful all-volunteer main-line steam operator. Various excursions throughout the midwest. Engineer-for-an-hour program.

Schedule: Call for a recorded message.

Admission/Fare: Varies according to excursion sponsor.

Locomotive/Rolling Stock: NKP 2-8-4 Berkshire steam locomotive no. 765; Lake Erie & Fort Wayne 0-6-0 no. 1; NKP wooden caboose no. 141; Wabash wooden caboose no. 2543; N&W wrecker no. 540019; 44-ton Davenport diesel no. 1231; NKP wooden boxcar no. 83047.

Special Events: Annual Open House, August.

Location/Directions: From New Haven take Dawkins Road east to Ryan Road, left to Edgerton Road, turn right and site is 1.5 miles on the right.

Site Address: 15808 Edgerton Road, New Haven, IN
Mailing Address: PO Box 11017, Fort Wayne, IN 46855
Telephone: (219) 493-0765
E-mail: info@steamloco765.org
Internet: www.steamloco765.org

Indiana, French Lick

FRENCH LICK, WEST BADEN & SOUTHERN RAILWAY
Train ride
Standard gauge

ALAN BARNETT

Description: A 20-mile, 1¾-mile round trip between the resort town of French Lick and Cuzco, site of Patoka Lake. The train traverses wooded Indiana limestone country and passes through one of the state's longest railroad tunnels.

Schedule: April through October: weekends and May 25 and September 7: 10 a.m., 1 and 4 p.m. November: 1 p.m. June through October: Tuesdays, 1 p.m.

Admission/Fare: Adults $8.00; children 3-11 $4.00; under 3 ride free.

Locomotive/Rolling Stock: 1947 General Electric 80-ton diesel no. 3; 1947 Alco RS-1 no. 4; open window Rock Island coaches.

Special Events: Wild West holdups are scheduled for many holiday weekends. Call or write for dates and times.

Nearby Attractions/Accommodations: French Lick Springs Resort.

Location/Directions: Trains depart the old Monon Passenger Depot on Highway 56 in French Lick.

Site Address: 1 Monon Street, French Lick, IN
Mailing Address: 1 Monon Street, French Lick, IN 47432
Telephone: (812) 936-2405 and (800) 74-TRAIN
Fax: (812) 936-2904

HESSTON STEAM MUSEUM
Train ride, museum
Various gauges

HESSTON STEAM MUSEUM

Description: Train rides from full scale to amusement-park size to hobby scale. Each railroad has 2 to 2.5 miles of mainline trackage. All live steam operation. Also see steam sawmill, steam light plant, 92-ton steam railroad crane, and more. All operational.

Schedule: Memorial Day weekend through Labor Day: Saturdays and Sundays. September through October: Sundays. Noon to 5 p.m.

Admission/Fare: Free admission except Labor Day weekend. Train rides, adults $3.00; children $2.00.

Locomotives/Rolling Stock: Darjeeling & Himalayan built by Atlas Works; New Mexico Lumber Shay built by Lima Locomotive.

Special Events: Whistle-Stop Days, Memorial Day weekend; Whistle Fest, July 4; Annual Steam Show, Labor Day weekend.

Nearby Attractions/Accommodations: Lighthouse Mall, Dunes National Lakeshore, Washington Park Beach/Zoo, Blue Chip Casino, charter boat fishing, Door Prairie Auto Museum, motels.

Location/Directions: South of Indiana-Michigan state line. Four miles east of State Road 39 north of LaPorte or south of New Buffalo to 1000 North, turn east, traveling for about 3 miles

Site Address: County Road 1000 North
Mailing Address: 2946 Mt. Clair Way, Michigan City, IN 46360
Telephone: (219) 872-7405 or (219) 872-5055
Fax: (219) 874-8239

THE CHILDREN'S MUSEUM
OF INDIANAPOLIS
Museum

ED LACEY

Description: The 356,000-square-foot facility is home to ten major galleries, including the newest addition of a large format CineDome theater and outdoor Festival Park area. Programs explore the physical and natural sciences, history, foreign cultures and the arts. Whenever possible, exhibits are "hands-on" or participatory in nature. The world's largest children's museum invites you to view the world from a seat in our CineDome theater, dig for fossils, try your skill at a rock-climbing wall, hop a ride on our turn-of-the-century carousel and sail through the cosmos in our SpaceQuest Planetarium.

Schedule: March 1 through Labor Day, daily 10 a.m. to 5 p.m. September through February, closed Mondays.

Admission/Fare: Museum–adults $8.00; seniors $7.00; children 2-17 $3.50. Group rates available. Additional fees for CineDome, SpaceQuest, and Lilly Theater.

Locomotive/Rolling Stock: Reuben Wells, a 35-foot long, 55-ton steam engine. It was used to push five to eight cars and freight up Madison Hill, the steepest U.S. railroad grade in 1868, in 15 minutes.

Location/Directions: Museum is located five minutes north of downtown at 30th and Meridian Streets. Free parking available in the museum lot on Illinois Street (one street west of Meridian).

Site Address: 3000 N. Meridian Street, Indianapolis, IN
Mailing Address: PO Box 3000, Indianapolis, IN 46206-3000
Telephone: (317) 924-5431
Fax: (317) 921-4000
E-mail: tcmi@childrensmuseum.org
Internet: www.childrensmuseum.org

CARTHAGE, KNIGHTSTOWN & SHIRLEY RAILROAD
Train ride
Standard gauge

CARTHAGE, KNIGHTSTOWN & SHIRLEY RAILROAD

Description: A ten mile, 1.25 hour round trip over the former Cleveland, Cincinnati, Chicago & St. Louis Michigan Division through scenic country, crossing the Big Blue River into Carthage, Indiana. Train leaves from the former NYC freight house in Knightstown.

Schedule: May through October: weekends and holidays, 11 a.m., 1, and 3 p.m. Fridays, 1 p.m.

Admission/Fare: Adults $6.00; children 3-11 $4.00; under age three ride free. Group rates available.

Locomotive/Rolling Stock: No. 215 45-ton GE, former Air Force no. 1215.

Location/Directions: Thirty three miles east of Indianapolis on U.S. 40; three miles out of I-70 on state route 109.

Site Address: 112 W. Carey Street, Knightstown, IN
Mailing Address: 112 W. Carey Street, Knightstown, IN 46148
Telephone: (317) 345-5561

LINDEN RAILROAD MUSEUM
Museum

LINDEN RAILROAD MUSEUM

Description: Operated by the Linden-Madison Township Historical Society, this museum is housed in the former Linden depot built by the Chicago, Indianapolis & Louisville Railway and the Toledo, St. Louis & Western Railroad in 1908. Restored to its 1950s appearance, the depot houses a collection of railroadiana from the Nickel Plate and Monon railroads. An HO model railroad club operates a 1950s depiction of Linden in the Monon baggage room. Both O and N gauge layouts are featured in the NKP baggage room.

Schedule: April through October: Wednesday through Sunday, 1 to 5 p.m. Group tours by appointment.

Admission/Fare: Adults $2.00, teens 13-17 $1.00, children 6-12 $.50, under age 6 are free.

Locomotive/Rolling Stock: Former Nickel Plate caboose no. 497; Fairmont A-3 motor car.

Special Events: Second Annual Civil War Weekend August 14-15.

Nearby Attractions/Accommodations: Old jail museum, Crawfordsville, Indiana.

Location/Directions: South of Lafayette on U.S. 231 and is 7.9 miles north of the Crawfordsville exit off I-74. The depot museum is across from Jane Stoddard Park in Linden.

*Coupon available, see coupon section.

         M

Site Address: 514 N. Main Street, Linden, IN
Mailing Address: PO Box 154, Linden, IN 47955
Telephone: (705) 339-7245 or (800) 866-3973
E-mail: weaver@tctc.com
Internet: http://www.tctc.com/~weaver/depot.htm

Indiana, Madison

JEFFERSON COUNTY HISTORICAL SOCIETY MUSEUM AND RAILROAD
Museum

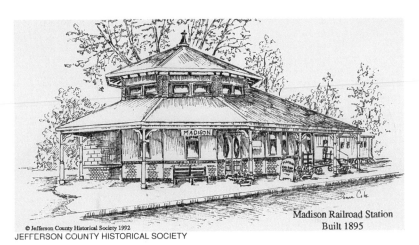

© Jefferson County Historical Society 1992
JEFFERSON COUNTY HISTORICAL SOCIETY

Madison Railroad Station
Built 1895

Description: Restored 1895 Pennsylvania Railroad station known for its 2½-story octagon waiting room topped by stained glass windows. View other local railroad memorabilia, civil war and steam boat displays.

Schedule: May 1 through October 31: Mondays through Saturdays 10 a.m. to 4:30 p.m., Sundays 1 to 4 p.m. November through April, weekdays only.

Admission/Fare: $3.00; youth 16 and under are free.

Locomotive/Rolling Stock: 1920 LM caboose

Special Events: Madison in Bloom, last weekend in April and first weekend in May.

Nearby Attractions/Accommodations: Clifty Falls State Park, Lanier Mansion, antique shops, wineries, bed & breakfast, Ohio River.

Location/Directions: Highways 56 and 421, located in downtown historic Madison.

       M

Site Address: 615 W. 1st Street, Madison, IN
Mailing Address: 615 W. 1st Street, Madison, IN 47250
Telephone: (812) 265-2335
Fax: (812) 273-5023
E-mail: jchs@seidata.com
Internet: www.seidata.com/~jchs

INDIANA TRANSPORTATION MUSEUM
Train ride, display
Standard gauge

JIM VAWTER

Description: Many railroad cars on display. Henry M. Flagler private car open on special occasions. Train rides through rural Hamilton county available weekends.

Schedule: April, May, September, and October: weekends, 10 a.m. to 5 p.m. Memorial Day through Labor Day: Tuesday through Sunday, 10 a.m. to 5 p.m. Trains run each weekend at 1:30 p.m.

Admission/Fare: Museum: adults $3.00; children 4-12 $2.00. Train: adults $7.00; children 4-12 $5.00. Children under 3 are free.

Locomotive/Rolling Stock: EMD F7 and FP7 diesels; 1918 Baldwin steam engine no. 587, former NKP; 8 stainless steel coaches from 1937 Santa Fe Scout.

Special Events: Fair Train during Indiana State Fair, August. Train rides to Atlanta New Earth Festival, September. Hamiltonian to restaurants in Cicero and Atlanta, Friday evenings.

Nearby Attractions/Accommodations: Conner Prairie Museum in Fishers, Children's Museum in Indianapolis, Motel 8 in Noblesville.

Location/Directions: Located 20 miles north of Indianapolis in Forest Park/Noblesville on State Road 19 just north of the intersection with State Road 32.

Site Address: 325 Cicero Road, Noblesville, IN
Mailing Address: PO Box 83, Noblesville, IN 46061-0083
Telephone: (317) 773-6000 recording
Fax: (317) 773-5530

HOOSIER VALLEY
RAILROAD MUSEUM, INC.
Train ride, museum
Standard gauge

BRUCE EMMONS

Description: Established in North Judson since 1988, the organization has been in the process of building the physical plant for a working railroad museum. The collection today consists of 30 pieces of railroad rolling stock. This includes the former 2-8-4 Chesapeake & Ohio steam locomotive no. 2789, which is under roof and being restored.

Schedule: Year round: Saturdays, 8 a.m. to 5 p.m.

Admission/Fare: No charge.

Locomotive/Rolling Stock: C&O 1947 Alco K-4 2-8-4 no. 2789; Erie 1947 Alco S-1 switcher no. 310; EL caboose no. C345; 30 pieces rolling stock.

Special Events: Appreciation Day/Open House, Annual Dinner. Dates to be announced.

Nearby Attractions/Accommodations: Tippecanoe River State Park, Bass Lake State Beach, Kersting's Cycle Center & Museum, Oak View Motel.

Location/Directions: Seventy miles southeast of downtown Chicago, Indiana 10 and 39.

        M

Site Address: 507 Mulberry Street, North Judson, IN
Mailing Address: PO Box 75, North Judson, IN 46366
Telephone: (219) 223-3834 and (219) 946-6499 eves.

Indiana, Wakarusa

OLD WAKARUSA RAILROAD
Train ride, display
Standard gauge

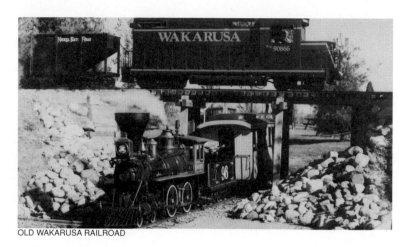

OLD WAKARUSA RAILROAD

Description: This railroad opened in 1989 on the grounds of the famous Come and Dine restaurant and gift shop. The train takes passengers on a 25-minute, 1.5 mile ride, traveling across two bridges, through a 100-foot curved tunnel, crossing city streets, and making a 10-minute stop at a miniature farm. On display are 30 to 40 fully restored antique farm tractors and other antiques and collectibles.

Schedule: April through October: Mondays through Saturdays, 11 a.m. to dark. Train departs every half hour.

Admission/Fare: Adults $3.00; children under age 5 are free.

Locomotive/Rolling Stock: One third scale 15 inch gauge 4-4-0 built in 1957 by Elmer and Norman Sandley; GP38 diesel hydraulic; 8 passenger coaches; stock cars; caboose; gondola; hopper.

Special Events: Pumpkin Trains, Winter Wonderland Trains. Call or write for information.

Location/Directions: Highway 19, on the grounds of Come and Dine restaurant.

Site Address: Highway 19, Wakarusa, IN
Mailing Address: PO Box 591, Wakarusa, IN 46573
Telephone: (219) 862-2714 and (219) 862-2136

BOONE & SCENIC VALLEY RAILROAD
IOWA RAILROAD HISTORICAL SOCIETY
Train ride, museum
Standard gauge

IOWA RAILROAD HISTORICAL SOCIETY

Description: Diesel trains weekdays for a 14-mile trip. Weekends motive power is steam on regular rails (the Wolf Train operates 22 miles of first-class service) and trolleys on demand.

Schedule: May 1 to Memorial Day: Saturdays 1:30 p.m. Memorial Day weekend through October 31: weekdays, 1:30 p.m., weekends, 11 a.m., 1:30, and 4 p.m. Wolf Train–weekends 12:15 p.m. Trolley–weekends on demand.

Admission/Fare: Diesel (weekdays)–adults $10.00; children 5-12 $5.00; under age 5 ride free in arms. Steam (weekends)–adults $12.00. Trolleys–$2.00. "Wolf Train" first class–$25.00.

Locomotive/Rolling Stock: No. 8419 Chinese steam locomotive, Datong, China; Diesel no. 1003 former C&NW; trolley no. 50 former CCW; passenger cars former Erie Lackawanna and Chicago & South Shore.

Special Events: Pufferbilly Days, second weekend after Labor Day; Thomas the Tank rides and Civil War Encampment, mid-summer.

Nearby Attractions/Accommodations: Mamie Eisenhower's birthplace, Union Pacific 186 foot high double-track bridge, antiquing, camping.

Location/Directions: I-35 to Ames, U.S. 30 west to Boone exit, north on Story street to 11th Street, turn west for 6 blocks.

Site Address: 225 10th Street, Boone, IA
Mailing Address: 225 10th Street, Boone, IA 50036
Telephone: (800) 626-0319
Fax: (515) 432-4253
E-mail: B&SVRR@tdsi.net
Internet: www.scenic-valleyrr.com

Iowa, Clear Lake

MASON CITY & CLEAR LAKE ELECTRIC
RAILWAY HISTORICAL SOCIETY
Train ride, display
Standard gauge

MASON CITY & CLEAR LAKE RAILWAY

Description: We are adjacent to the nation's oldest continuously operating, electrical freight railroad (private property). Opportunities to view and photograph the railroad in operation occur almost daily. One mile of electric travel from our carbarn and collection of historic trolley equipment and cars. Historic Baldwin-Westinghouse steeple cab power.

Schedule: Memorial Day through Labor Day: weekends, 12:30 to 4:30 p.m. Charters available April through October.

Admission/Fare: Adults $3.50; children under age 12 $2.00.

Locomotive/Rolling Stock: 1927 Chicago North Shore and Milwaukee Interurban no. 727; 1948 PCC trolley car; wooden trolley car (circa 1890s); 1900 electric sweeper car; Fairmont motor car.

Location/Directions: One-half mile east of I-35. East end of Main Street, Clear Lake, Iowa.

      M

Site Address: East Main Street, Clear Lake, IA
Mailing Address: PO Box 956, Clear Lake, IA 50428
Telephone: (515) 357-7433

Description: Operating O gauge toy train museum.

Schedule: Memorial Day to Labor Day: daily, 10 a.m. to 6 p.m.

Admission/Fare: Adults $4.50; seniors $4.00; children 3-12 $2.00; age two and under are free.

Locomotive/Rolling Stock: O gauge Lionel.

Nearby Attractions/Accommodations: Colfax Mineral Water Company and Pella Tulip Time, Knoxville. Sprint car racing, Walnut Creek National Wildlife Refuge, Jasper County Historical Museum, Living History Farms.

Location/Directions: I-80 exit 155, 2.5 miles north of Colfax on Highway 117.

*Coupon available, see coupon section.

Site Address: 3135 Highway 117N, Colfax, IA
Mailing Address: 3135 Highway 117N, Colfax, IA 50054
Telephone: (515) 674-3813

RAILSWEST RAILROAD MUSEUM
Museum, display, layout
HO

ROBERT HASTINGS

Description: The RailsWest Railroad Museum and HO model railroad are housed in an 1899 former Rock Island depot. The museum contains displays of historic photos, dining car memorabilia, uniforms, and many other interesting items used during the steam era. The 22 x 33 foot model railroad depicts scenery of the Council Bluffs/Omaha area, featuring train lines that served the heartland: Union Pacific; Chicago & Northwestern; Wabash; Chicago Great Western; Wabash, Rock Island; Milwaukee Road; Chicago, Burlington & Quincy.

Schedule: May: weekends 1 to 5 p.m. Memorial Day through Labor Day: Mondays, Tuesdays, Thursdays through Saturdays, 10 a.m. to 4 p.m. and Sundays, 1 to 5 p.m.

Locomotive/Rolling Stock: UP steam locomotive no. 814; CB&Q steam engine no. 915; CB&Q waycar no. 13855; CBQ Omaha Club car; Budd RPO former UP no. 5908; 1967 Rock Island caboose; UP boxcar no. 462536.

Special Events: Depot Days, September 25-26. Christmas at the Depot, November 27 through January 2, weekends 1 to 5 p.m.

Location/Directions: I-80 exit 3, travel north one mile or I-29 exit Manawa.

*Coupon available, see coupon section.

Omaha, NE

Site Address: 1512 S. Main Street, Council Bluffs, IA
Mailing Address: 72 Bellevue Avenue, Council Bluffs, IA 51503
Telephone: (712) 323-5182 depot and (712) 322-0612

DELMAR DEPOT MUSEUM
Museum

DELMAR DEPOT MUSEUM

Description: Restored depot with museum and caboose. Ongoing restoration.

Schedule: Call for information.

Admission/Fare: Free. Donations appreciated.

Locomotive/Rolling Stock: Caboose CC no. 199506.

Special Events: Festival of Lights, first Sunday in December.

Nearby Attractions/Accommodations: Quad Cities, Maquoketa Caves and Park, lime kilns.

Site Address: Main Street, Delmar, IA
Mailing Address: Delmar City Clerk, Delmar, IA
Telephone: (319) 674-4256
Fax: (319) 674-4262

FORT MADISON, FARMINGTON & WESTERN RAILROAD
Train ride, display

FORT MADISON, FARMINGTON & WESTERN RAILROAD

Description: An authentic re-creation of a pre-World War II branchline terminus. A country village, enginehouse with displays, an extensive collection of hand and motor cars, and the yard are on display. A wye is demonstrated and there are many restored pieces of rolling stock. The FMF&W is one of the most authentically operated and appearing railroads in the country. The ride is two miles through woods, up grade, and over a trestle.

Schedule: Memorial Day weekend through October: weekends and holidays, 12 to 5 p.m. Trains depart hourly on the half hour.

Admission/Fare: Adults $5.00; students $4.00; under age 5 are free. Price includes admission and ride.

Locomotive/Rolling Stock: Davenport diesel mechanical no. 348; 8-ton Vulcan no. 1; 1913 Baldwin no. 4; Edward Doodlebug no. 507; 30-ton steam crane no. 3; more.

Special Events: Antique Machinery Show, September 26, 27. Santa Train, December 6, 13, 20.

Nearby Attractions/Accommodations: Old Fort Madison, Catfish Bend Riverboat Casino, motels.

Location/Directions: Off Highway 2 between Fort Madison and Donnellson.

Radio frequency: 464.9750

Site Address: 2208 220th Street, Donnellson, IA
Mailing Address: 2208 220th Street, Donnellson, IA 52625
Telephone: (319) 837-6689
Fax: (319) 837-6080

MIDWEST CENTRAL RAILROAD
Train ride
36" gauge

SCOTT A. WILEY

Description: A one-mile steam train ride encircling the grounds of the Midwest Old Threshers Reunion. The all-volunteer Midwest Central is a non-profit, educational organization dedicated to the preservation and operation of narrow gauge steam railroad equipment. The Midwest Old Threshers Reunion is the world's largest steam show, featuring over 100 acres of exhibits including steam and gas tractors, antique cars, stationary steam, gas engines, horse power, recreated villages, working craft shows, and more.

Schedule: July 3-4: 10 a.m. to 5 p.m. September 2-6, 8:30 a.m. to 9:30 p.m.

Admission/Fare: Adults $2.00; children $1.00. Reunion–one day $7.00; five days $15.00.

Locomotive/Rolling Stock: 1891 Baldwin 2-6-0 Surrey, Sussex & Southhampton Railway no. 6; 1923 Lima three truck Shay, West Side Lumber no. 9; 1951 Henschel 0-4-0T no. 16; 1935 Vulcan gas mechanical switcher; three vintage speeders; five wooden coaches; wooden caboose; White Pass & Yukon steel caboose no. 903.

Special Events: Midwest Old Thresher's Reunion, September 3-7.

Location/Directions: From intersection of U.S. 34 and 218 proceed west to first traffic light (Walnut Street), then south 5 blocks to McMillan Park.

Site Address: Mt. Pleasant, IA
Mailing Address: Box 102, Mt. Pleasant, IA 52641
Telephone: (319) 385-2912

ABILENE & SMOKY VALLEY RAILROAD
Train ride
Standard gauge

ABILENE & SMOKY VALLEY RAILROAD

Description: A 1.5-hour, 10-mile round trip through Smoky Hill River Valley from historic Abilene to Enterprise, Kansas. Crosses the Smoky Hill River on high steel span bridge.

Schedule: Memorial Day through Labor Day: Tuesdays through Sundays. May, September through October: weekends. Dinner train specials. Call or write for more information.

Admission/Fare: Adults $7.50; children 3-11 $5.50. Dinner train prices vary. All prices subject to change without notice.

Locomotive/Rolling Stock: 1945 Alco S1; 1945 GE 44-ton; 1945 Whitcomb 45-ton side-rod; more.

Special Events: Abilene–Chisholm Trail Day, Saturday of first full weekend in October. Easter Bunny Train. Santa Claus Train. Call or write for details.

Nearby Attractions/Accommodations: Eisenhower Center, Dickinson County Heritage Center, C.W. Parker Carousel, Greyhound Hall of Fame, Great Plains Theater Festival, Abilene Community Theater.

Location/Directions: I-70 exit 275, south 2 miles on K-15 (Buckeye Street). Park in lot west of Eisenhower Center. (Shared lot with Greyhound Hall of Fame).

Site Address: 417 S. Buckeye, Abilene, KS
Mailing Address: PO Box 744, Abilene, KS 67410
Telephone: (785) 263-1077, (888) 426-6687 and (888) 426-6689 (reservations)
Fax: (785) 263-1066
Internet: www.ukans.edu/heritage/abilene/asvra.html

MIDLAND RAILWAY
Train ride
Standard gauge

ERNEST N. GRIFFIN

Description: This line was constructed in 1867 as the Leavenworth, Lawrence & Galveston, the first railroad south of the Kansas River. The Midland Railway is a volunteer operated intrastate common-carrier passenger railroad. Beginning in 1998 trains operate to the former town site of Norwood for an 11-mile round trip through scenic eastern Kansas farmland and woods.

Schedule: Memorial Day weekend through October: trains depart at 11:30 a.m., 1:30 & 3:30 p.m.

Fare/Admission: Adults $8.00, children ages 4-12 $4.00; under age 4 ride free. All-day fare (all ages) $15.00. Discounts for groups of 25 or more.

Locomotive/Rolling Stock: No. 524, 1946 EMD NW2, former Chicago, Burlington & Quincy; no. 142 RS-3M, former Missouri-Kansas-Texas; no. 460 44-t, former ATSF; more.

Special Events: Maple Leaf Festival, third weekend in October; Halloween Trains, last weekend in October. Railfans Weekend, TBA.

Location/Directions: About 30 miles southwest of Kansas City on U.S. 56 at the 1906 former AT&SF depot, 7 blocks west of downtown.

*Coupon available, see coupon section.

 Lawrence

Radio Frequency: 161.055

Site Address: 1515 High Street, Baldwin City, Kansas
Mailing Address: PO Box 412, Baldwin City, KS 66006
Telephone: (785) 594-6982
Fax: (816) 873-3387
Internet: www.tfs.net/~jashaw/rhs/midland.html

ELLIS RAILROAD MUSEUM
Train ride, museum, display , layout

Description: See railroad memorabilia: replica depot with office and wait-ing room, model railroad layout, doll museum.

Schedule: April 1 through October 1: Mondays through Saturdays, 9 a.m. to 5 p.m, Sundays, 1 to 5 p.m. November 1 through March 31: Mondays through Saturdays, 11 a.m. to 4 p.m, Sundays, 1 to 5 p.m. Train operates same hours weather permitting.

Admission/Fare: Adults $2.00; children 5-12 $1.00; under age 4 are free with adult.

Locomotives/Rolling Stock: UP caboose no. 25549; MOP FRT cars MP30307-MP3038.

Special Events: Riverfest, second Saturday in June.

Nearby Attractions/Accommodations: Walter P. Chrysler boyhood home and museum; Bukovina Society of the Americas Headquarters and Museum; Lakeside Campground, bathhouses and electrical hookups; Ellis House Inn; Alloway Restaurant.

Location/Directions: I-70 exit 145, 8 blocks south to museum.

Site Address: 911 S. Washington, Ellis, KS
Mailing Address: Box 82, Ellis, KS 67637
Telephone: (785) 726-4493
Fax: (785) 726-3294
E-mail: glenker@ruraltel.net

LIBERAL ROCK ISLAND DEPOT
Display

PETER LIMAS

Description: Mission-styled depot and hotel buildings built in 1911 and restored in 1998 with city, state, corporate and community support. Currently used for meetings, offices and Rock Island displays.

Schedule: Year round: Mondays through Fridays 8:30 a.m. to 5 p.m.

Admission/Fare: Free.

Special Events: Rock Island Depot Jubilee, third weekend in June.

Nearby Attractions/Accommodations: Land of Oz and Dorothy's House, Mid-America Air Museum, Baker Arts Center, Coronado Museum, Arkalon Park & Recreation Center, city parks.

Location/Directions: At junction of Highways 54 and 83 go north 6 blocks to Kansas Avenue to Rock Island Road

Site Address: 2 and 4 Rock Island Road, Liberal, KS
Mailing Address: PO Box 676, Liberal, KS 67905
Telephone: (316) 624-3855
Fax: (316) 624-3855

GREAT PLAINS TRANSPORTATION
MUSEUM, INC.
Museum

L. L. CLERICO

Description: The museum was established in 1985 with the help of the local National Railway Historical Society chapter to preserve and display transportation history as it relates to Kansas. The museum is one of the sponsors of the annual Air Capital Train Show. A former ATSF 3768 is the highlight of our outdoor display. The indoor display is housed in a former railroad hotel that is currently being remodeled.

Schedule: Year round: Saturdays, 9 a.m. to 4 p.m. April through October: Sundays, 1 to 4 p.m. Closed Christmas and New Year's Day.

Admission/Fare: Adults $3.50; children 5-12 $2.50. School and community groups rate available.

Locomotive/Rolling Stock: 4-8-4 no. 3768, former Atchison, Topeka & Santa Fe; electric no. 603, former Kansas Gas & Electric; NW2 diesel-electric no. 421, former Burlington Northern; Whitcomb 30-ton no. 3819, former Mobil Oil; heavyweight baggage car, former AT&SF.

Nearby Attractions/Accommodations: Historic Old Town District, shopping, entertainment and restaurant district, former Union station and depot.

Location/Directions: Wichita's Historic Old Town District.

*Coupon available, see coupon section.

Site Address: 700 E. Douglas Avenue, Wichita, KS (upper level)
Mailing Address: 700 E. Douglas Avenue, Wichita, KS 67202-3506
Telephone: (316) 263-0944

MY OLD KENTUCKY DINNER TRAIN
Dinner train

MY OLD KENTUCKY DINNER TRAIN

Description: A 1940s dinner train carries passengers 35 miles through Bluegrass countryside for lunch and dinner excursions. Chef travels on board for all meal preparation.

Schedule: Year round: schedule varies, call or write for details.

Admission/Fare: Lunch $36.95; dinner $59.95. Child and group rates available.

Locomotive/Rolling Stock: Two FP7A units; GP7 locomotive; three Budd dining cars; Budd kitchen car.

Special Events: Valentine's Day, Mother's Day, Thanksgiving, New Year's Eve, Mardi Gras.

Nearby Attractions/Accommodations: My Old Kentucky Home, Stephen Foster–The Musical, Jim Beam, several bed and breakfasts and hotels.

Location/Directions: Site is 32 miles from Louisville via I-65 and 60 miles from Lexington via Bluegrass Parkway.

Site Address: 602 N. Third Street, Bardstown, KY
Mailing Address: PO Box 279, Bardstown, KY 40004
Telephone: (502) 348-7300
Fax: (502) 348-7780

RAILWAY EXPOSITION CO.
Museum
Standard gauge

RAILWAY EXPOSITION CENTER

Description: Materials provided for self-guided exterior tours. Volunteer guides available most weekends to tour through selected interiors from our 80 piece collection of locomotives, freight and passenger cars.

Schedule: May through October: weekends 12:30 to 4:30 p.m. Closed holiday weekends. Call for recorded message.

Admission/Fare: Adults $4.00; children ages 10 and under $2.00.

Locomotive/Rolling Stock: PRR streamlined and Pullman heavyweight train sets; other regional equipment.

Special Events: Call for recorded message.

Nearby Attractions/Accommodations: Paramount Kings Island Amusement Park, Cincinnati Reds/Bengals. USAF Museum (Dayton). Museum Center at Cincinnati Union Terminal.

Location/Directions: Three miles south of Cincinnati, near I-275 and Kentucky Route 17.

   M

Site Address: 315 W. Southern Avenue, Covington, KY
Mailing Address: PO Box 15065, Covington, KY 41015
Telephone: (606) 491-7245

HARDIN SOUTHERN RAILROAD
Train ride, display
Standard gauge

HARDIN SOUTHERN RAILROAD

Description: This line is a working common-carrier railroad offering seasonal *Nostalgia Train* passenger service for a 2-hour, 18-mile journey to the past. Built in 1890, the railroad was once a portion of the Nashville, Chattanooga & St. Louis Railway's Paducah main line through the Jackson Purchase in western Kentucky. The railroad is a designated Kentucky State Landmark. Today's trip features the rural farms and lush forests of the Clarks River Valley.

Schedule: May 25 through October 31: weekends, midday and late afternoon.

Admission/Fare: Adults $9.75; children 3-12 $6.00. Tour, group, and charter rates available.

Locomotive/Rolling Stock: No. 863, 1940 Electro-Motive Corporation SW1, former Milwaukee Road; no. 4 Baldwin 1914 2-6-2 steam locomotive; air-conditioned coaches.

Special Events: Easter, Mother's Day, Halloween, Christmas.

Nearby Attractions/Accommodations: Land Between the Lakes National Recreation Area.

Location/Directions: In western Kentucky, southeast of Paducah via I-24 and State Route 641; 6 miles from the Tennessee Valley Authority's Land Between the Lakes National Recreation Area. Hardin is located at junction of Routes 641/80. Depot is on Route 80 in the center of town.

       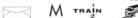

Site Address: Hardin, KY
Mailing Address: PO Box 20, Hardin, KY 42048
Telephone: (502) 437-4555
Fax: (502) 753-7006
E-mail: office@hsrr.com
Internet: www.hsrr.com

Kentucky, New Haven

KENTUCKY RAILWAY MUSEUM
Train ride, dinner train, museum, display, layout
Various gauges

ELMER KAPPELL

Description: Steam alternates weekends with diesel on a 22-mile, 1½-hour round trip through scenic Rolling Fork River Valley, from nostalgic New Haven to Boston, Kentucky. Ride over former Louisville & Nashville trackage. Our new brick depot is a replica of the original NH depot complete with station master's office from the 1930s. See more than 5,000 square feet of artifacts depicting Kentucky's railroad history.

Schedule: Museum–year round: daily. Train–April, May, September through November: weekends. June through August: Tuesdays through Sundays. Call or write for hours. Group tours by appointment. Dinner train–groups only.

Admission/Fare: Call or write for information.

Locomotive/Rolling Stock: No. 152, 1905 Rogers 4-6-2 no. 152, EMD E6 no. 77 (first diesel for the *Pan-American*), and 1925 Alco 0-8-0 no. 2152, all former L&N; former L&N and other open and closed window cars; diner "Kentucky Colonel," former Southern Pacific; more.

Special Events: Kentucky Homecoming Festival, May 29 through June 5. Murder Mystery Weekend, call for dates. Rolling Horse Iron Festival, September 11. Kentucky Bourbon Festival, September 18. Halloween. Christmas.

Location/Directions: I-65 exit 112 to Bardstown, then U.S. 31E south.

Site Address: 136 South Main Street, New Haven, KY
Mailing Address: PO Box 240, New Haven, KY 40051
Telephone: (502) 549-5470 and (800) 272-0152
Fax: (502) 549-5472
E-mail: kyrail@bardstown.com
Internet: www.rrhistorical.com/krm/

KENTUCKY CENTRAL RAILWAY
Train ride
Standard gauge

RUTH ANN COMBS

Description: The Kentucky Central Railway is operated by the Kentucky Central Chapter of the National Railway Historical Society. Trips typically originate in Paris and run to Carlisle, Ewing, or Maysville. The 50-mile "Bluegrass Route," now operated by the Transkentucky Transportation Railroad, was part of the original Kentucky Central Railway, which later became part of the Louisville & Nashville Railroad. It passes through some of Kentucky's most beautiful horse farms and through two tunnels.

Schedule: Write for information.

Admission/Fare: To be announced.

Locomotive/Rolling Stock: 1925 Baldwin 2-6-2, former Reader no. 11; no. 9, VO, 1000 Baldwin diesel, former LaSalle & Bureau County Railroad; three coaches, former Erie Lackawanna; KCR no. 1, former Southern Railway concession/observation car; bay-window caboose no. 225, former Southern Railway; caboose no. 904055, former Baltimore & Ohio.

Special Events: To be announced.

Nearby Attractions/Accommodations: Kentucky Horse Park, Claiborn Farm.

Location/Directions: U.S. 460 E (North Middletown Rd.)

     M TRAIN

Site Address: U.S. 460 East, North Middletown Rd., Paris, KY
Mailing Address: 1749 Bahama Rd., Lexington, KY 40509

BIG SOUTH FORK SCENIC RAILWAY
Train ride
Standard gauge

BIG SOUTH FORK SCENIC RAILWAY

Description: Interpretive exhibits at the Blue Heron Mining Community tell the stories of miners and their families living and working in the mining camp. Passengers enjoy a trip reminiscent of rail travel in the early 1900s as the Big South Fork Scenic takes them through the gorge area near Roaring Paunch Creek. The 3-hour ride features a 1½-hour stop at the restored mining community of Blue Heron, where oral inter- pretations are offered.

Schedule: May 1 through October 31: Wednesday through Friday, 10 a.m.; weekends, 10 a.m. and 2 p.m.

Admission/Fare: Adults $10.00; seniors $9.50; children $5.00.

Locomotive/Rolling Stock: Nos. 102 and 105, 1942 Alcos; open cars; caboose.

Special Events: To be announced.

Nearby Attractions/Accommodations: Cumberland Falls State Park, Big South Fork National River and Recreation Area.

Location/Directions: Kentucky 92, one mile west of U.S. 27 on State Route 92 and 33 miles south of Somerset, Kentucky.

*Coupon available, see coupon section.

Site Address: 21 Main Street, Stearns, KY
Mailing Address: Box 368, Stearns, KY 42647
Telephone: (800) GO-ALONG
Fax: (606) 376-5332

BLUEGRASS RAILROAD MUSEUM
Train ride
Standard gauge

BLUEGRASS RAILROAD MUSEUM

Description: The museum was founded in 1976 and includes displays of limestone sills from the Lexington & Ohio Railroad, built 1831-1835; an air-conditioned display car housing railroad artifacts; "Duncan Tavern" diner car; baggage express car; and caboose, former Southern Railway. The ride offers a 1½-hour, 11½-mile round trip through Kentucky's famed horse country. The trip includes a stop to view the Kentucky River Palisades and the 104-year-old Louisville Southern Railroad's "Young High Bridge," which is 281 feet high and 1,659 feet long.

Schedule: Early May through late October: Saturdays, 10:30 a.m., 1:30 and 3:30 p.m. Sundays, 1:30 and 3:30 p.m.

Admission/Fare: Adults $7.00; seniors $6.00; children 2-12 $4.00; under age 2 ride free unless occupying a seat. Prices may increase during special events.

Locomotive/Rolling Stock: 1953 Alco MRS-1s nos. 2043, 2086, and 1849; Fairbanks Morse H12-44, former U.S Army.

Special Events: Halloween Ghost Train, Santa Express, Hobo Days, Clown Days, and train robberies. Write for complete listing.

Location/Directions: Woodford County Park, U.S. 62 (Tyrone Pike).

P 🚌 ✳ ☕ 🚻 ✉ M arm TRAIN

Radio frequency: 160.275, 161.160, 160.500, 161.190

Site Address: Versailles, Kentucky
Mailing Address: PO Box 27, Versailles, KY 40383
Telephone: (606) 873-2476 and (800) 755-2476

DEQUINCY RAILROAD MUSEUM
Museum, display

DEQUINCY RAILROAD MUSEUM

Description: Nestled among tall pines at the beginning of Louisiana's foothills in north Calcasieu County, the city of DeQuincy was at the intersection of two major railroads in 1895. Its turn-of-the-century beginnings have been preserved, including two major historical land-marks–the All Saints Episcopal Church and the Kansas City Southern Railroad Depot. Both structures are on the National Register of Historic Places, and the depot now houses the railroad museum. There are a vintage caboose, a passenger coach, and a host of railroad artifacts.

Schedule: Year round: Mondays through Fridays, 9 a.m. to 4 p.m. and weekends, 1 to 4 p.m.

Admission/Fare: Free, donations appreciated.

Locomotive/Rolling Stock: Vintage caboose; steam engine no. 124; passenger coach.

Special Events: Louisiana Railroad Days, second weekend of April. Old Timers Reunion in City Hall, 10 a.m. Saturday during second weekend of April.

Nearby Attractions/Accommodations: Lake Charles, Casino gambling boats, golf.

Location/Directions: I-10 exit at DeQuincy, Louisiana 12, Louisiana 27 (27 runs parallel to I-10).

             arm M

Site Address: Lake Charles Avenue and Main Street, DeQuincy, LA
Mailing Address: PO Box 997, DeQuincy, LA 70633
Telephone: (318) 786-2823 and (318) 786-7113

LOUISIANA STATE RAILROAD MUSEUM
Museum, display, layout

GRETNA HISTORICAL SOCIETY

Description: Railroad artifacts, library, an HO layout and coin-operated HO. The Gretna Station was the starting point of all Texas-Pacific rails going west and northwest of the Mississippi River. Passengers boarded in New Orleans, the cars were ferried across the river and assembled into the train at Gretna Station. The station is restored to its 1905 appearance.

Schedule: Year round: Tuesdays through Saturdays, 10 a.m. to 3 p.m. Closed from 12 to 1 p.m. Call to confirm.

Admission/Fare: Adults $1.50; seniors, students, children $1.00; family $5.00 maxium.

Locomotive/Rolling Stock: In Mel Ott Park (½ mile away): Porter compressed air compound locomotive and box cab electric locomotive; special-built cradle car to deliver canisters of ammonia used to manufacture ice.

Special Events: Louisiana Railroad Festival, November. Mardi Gras celebration. Call or write for information.

Nearby Attractions/Accommodations: New Orleans Vieux Carre, Cabildo, Museum of Art.

Location/Directions: Fifteen minutes from downtown New Orleans. Over bridge on Bus. 90 west, exit 7 (Lafayette St.), continue two blocks past light, right on Huey P. Long Avenue to 3rd Street.

       New Orleans

Site Address: 3rd Street and Huey P. Long Avenue, Gretna, LA
Mailing Address: PO Box 8412, New Orleans, LA 70182
Telephone: (504) 283-8091
Fax: (504) 283-8091
E-mail: trainmax@aol.com
Internet: www.railroadmuseum.com

LOUISIANA TOY TRAIN MUSEUM
IN RIVERTOWN
Museum

RIVERTOWN

Description: This museum displays the largest collection of model trains dating from the early 1800s to the present day. Adjacent to the Illinois Central Gulf Tracks, the beautifully renovated turn-of-the-century facility offers visitors the unique opportunity to view hundreds of miniature cars as they rumble over tiny tracks past lighted depots, flag stops and toy towns. Designed for kids and hobbyists alike, the museum is a train lover's dream come true. There's also a children's "play scape" designed for early elementary and preschool visitors featuring a half-scale caboose playhouse, a make-believe circus, a train engine and "Dixie Diner" where a play meal can be enjoyed.

Schedule: Year round: Tuesdays through Saturdays, 9 a.m. to 5 p.m. Closed holidays.

Admission/Fare: Adults $3.00; seniors and children ages 2-12 $2.00. A special discounted pass to see all museums may be purchased at any museum.

Nearby Attractions/Accommodations: Rivertown has many great attractions including museums, theatres, shops and cafes.

Location/Directions: Call or write Rivertown Visitor Center for more information and Rivertown brochure with map. Located 2 minutes from New Orleans International Airport.

Site Address: 519 Williams Blvd., Rivertown, Kenner, LA
Mailing Address: Visitor Center, 405 Williams Blvd., Rivertown, Kenner, LA
Telephone: (504) 468-7223 museum or (504) 468-7231 visitor center

| Maine, Alna | WISCASSET, WATERVILLE & |
| (Sheepscot Station) | FARMINGTON RAILWAY MUSEUM |

Train ride, museum, display
24" gauge

BRUCE N. WILSON

Description: Ride a restored flatcar and caboose hauled by a 15-ton Plymouth diesel locomotive. A Model T inspection car originally SR&RL operates on special occasions. Museum is located on the original WW&F roadbed.

Schedule: Year round: Saturdays, 9 a.m. to 5 p.m. Memorial Day through Columbus Day weekend: Sundays, 12 to 5 p.m.

Admission/Fare: Train ride–adults $2.00; children $1.00. Museum–free.

Locomotive/Rolling Stock: 1891 Portland Forney no. 9; boxcar no. 309; flatcar no. 118; caboose no. 320.

Special Events: Annual picnic, second Saturday in August. Steam Weekend.

Nearby Attractions/Accommodations: Maine Coast Railroad, Boothbay Railway Village, Maine Narrow Gauge Railroad and Museum.

Location/Directions: Four miles north of Wiscasset on route 218, left on Cross Road.

*Coupon available, see coupon section.

Site Address: 97 Cross Road, Alna, ME
Mailing Address: PO Box 242, Alna, ME 04535
Telephone: (207) 586-5803

BIDDEFORD STATION
GREAT NORTHERN NARROW GAUGE RR
Train ride, museum, display, layout
Narrow gauge

RALPH DAY

Description: A two-foot gauge train ride and Great Northern Railroad Museum, theater, York County Model Railroad Club layout and Seashore Trolley Museum.

Schedule: May through December: Fridays through Sundays, 11 a.m. to 6 p.m. Memorial Day through Columbus Day: daily, 11 a.m. to 8 p.m.

Admission/Fare: Train ride–adults $3.00; seniors and children $2.00. Discount rates available.

Locomotive/Rolling Stock: Plymouth 15-ton no. 609; Brookville 15-ton no. 12; GN shay no. 1; GN caboose no. 256; GN ranch car no. 1244; Fairmont motor cars and trailers.

Special Events: Halloween Ghost Train up to age 12, Halloween week. Christmas Prelude, first week of December.

Nearby Attractions/Accommodations: Greater Portland area, Funtown USA, Old Orchard Beach Amusements, summer theaters, Maine coastal attractions, hotels.

Location/Directions: Maine Turnpike, exit 4 to US Route 1, turn south ¾ mile to Biddeford Station, which is on the left.

Site Address: US Route 1 (south) at Biddeford City Line
Mailing Address: PO Box 661, Biddeford, ME 04005-0661
Telephone: (207) 282-9255
Fax: (207) 967-5880

BOOTHBAY RAILWAY VILLAGE
Train ride
24" gauge

ROSS EDWARDS

Description: Ride a coal-fired, narrow gauge train through woods and a covered bridge, around a recreated village. View an exceptional antique vehicle exhibit and restored railroad structures and other buildings.

Schedule: May 29 through 31 and June 5 through October 10: daily, 9:30 a.m. to 5 p.m.

Admission/Fare: Adults $7.00; children $3.00; under age 2 are free. Group rates. Yearly memberships.

Locomotive/Rolling Stock: Locomotives: 1913, 1934, 1938 Henschels; Baldwin Plymouth locomotive; Ford Model T inspection car; rolling stock.

Special Events: Antique Engine Meet, first weekend in July. Antique Auto Days and Auction, third weekend in July. Maine Narrow Gauge Day, third Sunday in September. Columbus Day Weekend Craft Fair.

Nearby Attractions/Accommodations: Boothbay Harbor, restaurants, lodging, boat rides.

Location/Directions: On State Route 27, 8 miles from Route 1.

Site Address: Route 27, Boothbay, ME
Mailing Address: PO Box 123, Boothbay, ME 04537
Telephone: (207) 633-4727
E-mail: railvill@lincoln.midcoast.com
Internet: lincoln.midcoast.com/~railvill

SEASHORE TROLLEY MUSEUM
Train ride
Standard gauge

CHARLES WOOLNOUGH

Description: A 3¾-mile round trip takes passengers over the former Atlantic Shore Line interurban right-of-way, where they can experience the trolley era through the "National Collection" spanning a century of mass-transit vehicles. 1999 is our 60th year.

Schedule: May 1 through Memorial Day and October 12 though October 31: weekends. Memorial Day through October 12: daily. Hours are 10 a.m. to 4:30 p.m.

Admission/Fare: Adults $7.00; seniors $5.00; children (6-16) $4.00; family pass $25.00. Group rates: Adult $4.50; children (6-16) $3.00. Special admission prices, special events, call for specific information.

Special Events: Maine Museum Day, June. 60th Anniversary Celebration, July 5. Trolley Birthday, July. Moxie Day, July. Maine Antique Power, July. Fall Foliage Tours, September. Members Day, October.

Location/Directions: 1.5 miles off U.S. Route 1, 3 miles north of Kennebunkport, and 20 miles south of Portland. Short distance from exits 3 and 4 of the Maine Turnpike.

Site Address: 195 Log Cabin Road, Kennebunkport, ME
Mailing Address: PO Box A, Kennebunkport, ME 04046-1690
Telephone: (207) 967-2800 and (207) 967-2712
E-mail: carshop@gwi.net
Internet: www.gwi.net/trolley

OAKFIELD RAILROAD MUSEUM

Description: Oakfield Station has been restored to its original condition. Exhibits included hundreds of photographs dating back to the beginning of the Bangor & Aroostook Railroad in 1891. You'll see the building of this epic rail line through some of the most rugged terrain in the East. Other memorabilia include vintage signs and advertising pieces, signal lanterns, original railroad maps, telegraph equipment, newspapers chronicling the area's history, restored mail cars and a rejuvenated C-66 caboose. Railroad history lives at Oakfield Station.

Schedule: Memorial Day weekend through Labor Day: Saturdays 12 to 4 p.m. and Sundays 1 to 4 p.m.

Admission/Fare: Donations appreciated.

Locomotive/Rolling Stock: C-66 caboose.

Nearby Attractions/Accommodations: Restaurants and lodging.

Location/Directions: I-95 exit 60, turn right for 1 mile, turn left at hardware store, cross bridge, turn right to end of street.

    M

Site Address: Station Street, Oakfield, ME
Mailing Address: PO Box 62, Oakfield, ME 04763
Telephone: (207) 757-8575
E-mail: oakfield.rr.museum@ainop.com
Internet: www.ainop.com/users/oakfield.rr/

Maine, Phillips

SANDY RIVER & RANGELEY LAKES RAILROAD
DIVISION OF PHILLIPS HISTORICAL SOCIETY

Train ride, museum, display
24" gauge

KEN TEELE

Description: Ride on original roadbed in a restored coach and caboose powered by a replica of SR&RL no. 4. Take a trip back in time as you visit our roundhouse and view our roster.

Schedule: Train–June 6 through September 20; July 4, 5,18; August 1, 15, 20-22; September 5, 19, 25, 26; October 2, 3. Hours are 11 a.m. to 4 p.m., hourly departures. 9 p.m. train on August 20, 21.

Admission/Fare: Train–adults $3.00; seniors and children to age 12 $2.00; under age 6 are free with adult.

Locomotive/Rolling Stock: No. 4 replica; coaches nos. 5 and 6; five box-cars; two cabooses nos. 556 and 558; flatcar; toolcar; flanger; two Brookvilles; Plymouth; 1890 Laconia coach; 1912 MEC coach.

Special Events: Phillips Old Home Days, August 20-22.

Nearby Attractions/Accommodations: Stanley Museum Kingfield, Eastman Park and Small Falls. The Elcourt Bed and Breakfast, restaurants, motels, campgrounds.

Location/Directions: Located 18 miles north of Farmington on State Route 4.

Site Address: Bridge Hill Road, Phillips, ME
Mailing Address: PO Box B, Phillips, ME 04966
Telephone: (207) 779-1901
Fax: (207) 779-1901
E-mail: awb@ime.net

Maine, Portland

MAINE NARROW GAUGE RAILROAD COMPANY AND MUSEUM
Train ride, museum, display
24" gauge

J.E. LANCASTER

Description: A two-foot gauge train takes passengers on a 3-mile round trip along Casco Bay.

Schedule: February 14 through May 15 and October 15 through December 11: weekends. May 16 through October 14 and December 11 through January 1: daily. Also all Maine and New Hampshire school vacation weeks.

Admission/Fare: Train–adults $5.00; children $3.00. Museum–free.

Locomotive/Rolling Stock: No. 3, 1913 Vulcan 0-4-4T; no. 4, 1918 Vulcan 0-4-4T, former Monson; no. 8, 1924 Baldwin 2-4-4T, former B&SR; no. 1, 1949 General Electric B-B diesel electric 23-ton; Plymouth lokies.

Special Events: Railfair, Father's Day. Winterfest Christmas Light Spectacular. Send SASE for list of dates and events.

Nearby Attractions/Accommodations: Old Port shopping area, tour boats, ferry terminal, restaurants.

Location/Directions: Off Franklin Arterial, U.S. route 1A.

*Coupon available, see coupon section.

Radio frequency: 160.245

Site Address: 58 Fore Street, Portland, ME
Mailing Address: 58 Fore Street, Portland, ME 04101
Telephone: (207) 828-0814
Fax: (207) 879-6132
Internet: www.datamaine.com/mngrr/

BELFAST & MOOSEHEAD LAKE RAILROAD
Train ride

BELFAST & MOOSEHEAD LAKE RAILROAD

Description: Tourist excursions offering views of beautiful landscape and bodies of water.

Schedule: Call for information.

Admission/Fare: Adults $14.00; seniors $13.00; teens $10.00; children $7.00; age 2 and under are free.

Special Events: Call for information.

Nearby Attractions/Accommodations: Field of Dreams Outdoor Recreational Center, RAIL 1867 fine dining restaurant located at the Belfast Station in an antique southern rail car, Belfast park/picnic area at ocean front.

Location/Directions: Unity Station, Depot Street in Unity. Unity Belfast Station, Front Street in Belfast.

Site Address: Depot Street, Unity ME or Front Street, Belfast, ME
Mailing Address: One Depot Square, PO Box 555, Unity, ME 04988
Telephone: (800) 392-5500
Fax: (207) 948-5903
E-mail: bmlrr@uninets.net
Internet: www.mainguide.com/belfast/rail

Maine, Wiscasset

MAINE COAST RAILROAD
Train ride
Standard gauge

MAINE COAST RAILROAD

Description: Scenic train rides, charters, tour groups, special events, fall foliage tours.

Schedule: May 22 through June 20 and September 11 through October 17: weekends. June 21 through September 6: daily. Train departs at 11 a.m. and 2 p.m.

Admission/Fare: Adults $10.00; seniors $9.00; children 5-12 $5.00; age 4 and under are free. Group rates available.

Locomotive/Rolling Stock: Two Alco M420 no. 2002; Alco Rs11 no. 367; Alco 51 no. 950; 5 passenger cars; caboose; table car.

Special Events: Rail Fans Day, June. Bath Heritage Days, July. Brunswick Navel Air Show, July. Lobster Festival, August. Fall Foliage Specials, October.

Nearby Attractions/Accommodations: Located in Wiscasset, known as the prettiest village in Maine.

Location/Directions: Waterfront Park on Water Street, off Route 1.

Site Address: 51 Water Street, Wiscasset, ME
Mailing Address: PO Box 614, Wiscasset, ME 04578
Telephone: (207) 882-8000 and (800) 795-5404
Fax: (207) 882-7699

171

THE B&O RAILROAD MUSEUM
Train ride, museum, display, layout

THE B&O RAILROAD MUSEUM

Description: The B&O Railroad Museum's collection of locomotives, cars, artifacts, and archives originated as an exhibit at the 1893 Columbian Exposition in Chicago. A variety of equipment and interpretive exhibits, model railroads, toy-train exhibits, railroad artifacts are displayed, including 48 locomotives, 146 cars and 20 miscellaneous vehicles. Buildings include the 1851 Mt. Clare Station, the 1884 Annex Building, the 1884 covered passenger-car roundhouse, and a large 1870 car shop currently used for equipment storage. Excursion trains depart Mt. Clare Station for a 3-mile round trip over the first main line in America.

Schedule: Year round: daily, 10 a.m. to 5 p.m. Closed major holidays.

Admission/Fare: Museum admission–adults $6.50; seniors $5.50; children 12 and under $4.00; age 2 and under are free. Group rates are available.

Locomotive/Rolling Stock: Numerous; call or write for information.

Special Events: All Aboard Days, April and September. Thomas the Tank, summer. Holiday events, October through December.

Nearby Attractions/Accommodations: Orioles Park at Camden Yards, Baltimore Ravens Stadium, Inner Harbor.

Location/Directions: Corner of Pratt and Poppleton Streets, 10 blocks west of the Inner Harbor.

*Coupon available, see coupon section.

Site Address: 901 W. Pratt Street, Baltimore, MD
Mailing Address: 901 W. Pratt Street, Baltimore, MD 21223-2699
Telephone: (410) 752-2490
Fax: (410) 752-2499
E-mail: info@borail.org
Internet: www.borail.org

Maryland, Baltimore

BALTIMORE STREETCAR MUSEUM
Train ride
5'4½" gauge

ANDREW S. BLUMBERG

Description: Re-live rail transit in the city of Baltimore from 1859 to 1963 through a 14-car collection (12 electric, 2 horse-drawn). Cars operate over 1¼-mile round trip trackage. The Visitor's Center contains displays and a video presentation.

Schedule: June 1 through October 31: weekends. November 1 through May 31: Sundays. Hours are noon to 5 p.m.

Admission/Fare: Adults $5.00; seniors and children 4-11 $2.50; family $15.00 maximum.

Locomotive/Rolling Stock: No. 554, 1896 single-truck summer car, no. 1050, 1898 single-truck closed car and no. 264, 1900 convertible car, all Brownell Car Co.; no. 1164, 1902 double-truck summer car, no. 3828, 1902 double-truck closed car and no. 6119, 1930 Peter Witt car, all J.G. Brill Co.; no. 7407, 1944 Pullman-Standard PCC car.

Special Events: Mother's, Father's, and Grandparent's Days. Museum Birthday Celebration. Antique Auto Meets. Dixieland Concert. Tinsel Trolley, December. Call or write for more information.

Nearby Attractions/Accommodations: B&O Railroad Museum, Baltimore Museum of Industry, Maryland Science Center, National Aquarium.

Location/Directions: From Maryland and Lafayette Avenues, one block west on Lafayette to Falls.

        M arm

Site Address: 1901 Falls Road, Baltimore, MD
Mailing Address: PO Box 4881, Baltimore, MD 21211
Telephone: (410) 547-0264
Fax: (410) 547-0264
Internet: www.baltimoremd.com/streetcar/

173

BRUNSWICK RAILROAD MUSEUM

Description: Brunswick yards handled all B&O passenger and freight on the east-west main line. 863 feet of track in an interactive HO layout traces route from Washington, D.C., to Brunswick. Railroad artifacts include numerous historic photographs, tools, signals, equipment and uniforms. Exhibitions of circa 1900 life in a railroad town; women's and labor history.

Schedule: April through December: Saturdays 10 a.m. to 4 p.m. and Sundays 1 to 4 p.m. June through first weekend in October and Christmas week: Thursdays and Fridays 10 a.m. Closed major holidays.

Admission/Fare: Adults $4.00; seniors $2.50; children age 6 and up $2.00.

Special Events: Railroad History Days, first weekend in April. Railroad Days, first weekend in October. Victorian Christmas, weekend after Thanksgiving.

Nearby Attractions/Accommodations: Harper's Ferry Toy Train Museum, Walkersville Southern Railroad, River and Trail Outfitters, Potomac and Shenandoah expeditions and ski tours, C&O canal bike tours.

Location/Directions: From Washington, D.C.–I-270 north to I-340 west to Brunswick. From Baltimore–I-70 west to I340 west to Brunswick.

Site Address: 40 West Potomac Street, Brunswick, MD
Mailing Address: 40 West Potomac Street, Brunswick, MD 21716
Telephone: (301) 834-7100
Internet: www.bhs.edu/brun/rrmus/rrmus.html

Maryland, Chesapeake Beach

**CHESAPEAKE BEACH
RAILWAY MUSEUM**
Museum

CHESAPEAKE BEACH RAILWAY MUSEUM

Description: The CBRM preserves and interprets the history of the Chesapeake Beach Railway, which brought people from Washington, D.C. to the resorts of Chesapeake Beach and North Beach from 1900 until 1935. The museum exhibits photographs and artifacts of the railroad and resort.

Schedule: May 1 through September 30: daily, 1 to 4 p.m. April and October: weekends only. By appointment at all other times.

Admission/Fare: Free.

Locomotive/Rolling Stock: The CBR chair car "Dolores" is undergoing restoration by the museum staff and volunteers. Only one half of "Dolores" survives; it is the only known CBR rolling stock to survive.

Special Events: Annual Right of Way Hike, first Saturday in April (rain date second Saturday). Antique Vehicle Show, third Sunday in May. Bay Breeze Summer Concert Series, June through September, second Thursdays. Children's Summer Program Series, mid-June through mid-August, Thursdays. Christmas Open House, first Sunday in December.

Nearby Attractions/Accommodations: Chesapeake Beach Water Park, Breezy Point Beach and Campground, restaurants, antique/arts and crafts.

Location/Directions: From Washington's Capital Beltway–I-95 to Route 4 south. From Baltimore Beltway–I-695 to Route 301 south to Route 4 south. Left on Route 260, right on Route 261 to museum.

Site Address: 4155 Mears Avenue, Chesapeake Beach, MD
Mailing Address: PO Box 783, Chesapeake Beach, MD 20732
Telephone: (410) 257-3892

175

**WESTERN MARYLAND
SCENIC RAILROAD**
Train ride
Standard gauge

WESTERN MARYLAND SCENIC RAILROAD

Description: Take a 32-mile round trip from Cumberland to Frostburg, climbing 1,300 feet with grades of 2.8 percent through three horseshoe curves and a 900-foot tunnel. Layover at historic C&P Rail Depot.

Schedule: May through December: Tuesdays through Sundays. May through September departs at 11:30 a.m. October departs at 11 a.m. and 4 p.m. on Fridays through Sundays.

Admission/Fare: May through September: adults $16.50; seniors $15.00; children 12 and under $10.25. October through December: adults $18.50; seniors $18.00; children $11.25. Group rates available.

Locomotive/Rolling Stock: 1916 Baldwin 280 no. 734; Atlantic Coastline no. 850; Florida East Coast no. 851; Pennsylvania Railroad diner no. 1155; Central of Georgia combine no. 726; Norfolk & Western coach no. 540; two Southern coaches nos. 844 and 845; Seaboard coach no. 846; Union Pacific coach no. 2001; Santa Fe coach no. 1504; two Long Island coaches nos. 876 and 880; miscellaneous coaches and freight cars.

Special Events: Maryland Rail Fest, early fall. Murder Mystery Trains. Dinner Trains. Santa Express. Caboose rentals. Chartered Trains.

Nearby Attractions/Accommodations: Holiday Inn, Best Western, Comfort Inn, several bed and breakfasts, Rocky Gap State Park.

Location/Directions: I-68, exit 43C to Harrison Street to station.

Site Address: Cumberland, MD
Mailing Address: 13 Canal Street, Cumberland, MD 21502
Telephone: (301) 759-4400 or (800) 872-4650
Fax: (301) 759-1329
E-mail: trainmaster@miworld
Internet: www.wmsr.com

Maryland, Ellicott City

**ELLICOTT CITY B&O RAILROAD
STATION MUSEUM**
Museum, display, layout
HO, O, G

ELLICOTT CITY B&O RAILROAD STATION MUSEUM

Description: An historic railroad station and freight house, gift shop and library. See early railroad artifacts, B&O tools and equipment, 1927 caboose, tool car and hand car.

Schedule: Winter–Fridays 11 a.m. to 4 p.m.; Saturdays till 5 p.m.; Sundays 12 to 5 p.m.; Mondays 11 a.m. to 4 p.m. Summer–Wednesdays through Saturdays 11 a.m. to 4 p.m.; Sundays 12 to 5 p.m.; Mondays 11 a.m. to 4 p.m.

Admission/Fare: Adults $3.00; seniors $2.00; children under age 12 $1.00.

Locomotive/Rolling Stock: B&O I-5 caboose.

Nearby Attractions/Accommodations: Baltimore and Washington, D.C.

Location/Directions: Located in the historic district of Ellicott City, Main Street, Route 144.

Site Address: 2711 Maryland Avenue, Ellicott City, MD
Mailing Address: 2711 Maryland Avenue, Ellicott City, MD 21043
Telephone: (410) 461-1944
Fax: (410) 461-1944
Internet: www.ref.usc.edu/~gkoma

Maryland, Hagerstown   **HAGERSTOWN ROUNDHOUSE MUSEUM**
Museum, layout
O, HO, N

BILL KNODE

Description: Photos, artifacts and special displays mostly of Western Maryland Railway.

Schedule: Year round: Thursdays through Saturdays 1 to 5 p.m.

Admission/Fare: Adults $3.00; children age 12 and under $.50.

Locomotive/Rolling Stock: MRS-1 Alco Locos no. 2044, 2045; EMD mode 40 switcher; N&W and Reading cabooses; PRR B-60 baggage; Derby Club passenger car no. 714; Pullman Troop sleeper; Frick Co. flat car; Hagerstown & Frederick trolley car no. 168.

Special Events: Railroad Heritage Days, second week of May. Fall Foliage Excursions, October. Trains of Christmas, mid-December-January.

Nearby Attractions/Accommodations: Antietam Battlefield, Washington County Fine Arts Museum, Fort Frederick, Hagerstown Motor Speedway, Hagerstown Prime Outlets Shopping Mall.

Location/Directions: I-81, U.S. 11 north to museum; US 40, U.S. 11 south to museum.

       arm

Site Address: 300 S. Burhans Blvd., Hagerstown, MD
Mailing Address: PO Box 2858, Hagerstown, MD 21741-2858
Telephone: (301) 739-4665
Fax: (301) 739-5598

MARION STATION RAILROAD MUSEUM AND GIFT SHOPPE
Museum, display, layout
G, HO, N

MARION STATION RAILROAD MUSEUM

Description: Museum and gift shop located in a recently restored PRR passenger station. We carry railroad related gifts, trains, books, videos and more.

Schedule: May through December: Wednesdays through Fridays 9 a.m. to 5 p.m. and Saturdays 10 a.m. to 3 p.m. January through April: Saturdays 10 a.m. to 3 p.m.

Admission/Fare: Free.

Special Events: Strawberry Festival, June. Call for information.

Nearby Attractions/Accommodations: Early Americana Museum, Smith and Tangier Island Cruises, Janes Island State Park, Somers Cove Marina, Great Hope Golf Course, fishing and crabbing on the Chesapeake Bay.

Location/Directions: Located about 30 miles south of Salisbury, Maryland, on the Delmarva Peninsula, 6 miles east of the Chesapeake Bay.

Site Address: 28380 Crisfield-Marion Road, Marion, MD
Mailing Address: PO Box 320, Marion, MD 21838
Telephone: (410) 623-2420
Fax: (410) 623-2422
E-mail: marionstation@trainweb.com
Internet: www.trainweb.com/marionstation

**WESTERN MARYLAND RAILWAY
HISTORICAL SOCIETY, INC.**
Museum

DENNIS HETZNER, WMRHS COLLECTION

Description: The Western Maryland Railway Historical Society was founded in 1967 to preserve the heritage of the WM, now part of CSX. It has established a museum in the former general office building of the railway at Union Bridge, next to the Maryland Midland station. On exhibit are Western Maryland artifacts and an N scale model railroad. The museum includes a library and an archives collection which are available for research by appointment.

Schedule: Year round: Sundays 1 to 4 p.m. Other times by appointment. Closed Easter, Christmas, New Year's when they fall on a Sunday.

Admission/Fare: Donations appreciated.

Location/Directions: On Main Street (State Route 75) at railroad tracks.

    M

Site Address: 41 N. Main Street, Union Bridge, MD
Mailing Address: PO Box 395, Union Bridge, MD 21791
Telephone: (410) 775-0150

WALKERSVILLE SOUTHERN RAILROAD
Train ride
Standard gauge

PAUL J. BERGDOLT

Description: An 8-mile, one-hour round trip through the woods and rural farm country north of Frederick, Maryland.

Schedule: May through October: Saturdays and Sundays, departs at 11 a.m., 1 and 3 p.m. Also Memorial Day, July 4th, and Labor Day.

Admission/Fare: Adults $7.00; children 3-12 $3.50; under age 3 ride free unless occupying a seat.

Locomotive/Rolling Stock: Plymouth 0-4-0 no. 1; Davenport 0-4-0 no. 2; converted flatcar no. 11; coach no. 12, former troop sleeper; caboose no. 2827, former Wabash.

Special Events: Saturday Evening Mystery Trains, Father's and Mother's Day special, Zoo Choo Trains, Nature Trains, Civil War Days, Circus Days, Heritage Days, Ghost Trains, Santa Claus Specials. Call for details.

Nearby Attractions/Accommodations: Catoctin Mountain Zoological Park in Thurmont, Maryland.

Location/Directions: Two miles east on Biggs Ford Road, off U.S. Route 15, three miles north of Frederick. Located 50 miles west of Baltimore and 50 miles northwest of Washington, D.C.

Radio frequency: 160.6500 and 160.7250

Site Address: 34 W. Pennsylvania Avenue, Walkersville, MD
Mailing Address: PO Box 651, Walkersville, MD 21793-0651
Telephone: (301) 898-0899
Fax: (703) 533-0433
E-mail: grtucker@erols.com
Internet: eastend.csx.railfan/ws/index.html

Maryland, Wheaton

NATIONAL CAPITAL TROLLEY MUSEUM
Train ride
Standard gauge

KEN RUCKER

Description: Visit "From Streetcars to Light Rail," a computer-based exhibit, view an O gauge model of the trolley line from Rock Creek Loop to Chevy Chase Lake. Enjoy a 1¾-mile, 20-minute round trip in Northwest Branch Park on cars selected from the museum's collection of 15 streetcars. See the CTCo switch tower as you board at the Visitors Center Station.

Schedule: January 2 through November 30, Memorial Day, July 4, and Labor Day: weekends, 12 to 5 p.m. July and August: Wednesdays, 11 a.m. to 3 p.m. December 4-5, 11-12, 18-19, 25-26: 5 to 9 p.m.

Admission/Fare: Adults $2.50/5 rides $6.25; children 2-17 $2.00/5 rides $5.00; under age 2 are free.

Locomotive/Rolling Stock: DCTS 1101; CTCo 1053; TTC 4603; European trams; Washington work cars.

Special Events: Snow Sweeper Day, March 20. Cavalcade of Cars, April 18. Montgomery County History Day, July 11. Fall Open House, October 17. Holly Trolley Fest, December.

Nearby Attractions/Accommodations: Brookside Gardens, Sandy Spring Museum, Montgomery County Historical Society, nation's capitol.

Location/Directions: On Bonifant Road between Layhill Road (route 182) and New Hampshire Avenue (route 650), north of Wheaton.

*Coupon available, see coupon section.

Site Address: 1313 Bonifant Road, Silver Spring, MD
Mailing Address: 1313 Bonifant Road, Silver Spring, MD 20905-5955
Telephone: (301) 384-6088
Fax: (301) 384-6352
E-mail: nctm@dctrolley.org
Internet: www.dctrolley.org

Massachusetts, Beverly   **WALKER TRANSPORTATION COLLECTION**
BEVERLY HISTORICAL
SOCIETY & MUSEUM
Museum

WALKER TRANSPORTATION COLLECTION—O. C. LEONARD

Description: A collection of over 100,000 photographs depicting all forms of transportation in New England. The majority of the collection is railroad and streetcar related. There are also models, memorabilia, library, videos, and oral history transcripts to view and browse.

Schedule: Year round: Wednesdays, 7 to 10 p.m. or by appointment. Closed the week between Christmas and New Year's.

Admission/Fare: $2.00.

Nearby Attractions/Accommodations: Balch House, Beverly. House of Seven Gables, Salem. Numerous hotels and motels.

Location/Directions: I-95 north or south to route 128 north, exit 22 onto route 62 east, to Cabot Street for one mile.

    M

Site Address: 117 Cabot Street, Beverly, MA
Mailing Address: 117 Cabot Street, Beverly, MA 01915
Telephone: (978) 922-1186
E-mail: fletcher@tiac.com
Internet: www.tiac.net/users/fletcher

Massachusetts, Fall River

OLD COLONY AND FALL RIVER RAILROAD MUSEUM
Museum
Standard gauge

DAVID SOUZA

Description: The museum, located in railroad cars that include a renovated Pennsylvania Railroad coach, features artifacts of the New Haven, Penn Central, Conrail, Amtrak and other New England railroads.

Schedule: April 25 through June 27 and September through November 14: Saturdays 12 to 4 p.m. and Sundays 10 a.m. to 2 p.m. July 3 through September 6: Thursdays through Sundays 12 to 5 p.m.

Admission/Fare: Adults $2.00; seniors $1.50; children 5-12 $1.00; under age 5 are free. Group rates available.

Rolling Stock: Pennsylvania P-70 coach; no. 42 New Haven R.D.C. "Firestone"; New Haven 40' boxcar no. 33401; New York City N7B caboose no. 21052.

Special Events: Annual Railroad Show, third weekend in January. Fall River Celebrates America, mid-August.

Nearby Attractions/Accommodations: Battleship Cove (six warships on display), Marine Museum at Fall River, Heritage State Park, Fall River Carousel.

Location/Directions: The museum is located in a railroad yard at the corner of Central and Water Streets, across from the entrance to Battleship Cove.

     M

Site Address: 2 Water Street, Fall River, MA
Mailing Address: PO Box 3455, Fall River, MA 02722-3455
Telephone: (508) 674-9340
E-mail: railroadjc@aol.com

BERKSHIRE SCENIC RAILWAY
Train ride
Standard gauge

BERKSHIRE SCENIC RAILWAY

Description: Fifteen-minute short shuttle train ride within Lenox Station yard, with narrative of Berkshire railroading and Lenox Station history. Locomotive cab tours for youngsters. The museum is in the restored Lenox station. Restored former New York, New Haven & Hartford NE-5 caboose; Fairmont speeder and track-gang train; displays about Berkshire railroading history; railroad videos; exhibit of photos of Gilded-Age Berkshire cottages; three model railroads.

Schedule: May through October: weekends and holidays, 10 a.m. to 4 p.m. Lenox local shuttle trains operate half-hourly.

Admission/Fare: Adults $2.00; children under age 14 $1.00.

Locomotive/Rolling Stock: Diesel engines; passenger cars.

Special Events: Fire Apparatus Display, Gas Engine Show, Circus Day, Halloween Special, Santa Special. Call or write for information.

Nearby Attractions/Accommodations: Tanglewood, summer home of the Boston Symphony Orchestra.

Location/Directions: U.S. 7/20 to Housatonic Street, travel east 1.5 miles.

Site Address: Willow Creek Road, Lenox, MA
Mailing Address: PO Box 2195, Lenox, MA 01240
Telephone: (413) 637-2210
Fax: (518) 392-2225
E-mail: wordworks@taconic.net
Internet: www.regionnet.com/colberk/berkshirerailway.html

ADRIAN & BLISSFIELD RAILROAD
OLD ROAD DINNER TRAIN
Dinner train
Standard gauge

ADRIAN & BLISSFIELD RAILROAD

Description: This working, common-carrier freight and passenger railroad offers 14-mile, 1½-hour round trips from Blissfield to Lenawee Junction over a former New York Central line. The train travels through the village of Blissfield, crosses the River Raisin, and runs through Lenawee County farmland to Lenawee Junction. The "Old Road Dinner Train" is a 2- to 3-hour round trip featuring traditional, impeccable dining-car service including an elegant four-course dinner.

Schedule: Year round: dinner trains–call for information; excursion trains–July through August.

Admission/Fare: Dinner train–$60.00 per person. Excursions–adults $8.00; seniors $7.00; children 3-12 $6.00. Reservations recommended.

Locomotive/Rolling Stock: Nos. 1751 and 1752, 1957 EMD GP9s, former Grand Trunk Western/Central Vermont; no. 5197, 1937 *Canadian Flyer* coach, former Canadian National; no. 721; no. 3370, 1949 diner, former Union Pacific.

Special Events: Fall color tours, Santa Train, Snow Train, Easter Bunny Train, senior charters.

Location/Directions: U.S. 223 and Depot Street. Ten miles west of exit 5 off U.S. 23 and 20 miles northwest of Toledo.

Site Address: 301 E. Adrian Street, Blissfield, MI
Mailing Address: PO Box 95, Blissfield, MI 49228
Telephone: (888) GO-RAIL-1 and (888) SANTA-RR
Fax: (248) 626-4531
E-mail: ihswabash@msn.com

JUNCTION VALLEY RAILROAD

Description: The ride, more than 2 miles long, travels 22 feet down into a valley around a lake, over 865 feet of bridges and trestles, through a 100-foot tunnel, playground, and picnic area. Junction Valley Railroad is the "Largest Quarter-Size Railroad in the World." A 10-stall roundhouse with turntable; 5-track switchyard; railroad shops. The only diamond-crossing trestle in the world. Railroad hobby shop.

Schedule: Mid-May through Labor Day: Mondays through Saturdays, 10 a.m. to 6 p.m. Sundays, 1 to 6 p.m. September through October 4: weekends, 1 to 5 p.m. Railroad hobby shop open year round.

Admission/Fare: Adults $4.75; seniors $4.50; children $4.00. Special events fares are higher. Group rates available.

Locomotive/Rolling Stock: No. 1177 GP45; no. 333 SW1500; no. 4 Plymouth; no. 300 SW1500 booster unit; no. 5000 WS4A; no. 7000 WS4A; no. 6000 WS4B; no. 555 MP15. All are built ¼ size of their models.

Special Events: Opening Day balloon launch. Valley of Flags, July 4. Railroad Days, June 26-27, July 17-18, August 14-15. Halloween Spook Ride, October. Fantasyland Train Ride, December, and more.

Location/Directions: I-75, Bridgeport exit, head south for 2 miles. Located 5 miles west of historic Frankenmuth.

*Coupon available, see coupon section.

Site Address: 7065 Dixie Hwy., Bridgeport, MI
Mailing Address: 7065 Dixie Hwy., Bridgeport, MI 48722
Telephone: (517) 777-3480
Fax: (517) 777-4070

Michigan, Dearborn

HENRY FORD MUSEUM AND
GREENFIELD VILLAGE RAILROAD
Train ride
Standard gauge

E.J. GULASH

Description: The Greenfield Village Railroad offers a 2½-mile, 35-minute narrated circuit of the world-famous Greenfield Village in open-air passenger cars. While riding you will hear interpretations of the history of the village, its occupants and the railroad. The Henry Ford Museum, a general museum of American history occupying about 12 acres under one roof, contains a huge transportation collection, including the widely acclaimed "Automobile in American Life" exhibit. Greenfield Village is an 81-acre outdoor museum comprising more than 80 historic structures. Also at the site are 1941 Lima 2-6-6-6 no. 1601; a 1902 Schenectady 4-4-2; an 1858 Rogers 4-4-0; an 1893 replica of the "DeWitt Clinton"; 1909 Baldwin 2-8-0, former Bessemer & Lake Erie no. 154; a 1923 Canadian Pacific snowplow; a 1924 FGE reefer; and a 1925 Detroit, Toledo & Ironton caboose.

Schedule: Call or write for information.

Admission/Fare: Call or write for information.

Locomotive/Rolling Stock: No. 1, 1876 Ford Motor Co. 4-4-0 (rebuilt 1920s); no. 3, 1873 Mason-Fairlie 0-6-4T, former Calumet & Hecla Mining; no. 8, 1914 Baldwin 0-6-0, former Michigan Alkali Co.

Location/Directions: One-half mile south of U.S. 12 (Michigan Avenue) between Southfield Road and Oakwood Boulevard.

Dearborn

Site Address: Dearborn, MI
Mailing Address: PO Box 1970, Dearborn, MI 48121
Telephone: (313) 271-1620
Internet: www.hfmgv.org

GAIL JONES

Description: Operates along Washington Blvd. and Jefferson Ave. between the Renaissance Center and Grand Circus Park in downtown Detroit's central business district.

Schedule: Memorial Day through Labor Day: daily, 7:30 a.m. to 5:30 p.m.

Admission/Fare: 50 cents.

Locomotive/Rolling Stock: Seven closed; one open-air; one open-air double-decker; built 1895 to 1925 in England, Germany, Portugal, and the United States.

Special Events: Sports events, conventions, and festivals.

Nearby Attractions/Accommodations: New Tigers and Lions stadiums, Greektown, casinos.

Location/Directions: I-75 to I-375 (Civic Center) to Jefferson and Washington Blvd.

Site Address: 1551 Washington Blvd., Detroit, MI
Mailing Address: DDOT, 1301 E. Warren Ave., Detroit, MI 48207
Telephone: (313) 933-1300 and (888) DDOT BUS
Fax: (313) 833-5523

MICHIGAN RAILROAD HISTORY MUSEUM
AT DURAND UNION STATION, INC.
Museum, layout
HO

JIM KNEER

Description: A preserved Union Station, historic displays, library, archives, gift shop, active Amtrak station, busy railroad junction.

Schedule: Year round: Tuesdays through Sundays, 1 to 5 p.m. except Easter, Thanksgiving, and Christmas.

Admission: Donations appreciated.

Locomotive/Rolling Stock: GTW caboose.

Special Events: Durand Railroad Days, model railroad flea market. Call or write for dates.

Nearby Attractions/Accommodations: Crossroads Village and Huckleberry Railroad in Flint.

Location/Directions: I-69 exit 118 between Flint and Lansing.

 M

Site Address: 200 Railroad Street, Durand, MI
Mailing Address: PO Box 106, Durand, MI 48429
Telephone: (517) 288-3561
Fax: (517) 288-4114

MICHIGAN AUSABLE VALLEY RAILROAD
Train ride
16" gauge

MICHIGAN AUSABLE VALLEY RAILROAD

Description: A 1.5-mile, 20-minute scenic ride on a ¼ scale passenger train that runs through a jackpine forest, part of the Huron National Forest, and overlooks beautiful AuSable Valley. You will pass through a 115-foot wooden tunnel and over two wooden trestles, one over 220 feet long to view the wooded valley below. The MAV Railroad is also home to Schrader's Railroad Gift Catalog for railroad enthusiasts. You will find many one-of-a-kind items in the quaintly designed Railroad Depot Gift Shop from past and present catalogs.

Schedule: Memorial Day through Labor Day: weekends and holidays, 10 a.m to 5 p.m. Fall Color Tours–first two weekends in October. Diesels on Saturdays. Steam on Sundays and holidays only.

Admission/Fare: $3.00; children age 2 and under are free.

Locomotive/Rolling Stock: ¼ scale Hudson steam locomotive 4-6-4 no. 5661, built by E.C. Eddy of Fairview and formerly run on the Pinconning & Blind River Railroad; 7¼ scale 12 passenger streamline coaches.

Nearby Attractions/Accommodations: Huron National Forest, canoe ride National Scenic AuSable River, campgrounds, nature hikes.

Location/Directions: North on I-75 exit 202 onto M-33, north to Fairview. Turn south at blinker light in Fairview and go 3.5 miles south on Abbe Road.

Site Address: 230 S. Abbe Road, Fairview, MI
Mailing Address: 230 S. Abbe Road, Fairview, MI 48621
Telephone: (517) 848-2229
Fax: (517) 848-2240

HUCKLEBERRY RAILROAD
Train ride
Narrow gauge

Description: Steam locomotive and historic coaches depart from 1860s Crossroads Depot for 8-mile excursion. Route borders Mott Lake and crosses 26-foot trestle. Operated in conjunction with Crossroads Village, living history museum of 30 plus buildings and paddle wheel riverboat.

Schedule: May 17 through August 29: daily. September: weekends. October 8-10 and 15-31. November 26-28, December 2-5, 9-23 and 26-30.

Admission/Fare: Adults $9.25; seniors $8.25; children 4-12 $6.25; under age 3 are free.

Locomotive/Rolling Stock: No. 2 Baldwin 4-6-0 steam locomotive in service; 15 vintage wooden coaches.

Special Events: Halloween Ghost Train, October; Christmas at Crossroads, November and December; Bunny Train, April; Railfans Weekend, call for information.

Nearby Attractions/Accommodations: Crossroads Village, Genesee Belle Riverboat, Timber Wolf Campground, outlet shopping, many area motels and restaurants.

Location/Directions: North of Flint. I-475, exit 13, north on Saginaw Street, east on Stanley Road, south on Bray Road to Crossroads Village and Huckleberry Railroad.

*Coupon available, see coupon section.

Site Address: 6140 Bray Road, Flint, MI
Mailing Address: 5045 Stanley Road, Flint, MI 48506
Telephone: (810) 736-7100 and (800) 648-7275
Fax: (810) 736-7220
E-mail: gencopks@concentric.net
Internet: geneseecountyparks.org

THE GRAND TRAVERSE DINNER TRAIN
Dinner train

GRAND TRAVERSE DINNER TRAIN

Description: Relive the elegance of classic Pullman style rail dining aboard the nostalgic Grand Traverse Dinner Train. Amble over 45 miles of track through Northern Michigan countryside as we serve exquisite gourmet cuisine.

Schedule: January through May: weekends. June through October: 6 days per week. November through December: 4 days per week. Reservations required.

Admission/Fare: High season—dinner $65.00; lunch $50.00. Low season—dinner $62.00; lunch $47.50.

Locomotive/Rolling Stock: Two F7 diesel locomotives; two articulated passenger dining cars; one kitchen car.

Special Events: New Year's Eve Gala, Valentine's Day, Easter Sunday dinner, Mother's and Father's Day dinners, Halloween train rides, Thanksgiving Day dinner, Santa rides for kids, Victorian Christmas.

Nearby Attractions/Accommodations: Lodging, restaurants, golf, tennis, water sports, snow sports, camping, tall ship sailing vessels.

Location/Directions: Route 31 north from Grand Rapids to Traverse City. Station is located 4 blocks south of West Grand Traverse Bay.

*Coupon available, see coupon section.

Site Address: Eighth Street and Woodmere Avenue, Traverse City, MI
Mailing Address: 642 Railroad Place, Traverse City, MI 49686
Telephone: (616) 933-3768 and (888) 933-3768
Fax: (616) 933-5440
E-mail: gtdt@dinnertrain.com
Internet: www.dinnertrain.com

Michigan, Iron Mountain

IRON MOUNTAIN IRON MINE
Train ride
24" gauge

IRON MOUNTAIN IRON MINE

Description: Designated a Michigan Historical Site, the Iron Mountain Iron Mine offers guided underground tours by mine train. Visitors travel 2,600 feet into the mine to see mining demonstrations and the history of iron mining in Michigan's Upper Peninsula. Mining equipment dating from the 1870s is shown and explained.

Schedule: June 1 through October 15: daily, 9 a.m. to 5 p.m.

Admission/Fare: Adults $6.00; children 6-12 $5.00; children under 6 are free. Group rates available.

Locomotive/Rolling Stock: Electric locomotive and five cars.

Location/Directions: Nine miles east of Iron Mountain on U.S. 2.

*Coupon available, see coupon section.

Site Address: Iron Mountain, MI
Mailing Address: PO Box 177, Iron Mountain, MI 49801
Telephone: (906) 563-8077
E-mail: ironmine@uplogon.com
Internet: www.ironmountainironmine.com

MICHIGAN TRANSIT MUSEUM
                                                Train ride, museum
                                                Standard gauge

GARY J. MICHAELS

Description: This unique train ride is a 6-mile, 40-minute trip through farmlands and a park on trackage of the Selfridge Air National Guard Base. Eastbound, the train is controlled from "el" cars, with a diesel locomotive providing electricity. Westbound, the locomotive powers the train. Located on the route is the Selfridge Military Air Museum, with more than 20 military aircraft, plus photos, models, and memorabilia. A small donation for the museum is collected with the train fare. The group leases the Mt. Clemens Grand Trunk Railroad station, built in 1859, and operates it as a museum. The station is located at the Cass Avenue crossing of the Grand Trunk in Mt. Clemens.

Schedule: Train–late May through September: Sundays, 1, 2, 3, and 4 p.m.

Admission/Fare: Train–adults $6.00; children 4-12 $3.00. Museum–donations appreciated.

Locomotive/Rolling Stock: No. 1807 Alco S-1, former Alco plant switcher; more.

Special Events: Mt. Clemens Museum Days, first full weekend in March.

Nearby Attractions/Accommodations: Gibraltar Trade Center.

Location/Directions: Train–I-94 to North River Road, west to M-3, north to Joy Blvd., east to Joy Park. Station–I-94 to North River Road, west to M-3, south to Cass Avenue, west to tracks on north side.

Site Address: 200 Grand Avenue, Mt. Clemens, MI
Mailing Address: PO Box 12, Mt. Clemens, MI 48046
Telephone: (810) 463-1863
E-mail: grandtrunk@hotmail.com
Internet: www. alexxi.com/mtm

MICHIGAN STATE TRUST FOR RAILWAY PRESERVATION

Train ride
Standard gauge

AARNE FROBOM

Description: A 1941 steam locomotive in 1887 locomotive shop. Occasional events, exhibits, and excursions.

Schedule: Saturdays, 10 a.m. to 5 p.m. Occasional events as announced.

Admission/Fare: Free. Event prices as announced.

Locomotive/Rolling Stock: Pere Marquette 2-8-4 no. 1225 (Lima, 1941).

Special Events: Engineer-for-an-Hour program permits MSTRP members to operate Locomotive 1225.

Nearby Attractions/Accommodations: Durand Depot Museum, Historic Crossroads Village.

Location/Directions: Located in Tuscola and Saginaw Bay Railway Yard on South Oakwood Street, off Highway M-71 in southeast Owosso.

Site Address: 600 South Oakwood Street, Owosso, MI
Mailing Address: PO Box 665, Owosso, MI 48867-0665
Telephone: (517) 725-9464
Internet: http://www.shianet.org/~twelve25

Michigan, Soo Junction

TOONERVILLE TROLLEY, TRAIN AND BOAT TOURS
Train ride
24" gauge

TOONERVILLE TROLLEY, TRAIN AND BOAT TOURS

Description: Enjoy a 6½-hour train and boat tour to Tahquamenon Falls or 1 hour and 45 minute train only tour.

Schedule: Train and boat tour–June 15 through October 6: one trip daily, departs at 10:30 a.m. and return at 5 p.m. Train only tour–July through August: one trip daily, departs 12:45 to 2:30 p.m.

Admission/Fare: Train and boat tour–adults $20.00; children 6-15 $10.00; under age 6 are free. Train only tour–adults $10.00; children 6-15 $5.00; under age 6 are free.

Locomotive/Rolling Stock: Three Plymouth 5-ton locomotive no. 1; Plymouth 5-ton locomotive no. 2; Plymouth (Budda) 5-ton no. 3; 11 passenger cars home-made; assorted work cars.

Nearby Attractions/Accommodations: Mackinac Bridge, Soo locks, white fish, Point Shipwreck Museum, Newberry with lodging and restaurants.

Location/Directions: Off Highway M-28 at Soo Junction, 14 miles east of Newberry.

*Coupon available, see coupon section.

Site Address: Soo Junction, MI
Mailing Address: 5883 Co. Road 441, Newberry, MI 49868
Telephone: (888) 77-TRAIN

Michigan, Traverse City

SPIRIT OF TRAVERSE CITY
Train ride
15" gauge

LAUREN VAUGHN

Description: The "Spirit of Traverse City," an oil-fired, ¼-scale replica of a 4-4-2 steam locomotive pulls passengers in three open-air cars on a ⁹⁄₁₀-mile loop through the Clinch Park Zoo marina and beach. Provides scenic views of West Grand Traverse Bay and loads adjacent to the Con Foster Museum.

Schedule: May 29 through September 6 and September 11-12, 18-19: Daily, 10 a.m. to 4:30 p.m.

Admission/Fare: Adults $1.00; children 5-12 $.50; under age 5 are free.

Locomotive/Rolling Stock: "Spirit of Traverse City" no. 400 oil-fired 4-4-2 steam locomotive; three open-air passenger cars.

Special Events: Family Fun Day, June 6.

Nearby Attractions/Accommodations: Clinch Park Zoo, Clinch Park Beach, Con Foster Museum, motels, campgrounds, golf courses, more.

Location/Directions: On U.S. 31 (Grandview Parkway) at Cass Street, in downtown Traverse City on West Grand Traverse Bay.

*Coupon available, see coupon section.

Site Address: 100 E. Grandview Parkway, Traverse City, MI
Mailing Address: 625 Woodmere Avenue, Traverse City, MI 49686
Telephone: (616) 922-4910
Fax: (616) 941-7716

Michigan, Walled Lake

MICHIGAN STAR CLIPPER
DINNER TRAIN/COE RAIL
Dinner train
Standard gauge

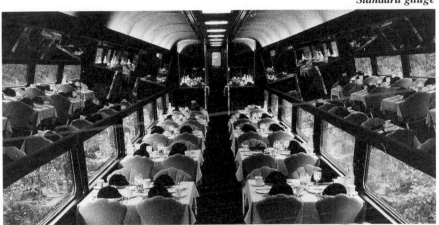

MICHIGAN STAR CLIPPER

Description: Adults enjoy a full 5-course meal, murder mystery, 50s-60s, jazz or Broadway musical entertainment all performed table-side while a relaxing yet very fun 3-hour journey takes you back in grand tradition to an era of fine rail dining and travel.

Schedule: Year-round: Tuesdays through Thursdays and Saturdays 7 to 10 p.m.; Fridays 7:30 to 10:30 p.m.; Sundays 5 to 8 p.m. Reservation required. Luncheons available for groups. Special fall tours.

Admission/Fare: $69.50 per person for everything except gratuity and bar service.

Locomotive/Rolling Stock: 1945 Alco S1; 1952 Alco S1; 1956 SW12 EMD; 1953 F7; *Michigan Star Clipper*–1952 Pennsylvania Railroad Keystone dining cars; kitchen car; power car; 1950s-vintage stainless steel sleepers; more.

Special Events: Casino nights, oldies revues, Friendship Day, romantic getaways on sleeper cars, more. Call for current specials.

Nearby Attractions/Accommodations: Located 6 minutes north of mall and shops, museums, Greenfield Village, antique shops, camp grounds.

Location/Directions: On Pontiac Trail just north of Maple Road, six minutes north of Novi/Walled Lake exit off I-96.

*Coupon available, see coupon section.

Site Address: 840 N. Pontiac Trail, Walled Lake, MI
Mailing Address: 840 N. Pontiac Trail, Walled Lake, MI 48390
Telephone: (248) 960-9440
Fax: (248) 960-9444
Internet: www.michiganstarclipper.com

LITTLE RIVER RAILROAD
Train ride
Standard gauge

CHARLES WILLER

Description: The Little River Railroad offers a 25-mile round trip steam excursion departing from White Pigeon Depot to Sturgis and return. The run goes through forest, farm and city scenery. Approximately a 2-hour 45-minute trip.

Schedule: Memorial Day weekend through October: Sundays and holidays, 2 p.m. departure.

Admission/Fare: Adults $15.00; children 3-11 $8.00; families $50.00 (2 adults, 3 or more children). Group rates for 20 or more.

Locomotive/Rolling Stock: No. 110, 1911 Baldwin 4-6-2, former Little River Railroad–the smallest standard-gauge Pacific locomotive ever built; combination car no. 2594, former Chicago & Alton; *Hiawatha* coaches, former Milwaukee Road; open-air cars; World War II troop car; cabooses, former Baltimore & Ohio.

Nearby Attractions/Accommodations: Shipshewana Auction, Dutchman Essenhaus–Amish cooking, Kalamazoo Air Museum.

Location/Directions: Indiana Toll Road, exit 107, north on Indiana 13 to U.S. 12, east to traffic light in White Pigeon. Go south and follow signs.

Site Address: 413 Elkhart Street, White Pigeon, MI
Mailing Address: 13187 SR 120, Middlebury, IN 46540
Telephone: (219) 825-9182
Internet: //2mm.com/info/rr/

IRONWORLD DISCOVERY CENTER

Description: A vintage electric trolley transports visitors to Mesaba Junction where a "location" house and mining equipment are on display.

Schedule: Mid-June through Labor Day: daily 9:30 a.m. to 5:00 p.m., departures every half-hour. Research center–year round: Mondays through Fridays 8 a.m. to 4:30 p.m.

Admission/Fare: Adults $7.00; seniors $6.00; students $5.00; families $25.00.

Locomotives/Rolling Stock: Two class W-2 trains from Melborne and Metropolitan Tramways, Board of Melbourne, Australia.

Special Events: International Polkafest, Minnesota Ethnic Days, International Button Box Festival. Call or write for information.

Nearby Attractions/Accommodations: Minnesota Museum of Mining, Hull Rust Mine Overview, Hibbing Park Hotel, Country Inn & Suites.

Location/Directions: Highway 169, five miles east of Hibbing.

Site Address: West Highway 169, Chisholm, MN
Mailing Address: PO Box 392, Chisholm, MN 55719
Telephone: (218) 254-3321 and (800) 372-6437
Fax: (218) 254-5235
E-mail: janette@ironworld.com
Internet: www.ironworld.com

END-O-LINE RAILROAD PARK
AND MUSEUM
Museum, display, layout

END-O-LINE RAILROAD PARK AND MUSEUM

Description: Rides on a manually operated turntable are given to all visitors. For the children, rides are also given on a 3½ gauge Hilfers Train. A working railroad yard including a rebuilt enginehouse on its original foundation, an original four-room depot, a water tower, an 1899 section-foreman's house, and an outhouse. The turntable, built in 1901 by the American Bridge Company and still operable, is the only one left in Minnesota on its original site. The section-foreman's house, a general store, and one-room schoolhouse can also be seen. A replica of the coal bunker was built in 1995 and is used for a picnic shelter and gift shop. The enginehouse has been lengthened to its original 90 feet. It contains various exhibits and displays of railroad artifacts, photographs, memorabilia and equipment. The freight room in the depot has an HO scale model train layout of the railroad yards in Currie. A bicycle/pedestrian paved pathway connects the railroad park to Lake Shetek State Park.

Schedule: Memorial Day through Labor Day: Mondays through Fridays, 10 a.m. to 12 p.m. and 1 to 5 p.m.; weekends, 1 to 5 p.m.; and by appointment. Last tour 4 p.m.

Admission/Fare: Adults $2.00; students $1.00; families $5.00.

Locomotive/Rolling Stock: 1923 Georgia Northern steam engine no. 102; more.

Location/Directions: Highway 30 to Currie, travel ¾ mile north on Cty. Road 38.

  🦽 Ⓟ 🚌 ✳ 📷 ⛩ ⛪ M

Site Address: 440 North Mill Street, Currie, MN
Mailing Address: 440 North Mill Street, Currie, MN 56123
Telephone: (507) 763-3708 and (507) 763-3113 (off season)

Minnesota, Dassel

THE OLD DEPOT RAILROAD MUSEUM
Museum

THE OLD DEPOT RAILROAD MUSEUM

Description: A former Great Northern depot built in 1913 is filled with railroad memorabilia and pictures. This 33-foot by 100-foot country depot has two waiting rooms, an agent's office, and a large freight room, as well as a full basement. Authentic recorded sounds of steam locomotives and the clicking of the telegraph key create the realistic feel of an old small-town depot. Items displayed include lanterns, telegraph equipment, semaphores, and other signals; section crew cars, a hand pump car, and a velocipede; tools and oil cans; depot and crossing signs; buttons, badges, service pins, and caps; a large date-nail collection; and many baggage carts. Also included are children's toy trains, an HO scale model railroad, and many railroad advertising items. Interpretation of the items is provided. Static ½-scale train on display.

Schedule: Memorial Day through October 1: Daily, 10 a.m. to 4:30 p.m.

Admission/Fare: Adults $2.50; children under age 12 $1.00.

Nearby Attractions/Accommodations: Six other museums along Highway 12.

Locomotive/Rolling Stock: Caboose; two boxcars.

Location/Directions: Fifty miles west of Minneapolis on U.S. Highway 12.

Site Address: 651 W. Highway 12, Dassel, MN
Mailing Address: 651 W. Highway 12, Dassel, MN 55325
Telephone: (320) 275-3876
Fax: (320) 275-3933

Minnesota, Duluth

LAKE SUPERIOR &
MISSISSIPPI RAILROAD
Train ride
Standard gauge

DAVE SCHAUER

Description: A historic 90-minute rail journey along the scenic St. Louis River. The railroad uses vintage equipment as well as on open safari car on its excursions.

Schedule: June 12 through September 5: weekends. Charters available seven days a week during season.

Admission/Fare: Adults $7.00; seniors $6.00; children $5.00.

Locomotive/Rolling Stock: GE 44-ton no. 46 diesel locomotive; restored full coach no. 85 and solarium coach no. 29, former DM&IR; safari car no. 100, rebuilt flatcar with railing and seating.

Nearby Attractions/Accommodations: Many hotels, restaurants, and attractions in the Duluth area.

Location/Directions: Six miles southwest of downtown Duluth on Grand Avenue, route 23, across from the Duluth Zoo and the Lake Superior Zoo. Train leaves from the Western Waterfront Trail; park in Western Waterfront Trail lot.

*Coupon available, see coupon section.

        M

Site Address: Western Waterfront Trail parking lot, Duluth, MN
Mailing Address: 506 W. Michigan Street, PO Box 16211, Duluth, MN 55802
Telephone: (218) 624-7549 and (218) 728-2262
Fax: (218) 728-6303
E-mail: captkatt@aol

Minnesota, Duluth

LAKE SUPERIOR RAILROAD MUSEUM
Train ride, dinner train, museum, display, layout
Standard gauge, narrow gauge, HO

BRUCE OJARD PHOTOGRAPHY

Description: The Lake Superior Railroad Museum has one of the largest and most diverse collections of railroad artifacts, including the Great Northern's famous "William Crooks" locomotive and cars of 1861; Northern Pacific Railway no. 1, The "Minnetonka" built in 1870; the Soo line's first passenger diesel, FP7 no. 2500A; Duluth, Missabe & Iron Range 2-8-8-4 no. 227, displayed with revolving drive wheels and recorded sound; Great Northern no. 400, the first production-model SD45 diesel; an 1887 steam rotary snowplow; other steam, diesel, and electric engines; a Railway Post Office car; a dining-car china exhibit; freight cars; work equipment; an operating electric single-truck street-car; and much railroadiana.

Schedule: Museum–year round. Train/trolley–Memorial Day weekend through Labor Day weekend. Tuesdays through Sundays, to 6 p.m.; Thursdays and Saturdays, 9:30 a.m. to 6:30 p.m.; Fridays to 8 p.m.

Admission/Fare: Combo tickets (museum and train)–$6.00 to $20.00.

Special Events: Steam train weekends.

Location/Directions: I-35 exit downtown Duluth/Michigan Street.

Radio frequency: 160.920

Site Address: 506 W. Michigan Street, Duluth, MN
Mailing Address: 506 W. Michigan Street, Duluth, MN 55802
Telephone: (218) 733-7590
Fax: (218) 733-7596
E-mail: isrm@cpinternet.com or nssr@cpinternet.com
Internet: www.duluth.com/isrm/

Minnesota, Duluth

NORTH SHORE SCENIC RAILROAD
Train ride, dinner train

TIM SCHANDEL

Description: Formerly the Duluth Missabe & Iron Range Railway's Lake Front Line, this railroad's 26 miles of track run between the Depot in downtown Duluth, along the Lake Superior waterfront, and through the residential areas and scenic woodlands of northeastern Minnesota to the Two Harbors Depot, adjacent to DM&IR's active taconite yard and ship-loading facility. The line offers 1½-, 2½-, and 6-hour round trips with departures from Duluth and Two Harbors.

Schedule: To Lester River–June through September: Mondays through Fridays, 12:30 and 3 p.m.; Saturdays 10 a.m. Pizza train–Wednesdays through Saturdays, 6:30 p.m. Two Harbors–Fridays and Saturdays, 10:30 a.m.

Admission/Fare: Lester River–adults $9.00; children $5.00. Pizza train–adults $16.00; children $11.00. Two Harbors–adults $17.00; children $8.00.

Locomotive/Rolling Stock: DM&IR SD18 no. 193; GN SD45 no. 400; GN NW5 no. 192; Soo Line FP7 no. 2500; DM&IR and GN coaches; more.

Special Events: Steam excursion weekends, elegant dinner trains, Grandma's Marathon Train.

Location/Directions: Duluth–Duluth Depot, Michigan Street, downtown. Two Harbors–Lake County Historical Society, 7th and Waterfront.

Radio frequency: 160.920

Site Address: 506 W. Michigan Street, Duluth, MN
Mailing Address: 506 W. Michigan Street, Duluth, MN 55802
Telephone: (218) 722-1273 and (800) 423-1273
Fax: (218) 733-7596
E-mail: nssr@cpinternet.com
Internet: www.duluth.com/isrm/

Minnesota, Excelsior

MINNESOTA TRANSPORTATION MUSEUM
EXCELSIOR STREETCAR LINE
Train ride
Standard gauge

LOUIS HOFFMAN

Description: A 1-mile, 10-minute round trip on the former M&StL/C&NW right-of-way through the quaint town of Excelsior, the former western terminal of the Twin City Rapid Transit Company's Excelsior suburban line. You can also enjoy a 2.5 hour cruise on beautiful Lake Minnetonka aboard the Minnehaha, a former Twin City Rapid Transit Excelsior-bound streetcars.

Schedule: May 13 through September 19: Thursdays 1 to 5 p.m.; weekends and holidays 11 a.m. to 3 p.m.

Admission/Fare: $1.00; children under age 5 are free.

Locomotive/Rolling Stock: No. 1 reproduction 1890s era open bench car; no. 78 1893 Duluth Street Railway Co.; no. 2 reproduction 1890s era open bench car under restoration; no. 1239 1907 Twin City Rapid Transit Co. under restoration..

Special Events: Excelsior's Farmer's Market every Thursday.

Nearby Attractions/Accommodations: Streetcar Steamboat Minnehaha, Excelsior Historical Society, Minnesota Landscape Arboretum, Old Log Theater.

Location/Directions: State Highway 7, Excelsior exit, turn left on Water Street to boarding platform.

   M arm   St. Paul

Site Address: Water Street and County Trail
Mailing Address: PO Box 17240, Nokomis Station, Minneapolis, MN 55417
Telephone: (651) 228-0263 or (800) 711-2591
Internet: www.mtmuseum.org

MINNESOTA TRANSPORTATION MUSEUM
COMO-HARRIET STREETCAR LINE
Train ride, museum
Standard gauge

LOUIS HOFFMAN

Description: A 2-mile, 15-minute round trip on a restored portion of the former Twin City Rapid Transit Company's historic Como-Harriet route. Streetcars operate over a scenic line through a wooded area between Lakes Harriet and Calhoun. This is the last operating portion of the 523-mile Twin City Lines system, abandoned in 1954. The Linden Hills Station, a re-creation of the 1900 depot located at the site, houses changing historical displays about electric railways in Minnesota.

Schedule: May 21 through September 6: weekends, holidays, 12:30 p.m. to dusk. Mondays through Fridays, 6:30 p.m. to dusk. May before Memorial weekend, September after Labor Day: weekends, 12:30 p.m. to dusk. October: weekends 12:30 to 5:00 p.m.

Admission/Fare: $1.25; children under age 5 are free. Chartered streetcars–$50.00 per one-half hour.

Locomotive/Rolling Stock: No. 265, 1915 Duluth Street Railway (TCRT Snelling Shops, St. Paul); no. 322 1946 Twin City Lines PCC; more.

Special Events: Linden Hills Neighborhood Fair, May 15-16.

Nearby Attractions/Accommodations: Lake Harriet Park, Bird Sanctuary

Location/Directions: I-35W, 46th Street west to Lake Harriet Parkway, follow parkway to west shore at Linden Hills Station. Metro routes 6 and 28.

*Coupon available, see coupon section.

St. Paul   Radio frequency: 161.355

Site Address: 2330 West 42nd Street, Minneapolis, MN
Mailing Address: PO Box 17240, Nokomis Station, Minneapolis, MN 55417
Telephone: (651) 228-0263 and (800) 711-2591
Internet: www.mtmuseum.org

MINNESOTA TRANSPORTATION MUSEUM
MINNEHAHA DEPOT
Museum, display

ERIC MORTENSEN, MINNESOTA HISTORICAL SOCIETY

Description: Built in 1875, the Minnehaha Depot replaced an even smaller Milwaukee Road depot on the same site. Milwaukee Road agents quickly nicknamed the depot the "Princess" because of its intricate architectural details. Until Twin City Rapid Transit Company streetcars connected Minnehaha Falls Park to the city, as many as 13 passenger trains per day served the depot. It remained in service, primarily handling freight, for many years. Located at the south end of CP Rail System's South Minneapolis branch, once a through route to the south, the depot sees occasional freight movements and often hosts visiting private cars. Visitors may tour the depot, which appears much as it did when in service as a typical suburban station. Exhibits include telegraphy demonstrations and historic photographs of the depot and its environs.

Schedule: May 23 through September 6. Sundays and holidays, 12:30 to 4:30 p.m.

Admission/Fare: Donations appreciated.

Special Events: Annual Open House, May 17.

Nearby Attractions/Accommodations: Fort Snelling State Park. Historic Fort Snelling. Mall of America.

Location/Directions: In Minnehaha Falls Park just off State Highway 55 (Hiawatha Avenue). Metro routes 7 and 20.

 St. Paul

Site Address: 4926 Minnehaha Avenue, Minneapolis, MN
Mailing Address: PO Box 17240, Nokomis Station, Minneapolis, MN 55417
Telephone: (651) 228-0263 and (800) 711-2591
E-mail: corbin@plethora.net
Internet: www.mtmuseum.org

VICTOR HAND

Description: North Star Rail, Inc. operates a day-long steam powered excursion over various Class 1 railroads.

Schedule: Varies with trip. Call or write for information.

Admission/Fare: Varies. Reservations recommended.

Locomotive/Rolling Stock: No. 261 1944 Alco 4-8-4, former Milwaukee Road class S3, leased to North Star Rail by the National Railroad Museum in Green Bay, Wisconsin.

Site Address: Minneapolis, MN
Mailing Address: 4322 Lakepoint Court, Shoreview, MN 55126
Telephone: (651) 490-1985
Fax: (651) 490-1985 (call first)
E-mail: friends261aol.com
Internet: www.261.com

MINNESOTA ZEPHYR LIMITED
Dinner train
Standard gauge

MINNESOTA ZEPHYR LIMITED

Description: The *Minnesota Zephyr* dining train steeps passengers in the ambience of 1940s railroad travel. The 3½-hour journey begins on the Stillwater & St. Paul Railroad, built more than 120 years ago and later acquired by the Northern Pacific Railroad. The 7-mile line first parallels the St. Croix River, then swings west through Dutchtown along scenic Brown's Creek, climbing 250 feet on grades up to 2.2 percent. The tracks pass open fields to the Oak Glen Country Club, the summit area, then head onward to Duluth Junction. The *Zephyr* stops at the junction to prepare for the return to Stillwater. Stillwater Depot, which opened in 1993, features displays about the history of Stillwater and the logging and rail industry.

Schedule: Year round: Mondays through Saturdays, 7:30 p.m; Sundays and afternoon trips, 12 p.m. Call or write for more information.

Admission/Fare: $58.50 for excursion and dinner. Semi-formal attire requested. Reservations required. Family Day–$14.95 children.

Special Events: Family Day 45-minute trip with lunch, Saturdays.

Locomotive/Rolling Stock: Two 1951 diesel-electric engines: no. 788, a 1,750-horsepower FP9, and no. 787, a 1,500-horsepower F7; five dining cars.

Location/Directions: Follow Highway 36 east from the Twin Cities to Stillwater.

Site Address: 601 N. Main Street, Stillwater, MN
Mailing Address: PO Box 573, Stillwater, MN 55082
Telephone: (612) 430-3000 and (800) 992-6100
Internet: mnzephyr.com

LAKE COUNTY HISTORY
AND RAILROAD MUSEUM
Train ride, museum
Standard gauge

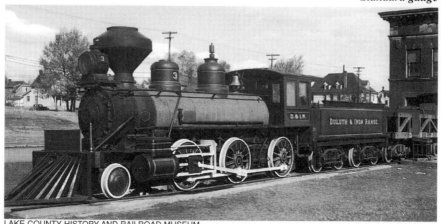

LAKE COUNTY HISTORY AND RAILROAD MUSEUM

Description: Visit our turn-of-the-century railroad depot with exhibits relating to the early railroad, logging, and shipping history of the area. The "3-Spot," former Duluth & Iron Range 2-6-0 no. 3, the first engine on the D&IR; a 2-8-8-4, former D&IR no. 229 is also on display. Visitors can also see the *Edna G.*, the last coal-fired tug on the Great Lakes; ore-loading docks; and Great Lakes ore boats.

Schedule: Mid-May through mid-October: daily, 9 a.m.-5 p.m.

Admission/Fare: Adults $2.00; children 9-17 $1.00.

Locomotive/Rolling Stock: 1943 steam engine with coal car no. 229 DM&IR "The Mallet"; steam engine with coal car D&IR Baldwin; 1883 Burnham Parry M4 no. 6649; D&IR no. 251 flatbed car and no. 22 caboose.

Special Events: Summer Solstice Party, longest day of year. Heritage Days, mid-July. Folk Festival, mid-July. Steam Train Days, August.

Nearby Attractions/Accommodations: Lighthouse, *Edna G.* Tugboat, ore docks, Sandpaper Museum.

Location/Directions: Downtown Two Harbors.

Site Address: Waterfront Drive and South Avenue, Two Harbors, MN
Mailing Address: PO Box 313, Two Harbors, MN 55616
Telephone: (218) 834-4898

CASEY JONES MUSEUM

Description: The Casey Jones Railroad Museum State Park is housed in an antique railroad depot located less than one mile from the site of the crash that killed Casey Jones. In addition to Casey Jones memorabilia, the museum features exhibits chronicling the development and importance of railroads in Mississippi. Authentic steam engine no. 841 is displayed adjacent to the museum.

Schedule: Year round: daily 8 a.m. to 4 p.m. except Wednesdays and Saturdays till noon. Closed Sundays.

Admission/Fare: Adults $1.00; children $ .50.

Nearby Attractions/Accommodations: Holmes County State Park, Little Red Schoolhouse, Hillside NWR, Morgan Break NWR, Panther Swamp NWR.

Location/Directions: I-55 exit 133, east for one mile. Vaughan is 33 miles north of Jackson.

Site Address: 10901 Vaughan Road, No. 1, Vaughan, MS
Mailing Address: 10901 Vaughan Road, No. 1, Vaughan, MS 39179
Telephone: (601) 673-9864
Fax: (601) 653-6693

KANDIYOHI COUNTY HISTORICAL SOCIETY

Description: This historical center is located in the former Great Northern Division of Willmar. Summer guests can climb into the cab of the majestic 2523. The center also features a Great Northern depot built at the turn of the century, railroad exhibits, and other attractions.

Schedule: Summer: weekdays, 9 a.m. to 5 p.m. and weekends, 1 to 5 p.m. Winter: weekdays, 9 a.m. to 5 p.m.

Admission/Fare: Free.

Locomotive/Rolling Stock: Great Northern 2523 P2 class Baldwin.

Nearby Attractions/Accommodations: Little Crow Lake Region, resorts and motels, fishing.

Site Address: 610 N. Business 71, Willmar, MN
Mailing Address: 610 NE Highway 71, Willmar, MN
Telephone: (320) 235-1881

BELTON, GRANDVIEW & KANSAS CITY RR CO.
THE "LEAKY ROOF" ROUTE
Train ride, museum, display
Standard gauge

DAVID HOLLAND

Description: Two former Frisco static steam locomotives (2-10-0) no. 1632 and (2-8-0) no. 5, several freight and passenger cars representing various midwestern railroads. Last remaining trackage (56# rail) from the former Kansas City, Clinton & Springfield "Leaky Roof" Railroad. Interpretive displays housed in cases in the former Norfolk & Western baggage express car no. 873. Railroad-related videos shown continuously in the former Santa Fe instruction/theater car no. 80. Train ride is approximately five miles round trip.

Schedule: May through October: weekends and holidays, departs at 2 p.m., ticket sales 1 p.m. Group specials available.

Admission/Fare: Train–adults $5; children age 3 and under free if not occupying a seat.

Locomotive/Rolling Stock: 1956 former B&O GP9 no. 102; 1920 former Erie, Delaware & Lackawanna open-window commuter coach no. 4364; 1972 former Missouri Pacific wide-vision cupola caboose no. 13562.

Special Events: Easter Egg Express, April. Belton Community Days, June. Gold Rush and Confusion Creek, summer. Pumpkin Patch Express, October.

Location/Directions: About 8 miles south of I-435/I-470 and Hwy 71.

Site Address: 502 Walnut, Belton, MO
Mailing Address: 502 Walnut, Belton, MO 64012-2516
Telephone: (816) 331-0630

BRANSON SCENIC RAILWAY
Train ride
Standard gauge

BRANSON SCENIC RAILWAY

Description: This railway operates a 40-mile, 1¾-hour round trip through the Ozark foothills over the former Missouri Pacific White River Route, now operated by the Missouri & North Arkansas Railroad. Most trips take passengers south into Arkansas, across Lake Taneycomo and two high trestles and through two tunnels. The original 1906 Branson depot houses the railway's ticket office, waiting room, gift shop, and business offices.

Schedule: Excursions–Mid-March through mid-December: 9 and 11:30 a.m., 2 and 5 p.m. Dinner train–May through December: Saturdays 5 p.m.

Admission/Fare: Adults $18.50; seniors $17.50; student 13-18 $13.50; children 4-12 $8.75; age 3 and under are free if not occupying a seat. Group rates available.

Locomotive/Rolling Stock: No. 98 F9PH BSR no. 265; GP30M BSR, former B&O; Silver Garden dome car, former CBQ; Silver Island dome, former CBQ.

Special Events: Downtown see Plumb Nellie Days and Fiddler's Contest.

Nearby Attractions/Accommodations: Theme park, historic downtown, restaurants, flea market, crafts festivals, lake, campgrounds, lodging.

Location/Directions: Downtown Branson, ¾ mile east of U.S. 65.

Site Address: 206 E. Main Street, Branson, MO
Mailing Address: PO Box 924, Branson, MO 65615
Telephone: (417) 334-6110 and (800) 2TRAIN2
Fax: (417) 336-3909

SILVER DOLLAR CITY THEME PARK
Train ride

SILVER DOLLAR CITY

Description: The Silver Dollar Steam Train takes guests on a fun-filled trip back to the 1890s on a tour through the splendid Ozark Mountains.

Schedule: April 7 through December 30: departures every 30 minutes. Days of operation vary with operation of theme park.

Admission/Fare: Free with paid admission to theme park.

Locomotive/Rolling Stock: 1938 engine no. 13 Orenstein 2-4-0, Koppel, Germany; 1934 engine no. 43 Orenstein 2-4-0, Koppel, Germany; 1940 engine no. 76 2-4-0, Germany.

Special Events: Sing-Along Steam Train (caroling rides) during Old Time Christmas, November and December.

Location/Directions: Highway 76, approximately 5 miles west of Branson.

Site Address: Silver Dollar City Theme Park, West Hwy 76, Branson, MO
Mailing Address: HC 1, Box T91, Branson, MO 65616
Telephone: (800) 952-6626
Internet: www.silverdollarcity.com

SIX FLAGS OVER ST. LOUIS
Train ride
36" gauge

SIX FLAGS OVER ST. LOUIS

Description: The narrow gauge Six Flags Railroad was built and first operated in 1971. It consists of one 25-ton steam locomotive, a tender, four passenger cars, and a caboose. The engine is a propane-fueled steam locomotive manufactured by Crown Metal Company.

Schedule: Runs continuously around park, stopping at two stations.

Admission/Fare: Park admission required.

Locomotive/Rolling Stock: One 25-ton narrow gauge steam locomotive; open passenger cars; enclosed caboose.

Location/Directions: I-44 and Allentown Road, west of St. Louis.

Site Address: Eureka, MO
Mailing Address: PO Box 60, Eureka, MO 63025
Telephone: (314) 938-5300

**Missouri, Glencoe
(Wildwood)**

WABASH FRISCO & PACIFIC RAILWAY
"THE UNCOMMON CARRIER"
Train ride
12" gauge

DAVID J. NEUBAUER

Description: A 2-mile, 30-minute round trip over a former Missouri Pacific right-of-way along the scenic Meramec River through wooded areas and over three bridges. 1999 is the 60th anniversary of our founding in 1939.

Schedule: May through October: Sundays, 11:15 a.m. to 4:15 p.m.

Admission/Fare: $2; children under age 3 ride free. No reservations.

Locomotive/Rolling Stock: Eight steam locomotives; 1907 no. 171 4-4-0 and coal burner; no. 180 4-4-0 coal; no. 102 2-6-2 coal; no. 300 4-4-2 oil; no. 400 4-6-2 oil; no. 434 4-6-4 oil; no. 350 4-4-4 coal being rebuilt as 4-6-4; no. 401 4-6-2 coal.

Special Events: Member's Day, June.

Nearby Attractions/Accommodations: Museum of Transportation, Union Pacific and Burlington Northern Santa Fe main lines, Eureka, Missouri.

Location/Directions: Twenty-five miles west of St. Louis. I-44 (Eureka), exit 264, north on Route 109 for 3.5 miles to Old State Road, make two right turns to depot on Washington Street and Grand Avenue.

*Coupon available, see coupon section.

         Radio frequency: 151.955

Site Address: Foot of Washington and Grand Avenue, Wildwood, MO
Mailing Address: 1569 Ville Angela Lane, Hazelwood, MO 63042-1630
Telephone: (314) 587-3538 and (314) 351-9385
Internet: http://home.stlnet.com/~shahriary/wfp

ST. LOUIS, IRON MOUNTAIN & SOUTHERN RAILWAY

Train ride, dinner train
Standard gauge

ST. LOUIS, IRON MINE & SOUTHERN RAILWAY

Description: Steam-powered train takes passengers on one of two round trips over a former Missouri Pacific branch line: a 10-mile, 1.5 hour sightseeing trip to Gordonville; or a 20-mile, 2-hour dinner trip to Dutchtown.

Schedule: April through October: Gordonville trip–Saturdays, 11 a.m., 2 p.m. and Sundays, 1 p.m. Summer: add Wednesdays and Fridays, 1 p.m. Saturdays dinner or murder mystery, 5 p.m. Charters available.

Admission/Fare: Adults $12.50; children $6.00; dinner $24.50; murder mystery $37.00.

Locomotive/Rolling Stock: No. 5, 1946 Porter 2-4-2, former Central Illinois Public Service, former Crab Orchard & Egyptian; 1945 New York Central coach no. 4452, former Baltimore & Ohio; more.

Special Events: New Year's Eve Murder Mystery, Valentine's Dinner Train, Mother's and Father's Day Excursions, Halloween Express, Santa Express, Hobo Days, James Gang Robberies, Magic Show, more.

Nearby Attractions/Accommodations: Bollinger Mill and Covered Bridge, Trail of Tears State Park, Veteran's War Memorial, The Oliver House Historic Home, Old McKendree Chapel, Mississippi River scenic overview, Civil War sites, Glenn House Historic Home.

Location/Directions: I-55, exit 99, 4 miles south on Highway 61 at 25.

*Coupon available, see coupon section.

♿ 🅿 🚌 ✳ ☕ 🍴 📷 🎪 ✉ M

MasterCard VISA **Radio frequency: 168.45**

Site Address: 252 E. Jackson Blvd., Jackson, MO
Mailing Address: PO Box 244, Jackson, MO 63755
Telephone: (573) 243-1688 and (800) 455-RAIL
Fax: (573) 243-5355
Internet: www.rosecity.net/trains

GARY CHILCOTE

Description: Patee House Museum was headquarters for the Pony Express, in 1860. The former hotel is now a museum of communications and transportation featuring a steam locomotive, mail car, antique cars, trucks, fire trucks, buggies and wagons. On the grounds is the Jesse James Home where the outlaw was killed.

Schedule: April through October, daily 10 a.m. to 5 p.m. during summer months; otherwise, 10 a.m. to 4 p.m. November through March, weekends only.

Admission/Fare: Adults $3.00; seniors $2.50; students ages 6-17 $1.50; under age 6 are free with family.

Locomotive/Rolling Stock: 1892 Baldwin 4-4-0 no. 35, backdated by Burlington in 1933 to resemble Hannibal & St. Joseph locomotive no. 35.

Special Events: Pony Express/Jesse James Weekend, first weekend in April. Pony Express rerun, June.

Nearby Attractions/Accommodations: Home of Jesse James, Pony Express Museum, Doll Museum, Firefighters Museum, Old Smokehouse Restaurant.

Location/Directions: From Highway 36 take the 10th Street exit, follow 10th Street north to right on Mitchell to 12th Street.

*Coupon available, see coupon section.

         M

Site Address: 1202 Penn, St. Joseph, MO
Mailing Address: Box 1022, St. Joseph, MO 64502
Telephone: (816) 232-8206
Fax: (816) 232-8206
Internet: www.ponyexpress.net/~breeze/PateeHouse/

Missouri, St. Louis   **AMERICAN RAILWAY CABOOSE HISTORICAL EDUCATIONAL SOCIETY, INC. (A.R.C.H.E.S.)**
Cabooseum
Standard gauge

RICHARD A. EICHHORST

Description: The Caboose Museum has at least one of their 30 "cabeese" on display at any given time. While a permanent location is being planned, the equipment is stored at ten different locations in Missouri and Illinois. Some of these cabooses are on loan to other rail museums. In addition to the interpretive center that is open to the public, ARCHES is an international association with members in 33 states and Canada. The members are compiling *Catalog of Captive Cabeese*, which lists the location of cabooses in North America that are no longer in active service.

Schedule: April 3, May 1, June 5, July 3, August 7, September 4, and October 2: 1 to 4 p.m.

Admission/Fare: Donations appreciated.

Cabooses: A&S, B&O, C&O, C&NW, CC, CGW, C&NW, Essex Terminal, Frisco, IC, Manufacturers, N&W, RI, Southern, TRRA, and Union Pacific.

Special Events: Caboose Chili Cook-off, Caboose Chase excursions, Santa on Amtrak, Rail Caboose tours.

Location/Directions: Varies, call or write for information.

St. Louis & Kirkwood, MO / Alton, IL

Site Address: St. Louis, MO
Mailing Address: PO Box 2772, St. Louis, MO 63116
Telephone: (314) 752-3148

MUSEUM OF TRANSPORTATION
Museum
Standard gauge

MUSEUM OF TRANSPORTATION

Description: The museum houses one of the largest and best collections of transportation vehicles in the world, according to the Smithsonian Institution. With over 70 locomotives, the museum has one of the most complete collections of American rail power, and its collection of automobiles, buses, streetcars, aircraft, horsedrawn vehicles, and river boat material reflects the ever-changing nature of transportation.

Schedule: Year round: daily, 9 a.m. to 5 p.m. Closed Thanksgiving, Christmas, and New Year's Day.

Admission/Fare: Adults $4; seniors and children 5-12 $1.50.

Locomotive/Rolling Stock: UP Big Boy no. 4006; UP Centenial no. 6944; N&W Y6A no. 2156; Reading "Black Diamond"; GM FT no. 103; Milwaukee Road E 2; 35 steam locomotives, 29 internal combustion; 9 electric locomotives; 23 passenger cars; 54 freight cars.

Special Events: Annual Transportation Celebration, first weekend in August. Family Fall Festival, second Sunday in October.

Nearby Attractions/Accommodations: St. Louis Arch, Grant's Farm, Science Center, Zoo, Magic House.

Location/Directions: I-270, exit Dougherty Ferry Rd., west for 1 mile, left on Barrett Station.

*Coupon available, see coupon section.

          M  Kirkwood

Site Address: 3015 Barrett Station Rd., St. Louis, MO
Mailing Address: 3015 Barrett Station Rd., St. Louis, MO 63122
Telephone: (314) 965-7998
Fax: (314) 965-0242

FRISCO RAILROAD MUSEUM
Museum
Standard gauge

FRISCO RAILROAD MUSEUM

Description: This museum, located at station 238 on the Frisco's former Lebanon Subdivision, Eastern Division, is housed in a building originally constructed by the Frisco Railway in 1943 as a Centralized Traffic Control command center. It is the only facility in the country devoted exclusively to the preservation and display of the history and memorabilia of the Frisco Railway. The facility displays more than 2,000 items of Frisco and Frisco-related memorabilia, representing a wide range of operations, equipment, and services. In addition, it has the largest archive of historical, technical, and photographic information about the Frisco currently available to the public through its "Frisco Folks" membership program.

Schedule: Tuesday through Saturday, 10 a.m. to 5 p.m.

Admission/Fare: Adults $2.00; children under 12 $1.00. Group discounts.

Locomotive/Rolling Stock: Caboose no. 1159; boxcar no. 10055; side-door caboose no. 1156; no. 1551 diner-lounge "Oklahoma City" available for meetings, banquets, parties, special events. All former Frisco.

Special Events: Frisco Days, April; Christmas Open House, featuring large collection of train-related ornaments, held 2 weeks before Christmas.

Location/Directions: At 543 East Commercial Street. Take exit 80 A/B off I-44, travel south on business 65 1.3 miles to Commercial Street (third light), then travel west 1.3 miles.

           M

Site Address: 543 East Commercial Street, Springfield, MO
Mailing Address: 543 East Commercial Street, Springfield, MO 65803
Telephone: (417) 866-SLSF (7573)
E-mail: amunhotep@aol.com
Internet: www.frisco.org

IZAAK WALTON INN
Historic railroad inn

KYLE BREHM

Description: Historic railroad hotel with dining room, bar, railroad antiques and memorabilia. Built by the Great Northern Railroad in 1939.

Schedule: Year round: daily, 7 a.m. to 10 p.m.

Special Events: Annual Essex Express Railfan Weekend, first weekend in May.

Nearby Attractions/Accommodations: Glacier National Park, Montana main line of BNSF originally Great Northern line.

Location/Directions: On southern tip of Glacier National Park off Highway 2 between East and West Glacier.

Site Address: 123 Izaak Walton Inn Road, Essex, MT
Mailing Address: PO Box 653, Essex, MT
Telephone: (406) 888-5700
Fax: (406) 888-5200
E-mail: izaakw@digisys.net
Internet: www.vtown.com/izaakw

MONTANA HERITAGE COMMISSION
Train ride
30"

MONTANA HERITAGE COMMISSION

Description: Tourist train with open air cars operates along Alder Gulch between Nevada City and Virginia City, Montana.

Schedule: Memorial Day through Labor Day.

Admission/Fare: Adults $5.00.

Location/Directions: State Highway 287 between Ennis and Sheridan, Montana.

Site Address: Nevada City, MT
Mailing Address: PO Box 201201, Helena, MT 59620-1201
Telephone: (406) 443-2081

CHARLIE RUSSELL
CHEW-CHOO DINNER TRAIN
Dinner train
Standard gauge

CHERIE NEUDICK

Description: A 3.5-hour ride through a half-mile long tunnel, over three trestles, and past an abundance of wildlife. A full course prime rib dinner is served. Also, a train robbery and other entertainment.

Schedule: June through September: Saturdays.

Admission/Fare: $69.00; New Year's Eve train $99.00.

Locomotive/Rolling Stock: Five Budd-built NSSR passenger cars; diesel locomotive.

Special Events: Christmas Train, second Saturday in December. New Year's Eve Train. Valentine Train.

Nearby Attractions/Accommodations: Two golf courses, historical sites, fishing, water slide, third largest fresh water spring in the world, mountains.

Location/Directions: Highway 87, Highway 191 north, Highway 426.

Site Address: 408 E. Main, Lewistown, MT
Mailing Address: PO Box 818, Lewistown, MT 59457
Telephone: (406) 538-5436
Fax: (406) 538-5437
E-mail: lewchamb@lewistown.net
Internet: www.lewistownchamber.com

FREMONT & ELKHORN VALLEY RAILROAD
NATIONAL RAILWAY HISTORICAL SOCIETY
NEBRASKA CHAPTER
Train ride

FREEMONT & ELKHORN VALLEY RAILROAD

Description: Take a ride through history on a 30-mile round trip from Fremont to Hooper over rails laid in 1869. Ride on cars built in 1924 and 1925. Enjoy the scenic Elkhorn Valley.

Schedule: Call or write for information.

Admission/Fare: Call or write for information.

Locomotive/Rolling Stock: EMD no. 1219 locomotive; no. 1938 Burlington RPO baggage car; 1925 "Lake Bluff" passenger car; 1927 "Fort Andrew" passenger car; 1957 flatcar.

Special Events: Civil War reenactments, Memorial Day weekend, third week in August, and July 4. John C. Freemont Days, second weekend of July. Harvest Days, second and third week of October. Halloween activities, last weekend in October and Halloween night. December, Santa Runs (reservations required).

Nearby Attractions/Accommodations: Railway Museum, May Museum, Old Poor Farm, antique shopping, Motor Plex, historical Main Street.

Location/Directions: Approximately 35 miles west of Omaha. Highway 275 exit Military Avenue, travel west through Fremont, turn north on Somers Avenue.

P   🚌   ✳   ☕   🎋   🚂   ✉   M   arm

Site Address: 1835 N. Somers Avenue, Fremont, NE
Mailing Address: PO Box 191, Fremont, NE 68026
Telephone: (402) 727-0615
Fax: (402) 727-0615
E-mail: fevr@geocities.com
Internet: www.geocities.com/heartland/hills/4184/fevr.html

FREMONT DINNER TRAIN
Dinner train
Standard gauge

BRUCE EVELAND

Description: An operating restaurant on wheels featuring a 30-mile trip, three to five course dinners, movies and optional dinner theater shows.

Schedule: April through October: Fridays and Saturdays, 7:30 to 10:45 p.m.; Sundays, 1:30 to 4:45 p.m. November through March: Saturdays, 6:30 to 9:45 p.m.

Admission/Fare: Adults: Sundays, $38.95; evenings $59.95; child rates on Sundays.

Locomotive/Rolling Stock: N&W power car no. 410; two converted cars, former CN; one converted car, former IC; one partially converted car, former Milwaukee.

Special Events: Murder Mysteries, Melodramas, U.S.O. Shows, Wine Tastings, Valentine's Day, July 4th, Halloween, New Year's Eve.

Nearby Attractions/Accommodations: Museum and antique shop district, opera house, poor farm, lakes.

Location/Directions: Site is in the northwest corner of Fremont, 35 miles northwest of Omaha and 50 miles north of Lincoln.

Site Address: 1835 N. Somers Avenue, Fremont, NE
Mailing Address: 650 N. "H," Fremont, NE 68025
Telephone: (402) 727-8321 and (800) 942-7245
Fax: (402) 727-0915

STUHR MUSEUM OF THE PRAIRIE

Description: A 200-acre living history museum tells the story of the early town builders in the late 1800s and early 1900s.

Schedule: May 1 through October 15: daily 9 a.m. to 5 p.m., July and August till 5:30 p.m. October 15 through April 30: Mondays through Saturdays, 9 a.m. to 5 p.m., Sundays 1 to 5 p.m.

Admission/Fare: May-October: adults $6.40; children $3.75; under age 7 are free. October-April: adults $4.25; children $2.15.

Locomotive/Rolling Stock: Seven acre railyard; 1901 locomotive; 1908 narrow gauge locomotive; other rolling stock and equipment.

Special Events: Call or write for information.

Location/Directions: I-80, exit 312, 4 miles north.

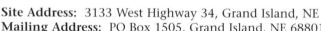

Site Address: 3133 West Highway 34, Grand Island, NE
Mailing Address: PO Box 1505, Grand Island, NE 68801
Telephone: (308) 385-5316
Fax: (308) 385-5028
Internet: www.stuhrmuseum.org

DURHAM WESTERN HERITAGE MUSEUM
Museum

DURHAM WESTERN HERITAGE MUSEUM

Description: Housed in the former Union Pacific Train Station Durham WHM explores the history of Omaha through interactive exhibits and displays, as well as bringing regional, national and world-renowned touring exhibitions to Omaha. In cooperation with the former UP Museum the DWHM displays the Union Pacific collection, including 6 train cars.

Schedule: Tuesdays through Saturdays, 10 a.m. to 5 p.m. and Sundays 1 to 5 p.m. Closed Mondays and most major holidays.

Admission/Fare: Adults $3.00; seniors $2.50; children ages 5-12 $2.00; under age 5 are free.

Locomotives/Rolling Stock: Baldwin 4-6-0 1243; Pullman 6-4-6 National Command; Pullman 1914 business car; Pullman 1949 barber shop lounge SP2906.

Special Events: Christmas, weekends in December. Ethnic Holiday Festival, December. Railroad Days, March.

Nearby Attractions/Accommodations: Joslyn Art Museum, Henry Dorely Zoo, Omaha Royals baseball, Strategic Air Command Museum, more.

Location/Directions: I-80, exit 13th Street, north to Pacific Street, east to 10th Street, go 1 block north.

*Coupon available, see coupon section.

Site Address: 801 S. 10th Street, Omaha, NE
Mailing Address: 801 S. 10th Street, Omaha, NE 68108
Telephone: (402) 444-5071
Fax: (402) 444-5391

Nebraska, Omaha

OMAHA ZOO RAILROAD
Train ride
30" gauge

AARON ZORKO

Description: Two live steam locomotives operate on 2.5 miles of track through the zoo grounds. The train ride gives a panoramic view of the zoo and animals. The Union Pacific Engine House provides excellent maintenance for this state-of-the-art steam operated railroad.

Schedule: Memorial Day through Labor Day: daily, 11 a.m. to 4 p.m. April, May, September and October: weekends only.

Admission/Fare: Zoo admission: adults $7.25; seniors $5.75; children $3.75. Train fare: adults $2.50; children $1.50.

Locomotives/Rolling Stock: Locomotive 395-104 Krauss built 1890 0-6-2T; locomotive 119 Crown built 1968 4-4-0; open air coaches; caboose.

Special Events: Ice Cream Safari; Critter Ride (bike around zoo); Holiday Wildlights.

Nearby Attractions/Accommodations: Rosenblatt Baseball Stadium (home of Omaha Royals), Omaha Community Playhouse, Omaha Children's Museum, The Old Market, Central Park Mall.

Location/Directions: I-80, exit 13th Street south, east on Bert Murphy Avenue. Adjacent to Rosenblatt Stadium.

Site Address: 3701 S. 10th Street, Omaha, NE
Mailing Address: 3701 S. 10th Street, Omaha, NE 68107-2200
Telephone: (402) 733-8401
Fax: (402) 733-7868
E-mail: market@omahazoo.com
Internet: www.omahazoo.com

NEVADA STATE RAILROAD MUSEUM
Museum
Standard and narrow gauge

NEVADA STATE RAILROAD MUSEUM

Description: The Nevada State Railroad Museum houses over 50 pieces of railroad equipment from Nevada's past and is considered one of the finest regional railroad museums in the country. Included in the collection are 5 steam locomotives and several restored coaches and freight cars. The bulk of the equipment is from the Virginia & Truckee Railroad, America's richest and most famous short line. Museum activities include operation of historic railroad equipment, hand car races, lectures, an annual railroad history symposium, changing exhibits, and a variety of special events.

Schedule: Year round: daily, 8:30 a.m. to 4:30 p.m.

Admission/Fare: $2.00; under age 18 are free.

Locomotive/Rolling Stock: No. 25, 1905 Baldwin 4-6-0; no. 18, "Dayton," 1873 Central Pacific 4-4-0; and no. 22, "Inyo," 1875 Baldwin 4-4-0; all former V&T. No. 1, "Glenbrook," 1875 Baldwin narrow-gauge 2-6-0, former Carson & Tahoe Lumber & Fluming Co.; no. 8, 1888 Cooke 4-4-0, former Dardanelle & Russellville; no. 1, "Joe Douglass," 1882 Porter narrow gauge 0-4-2T, former Dayton, Sutro & Carson Valley. Coaches nos. 3, 4, 8, 11, 12, 17 and 18, express/mail nos. 14 and 21, caboose-coaches nos. 9, 10 and 15, and eleven freight cars, all former V&T; more.

Location/Directions: Highways 50 and 395, at the south end of town.

     M arm ᵀᴿᴬᴵᴺ

Site Address: 2180 South Carson Street, Carson City, NV
Mailing Address: 2180 South Carson Street, Carson City, NV 89710
Telephone: (702) 687-6953
Internet: pages.prodigy.com/jbryant/ncvrr.htm

Nevada, East Ely

NEVADA NORTHERN RAILWAY MUSEUM
Train ride
Standard gauge

JACK SWANBERG

Description: Keystone Route–A 14-mile, 1.5-hour round trip to the historic mining district of Keystone, passing downtown Ely, tunnel No. 1, the ghost town of Lane City, and Robinson Canyon. Highline Route–A 22-mile, 1½-hour round trip with exciting overviews of the scenic Steptoe Valley, high in the foothills. Displays consist of steam, diesel, and electric locomotives; 1907 steam rotary snowplow; 1910 Jordan spreader; more than 60 pieces of antique passenger, freight, and work equipment; general offices; depot; machine shops; roundhouse.

Schedule: Memorial Day through Labor Day: most Saturdays and some Sundays.

Admission/Fare: Call or write for information.

Locomotive/Rolling Stock: No. 40, 1910 Baldwin 4-6-0, Nevada Northern Railway; no. 93, 1909 Alco 2-8-0; no. 105, Alco RS-2, and no. 109, Alco RS-3, both former Kennecott Copper Co.

Location/Directions: In eastern Nevada on U.S. 93.

Site Address: East Ely Depot, 1100 Avenue A, East Ely, NV
Mailing Address: PO Box 150040, East Ely, NV 89315
Telephone: (702) 289-2085
Internet: www.artcom.com/museums/nv/mr/89315-00.htm

EUREKA & PALISADE RAILROAD
Train ride
36" gauge

DANIEL MARKOFF

Description: Occasional historic display and operation on various host railroads.

Schedule: Call or write for details.

Admission/Fare: Call or write for details.

Locomotive/Rolling Stock: 1875 Baldwin Locomotive Works 4-4-0 American "Eureka."

Special Events: Call or write for details.

  TRAIN

Site Address: Las Vegas, NV
Mailing Address: 820 S. 7th Street, Suite A, Las Vegas, NV 89101
Telephone: (702) 383-3327

VIRGINIA & TRUCKEE RAILROAD CO.
Train ride
Standard gauge

VIRGINIA & TRUCKEE RAILROAD CO.

Description: A 5-mile round trip from Virginia City to the town of Gold Hill through the heart of the historic Comstock mining region. A knowledgeable conductor gives a running commentary of the area and of the 126-year-old railroad.

Schedule: May 22 through October 17.

Admission/Fare: Adults $4.75; children 5-12 $2.50; children under age 4 ride free; all-day pass $9.50.

Locomotive/Rolling Stock: 1916 Baldwin 2-8-0 no. 29, former Longview Portland & Northern; 1907 Baldwin 2-6-2 no. 8, former Hobart Southern; 1888 Northwestern Pacific combine and coach; former Tonopah & Tidewater coach; former Northern Pacific caboose; 1919 0-6-0 no. 30, former Southern Pacific.

Special Events: Party and Night train, once a month during season.

Nearby Attractions/Accommodations: Historic Virginia City, mines, mansions, shops.

Location/Directions: Twenty-one miles from Reno, 17 miles from Carson City.

*Coupon available, see coupon section.

Site Address: Washington and "F" Streets, Virginia City, NV
Mailing Address: PO Box 467, Virginia City, NV 89440
Telephone: (702) 847-0380

Guide to Tourist Railroads and Museums
1999 GUEST COUPONS

ROARING CAMP & BIG TREES RR
Regular price: Adults $13.75, children $9.50
With coupon: Adults $12.38, children $8.55
Valid April 1999 through March 2000

CALIFORNIA WESTERN RR
**With coupon: Buy one admission get
equal price admission free**
Valid April 1999 through March 2000
Maximum discount 2 persons per coupon

LOMITA RAILROAD MUSEUM
Regular price: Adults $1, children $1
With coupon: Adults $.50, children $.50
Valid April 1999 through March 2000

SAN DIEGO
MODEL RAILROAD MUSEUM
Regular price: Adults $3, seniors $2.50
With coupon: Adults $2, seniors $2
Valid April 1999 through March 2000

TRAIN TOWN
Regular price: Adults $3.50, seniors/children $2.50
With coupon: Adults $1.75, seniors/children $1.25
Valid April 1999 through March 2000

CRIPPLE CREEK AND VICTOR
Regular price: Adults $7.50, seniors $6.75, children $3.75
**With coupon: Adults $7, seniors $6.25,
children $3.25**
Valid April 1999 through March 2000
Maximum discount 4 persons per coupon

ESSEX STEAM TRAIN
Regular price: Adults $15, children $7.50
With coupon: Adults $13, children $6.50
Valid April 1999 through March 2000
Maximum discount 4 persons per coupon

QUEEN ANNE'S RAILROAD
Regular price: Adults $54.95
With coupon: Adults $47.95
Valid April 1999 through March 2000

WEST CHESTER RAILROAD
Regular price: Adults $9, children $5
With coupon: Adults $8, children $4
Valid April 1999 through March 2000

RAILROAD MUSEUM OF SO. FLORIDA
TRAIN VILLAGE
Regular price: Adults $2.50, seniors $2.50
With coupon: Adults $2, seniors $2
Valid April 1999 through March 2000
Maximum discount 2 persons per coupon

SEMINOLE GULF RAILWAY
Regular price: Adults $39.98 plus tax
With coupon: Adults $29.98 plus tax
Sunday Twilighter Dinner Train, 5:30 p.m.
Valid April 1999 through March 2000

FLORIDA GULF COAST RR MUSEUM
Regular price: Adults $8
With coupon: Adults $7
Valid April 1999 through March 2000

Guide to Tourist Railroads and Museums
1999 GUEST COUPONS

CYPRESS GARDENS
Regular price: Adults $30.95, seniors $26.30, children $20.95
With coupon: Adults $27.70, seniors $22.05, children $17.70
Valid April 1999 through March 2000
PLU CODE 969

KENNESAW CIVIL WAR MUSEUM
With coupon: Buy one admission get equal price admission free
Valid April 1999 through March 2000

HISTORIC RAILROAD SHOPS
Regular price: Adults $2.50, seniors/children $2
With coupon: Adults $2, seniors/children $1.60
Valid April 1999 through March 2000

NORTHERN PACIFIC DEPOT RR MUSEUM
Regular price: Adults $2, seniors $1.50, children $1
With coupon: Adults $1, seniors $1, children $.50
Valid April 1999 through March 2000
Maximum discount $7 per coupon

HISTORIC PULLMAN FOUNDATION
With coupon: Buy one admission get equal price admission free
Valid April 1999 through March 2000
Maximum discount 2 persons per coupon

MONTICELLO RAILWAY MUSEUM
Regular price: Adults $6, seniors/children $4
With coupon: Adults $5.50, seniors/children $3.50
Valid April 1999 through March 2000
Maximum discount 4 persons per coupon

RAYVILLE RAILROAD MUSEUM
With coupon: Buy one admission get equal price admission free
Valid April 1999 through March 2000

VALLEY VIEW MODEL RAILROAD
Regular price: Adults $4, seniors $ 3.50, children $2
With coupon: Adults $3, seniors $2.50, children $1.50
Valid April 1999 through March 2000
Maximum discount 6 persons per coupon

WHITEWATER VALLEY RAILROAD
Regular price: Adults $12, children $6
With coupon: Adults $11, children $5
Valid April 1999 through March 2000
Maximum discount 4 persons per coupon

LINDEN RAILROAD MUSEUM
Regular price: Adults $2, children $1
With coupon: Adults $1, children $.50
Valid April 1999 through March 2000
Maximum discount 5 persons per coupon

TRAINLAND U.S.A.
Regular price: Adults $4.50, seniors $4, children $2
With coupon: Adults $3.50, seniors $3, children $1.50
Valid April 1999 through March 2000

RAILSWEST RAILROAD MUSEUM
Regular price: Adults $3, children $1.50
With coupon: Adults $2.50, children $1.25
Valid April 1999 through March 2000
Maximum discount 4 persons per coupon

KENNESAW CIVIL WAR MUSEUM KENNESAW, GA GUIDE TO TOURIST RAILROADS AND MUSEUMS 1999 GUEST COUPON	**CYPRESS GARDENS** WINTER HAVEN, FL GUIDE TO TOURIST RAILROADS AND MUSEUMS 1999 GUEST COUPON
NORTHERN PACIFIC DEPOT **RR MUSEUM** WALLACE, ID GUIDE TO TOURIST RAILROADS AND MUSEUMS 1999 GUEST COUPON	**HISTORIC RAILROAD SHOPS** SAVANNAH, GA GUIDE TO TOURIST RAILROADS AND MUSEUMS 1999 GUEST COUPON
MONTICELLO RAILWAY MUSEUM MONTICELLO, IL GUIDE TO TOURIST RAILROADS AND MUSEUMS 1999 GUEST COUPON	**HISTORIC PULLMAN FOUNDATION** CHICAGO, IL GUIDE TO TOURIST RAILROADS AND MUSEUMS 1999 GUEST COUPON
VALLEY VIEW MODEL RAILROAD UNION, IL GUIDE TO TOURIST RAILROADS AND MUSEUMS 1999 GUEST COUPON	**RAYVILLE RAILROAD MUSEUM** MONTICELLO, IL GUIDE TO TOURIST RAILROADS AND MUSEUMS 1999 GUEST COUPON
LINDEN RAILROAD MUSEUM LINDEN, IN GUIDE TO TOURIST RAILROADS AND MUSEUMS 1999 GUEST COUPON	**WHITEWATER VALLEY RAILROAD** CONNERSVILLE, IN GUIDE TO TOURIST RAILROADS AND MUSEUMS 1999 GUEST COUPON
RAILSWEST RAILROAD MUSEUM COUNCIL BLUFFS, IA GUIDE TO TOURIST RAILROADS AND MUSEUMS 1999 GUEST COUPON	**TRAINLAND U.S.A.** COLFAX, IA GUIDE TO TOURIST RAILROADS AND MUSEUMS 1999 GUEST COUPON

Guide to Tourist Railroads and Museums
1999 GUEST COUPONS

MIDLAND RAILWAY
Regular price: Adults $8, children $4
With coupon: Adults $7, children $3
Valid April 1999 through March 2000
Maximum discount 2 persons per coupon

GREAT PLAINS TRANSPORTATION MUSEUM
With coupon: Buy one admission get equal price admission free
Valid April 1999 through March 2000
Maximum discount 4 persons per coupon

BIG SOUTH FORK SCENIC RAILWAY
With coupon: Buy one admission get equal price admission free
Valid April 1999 through March 2000
Maximum discount 2 persons per coupon

WISCASSET, WATERVILLE & FARMINGTON
Regular price: Adults $2
With coupon: Adults $1
Valid April 1999 through March 2000

MAINE NARROW GAUGE RAILROAD
Regular price: Adults $5, seniors $4, children $3
With coupon: Adults $4.50, seniors $3.50, children $2.50
Valid April 1999 through March 2000

THE B&O RAILROAD MUSEUM
Regular price: Adults $6.50, seniors $5.50, children $4
With coupon: Adults $5.50, seniors $4.50, children $3
Valid April 1999 through March 2000
Maximum discount 1 person per coupon
Not valid for specials events or with any other offer

NATIONAL CAPITAL TROLLEY MUSEUM
With coupon: Buy one admission get equal price admission free
Valid April 1999 through March 2000
Maximum discount 1 per coupon

JUNCTION VALLEY RAILROAD
Regular price: Adults $4.75, seniors $4.50, children $4
With coupon: Adults $4.25, seniors $4.05, children $3.60
Valid April 1999 through March 2000

HUCKLEBERRY RAILROAD
Regular price: Adults $9.25, seniors $8.25, children $6.25
With coupon: Adults $7.75, seniors $7, children $5
Valid April 1999 through March 2000

GRAND TRAVERSE DINNER TRAIN
Regular price: Adults $65/$50, children $55/$40
With coupon: Adults $62/$47, children $52/$37
High season 9/15-10/31/low season 11/1-9/14
Valid April 1999 through March 2000

IRON MOUNTAIN IRON MINE
Regular price: Adults $6, children $5
With coupon: Adults $5, children $4
Valid April 1999 through March 2000

TOONERVILLE TROLLEY
Regular price: Adults $20, seniors $19, children $10
With coupon: Adults $19, seniors $18, children $9
6.5 hour tour
Valid April 1999 through March 2000

**GREAT PLAINS
TRANSPORTATION MUSEUM**
WICHITA, KS
GUIDE TO TOURIST RAILROADS AND MUSEUMS
1999 GUEST COUPON

MIDLAND RAILWAY
BALDWIN CITY, KS
GUIDE TO TOURIST RAILROADS AND MUSEUMS
1999 GUEST COUPON

**WISCASSET,
WATERVILLE & FARMINGTON**
ALNA, ME
GUIDE TO TOURIST RAILROADS AND MUSEUMS
1999 GUEST COUPON

BIG SOUTH FORK SCENIC RAILWAY
STEARNS, KY
GUIDE TO TOURIST RAILROADS AND MUSEUMS
1999 GUEST COUPON

THE B&O RAILROAD MUSEUM
BALTIMORE, MD
GUIDE TO TOURIST RAILROADS AND MUSEUMS
1999 GUEST COUPON

MAINE NARROW GAUGE RAILROAD
PORTLAND, ME
GUIDE TO TOURIST RAILROADS AND MUSEUMS
1999 GUEST COUPON

JUNCTION VALLEY RAILROAD
BRIDGEPORT, MI
GUIDE TO TOURIST RAILROADS AND MUSEUMS
1999 GUEST COUPON

NATIONAL CAPITAL TROLLEY MUSEUM
WHEATON, MD
GUIDE TO TOURIST RAILROADS AND MUSEUMS
1999 GUEST COUPON

GRAND TRAVERSE DINNER TRAIN
GRAND TRAVERSE, MI
GUIDE TO TOURIST RAILROADS AND MUSEUMS
1999 GUEST COUPON

HUCKLEBERRY RAILROAD
FLINT, MI
GUIDE TO TOURIST RAILROADS AND MUSEUMS
1999 GUEST COUPON

TOONERVILLE TROLLEY
SOO JUNCTION, MI
GUIDE TO TOURIST RAILROADS AND MUSEUMS
1999 GUEST COUPON

IRON MOUNTAIN IRON MINE
IRON MOUNTAIN, MI
GUIDE TO TOURIST RAILROADS AND MUSEUMS
1999 GUEST COUPON

Guide to Tourist Railroads and Museums
1999 GUEST COUPONS

SPIRIT OF TRAVERSE CITY
**With coupon: Buy one admission get
equal price admission free**
Valid April 1999 through March 2000
Maximum discount 2 persons per coupon

MICHIGAN STAR CLIPPER
Regular price: Adults $69.50
With coupon: Adults $59.50
Specific dates and departures only, call for details
Valid April 1999 through March 2000

LAKE SUPERIOR
& MISSISSIPPI RAILROAD
Regular price: Adults $7, seniors $6, children $5
With coupon: Adults $6, seniors $5, children $4
Valid April 1999 through March 2000

COMO-HARRIET STREETCAR LINE
Regular price: Adults $1.25
With coupon: Adults $1
Valid April 1999 through March 2000
Maximum discount 4 persons per coupon

WABASH FRISCO & PACIFIC RAILWAY
Regular price: Adults $2
With coupon: Adults $1.50
Valid April 1999 through March 2000

ST. LOUIS IRON MOUNTAIN & SOUTHERN
Regular price: Adults $12.50, children $6
With coupon: Adults $11.50, children $5
Valid April 1999 through March 2000
Maximum discount 2 persons per coupon

PATEE HOUSE MUSEUM
Regular price: Adults $3, seniors $2.50, children $1.50
With coupon: Adults $2.50, seniors $2, children $1
Valid April 1999 through March 2000

MUSEUM OF TRANSPORTATION
**With coupon: Buy one admission get
equal price admission free**
Valid April 1999 through March 2000
Maximum discount 2 persons per coupon

DURHAM
WESTERN HERITAGE MUSEUM
**With coupon: Buy one admission get
equal price admission free**
Valid April 1999 through March 2000
Maximum discount 1 person per coupon

VIRGINIA & TRUCKEE RAILROAD CO.
Regular price: Adults $4.75, children $2.50
With coupon: Adults $4, children $2.50
Valid April 1999 through March 2000
Maximum discount 6 persons per coupon

HOBO RAILROAD
Regular price: Adults $8, children $5.50
With coupon: Adults $7, children $4.50
Valid April 1999 through March 2000

CONWAY SCENIC RAILROAD
**With coupon: $.50 off Conway departure or
With coupon: $1 off Bartlett departure or
With coupon: $2 off Crawford Notch departure**
Valid April 1999 through March 2000
Discount applies to entire group

Guide to Tourist Railroads and Museums
1999 GUEST COUPONS

CAFE LAFAYETTE DINNER TRAIN
With coupon: Adults $2 discount,
children $1 discount
Valid April 1999 through March 2000

NORTHLANDZ
With coupon: Free ride on outside train with paid
admission to Northlandz
Valid April 1999 through March 2000

BLACK RIVER & WESTERN RAILROAD
With coupon: Buy one admission get
equal price admission free
Valid April 1999 through March 2000
Maximum discount 1 person per coupon

NEW YORK & LAKE ERIE RAILROAD
Regular price: Adults $9, seniors $8.50, , children $4.50
With coupon: Adults $7, seniors $6.50,
children $2.50
Valid April 1999 through March 2000
Maximum discount 4 persons per coupon

TROLLEY MUSEUM OF NEW YORK
Regular price: Adults $3, seniors/children $2
With coupon: Adults $1, seniors/children $1
Valid April 1999 through March 2000

**NORTHEASTERN
NEW YORK RAILROAD**
Regular price: Adults $10, seniors $9, children $5
With coupon: Adults $9, seniors $8, children $4.50
Valid April 1999 through March 2000

DELAWARE & ULSTER RAILRIDE
With coupon: Buy one admission get
equal price admission free
Valid April 1999 through March 2000
Maximum discount 2 persons per coupon

**NORTH CAROLINA
TRANSPORTATION MUSEUM**
Regular price: Adults $5, seniors/children $4
With coupon: Adults $4, seniors/children $3
Valid April 1999 through March 2000

WILMINGTON RAILROAD MUSEUM
With coupon: Buy one admission get
equal price admission free
Valid April 1999 through March 2000
Maximum discount 2 persons per coupon

FORT LINCOLN TROLLEY
Regular price: Adults $5
With coupon: Adults $4
Valid April 1999 through March 2000

**CARROLLTON-ONIEDA-MINEVA
RAILROAD**
Regular price: Adults $10, children $8
With coupon: Adults $9, children $7
Valid April 1999 through March 2000

BUCKEYE CENTRAL SCENIC RAILROAD
Regular price: Adults $6, children $5
With coupon: Adults $5, children $4
Valid April 1999 through March 2000
Maximum discount 6 persons per coupon

Guide to Tourist Railroads and Museums
1999 GUEST COUPONS

HARMAR STATION
Regular price: Adults $5, seniors $4
With coupon: Adults $4, seniors $3
Valid April 1999 through March 2000
Maximum discount 1 person per coupon

LUCAS COUNTY/MAUMEE VALLEY HISTORICAL SOCIETY
Regular price: Adults $3.50, children $1.50
With coupon: Adults $3, children $1.25
Valid April 1999 through March 2000

HOCKING VALLEY SCENIC RAILWAY
With coupon: $.50 off regular admission
Valid April 1999 through March 2000

TROLLEYVILLE U.S.A.
Regular price: Adults $6, seniors $4, children $3
With coupon: Adults $5, seniors $3, children $2
Valid April 1999 through March 2000

TOLEDO LAKE ERIE & WESTERN RAILROAD
Regular price: Adults $8, seniors $7, children $4.50
With coupon: Adults $7, seniors $5, children $3
Valid April 1999 through March 2000

HUGO HERITAGE RAILROAD
Regular price: Adults $20, seniors $17, children $13
With coupon: Adults $15, seniors $13, children $10
Valid April 1999 through March 2000

OREGON ELECTRIC RAILWAY HISTORICAL SOCIETY
Regular price: Adults $6, seniors $5, children $3
With coupon: Adults $5, seniors $3, children $2
Valid April 1999 through March 2000

ALTOONA RAILROADERS MEMORIAL MUSEUM
Regular price: Adults $10, seniors $9, children $5.50
With coupon: Adults $9, seniors $8, children $5
Valid April 1999 through March 2000

BIG BEAR FARM
Regular price: Adults $5.50, seniors $3.50
With coupon: Adults $4.50, seniors $2.50
Valid April 1999 through March 2000
Maximum discount 1 person per coupon

STOURBRIDGE LINE RAIL EXCURSIONS
Regular price: Adults $17.50, seniors $16.50, children $11
With coupon: Adults $16.50, seniors $15.50, children $10
Groups of 4 or more additional $1 off per ticket
Valid April 1999 through March 2000

OLD MAUCH CHUNK MODEL TRAIN
With coupon: Buy one admission get equal price admission free
Valid April 1999 through March 2000
Maximum discount 1 person per coupon

WANAMAKER KEMPTON & SOUTHERN
Regular price: Adults $5, children $3
With coupon: Adults $4.75, children $2.75
Valid April 1999 through March 2000
Maximum discount 5 persons per coupon

LUCAS COUNTY/MAUMEE VALLEY HISTORICAL SOCIETY MAUMEE, OH GUIDE TO TOURIST RAILROADS AND MUSEUMS 1999 GUEST COUPON	**HARMAR STATION** MARIETTA, OH GUIDE TO TOURIST RAILROADS AND MUSEUMS 1999 GUEST COUPON
TROLLEYVILLE U.S.A. OLMSTED TOWNSHIP, OH GUIDE TO TOURIST RAILROADS AND MUSEUMS 1999 GUEST COUPON	**HOCKING VALLEY SCENIC RAILWAY** NELSONVILLE, OH GUIDE TO TOURIST RAILROADS AND MUSEUMS 1999 GUEST COUPON
HUGO HERITAGE RAILROAD HUGO, OK GUIDE TO TOURIST RAILROADS AND MUSEUMS 1999 GUEST COUPON	**TOLEDO LAKE ERIE & WESTERN RAILROAD** WATERVILLE AND GRAND RAPIDS, OH GUIDE TO TOURIST RAILROADS AND MUSEUMS 1999 GUEST COUPON
ALTOONA RAILROADERS MEMORIAL MUSEUM ALTOONA, PA GUIDE TO TOURIST RAILROADS AND MUSEUMS 1999 GUEST COUPON	**OREGON ELECTRIC RAILWAY HISTORICAL SOCIETY** LAKE OSWEGO, OR GUIDE TO TOURIST RAILROADS AND MUSEUMS 1999 GUEST COUPON
STOURBRIDGE LINE RAIL EXCURSIONS HONESDALE, PA GUIDE TO TOURIST RAILROADS AND MUSEUMS 1999 GUEST COUPON	**BIG BEAR FARM** HONESDALE, PA GUIDE TO TOURIST RAILROADS AND MUSEUMS 1999 GUEST COUPON
WANAMAKER KEMPTON & SOUTHERN KEMPTON, PA GUIDE TO TOURIST RAILROADS AND MUSEUMS 1999 GUEST COUPON	**OLD MAUCH CHUNK MODEL TRAIN** JIM THORPE, PA GUIDE TO TOURIST RAILROADS AND MUSEUMS 1999 GUEST COUPON

Guide to Tourist Railroads and Museums
1999 GUEST COUPONS

EAST PENN RAIL EXCURSIONS
Regular price: Adults $8, seniors $7, children $4
With coupon: Adults $7, seniors $6, children $3
Valid April 1999 through March 2000

BRANDYWINE SCENIC RAILWAY
Regular price: Adults $8, seniors $7, children $6
With coupon: Adults $7, seniors $6, children $5
Valid April 1999 through March 2000
Maximum discount 2 persons per coupon

EAST BROAD TOP RAILROAD
**With coupon: Buy one admission get
equal price admission free**
Valid April 1999 through March 2000
Maximum discount 1 person per coupon

STEWARTSTOWN RAILROAD
With coupon: $1 off admission
Valid April 1999 through March 2000
Maximum discount 2 persons per coupon

PENNSYLVANIA TROLLEY MUSEUM
**With coupon: Buy one admission get
equal price admission free**
Valid April 1999 through March 2000
Maximum discount 1 person per coupon

TIOGA CENTRAL RAILROAD
Regular price: Adults $10, seniors $9, children $5
With coupon: Adults $9, seniors $8, children $4
Valid April 1999 through March 2000

DINNER TRAINS OF NEW ENGLAND
With coupon: $10 off dinner for two
Valid April 1999 through March 2000

WHETSTONE VALLEY EXPRESS
Regular price: Adults $14, children $9
With coupon: Adults $13, children $8
Valid April 1999 through March 2000

CASEY JONES MUSEUM
Regular price: Adults $4, seniors $3.50, children $3
With coupon: Adults $3, seniors $2.50, children $2
Valid April 1999 through March 2000
Maximum discount 2 persons per coupon

AUSTIN & TEXAS CENTRAL RAILROAD
**With coupon: Buy one admission get
equal price admission free**
Hill Country Flyer, coach fare
Valid April 1999 through March 2000
Maximum discount $24 per coupon

RAILROAD AND PIONEER MUSEUM
**With coupon: Buy one admission get
equal price admission free**
Valid April 1999 through March 2000
Maximum discount 6 persons per coupon

VIRGINIA
MUSEUM OF TRANSPORTATION
**With coupon: Buy one admission get
equal price admission free**
Valid April 1999 through March 2000
Maximum discount 2 persons per coupon

BRANDYWINE SCENIC RAILWAY
NORTHBROOK, PA
GUIDE TO TOURIST RAILROADS AND MUSEUMS
1999 GUEST COUPON

EAST PENN RAIL EXCURSIONS
KUTZTOWN, PA
GUIDE TO TOURIST RAILROADS AND MUSEUMS
1999 GUEST COUPON

STEWARTSTOWN RAILROAD
STEWARTSTOWN, PA
GUIDE TO TOURIST RAILROADS AND MUSEUMS
1999 GUEST COUPON

EAST BROAD TOP RAILROAD
ROCKHILL FURNACE, PA
GUIDE TO TOURIST RAILROADS AND MUSEUMS
1999 GUEST COUPON

TIOGA CENTRAL RAILROAD
WELLSBORO, PA
GUIDE TO TOURIST RAILROADS AND MUSEUMS
1999 GUEST COUPON

PENNSYLVANIA TROLLEY MUSEUM
WASHINGTON, PA
GUIDE TO TOURIST RAILROADS AND MUSEUMS
1999 GUEST COUPON

WHETSTONE VALLEY EXPRESS
MILBANK, SD
GUIDE TO TOURIST RAILROADS AND MUSEUMS
1999 GUEST COUPON

DINNER TRAINS OF NEW ENGLAND
NEWPORT, RI
GUIDE TO TOURIST RAILROADS AND MUSEUMS
1999 GUEST COUPON

AUSTIN & TEXAS CENTRAL RAILROAD
AUSTIN, TX
GUIDE TO TOURIST RAILROADS AND MUSEUMS
1999 GUEST COUPON

CASEY JONES MUSEUM
JACKSON, TN
GUIDE TO TOURIST RAILROADS AND MUSEUMS
1999 GUEST COUPON

VIRGINIA
MUSEUM OF TRANSPORTATION
ROANOKE, VA
GUIDE TO TOURIST RAILROADS AND MUSEUMS
1999 GUEST COUPON

RAILROAD AND PIONEER MUSEUM
TEMPLE, TX
GUIDE TO TOURIST RAILROADS AND MUSEUMS
1999 GUEST COUPON

Guide to Tourist Railroads and Museums
1999 GUEST COUPONS

CHELAN COUNTY HISTORICAL SOCIETY
Regular price: Adults $3, seniors/children $2
With coupon: Adults $1, seniors/children $1
Valid April 1999 through March 2000

CHEHALIS-CENTRALIA RAILROAD ASSN
Regular price: Adults $7, seniors $6, children $5
With coupon: Adults $6, seniors $5, children $4
Valid April 1999 through March 2000

YAKIMA VALLEY RAIL AND STEAM MUSEUM
Regular price: Adults $2, seniors/children $1
With coupon: Adults $1, seniors/children $.50
Valid April 1999 through March 2000

CASS SCENIC RAILROAD STATE PARK
With coupon: Buy one admission get equal price admission free
Valid April 1999 through March 2000
Maximum discount 1 person per coupon

COLLIS P. HUNTINGTON RAILROAD
Regular price: Adults $99, children $69
With coupon: Adults $89, children $62
Valid April 1999 through March 2000
Maximum discount 2 persons per coupon

NATIONAL RAILROAD MUSEUM
With coupon: Buy one admission get equal price admission free
Valid April 1999 through March 2000
Maximum discount 1 person per coupon

CAMP FIVE MUSEUM
Regular price: Adults $14
With coupon: Adults $13
Valid April 1999 through March 2000

KETTLE MORAINE RAILWAY
Regular price: Adults $9, children $5
With coupon: Adults $8, children $4.50
Valid April 1999 through March 2000

OSCEOLA & ST. CROIX VALLEY RAILROAD
Regular price: Adults $12, seniors $11, children $7
With coupon: Adults $11, seniors $10, children $6
Valid April 1999 through March 2000

RAILROAD MEMORIES MUSEUM
Regular price: Adults $3, children $.50
With coupon: Adults $2.50, children $.25
Valid April 1999 through March 2000

BC RAIL LTD
With coupon: Buy one admission get equal price admission free
Round trip, coach fare
Valid April 1999 through March 2000
Maximum discount 1 person per coupon

KETTLE VALLEY STEAM RAILWAY
Regular price: Adults $11, seniors $10, children $8.50
With coupon: Adults $10, seniors $9, children $7.50
Valid April 1999 through March 2000
Maximum discount 1 person per coupon

New Hampshire, Bretton Woods

THE MOUNT WASHINGTON COG RAILWAY
Train ride
4'8"gauge

THE MOUNT WASHINGTON COG RAILWAY

Description: Climb aboard the World's first mountain climbing cog railway to the summit of Mount Washington, the highest peak in the Northeast. Rain or shine, this three-hour round trip journey on one of seven enclosed and heated coaches is a truly unique vacation experience for all ages. Visit our new Base Station with museum, restaurant and gift shop. National Historic Engineering Landmark built in 1869.

Schedule: Early May through early November: call for schedule. Reservations recommended.

Admission/Fare: Adults $39.00; seniors $35.00; children ages 6-12 $26.00; under age 6 are free unless occupying a seat.

Locomotive/Rolling Stock: Seven coal-fired steam engines; seven enclosed heated coaches; one speeder.

Nearby Attractions/Accommodations: The Mount Washington Hotel & Resort, over 12 family attractions within 30 miles, outlet shopping, and hiking.

Location/Directions: Located in the heart of New Hampshire's White Mountains at the base of the Presidential Mountain Range. I-93, exit 35, route 3N, Route 302E to Cog Railway Base Road. Site is located 165 miles from Boston, Massachusetts, and 105 miles from Manchester, New Hampshire.

Site Address: Base Road, Mt. Washington, NH
Mailing Address: Base Road, Mt. Washington, NH 03589
Telephone: (800) 922-8825 and (603) 278-5404
Fax: (603) 278-5830

HARTMANN MODEL RAILROAD, LTD.
Display

HARTMANN MODEL RAILROAD, LTD.

Description: Housed in two buildings, each 8,000 square feet, is a railroad display for all ages. This site features many operating layouts, from G to Z scales, including a replica of Crawford Notch, New Hampshire, in the mid 1950s to early 1960s. Visitors can see several other detailed operating layouts with trains winding through tunnels, over bridges, and past miniature stations and buildings, and Thomas the Tank Engine operates by a light-sensor system. Also on display are about 5,000 model locomotives and coaches, American and European. Come and see our operating outdoor railroad and take a ride with us.

Schedule: Year round: daily, 10 a.m. to 5 p.m. Closed Easter, Mother's Day, Thanksgiving, Christmas Day.

Admission/Fare: Adults $5.00; seniors $4.00; children ages 5-12 $3.00; group rates available.

Location/Directions: Four miles north of North Conway.

Site Address: Town Hall Road and Route 302/16, Intervale, NH
Mailing Address: PO Box 165, Intervale, NH 03845
Telephone: (603) 356-9922
Fax: (603) 356-9958
E-mail: hartmann@landmarknet.net

New Hampshire, Lincoln

HOBO RAILROAD
· Train ride, dinner train
Standard gauge

ALLAN POMMER

Description: A 1.25-hour train ride in a woodsy setting along the Pemigewasset River. As you travel along in our vintage cars treat yourself to one of our unique specialties: a Hobo picnic lunch, a Friendly's ice cream sundae, or the Mountain View Dinner Train.

Schedule: May, June, October, December: weekends. July through September: daily departures at 11 a.m., 1 and 3 p.m. Dinner train–departs 7 p.m.

Admission/Fare: Adults $8.00; seniors $7.00; children ages 4-11 $5.50; under age 4 are free. Dinner train–38.95 per person.

Locomotive/Rolling Stock: Former PT S1 1008; former B&M S1 1186; former MEC S1 959; former U.S. Army GE 44-ton 2; former DL&W coaches 1001-1004; former B&M RDC coaches.

Location/Directions: I-93 exit 32 on Main Street (Route 112). Across the street from McDonald's.

*Coupon available, see coupon section.

Radio frequencies: 160.470

Site Address: Railroad Street, Lincoln, NH
Mailing Address: PO Box 9, Lincoln, NH 03251
Telephone: (603) 745-2135
Fax: (603) 745-9850
E-mail: www.hoborr.together.net
Internet: www.hoborr.com

WHITE MOUNTAIN CENTRAL RAILROAD
Train ride
Standard gauge

CHET BRICKET

Description: A facsimile of an 1890s railroad station, a wooden caboose, boxcars, and flatcars. Other exhibits include a fire museum, an Americana museum, a haunted house, an antique photo parlor, a 1920s-era garage, an illusion building, "Merlin's Mansion," and much more. Enjoy a 2-mile, 30-minute ride through the scenic White Mountains, leaving from the beautiful depot at Clark's Trading Post. The train crosses a 120-foot covered bridge and climbs a 2 percent grade into the woods.

Schedule: Memorial weekend through late June: weekends only. Late June through Labor Day: daily 10 a.m. to 5 p.m. Labor Day through Columbus Day: weekends 10 a.m. to 4 p.m.

Admission/Fare: $7.00 per person ages 6 years and up.

Locomotive/Rolling Stock: No. 4, 1927 2-truck Heisler, former International Shoe Co.; no. 6, Climax, former Beebe River Railroad; no. 3, former East Branch & Lincoln.

Nearby Attractions/Accommodations: Loon Mountain gondola, Lost River.

Location/Directions: I-93 exit 33 south.

Site Address: Clark's Trading Post, Route 3, Lincoln, NH
Mailing Address: Box 1, Lincoln, NH 03251
Telephone: (603) 745-8913

New Hampshire, Meredith/Weirs Beach

WINNIPESAUKEE SCENIC RAILROAD
Train ride
Standard gauge

WINNIPESAUKEE SCENIC RAILROAD

Description: This line operates 1- and 2-hour excursions over former Boston & Maine track between Meredith and Lakeport. Passengers view unsurpassed scenery along the shores of New Hampshire's largest lake, Lake Winnipesaukee, in the comfort of climate-controlled coaches. Dining service is available during the summer, and the Ice Cream Parlor Car offers ice cream sundaes aboard the train. Fall foliage tours are 3-hour round trips to Plymouth. An 1893 former B&M baggage car serves as the ticket office; cabooses and other rolling stock are also on exhibit.

Schedule: May, June, September, October: weekends. July through August: daily departures 10:30 a.m., 12:30, 2:30, 4:30 p.m. Daily trains from Weirs Beach every hour on the hour from 11 a.m. to 5 p.m.

Admission/Fare: Two hour ride–adults $8.50; seniors $7.50; children ages 4-11 $6.50; under age 4 are free. One-hour rides–adults $7.50; children ages 4-11 $5.50; under age 4 are free. Dinner train–$38.95 per person.

Locomotive/Rolling Stock: Former PT S1 1008; former B&M S1 1186; former MEC S1 959; former U.S. Army GE 44-ton 2; former DL&W coaches 1001-1004; former B&M RDC coaches.

Location/Directions: In the heart of New Hampshire's Lake Region, located just off Route 3 in downtown Meredith. The Weirs Beach ticket office is located on the Weirs Beach boardwalk (Lakeside Avenue).

Radio frequencies: 161.550

Site Address: Mill Street, Meredith, NH
Mailing Address: PO Box 9, Lincoln, NH 03251
Telephone: (603) 745-2135
Fax: (603) 745-9850
E-mail: www.hoborr.together.net
Internet: www.hoborr.com

New Hampshire, North Conway   **CONWAY SCENIC RAILROAD**
Train ride, dinner train, museum,
display, and layout
Standard gauge

LES MACDONALD

Description: "Valley Train" travels south to Conway over former Boston & Maine Railroad branchline through farmlands in the Mount Washington Valley and west over former Maine Central Mountain Subdivision to Bartlett. "Notch Train" provides excursion service west from North Conway through spectacular Crawford Notch to Crawford Depot and Fabyan Station.

Schedule: Valley Train–May 15 through October 24: daily. Mid-April through mid-May, November, December: weekends. Notch Train–June 22 through September 11: Tuesdays through Saturdays. September 14 through October 15: daily.

Admission/Fare: Valley Train–adults from $8.50; children ages 4-12 from $6.00; under age 4 price varies with destination. North Train–adults from $30.00; children ages 4-12 from $16.00; under age 4 from $5.00.

Locomotive/Rolling Stock: No. 7470, 1921 Grand Trunk 0-6-0, former Canadian National; no. 15, 1945 44-ton GE, former Maine Central; more.

Nearby Attractions/Accommodations: Four-season destination resort in New Hampshire's White Mountains.

Location/Directions: Route 16/302 and Norcross Circle in the heart of North Conway village. Depot faces Village Park.

*Coupon available, see coupon section.

Radio frequency: 161.250

Site Address: Route 16/302 and Norcross Circle, North Conway Village, NH
Mailing Address: PO Box 1947, North Conway, NH 03860
Telephone: (603) 356-5251
E-mail: info@conwayscenic.com
Internet: www.conwayscenic.com

**CAFE LAFAYETTE
DINNER TRAIN**
Dinner train
Standard gauge

CHET BURAK

Description: Experience a leisurely two-hour evening train ride spent criss-crossing the picturesque Pemigewasset River. As dinner is served period music keeps time with the rail's rhythmic rumbling. See magnificent mountain vistas and lush New England forests during this 20-mile round trip. After dinner, with the compartment lights down low, watch a dramatic New England sunset outside your window.

Schedule: Mother's Day through last Saturday in October and December. Call for details.

Admission/Fare: Adults $38.95; children 4-11 $19.95; age 3 and under $5 minimum.

Locomotive/Rolling Stock: 1923 Pennsylvania Railroad caboose; 1924 Pullman dining car no. 221, former NYC; 1953 Army kitchen car; 1954 CN cafe coach no. 3207.

Nearby Attractions/Accommodations: Heart of the White Mountain National Forest, Old Man of the Mountain, Franconia Notch State Park.

Location/Directions: I-93, exit 32 on Route 112 midway between Lincoln and North Woodstock, New Hampshire.

*Coupon available, see coupon section.

Site Address: Route 112, North Woodstock, NH
Mailing Address: RR1 Box 85, Lincoln, NH 03251
Telephone: (603) 745-3500 and (800) 699-3501 (outside NH)
Fax: (603) 745-3535
Internet: www.cafelafayette.com

KLICKETY KLACK
MODEL RAILROAD
Layout
HO, N

KLICKETY KLACK MODEL RAILROAD

Description: Operate a turntable, a quarry train and carnival rides; visit a circus, castle, lighthouse and village; see a smoking factory and shop chimneys; experience four seasons and day/night in two rooms. All of this is possible at Klickety-Klack, where 24 HO and N scale trains run over 1500 feet of track. This miniature collection includes 150 locomotives, 400 freight and passenger cars, 1500 "people" and much more. This railroad represents over 70,000 hours of work by many dedicated people.

Schedule: July 1 through Labor Day: Mondays through Saturdays, 10 a.m. to 5:30 p.m. September through June: Thursdays through Saturdays, 10 a.m. to 5 p.m. Closed the last week in April.

Admission/Fare: Adults $4.00; children 3-12 $3.00.

Nearby Attractions/Accommodations: Mount Washington, New Hampshire lake region.

Location/Directions: At the junction of Routes 28 and 109A.

Site Address: 8 Elm Street, Wolfeboro Falls, NH
Mailing Address: PO Box 205, Wolfeboro Falls, NH 03896
Telephone: (603) 569-5384

CAPE MAY SEASHORE LINES
Train ride
Standard gauge

JOE OSCIAK

Description: The Seashore Lines offers a 20-mile, 1¼-hour round trip on the former Reading Company's famous steel speedway to the Jersey seashore.

Schedule: Call or write for information.

Admission/Fare: Call or write for information.

Locomotives/Rolling Stock: Eight Budd RDC1s, former Pennsylvania-Reading Seashore Lines; two RDC9s, former Boston & Maine; Alco/EMD RS3m, former Pennsylvania Railroad; EMD GP9, former PRR; P-RSL P70 coaches, former PRR.

Nearby Attractions/Accommodations: Victorian Cape May City, Wildwood Beaches, Boardwalk and Amusement Piers, Cape May Light House, Cape May-Lewes Ferry, Cape May County Park and Zoo, historic Cold Spring Village, Mid-Atlantic Center for the Arts, and Middle Township Performing Arts Center.

Special Events: Railroad Days, July. Halloween Trains, October. The Santa Express, December.

Location/Directions: 4-H Fairgrounds Station–Route 675, Cape May Court House. Cape May Court House Station–Route 615/Mechanic Street. Cold Spring Station–Route 9, Cold Spring. Cape May Rail Terminal–Lafayette Street, Cape May City.

P   **Radio frequency:** 161.160

Site Address: Rio Grande, NJ
Mailing Address: PO Box 152, Tuckahoe, NJ 08250-0152
Telephone: (609) 884-2675
Fax: (609) 567-5847

New Jersey, Farmingdale

THE NEW JERSEY MUSEUM OF TRANSPORTATION, INC.
Train ride
36" gauge

THE NEW JERSEY MUSEUM OF TRANSPORTATION INC.

Description: The ride is 12 minutes, two times around a 3,300-foot loop track. Equipment from museum collection is on display.

Schedule: Steam train–June through September: weekends. Diesel train–April, May, and October: weekends; July and August, weekdays. 12 to 4:30 p.m., departures every 30 minutes.

Admission/Fare: $2.00 per person; under age 2 are free. Higher fare for special events.

Locomotive/Rolling Stock: Surry, Sussex & Southampton no. 26, 1920 Baldwin 2-6-2; Ely-Thomas Lumber Co. no. 6, 1927 Lima Class B Shay; Cavan & Leitrim Railway (Ireland) no. 3L, 1887 Robert Stevenson 4-4-0T; U.S. Army no. 7751, 1942 GE 25 ton diesel-electric; U.S. Steel no. 45, 1950 GE 50 ton diesel-electric; Newfoundland Railway (CN) no. 502, 1902 wood coach; Central Railroad of NJ no. 91155 1874/1903 caboose.

Special Events: Railroaders' Day, Sunday after Labor Day. Christmas Express, four weekends after Thanksgiving.

Nearby Attractions/Accommodations: Allaire State Park, including Historic Allaire Village, nature center, playground campgrounds. North Jersey Coast shore attractions.

Location/Directions: Route 524, Wall Township, 2 miles west of Garden State Parkway exit 98, 2 miles east of I-195 exit 31.

   M TRAIN

Site Address: Allaire State Park, Route 524, Wall Township, NJ
Mailing Address: PO Box 622, Farmingdale, NJ 07727
Telephone: (732) 525-9251

NORTHLANDZ GREAT AMERICAN RAILWAY, DOLLHOUSE MUSEUM, & ART GALLERY

Train ride, museum, display and layout

NORTHLANDZ

Description: The world's largest miniature railway (Guinness) running over 100 trains, 3.5 story high mountains. Doll museum, art gallery and 3 foot outside railroad.

Schedule: Year round: daily 10 a.m. to 6 p.m.

Admission/Fare: Adults $13.75; children $7.75; under age 2 are free.

Special Events: Christmas Festival with thousand of lights and decorations, live music and Santa Claus Special on outside train.

Nearby Attractions/Accommodations: Ramada Inn, Black River and Western Tourist Railroad, New Hope & Ivy Tourist Railroad.

Location/Directions: Western New Jersey. Highway 202, 2 miles north of Flemington Traffic Circle. One hour from New York City and one hour from Philadelphia.

*Coupon available, see coupon section.

Site Address: 495 Highway 202, Flemington, NJ
Mailing Address: 495 Highway 202, Flemington, NJ 08822
Telephone: (908) 782-4022
Fax: (908) 782-5131
Internet: www.northlandz.com

**BLACK RIVER &
WESTERN RAILROAD**
Train ride

SEAN SIMON

Description: The Black River & Western is a steam/diesel excursion through the rolling hills of Hunterdon County. The 1.5 hour ride travels between Flemington and Ringoes. Saturday night trains to historic Lambertville during the summer.

Schedule: April through December: weekends 11:30 a.m., 1, 2:30 and 4 p.m. July through August: add Thursdays and Fridays. Trains depart Flemington Station.June through Labor Day: Saturday Night Special, departs Flemington at 7 p.m., dinner in Lambertville, return to Flemington at 11:40 p.m. Trains depart Flemington Station.

Admission/Fare: Adults $8.00; children $4.00. Groups/private charters available.

Locomotive/Rolling Stock: 1937 Alco 2-8-0 no. 60; 1956 EMD GP9 no. 752; 1950 EMD GP7 no. 780; nos. 320-323 commuter cars, former Central of New Jersey; nos. 301-305 "Wyatt Earp" cars, former Delaware, Lackawanna & Western; more.

Special Events: Easter Bunny, April. Train Robbery, May 15-16 and September 18-19. Railroad Days, July 17-18. Spooky Special, October 30-31. Santa Express, November 26-28, December 4-5 and 11-12.

Location/Directions: Route 202 to Flemington Circle, 12W, after railroad tracks turn right on Stangl Road.

*Coupon available, see coupon section.

Site Address: Route 12, Stangl Road, Flemington, NJ
Mailing Address: PO Box 200, Ringoes, NJ 08551
Telephone: (908) 782-6622
E-mail: blackriverrr@mailexcite.com
Internet: www.voicenet.com/~prw2/

HAZLET TRAIN STOP

Description: A large prewar and postwar train collection on display and a 25 x 28-foot operating layout.

Schedule: Summer: Wednesday through Saturday, 10 a.m. to 5 p.m.; Winter: Tuesday through Saturday, 10 a.m. to 6 p.m., and Sunday 1 to 5 p.m.

Admission/Fare: Adults $3.00; students $1.00; children ages 9 and under $.50.

Locomotive/Rolling Stock: Lionel, MTH, Marklin, LGB, Thomas the Tank Engine, HO, N, and Z.

Nearby Attractions/Accommodations: Boardwalk, ocean bathing.

Location/Directions: Garden State Parkway, exit 117 (Route 35 south), turn right on Hazlet Avenue, past railroad tracks turn right on Brailley Lane.

Site Address: 25 Brailley Lane, Hazlet, NJ
Mailing Address: 25 Brailley Lane, Hazlet, NJ 07730
Telephone: (732) 264-7429
Fax: (732) 888-7750
E-mail: HTS2250@aol.com

PAUL CAPRENITO

Description: Museum of local railroad history and an information center for the state transportation museum to be located at Phillipsburg.

Schedule: May 1 through October 1: Sundays.

Admission/Fare: Museum–free. Train–$.50.

Locomotive/Rolling Stock: IR former USA GE 44-tonner; L&HR caboose nos. 16, 18; CNT caboose no. 91197; L&HR 105 flanger; L&HR 1600 lowside gondola; Centerville & Southwestern 2" scale miniature railroad with two locomotives and 31 cars.

Special Events: Riverfest, early June. Old Towne Festival, late July.

Nearby Attractions/Accommodations: Crayola Factory, Two Rivers Landing Canal and Museum.

Location/Directions: Off South Main Street (Route 22) across from Joe's Steak Shop.

     M

Site Address: Cross Street and Pine Alley, Phillipsburg, NJ
Mailing Address: 292 Chambers Street, Phillipsburg, NJ 08805
Telephone: (908) 213-1722

New Jersey, Whippany

WHIPPANY RAILWAY MUSEUM
Museum
Standard gauge

PAUL TUPACZEWSKI

Description: Visit the Whippany Railway Museum, headquarted in the restored 1904 freight house of the Morristown & Erie, with its outstanding collection of railroad artifacts and memorabilia. Take a leisurely stroll through a railroad yard lost in time, complete with fieldstone depot, coal yard, wooden water tank and historic rail equipment. The museum also features one of the largest operating Lionel layouts in the area. Educational and fun for all ages.

Schedule: April through October: Sundays, 12 to 4 p.m.

Admission/Fare: Museum–adults $1.00; children under age 12 $.50. Special event train fare–adults $7.00; children under age 12 $4.00.

Locomotive/Rolling Stock: Morris County Central no. 4039, an 0-6-0 built in 1942 by the American Locomotive Company; railbus no. 10 built in 1918 by the White Motor Company for the Morristown & Erie; more.

Special Events: Easter Bunny Express, Railroad Festival, Halloween Chills, Santa Claus Special, more. Call or write for details.

Nearby Attractions/Accommodations: Morris Museum, Gen. Washington's headquarters, Jockey Hollow National Historic Site, Hanover Marriott (Whippany), Ramada Hotel (E. Hanover), Parsippany Hilton (Parsippany).

Location/Directions: At the intersection of Route 10 west and Whippany Road in Morris County.

        Newark & Metropark Sta.
Radio frequency: 160.230

Site Address: 1 Railroad Plaza, Whippany, NJ
Mailing Address: PO Box 16, Whippany, NJ 07981-0016
Telephone: (973) 887-8177
E-mail: paultup@interactive.net
Internet: www.interactive.net/~paultup/wrym.html

TOY TRAIN DEPOT
Train ride, museum, display and layout
12" and 16" gauge

RON KELLER

Description: A museum of model and toy trains. Layouts in Z, N, HO and O gauge. A gift shop of model supplies and train memorabilia.

Schedule: Year round: Wednesdays through Sundays, 12 to 5 p.m.

Admission/Fare: Museum–adults $2.00; children age 12 and under $1.50. Train–adults $2.00; children age 12 and under $1.50.

Special Events: Cottonwood Festival, Labor Day weekend. Railroad Days, Cloudcroft, New Mexico Balloon Rally.

Nearby Attractions/Accommodations: Oliver Lee State Park (campground), Alameda Park and Zoo, White Sands National Monument, Sunspot Observatory, Space Hall of Fame, Trinity Site.

Location/Directions: I-40 to Vaughn, New Mexico, U.S. 54 south to Alamogordo; or I-25 to Las Cruces, New Mexico, U.S. 70/82 east to Alamogordo. I-10 to El Paso, Texas, U.S. 54 north to Alamogordo. Alameda Park located on N. White Sands Blvd. (U.S. 54/70/82).

Site Address: 1991 N. White Sands Blvd., Alamogordo, NM
Mailing Address: 1991 N. White Sands Blvd., Alamogordo, NM 88310
Telephone: (505) 437-2855
Internet: www.quick.com/t/toy

New Mexico, Chama	**CUMBRES & TOLTEC SCENIC RAILROAD**
Colorado, Antonito	*Train ride*
	36" gauge

ALEX MAYES

Description: Steam trains travel over highly scenic former Denver & Rio Grande Western narrow-gauge trackage. The 64-mile line crosses Cumbres Pass (elevation 10,015 feet) and goes through spectacular Toltec Gorge, over high bridges, and through two tunnels. Passengers may choose to ride either the Colorado Limited from Antonito to Osier, Colorado, via Toltec Gorge or the New Mexico Express from Chama, New Mexico, to Osier via Cumbres Pass or ride the full length of the trip.

Schedule: Mid-May through mid-October: daily, departs Chama 10:30 a.m. to 4:30 p.m., departs Antonito 10 a.m. to 5 p.m.

Admission/Fare: Round trip: adults $34.00; children under 12 $17.00. Through trips from either terminal with return by van: adults $52.00, children $27.00. Reservations recommended for all trips.

Locomotive/Rolling Stock: Nos. 463, 484, 487, 488, 489, 497, 1925 Baldwin 2-8-2s, former D&RGW.

Special Events: Big Horn Tent Camp, Pony Express Race, Great Beat the Train over the Mountain Bicycle Race, dinner train.

Nearby Attractions/Accommodations: Ghost Ranch Museum/Georgia O'Keefe, Heron Lake, El Vado Lake.

Location/Directions: Stations at Chama, New Mexico, and Antonito, Colorado.

Site Address: 500 Terrace Avenue, Chama, NM
Mailing Address: PO Box 789, Chama, NM 87520
Telephone: (505) 756-2151 and (888) CUMBRES
Fax: (505) 756-2694

New Mexico, Clovis

CLOVIS DEPOT
MODEL TRAIN MUSEUM
Museum, display, layout

PHIL WILLIAMS

Description: The Clovis Depot has been restored to its condition in the 1950-60 era and has displays of historic documents and memorabilia covering its use and the history of the AT&SF in New Mexico along the "Belen Cutoff" since the turn of the century. Also featured are nine model railroad layouts depicting the history of toy trains, the development of the railroad in both Australia and Great Britain and the Clovis Yard and adjacent city in the 1950-60 time frame. Live BNSF train operations can be viewed from the dispatcher's position and platform with some 75-100 trains passing each day. We provide a one hour guided tour of the museum and model railroad layouts, including running the model trains and other displays.

Schedule: June through August: daily 12 to 5 p.m. Rest of year: Wednesdays through Sundays, 12 to 5 p.m. Closed September, February, Easter, Thanksgiving, Christmas, and New Year's Eve.

Admission/Fare: Call or write for information.

Locomotive/Rolling Stock: Fairmont Railway motor car.

Nearby Attractions/Accommodations: Blackwater Draw Museum, Blackwater Draw Archaeological site, Norman Petty Studios.

Location/Directions: In a restored ATSF passenger depot adjacent to BNSF main line, two blocks west of Main Street on U.S. 60/84.

Site Address: 221 West First Street, Clovis, NM
Mailing Address: 221 West First Street, Clovis, NM 88101
Telephone: (505) 762-0066 and (888) 762-0064
E-mail: philipw@3lefties.com
Internet: www.clovisdepot.com

SANTA FE SOUTHERN RAILWAY
Train ride, dinner train
Standard gauge

MARK ROUNDS

Description: Passenger, group and charter excursions on vintage cars from the teens to 1950s. Round trip from Santa Fe through beautiful high desert scenery to the village of Lamy.

Schedule: Scenic day trains–year round, call or write for information. Sunset dinner trains–April through October, Friday and Saturday nights.

Admission/Fare: Scenic day trains–adults $25.00; seniors $20.00; children 3-13 $13.00; age 2 and under are free. Sunset dinner trains–$45.00.

Locomotive/Rolling Stock: GP16, no. 93, former L&N no. 1850; no. 1158, former CNJ Coach; no. 144, former GN Coach; no. 4014, former SP Coach; no. 1370 "Acoma," former AT&SF Superchief; more.

Special Events: Murder Mysteries, Valentine's Day, Father's Day, Halloween, Santa trains, caroling trains, New Year's.

Nearby Attractions/Accommodations: Historic district, museums, Plaza shopping and dining.

Location/Directions: Heart of Santa Fe in the century old Santa Fe Depot, 10 minute walking distance from the Plaza.

Radio frequency: 160.290

Site Address: 410 South Guadalupe Street, Santa Fe, NM
Mailing Address: 410 South Guadalupe Street, Santa Fe, NM 87501
Telephone: (505) 989-8600 or (800) 989-8600
Fax: (505) 983-7620
E-mail: depot@sfsr.com
Internet: www.sfsr.com

ARCADE & ATTICA RAILROAD
Train ride
Standard gauge

PETER SWANSON

Description: The A&A, a common-carrier railroad that has been in existence since 1881, offers a 15-mile, 2-hour round trip over the historic trackage to Curriers. Open-end steel coaches and combination cars from the Delaware, Lackawanna & Western Railroad. A 16 x 16-foot HO model railroad is displayed in the Arcade Depot.

Schedule: Memorial weekend through October: weekends and holidays, 12:30 and 3 p.m. July through August: Wednesdays, 12:30 and 3 p.m.; Fridays 1 p.m.. First three weekends in October: 12, 2, and 4 p.m. Fridays, 12 p.m.

Admission/Fare: Adults $8.50; seniors $7.50; children 3-11 $5.00; children under age 3 are free.

Locomotive/Rolling Stock: 1917 Baldwin 4-6-0 no. 14, former Escanaba & Lake Superior; 1920 Alco (Cooke) 2-8-0 no. 18, former Boyne City Railroad.

Special Events: Civil War Train Capture, Children's Trains, Murder Mystery Runs, Special Fall Foliage Runs, Christmas Trains, and Winter Runs.

Nearby Attractions/Accommodations: Letchworth State Park, The Farm Craft Village, Wyoming Gas Light Village, Byrncliff Resort, Hillside Inn, Glen Iris Inn.

Location/Directions: In western New York, midway between Buffalo and Olean. Train departs from Arcade Depot in center of town, at routes 39 and 98.

Site Address: 278 Main Street, Arcade, NY
Mailing Address: PO Box 246, Arcade, NY 14009
Telephone: (716) 496-9877
Fax: (716) 492-0100

NEW YORK TRANSIT MUSEUM
Train ride, museum

NEW YORK TRANSIT MUSEUM ARCHIVES

Description: Housed in an historic subway station, the New York Transit Museum collects, preserves, exhibits and interprets the history, sociology and technology of public transportation systems in the New York region. This region is served by the Metropolitan Transportation Authority and includes bridges, tunnels, subways and buses.

Schedule: Year round: Tuesdays through Fridays 10 a.m. to 4 p.m.; weekends 12 to 5 p.m. Closed Mondays and major holidays.

Admission/Fare: Adults $3.00; seniors and children ages 3-7 $1.50. Seniors are free on Wednesdays 12 to 4 p.m. Museum members and MTA employees are free.

Locomotive/Rolling Stock: Twenty vintage railcars. Rolling stock dates back to 1904 to late 1960s subway cars. Money Car G on display and is on extended loan from Branford Electric Railway Assoc./Shoreline Trolley Museum.

Special Events: Behind-the-scenes Lunchtime Tours. Annual Bus Festival. Vintage railcar excursions throughout the year. Call or write for information.

Nearby Attractions/Accommodations: Manhattan, Brooklyn Marriott.

Location/Directions: Accessible via bus or subway.

     M

Site Address: Boerum Place & Schermerhorn Streets, Brooklyn Hts., NY
Mailing Address: 130 Livingston Street, Room 9001, Brooklyn, NY 11201
Telephone: (718) 243-8601
Internet: www.mta.nyc.ny.us/

New York, Camillus **MARTISCO STATION MUSEUM**
CENTRAL NEW YORK CHAPTER NRHS
Museum, display, layout
1½" gauge

CENTRAL NEW YORK CHAPTER NRHS

Description: The Martisco Station Museum is a brick Victorian structure erected in 1870 for the New York Central and Hudson River Railroad. Located in a picturesque setting, the restored 2-story passenger station houses a collection of railroad mementos of the local area. The adjacent former Pennsylvania Railroad diner houses additional displays. Presently the track passing the station is used 5 days per week by the Finger Lakes Railway.

Schedule: May through October: Sundays 1 to 5 p.m.

Admission/Fare: Donations appreciated.

Locomotive/Rolling Stock: 0-4-0 steam narrow gauge; PRR diner.

Special Events: Christmas at the Station, December.

Location/Directions: New York Route 174, halfway between the villages of Camillus and Marcellus, at the end of Martisco Road.

Site Address: Martisco Road, Camillus, NY
Mailing Address: PO Box 229, Marcellus, NY 13108-0229
Telephone: (315) 488-8208
Fax: (315) 487-2849
E-mail: CNYNRHS@aol.com
Internet: www.rrhistorical.com/cnynrhs

New York, Central Square

**CENTRAL SQUARE STATION MUSEUM
CENTRAL NEW YORK CHAPTER NRHS**
Museum, display

CENTRAL NEW YORK CHAPTER NRHS

Description: The Central New York Chapter NRHS is a former joint station of the New York Ontario & Western Railway and the New York Central Railroad built in 1902. The restored one-story wood passenger station houses a collection of railroad artifacts from the local area. The Conrail (CSX) Montreal Secondary track passes next to the station and is active 7 days a week.

Schedule: May through October: Sundays 12 to 5 p.m.

Admission/Fare: Donations appreciated.

Locomotive/Rolling Stock: 0-4-0T steam engine from Solvay Process Quarry in Jamesville, New York; 0-4-0 narrow gauge steam engine from quarry in Leroy, New York; 25-ton industrial switcher; Huntington & Broad Top Railroad combination baggage/coach, former gas electric car.

Special Events: Christmas at the Station, December.

Location/Directions: Route 11, to village of Central Square, to the south of the business district, at the end of Railroad Street.

      M

Site Address: Railroad Avenue, Central Square, NY
Mailing Address: PO Box 229, Marcellus, NY 13108-0229
Telephone: (315) 488-8208
Fax: (315) 487-2849
E-mail: CNYNRHS@aol.com
Internet: www.rrhistorical.com/cnynrhs

New York, Cooperstown

COOPERSTOWN & CHARLOTTE VALLEY RAILROAD

Train ride, dinner train, museum, display
Standard gauge

JAMES E. LOUDON

Description: A 16-mile round trip from Cooperstown to Milford and back. Milford is the site of the Milford Park Railway, a home-built narrow gauge railroad. The 1869 depot in Milford contain a gift shop and small museum. The entire operation is run by the Leatherstocking Railway Museum, which is owned by the Leatherstocking Railway Historical Society and the Leatherstocking Chapter NRHS.

Schedule: Tentatively Memorial Day weekend through October 31: call for information.

Admission/Fare: Train–adults $8.00; children $6.00. Museum–free

Locomotive/Rolling Stock:

Special Events: Milford Rail Days, first weekend in June.

Nearby Attractions/Accommodations: National Baseball Hall of Fame, The Farmers Museum, James Fenimore Cooper House, Otesaga Resort Hotel, Glimmerglass State Park, National Soccer Hall of Fame.

Location/Directions: I-88, north on Route 28 for approximately 8 miles to Milford. Then head east on Route 166 about one block to the railroad crossing.

Site Address: Cooperstown, NY
Mailing Address: PO Box 681, Oneonta, NY 13820
Telephone: (607) 432-2429
Fax: (607) 433-0747
E-mail: bruce101@aol.com
Internet: www.rrhistorical.com/nrhs/leth/lrhs.html

ALCO BROOKS RAILROAD DISPLAY
Display
Standard gauge

HISTORICAL SOCIETY OF DUNKIRK

Description: Located at the Chautauqua County Fairgrounds since 1987, features an original Alco-Brooks steam locomotive, a wood-sided boxcar housing displays of Chautauqua County commerce and railroads along with a gift shop, and a restored wooden caboose. Other items of interest at the site are a Nickel Plate work car, an Erie Railroad concrete telephone booth, a New York Central harp switch stand, a Pennsylvania Railroad cast-iron crossing sign, a DAV&P land line marker, and an operating crossing flasher.

Schedule: June 1 through August 31: Saturdays, 1 to 3 p.m. weather permitting. Open daily during special events or by appointment.

Admission/Fare: Donations appreciated.

Locomotive/Rolling Stock: 1916 Alco-Brooks 0-6-0 no. 444, former Boston & Maine; 1907 Delaware & Hudson 22020 wood-sided boxcar; 1905 New York Central 19224 wooden caboose.

Special Events: Chautauqua County Antique Auto Show and Flea Market, May 14-16. Chautauqua County Fair, July 26 through August 1.

Nearby Attractions/Accommodations: Dunkirk Historical Museum, Dunkirk Lighthouse, Chautauqua Institution, Four Points Hotel Sheraton, Brookside Manor bed and breakfast.

Location/Directions: I-90, exit 59, to Chautauqua County Fairgrounds.

     Dunkirk

Site Address: 1089 Central Ave., Chautauqua County Fairgrounds, Dunkirk, NY
Mailing Address: Historical Society of Dunkirk, 513 Washington Ave., Dunkirk, NY 14048
Telephone: (716) 366-3797
E-mail: davrr@netsync.net

New York, Gowanda

NEW YORK & LAKE ERIE RAILROAD
Train ride
Standard gauge

KEVIN ARGUE

Description: Rail excursions over former Erie Railroad trackage. "The Flyer" makes a 20-mile, 2¾-hour round trip to South Dayton over a steep grade and through the Old Stone Tunnel built in 1860. "The Country Traveler" makes a 30-mile, 4-hour round trip to Cherry Creek. Intermediate station stops are made at both stations.

Schedule: "The Flyer"–mid-June through mid-October: weekends, 1 p.m. "The Country Traveler"–July through August and selected dates in June and October: Wednesdays 1 p.m. Write or call for complete schedule.

Admission/Fare: "The Flyer"–adults $9.00; seniors $8.50; children ages 3-11 $4.50. "The Country Traveler"–adults $13.50; seniors $13.00; children ages 3-11 $6.00.

Locomotive/Rolling Stock: 1965 Alco C425 no. 1013, former N&W; two rebuilt coaches, former B&O; three electric coaches, former Lackawanna Electric; one dining car, former VIA; one open flatcar; more.

Special Events: Peter Cottontail Express, Great Train Robbery, Kids Day, Ghost & Goblin Party Train, Teddy Bear's Picnic, Santa Trains, Christmas in July, Hobo's Holiday Train, Murder Mystery Specials.

Location/Directions: Turn off Routes 62 and 39 at S. Water Street. Follow ½ mile to Commercial Street and station.

*Coupon available, see coupon section.

Site Address: 50 Commercial Street, Gowanda, NY
Mailing Address: PO Box 309, Gowanda, NY 14070
Telephone: (716) 532-5716
Fax: (716) 532-9128
E-mail: nyle@shortlineservices.com/nyle
Internet: www.shortlineservices.com/nyle

New York, Hyde Park

HUDSON VALLEY RAILROAD SOCIETY/RAILROAD STATION
Museum, display, layout
HO, N

LARRY LALIBERTE

Description: Restoration of 1914 railroad station by model railroad club. Museum relates history of station and the Roosevelt and Vanderbilt connection. Operating display layouts.

Schedule: Year round: Mondays 7 to 10 p.m. Mid-June through mid-September: weekends 11 a.m. to 5 p.m. Open Memorial Day and July 4.

Admission/Fare: Donations appreciated.

Nearby Attractions/Accommodations: Franklin Delano Roosevelt home and library, Vanderbilt mansion, Old Rhinebeck Aerodome, bicycle tours, hiking trails, golf course, river tours, Mills-Narrie State Park, hotels, motels, bed and breakfast, restaurants.

Location/Directions: East on East Market Street from U.S. 9 (historic signs posted on U.S 9) to bottom of hill. Station in Town Park on right.

        M

Site Address: Riverfront Park, River Road, Hyde Park, NY
Mailing Address: Dutch Village 3D, Kingston, NY 12401
Telephone: (914) 297-0901 and (914) 331-9233
Fax: (914) 297-0901
E-mail: revaul@aol.com

New York, Kingston

TROLLEY MUSEUM OF NEW YORK
Train ride
Standard gauge

THE TROLLEY MUSEUM OF NEW YORK

Description: This museum was established in 1955 and moved to its present location in 1983, becoming part of the Kingston Urban Cultural Park. A 2.5-mile, 40-minute round trip takes passengers from the foot of Broadway to Kingston Point, with stops at the museum in both directions. A gas-powered railcar operates on private right-of-way and in-street trackage along Rondout Creek to the Hudson River over part of the former Ulster & Delaware Railroad main line. An exhibit hall features trolley exhibits and a theater.

Schedule: Memorial weekend to Columbus Day: 12 to 5 p.m. Last ride departs at 4:30 p.m. Charters available.

Admission/Fare: Adults $3.00; seniors and children $2.00.

Locomotive/Rolling Stock: Eleven trolleys; eight rapid transit cars; Whitcomb diesel-electric; Brill model 55 interurban.

Special Events: Shad Festival, May 1-2; Mother's Day, May 9, (moms ride free); Father's Day, June 20 (dads ride free); Santa Days, December 4-5.

Nearby Attractions/Accommodations: Hudson River Maritime Museum, Senate House, Catskill Mountains, Urban Cultural Park.

Location/Directions: In the historic Rondout Waterfront area of Kingston. Call or write for directions or see map on web page.

*Coupon available, see coupon section.

 Radio Frequency: 462.175

Site Address: 89 East Strand, Kingston, NY
Mailing Address: PO Box 2291, Kingston, NY 12402
Telephone: (914) 331-3399
Internet: www.mhrcc.org/kingston/kgntroll.html/

MEDINA RAILROAD MUSEUM
Museum

MEDINA RAILROAD MUSEUM

Description: Located in a 1905 NYC freight depot. Displays include rail maintenance tools, models, equipment and memorabilia. We have a portable HO scale layout on loan and a 200 x 14-foot HO scale layout is under construction.

Schedule: Year round: Mondays through Saturdays 12 to 7 p.m. and Sundays 12 to 5 p.m.

Admission/Fare: Adults $5.00; seniors $4.00; children $3.00.

Locomotive/Rolling Stock: Five 1948 Budd coaches, former NYC Empire State Express coaches from WNY Railway Historical Society; Nickel Plate Road RS11 Alco Diesel 1952 owned by Genesee Valley Transportation.

Special Events: Harvest Festival and 34 mile rail excursions, October 25.

Nearby Attractions/Accommodations: Niagara Falls, Buffalo, Rochester, Darien Lakes Amusement Park, Lakeside Beach State Park.

Location/Directions: North of I-90, exit 48A, village of Medina at is at intersection of New York 63 and New York 31.

      M

Site Address: 530 West Avenue, Medina, NY
Mailing Address: 530 West Avenue, Medina, NY 14103
Telephone: (716) 798-6106

CATSKILL MOUNTAIN RAILROAD
Train ride
Standard gauge

CATSKILL MOUNTAIN RAILROAD

Description: This railroad, which operates over trackage of the former Ulster & Delaware Railroad (later the Catskill Mountain branch of the New York Central), offers a 6-mile, 1-hour round trip to Phoenicia along the scenic Esopus Creek, through the heart of the beautiful Catskill Mountains. Tourists, inner-tubers, and visitors interested in canoeing or fishing may ride one way or round trip; round-trip passengers may stay at Phoenicia to visit shops and restaurants and return on a later train.

Schedule: May 29 through September 6: 11 a.m. to 5 p.m. September 11 through October 11: 12 to 4 p.m.

Admission/Fare: Round trip: adults $6.00; children 4-11 $2.00; under age 4 are free. One way: adults $4.00; children 4-11 $2.00; under age 4 are free.

Locomotive/Rolling Stock: No. 1, "The Duck," 1942 Davenport 38-ton diesel-mechanical, former U.S. Air Force; no. 2, "The Goat," H.K. Porter 50-ton diesel-electric, former U.S. Navy; no. 2361, 1952 Alco RS-1, former Wisconsin Central (Soo Line).

Special Events: Fall Foliage Trains and others; call for schedule.

Location/Directions: New York State Thruway, exit 19 (Kingston), and travel west 22 miles on Route 28 to the railroad depot in Mt. Pleasant.

♿ Ⓟ 🚌 ✳ ☕ ⛩ ✉ TRAIN

Site Address: Mt. Pleasant, NY
Mailing Address: PO Box 46, Mt. Pleasant, NY 12481
Telephone: (914) 688-7400

UPPER HUDSON RAILROAD/ RIVERSIDE STATION

Train ride, museum

RIVERSIDE STATION

Description: Nestled in the Adirondack Mountains of upstate New York along the Hudson River is the Riverside Train Depot, a former Delaware & Hudson station built in 1913, filled with railroad memorabilia and pictures. This depot replaced a smaller Adirondack Company railway station that was built in 1870. The station was restored to its original charm in 1995 and consists of a ticket agent's office, waiting room, and baggage room. The baggage room is now home to a gift shop/train store. In the old waiting room you can relax and enjoy train videos that are shown continuously. In the yard there is a vintage caboose that now serves as a refreshment stand.

Schedule: May through October. Call or write for more information.

Admission/Fare: Free

Locomotive/Rolling Stock: Vintage caboose operates as snack bar and ice cream shop.

Special Events: Annual Whitewater Derby, first weekend in May.

Nearby Attractions/Accommodations: Loon Lake, Friends Lake, Schroon Lake, and Lake George.

Location/Directions: Route 8 at Hudson River, 7 miles west on Route 8 from northway exit 25.

Site Address: Riparius, NY
Mailing Address: PO Box 4, Riparius, NY 12862
Telephone: (518) 494-5635

New York, Old Forge **ADIRONDACK SCENIC RAILROAD**
Train ride
Standard gauge

ADIRONDACK SCENIC RR

Description: Scenic rail excursions of various lengths from Utica Comtrak Connection into the Adirondacks with flagstop service. One hour scenic excursions from Old Forge Canoe and Rail, bike/hike and rail, group packages.

Schedule: May through November: Call for schedule information.

Admission/Fare: Varies depending on routes and packages, call for price information.

Locomotive/Rolling Stock: New York Central no. 8223 Alco RS-3 diesel; no. 2064, former Lehigh Valley C-420 no. 408; SW-1 diesel no. 705, former Louisville & Nashville; VIA Rail intercity cars; commuter cars; open-air observation cars.

Special Events: Train robberies. Railfan Day, Father's Day weekend. World-class Boilermaker Race in Utica, July

Nearby Attractions/Accommodations: F.X. Matt Brewery, Historic Mohawk Valley, shopping, canoeing, boating, scenic boat cruises on Fulton Chain of Lakes and Raquette Lake.

Location/Directions: Route 28 in Old Forge on Main Street, 46 miles north of Utica.

Radio frequency: 160.440

Site Address: Thendara Station, Old Forge, NY
Site Address: Union Station, Utica, NY
Mailing Address: PO Box 84, Thendara, NY 13472
Telephone: (315) 724-0700 and (315) 369-6472
Fax: (315) 369-2479

TIOGA SCENIC RAILROAD
Train ride
Standard gauge

THOMAS TRENCANSKY

Description: Experience the beautiful landscape of the Southern Finger Lake region while enjoying fine dining on board the train. A 1¾-hour round trip from Owego to Newark Valley over tracks of the former Southern Central, constructed beginning in 1868 to connect southern New York with the Great Lakes.

Schedule: July through October: weekends 1 p.m.

Admission/Fare: Excursions–adults $8.00; seniors $7.50; children 3-11 $5.00. Meals–lunch $15.00 and $23.00; dinner $29.00. Dinner theater available. Call or write for more information.

Locomotive/Rolling Stock: Tioga Scenic Railroad SW1, EMD locomotive no. 40, 600 hp.

Special Events: Many throughout the season. Call or write for information.

Nearby Attractions/Accommodations: Tioga Park (country western theme park), Econo Lodge, Treadway Inn.

Location/Directions: Twenty miles west of Binghamton, route 17, exit 64.

Site Address: 25 Delphine Street, Owego, NY
Mailing Address: 25 Delphine Street, Owego, NY 13827
Telephone: (607) 687-6786
Fax: (607) 687-6817
Internet: www.railroad.net/tsrr/

EMPIRE STATE RAILWAY MUSEUM
Museum, display

EMPIRE STATE RAILWAY MUSEUM

Description: This is an all-volunteer membership organization dedicated to bringing alive the history of Catskill Mountain railroads, their people and the town they served. Museum is located in former Ulster & Delaware station celebrating its 100th anniversary in 1999.

Schedule: Memorial Day through Columbus Day: weekends and holidays 10 a.m. to 4 p.m.

Admission/Fare: Suggested donation–adults $3.00; seniors and students $2.00; children under age 12 $1.00; families $5.00.

Locomotive/Rolling Stock: No. 23, 1910 Alco 2-8-0, former Lake Superior & Ishpeming; 1920 D&H dining car Lion Gardner; 1890 PRR 4-wheel bobber caboose; 1926 CV autocarrier; 1920 B&M railway post office car.

Special Events: 100th anniversary birthday party with lectures and slide shows throughout the year, Santa Claus Special.

Nearby Attractions/Accommodations: Catskill Mountain Railroad, Delaware Ulster rail ride, New York state campgrounds at Woodland Valley and Wilson State Park, hiking, fishing in Catskill Forest Preserve, tube rides on Esopus Creek.

Location/Directions: New York State Thruway, exit 19, Route 28 west to Phoenicia.

Site Address: Off High Street, Phoenicia, NY
Mailing Address: PO Box 455, Phoenicia, NY 12464
Telephone: (914) 688-7501
Internet: www.esrm.com

New York, Rochester

JIM DIERKS

Description: Site includes trolleys, rail and road vehicles, related artifacts and exhibits, an 11 x 21 operating HO model railroad and a video/photo gallery. A 2-mile ride connects with the Rochester & Genesee Valley Railroad Museum, departing every half-hour.

Schedule: Museum–year round, Sundays, 11 a.m. to 5 p.m. Groups by appointment. Ride–May through October, weather permitting.

Admission/Fare: Adults $5.00; seniors $4.00; students ages 5-15 $3.00. Includes entry to NYMT, Rochester & Genesee Valley Railroad Museum, and ride. Lower rates November through April.

Locomotive/Rolling Stock: Rochester & Eastern interurban car no. 157; North Texas Trac. interurban car no. 409; P&W cars nos. 161 and 168; five other trolleys; Alco-Cooke 0-4-0 no. 47; G&W caboose no. 8; more.

Special Events: Transportation Day, mid-May; Antique Truck Show, July; Railroad Days, August.

Nearby Attractions/Accommodations: Finger Lakes Region, Niagara Falls, Arcade & Attica Railroad, Genesee County Museum, George Eastman House Museum of Photography.

Location/Directions: I-90, exit 46, south 3 miles on I-390, exit 11. Route 251 west 1.5 miles, right on East River Road, 1 mile to museum entrance.

        arm M

 Radio Frequency: 160.440

Site Address: 6393 East River Road, W. Henrietta, NY
Mailing Address: PO Box 136, W. Henrietta, NY 14586
Telephone: (716) 533-1113
Internet: www.rochester.ny.us/railmuseum.html

ROCHESTER & GENESEE VALLEY RAILROAD MUSEUM
Museum
Standard gauge

CHRISTOPHER HAUF

Description: The museum, housed in a restored 1908 Erie Railroad station, displays railroad artifacts from western New York railroads. On outdoor tracks are a number of railroad cars and diesel locomotives open for display. Museum has tours and track car rides.

Schedule: May through October: Sundays, 11 am. to 5 p.m. Visits at other times by appointment.

Admission/Fare: Adults $5.00; seniors $4.00; children 5-15 $3.00.

Locomotive/Rolling Stock: 1946 GE 80-ton diesel, former Eastman Kodak; 1953 Alco RS-3, former Lehigh Valley; 1953 Alco S-4, former Nickel Plate; 1941 GE 45-ton, former Rochester Gas & Electric; Fairbanks-Morse H12-44, former U.S. Army.

Nearby Attractions/Accommodations: Strong Museum, Eastman House, Genesee Country Museum, Frontier Stadium, New York Museum of Transportation.

Location/Directions: I-390 exit 11. Take route 251 west to East River Road, turn right, travel two miles to museum entrance.

Site Address: 6393 East River Rd, Henrietta, NY
Mailing Address: PO Box 664, Rochester, NY 14603
Telephone: (716) 533-1431 and (716) 533-1113
Fax: (716) 425-8587
E-mail: mikeb86393@aol.com
Internet: www.rochester.ny.us/railmuseum.html

ROSCOE ONTARIO & WESTERN RAILWAY MUSEUM
Museum

ROSCOE O&W RAILWAY MUSEUM

Description: This museum was established under the charter of the Ontario & Western Railway Historical Society in 1984 in a former Erie Railroad caboose. The O&W railway festival, first held in August of that year, has since become an annual event. The museum complex consists of a restored O&W caboose, watchman's shanties, and the O&W station motif building. The museum contains displays of O&W memorabilia and other railroadiana, as well as local-history displays that show the impact of the O&W on community life, hunting, fishing, farming, tourism, and local industry. The museum is maintained and operated by members of the Roscoe NYO&W Railway Association. The Archives Center of the history of the Ontario & Western Railway is located in Middletown, New York.

Schedule: Memorial weekend through Columbus Day: Saturday and Sunday, 11 a.m. to 3 p.m.

Admission/Fare: Donations welcomed.

Special Events: O&W Festival and Craft Fair, July 24-25. Call or write for information on other events.

Nearby Attractions/Accommodations: Call or write for information on overnight accommodations.

Location/Directions: Railroad Avenue.

Site Address: Historic Depot Street on Railroad Avenue, Roscoe, NY
Mailing Address: PO Box 305, Roscoe, NY 1776-0305
Telephone: (607) 498-5500
E-mail: artrobb@mhv.net
Internet: www.nyow.org/museum.html

SALAMANCA RAIL MUSEUM ASSOCIATION

Description: Fully restored BR&P depot and freight house. Artifacts and photographs tell the history of railroads in western New York and Pennsylvania. For children, the museum grounds offer the permanent display of a boxcar, a crew camp car, and the chance to explore two cabooses.

Schedule: April through December: Mondays through Saturdays, 10 a.m. to 5 p.m. and Sundays, 12 to 5 p.m. Closed Mondays in April, October, November, and December.

Admission/Fare: Donations appreciated.

Locomotive/Rolling Stock: B&O caboose; P&WV caboose; Erie crane crew car; Conrail boxcar; Jordan spreader; DL&W electric commuter coach.

Nearby Attractions/Accommodations: Allegany State Park, Seneca Iroquois National Museum, Holiday Valley Summer-Winter Resort, Chautauqua Institution.

Location/Directions: Downtown Salamanca on New York route 17/U.S. Route 219.

       M

Site Address: 170 Main Street, Salamanca, NY
Mailing Address: 170 Main Street, Salamanca, NY 14779
Telephone: (716) 945-3133

NORTHEASTERN NEW YORK RAILROAD PRESERVATION GROUP (NE RAIL)
Train ride
Standard gauge

GEORGE LERRIGO

Description: On this line, the *Batten Kill Rumbler* takes passengers on a scenic, 2-hour and 10-minute, 13-mile round trip along the Batten Kill River. An hour layover allows exploration of Shushan, New York with two museums. At secluded River Park, a picnic park is available by prior arrangement.

Schedule: Call or write for information.

Admission/Fare: Adults $10.00; seniors $9.00; children ages 3-12 $5.00; under age 3 are free.

Locomotive/Rolling Stock: No. 605, 1950 Alco; no. 4116, 1952 Alco RS-3; four steel coaches, former NYC.

Special Events: Children's Theater at River Park. Ride 'n Dine Halloween Train. Santa Trains.

Location/Directions: I-87 to Route 29, at Saratoga Springs east to Salem. Left on Route 22, north to village and station.

*Coupon available, see coupon section.

Saratoga Springs and Albany Rensselaer   **Radio frequency: 160.905**

Site Address: 232 Main Street, Salem, NY
Mailing Address: One Elbow Street, PO Box 148, Greenwich, NY 12834
Telephone: (518) 854-3787 (Salem station) and (518) 692-2191 (office)
Fax: (518) 692-0271
E-mail: wcormier@sover.net

RAIL CITY HISTORICAL MUSEUM
Museum

BOB GROMAN

Description: Site of the first steam-operating railroad museum in the U.S. Housed in the former RWO&NYC depot from Deer River, New York, the Rail City Historical Museum contains an extensive collection of steam-era photographs, displays of railroad timetables, brochures, posters, artifacts and a unique railroad gift store. In addition, the museum features the history of Rail City Museum.

Schedule: June 28 to Labor Day: daily, Mondays through Saturdays, 10 a.m. to 5 p.m. and Sundays 11 a.m. to 5 p.m. May, June, September, through mid-October: weekends only.

Admission/Fare: Adults $3.00; seniors $2.00; children 12 and under are free with an adult. Group rates available.

Special Events: Rail City Day, September. 18. Call for schedule.

Nearby Attractions/Accommodations: Lake Ontario shoreline, charter trout and salmon fishing, Southwick Beach State Park, Sackett's Harbor Battlefield (1812), Elms Golf Course, Salmon River Fish Hatchery, Lindsey Corner Restaurant, Deer Creek Motel, Port Lodge Motel and Colonial Court Campground.

Location/Directions: Fifty miles north of Syracuse. I-81, exit 37 (Sandy Creek), west to Main Street (Route 11), north on Ellisburg Road, west on Hadley Road, north on Route 3 for 1 mile to museum on left.

    M arm

Site Address: Route 3 "Seaway Trail," Sandy Creek, NY
Mailing Address: 162 Stanley Drive, Sandy Creek, NY 13145
Telephone: (315) 387-2932 (May-Oct.) and (315) 387-5720 (Nov.-Apr.)
Fax: (315) 387-5720 (June-Oct.) and (315) 635-6250 (Nov.-May)

DELAWARE & ULSTER RAILRIDE
Train ride, museum, display
Standard gauge

AARON KELLER

Description: Nineteen miles of rail offering a 1-hour or 1-hour 45-minute trip through the scenic Catskill Mountains. Operates on the route of the historic Ulster & Delaware Railroad.

Schedule: May 29 through October 24: weekends and holidays. June 30 through September 6: Wednesdays through Sundays. Departs at 10:30 a.m., 1 and 2:30 p.m.

Admission/Fare: Short trip–adults $7.00; seniors $5.50; children $4.00; under age 3 ride free. Long trip–adults $10.00; seniors $7.50; children $5.00; under age 3 ride free.

Locomotive/Rolling Stock: D&H no. 5017 RS36 Alco; no. 5106 1953 Alco S-4, former Chesapeake & Ohio; no. 1012 1954 Alco S-4, former Ford Motor Co.; M-405 1928 J.G. Brill Co. diesel-electric rail car, former New York Central; two slat cars with benches, former PRR; two boxcars, former NYC; 44-ton locomotive, former Western Maryland.

Special Events: Train Robberies, Teddy Bear Runs, Tractor Pulls, Twilight Runs, Fall Foliage, Halloween Train.

Location/Directions: Route 28, in Arkville, 45 miles west of New York State Thruway.

*Coupon available, see coupon section.

Radio frequency: 161.385

Site Address: Route 28, Arkville, NY
Mailing Address: PO Box 310, Stamford, NY 12167
Telephone: (800) 225-4132 and (914) 586-DURR
Fax: (607) 652-2822
Internet: www.durr.org

RENSSELAER MODEL RAILROAD EXHIBIT

Description: A 500-linear-foot historical railroad exhibit of some 40 connected scale dioramas of local scenes set in 1950.

Schedule: Call or check web page for upcoming dates.

Admission/Fare: $5.00 per person, not for children under 48 inches tall.

Location/Directions: Opposite Troy High School, RPI Campus, in Davison Hall basement.

Site Address: RPI Campus, Davison Hall, Troy, NY
Mailing Address: c/o RPI Student Union, Troy, NY 12180-3590
Telephone: (518) 276-2971
Fax: (518) 276-6920
E-mail: mrrs@rp.edu
Internet: www.rpi.edu/web/railroad

CHILDREN'S MUSEUM

Description: A children's museum with hands-on interactive displays concerning science, natural science, history and culture. Frequent craft activities and events.

Schedule: September through June: Tuesdays through Saturdays 10 a.m. to 4:30 p.m. and Sundays 12 to 4:30 p.m. July through August: Tuesdays through Saturdays 9 a.m. to 3:30 p.m. and Mondays 1 to 4:30 p.m. Closed Sundays.

Admission/Fare: $2.50 per person.

Locomotive/Rolling Stock: Engine; dining car; caboose.

Special Events: Christmas on Main Street, Saturday after Thanksgiving.

Nearby Attractions/Accommodations: Train station next door, restaurants.

Location/Directions: Thruway exit 31, follow Genesee Street, take Broad Street exit, left on Railroad Street, left on Main Street.

   M

Site Address: 311 Main Street, Utica, NY
Mailing Address: 311 Main Street, Utica, NY 13502
Telephone: (315) 724-6129 office and (315) 724-6128 information
Fax: (315) 724-6120 (call first)

TWEETSIE RAILROAD
Train ride
36" gauge

TWEETSIE RAILROAD

Description: The Tweetsie Railroad is a theme park centered on a three-mile train ride. Visitors can enjoy the train show, live entertainment, rides, mountain crafts, and a petting zoo.

Schedule: Call or write for information.

Admission/Fare: Call or write for information.

Locomotive/Rolling Stock: No. 12, 1917 Baldwin 4-6-0, former Tennessee & Western North Carolina; no. 190, 1943 Baldwin 2-8-2, former White Pass & Yukon.

Location/Directions: Between Boone and Blowing Rock on U.S. 221-321. Take Milepost 291 exit off the Blue Ridge Parkway.

Site Address: Blowing Rock, NC
Mailing Address: PO Box 388, Blowing Rock, NC 28605
Telephone: (704) 264-9061

GRAY LACKEY

Description: Eight-mile round trip over 4 miles of the original Norfolk Southern Railway's Durham Branch on a diesel-powered train with open cars and cabooses. Other equipment and displays at this site.

Schedule: May through December: first Sunday of month, departures at 12, 1, 2, 3, and 4 p.m.

Admission/Fare: Adults $5.00; children $3.00.

Locomotive/Rolling Stock: 80-ton GE and Whtcomb; 45-ton GE; 50-ton Whitcomb; Heisler steam engine under restoration; cabooses, freight cars.

Special Events: Halloween Train, Santa Claus Train.

Nearby Attractions/Accommodations: Jordan Lake, camping, fishing, boating, Shearon Harris Nuclear Power Plant tours, Ramada Inn in Apex, North Carolina.

Location/Directions: Eight miles south of Apex on State Route 1011. In Bonsal turn right on Daisey Street, 300 feet on left.

     M arm

Radio frequency: 160.425

Site Address: 102 Daisey Street, Bonsal, NC
Mailing Address: PO Box 40, New Hill, NC 27562
Telephone: (919) 362-5416
E-mail: nhvry@mindspring.com
Internet: www.mindspring.com/~nhvry

GREAT SMOKY MOUNTAINS RAILWAY
Train ride, dinner train
Standard gauge

LAVIDGE AND ASSOCIATES

Description: Departures from Dillsboro, Bryson City and Andrews, North Carolina. Enjoy scenic train rides amid beautiful mountain scenery. Dillsboro departures feature a scenic journey along the Tuckasegee River. Bryson City morning departures offer an optional luncheon or white water rafting. Andrews departures on Saturday mornings offer an optional luncheon, evenings include a southern BBQ. Twilight Dinner Train departs Dillsboro and features gourmet delicacies aboard restored dining cars.

Schedule: Mid-March through December: schedule varies with season. Call or write for schedule and reservations.

Admission/Fare: Adults $19.95 and up; children under age 13 $9.95 and up. Steam Days add $5.00 per adult. Reservations recommended. Excursion trains depart from Dillsboro, Bryson City, and Andrews.

Locomotive/Rolling Stock: No. 1702, 1942 Baldwin 2-8-0, former U.S. Army; nos. 711 and 777, EMD GP7s; nos. 210 and 223, EMD GP35s.

Special Events: Santa Express featuring the story of "Polar Express," December 2-19.

Nearby Attractions/Accommodations: Smoky Mountains National Park, Cherokee Indian Reservation, Biltmore estate, white water rafting.

Location/Directions: From Ashville–I-40 west to exit 27 to U.S. 74 west. Exit 81 for Dillsboro, or exit 67 for Bryson City.

Site Address: 119 Front Street, Dillsboro, NC or Depot Street, Bryson City, NC
Mailing Address: PO Box 397, Dillsboro, NC 28725
Telephone: (800) 872-4681 or (828) 586-8811
Fax: (828) 586-8806
E-mail: gsmr@dnet.net
Internet: www.gsmr.com

NORTH CAROLINA TRANSPORTATION MUSEUM AT HISTORIC SPENCER SHOPS

Train ride, museum
Standard gauge

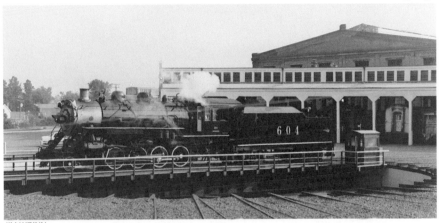

JIM WRINN

Description: The North Carolina Transportation Museum is the largest museum in the southeast devoted to telling the story of railways, aviation and motorized vehicles. The museum is housed in buildings once part of Southern Railway's largest steam repair complex, including one of America's largest remaining roundhouses.

Schedule: November through March: Tuesdays through Saturdays 10 a.m. to 4 p.m. and Sundays 1 to 4 p.m. April through October: Sundays 1 to 5 p.m. and Mondays through Saturdays 9 a.m. to 5 p.m.

Admission/Fare: Train ride–adults $5.00; seniors and children 3-12 $4.00. Turntable ride–$.50 per person.

Locomotive/Rolling Stock: No. 604, 1926 Baldwin 2-8-0, former Buffalo Creek & Gauley no. 4; no. 6900, EMD E8, and no. 6133, EMD FP7, all former SR; no. 1925, 1925 Lima 3-truck Shay, former Graham County Railroad; no. 1616, AS-416 diesel, former Norfolk Southern; no. 620, EMD GP9 diesel, former Norfolk & Western.

Special Events: Rail Days, June 5-6. Antique Truck Show, September 18. Antique Car Show, October 16. Santa Train, December 11-12, 18-19.

Nearby Attractions/Accommodations: North Carolina Zoo, boating, hiking.

Location/Directions: I-85 exit 79 (Spencer). Follow signs to museum.

*Coupon available, see coupon section.

Radio frequency: 160.695

Site Address: 411 S. Salisbury Avenue, Spencer, NC
Mailing Address: PO Box 44, Spencer, NC 28159
Telephone: (704) 636-2889
Fax: (704) 639-1881
E-mail: nctrans@tarheel.net
Internet: www.nctrans.org

CHARLES KERNAN

Description: Recapture the essence of railroad days as you climb aboard a 1910 steam locomotive, wander through a bright red caboose, explore extensive artifacts and photographs, or visit our model train displays.

Schedule: Year round: Mondays through Saturdays, 10 a.m. to 5 p.m. Sundays, 1 to 5 p.m. Closed Wednesdays. Hours subject to change, please call ahead.

Admission/Fare: Adults $3.00; seniors/military $2.00; children 6-12 $1.50; under age 5 are free; museum members are free. Group rates available if pre-arranged.

Locomotive/Rolling Stock: 1910 Baldwin steam locomotive 4-6-0 no. 250; ACL caboose no. 019983; 1963 RF&P boxcar no. 2379.

Special Events: Annual Model Railroad and Memorabilia Show. Halloween Haunted House. Azalea Festival, April. River Fest, October.

Nearby Attractions/Accommodations: U.S.S. Battleship North Carolina, Fort Fisher State Historical Site, beaches.

Location/Directions: Highway 17 to downtown Wilmington (turns into Market Street), follow to Water Street, turn right, 4 blocks ahead.

*Coupon available, see coupon section.

        M

Site Address: 501 Nutt Street, Wilmington, NC
Mailing Address: 501 Nutt Street, Wilmington, NC 28401
Telephone: (910) 763-2634
Fax: (910) 763-2634 (call first)
Internet: www.wilmington.org/railroad

FORT LINCOLN TROLLEY

Description: A 9-mile round trip from Mandan to Ft. Abraham Lincoln State Park along the Heart River.

Schedule: Memorial Day through Labor Day: daily departures 1, 2, 3, 4, 5 p.m.

Admission/Fare: Adults $5.00; children 6-12 $3.00; age 5 and under are free.

Locomotive/Rolling Stock: American Car Co. single track semi-convertible street car no. 102; reproduction single track open steetcar.

Nearby Attractions/Accommodations: Lewis and Clark Riverboats, Mandan Railroad Museum.

Location/Directions: On 3rd Street in southeast Mandan.

*Coupon available, see coupon section.

Site Address: 3rd Street, S.E. Mandan, ND
Mailing Address: 29 Captain Leach Drive, Mandan, ND 58554
Telephone: (701) 663-9018

BONANZAVILLE, U.S.A.
Display, layout
Standard gauge

R.A. YOUNG

Description: A 15-acre historical pioneer village with static displays of the Embden, North Dakota, Depot and train shed and the Kathryn, North Dakota, Depot with Spud Valley Model Railroad layout. See 40 other buildings serving as small museums representing life in the Red River Valley between 1880 and 1920.

Schedule: Memorial weekend through September 30: daily, 9 a.m. to 5 p.m.

Admission/Fare: Adults $6.00; students $3.00; under age 6 are free.

Locomotive/Rolling Stock: Rome locomotive 4-4-0; Northern Pacific wood caboose no. 1628; Burlington Northern, former Midland Continental; wood russell plow, former NP; NP steel 80-ton heavy-weight passenger coach, no. 1360.

Special Events: Pioneer Days, third weekend in August.

Nearby Attractions/Accommodations: Cass County Campground, Sunset Motel, Days Inn, Speedway Restaurant, Jiggs Homestyle Restaurant.

Location/Directions: I-94, exit 343 to West Fargo.

Site Address: 1351 W. Main Avenue, West Fargo, ND
Mailing Address: PO Box 719, West Fargo, ND 58078
Telephone: (701) 282-2822
Fax: (701) 282-7606
E-mail: bvillel@juno.com

Ohio, Carrollton

CARROLLTON-ONEIDA-MINERVA RAILROAD
ELDERBERRY LINE
Train ride
Standard gauge

CARROLLTON-ONEIDA-MINERVA RAILROAD, ELDERBERRY LINE

Description: Travel 14 miles between Carrollton and Minerva through areas of light industry, farmland, marshland, and forest. One-hour layover in Minerva.

Schedule: Mid-June through October: weekends. December: Christmas runs. Call for information and schedules.

Admission/Fare: Adults $10.00; children 2-12 $8.00. Group rates available.

Locomotive/Rolling Stock: 1952 Alco RS-3 locomotive; 1926 ES New Jersey coach; three 1937 coaches, former Canadian.

Special Events: Father's Day, Fourth of July, Great Trains Festival.

Nearby Attractions/Accommodations: Atwood Lodge, sailing, fishing, Pro Football Hall of Fame, McKinley's monument.

Location/Directions: Site is 100 miles south of Cleveland, 25 miles south of Canton, and 60 miles west of Pittsburgh, Pennsylvania.

*Coupon available, see coupon section.

Site Address: 203 2nd Street NW, Carrollton, OH
Mailing Address: 220 Wayne Avenue, Carrollton, OH 44615
Telephone: (330) 627-2282
Fax: (330) 627-3624

Ohio, Cincinnati

CINCINNATI RAILROAD CLUB
Museum, display

DALE W. BROWN

Description: Founded in 1938, this club has an exhibit in Cincinnati Union Terminal's former control tower A, which was the operating and dispatching center for terminal operations from 1933 to 1973. The tower overlooks the busy Norfolk Southern and CSX yards, main lines and the former Southern Railway bridge to Kentucky. The tower was restored in 1991 for CRRC as their display and meeting location. The club has displays and an extensive library and photo collection.

Schedule: Memorial Day to Labor Day: Saturdays 10 a.m. to 5 p.m., Sundays 12 to 5 p.m. October through June: Saturdays 10 a.m. to 4 p.m., third Sunday of each month 12 to 4 p.m.

Admission/Fare: Free; $3.00 parking in Museum Center lot.

Locomotive/Rolling Stock: Trolley car no. 2435, former Cincinnati Street Railway.

Special Events: Summerail 99 and Railroadiana Show & Sale, August 7. Pre-Summerail slide show, August 6. Call or write for information.

Nearby Attractions/Accommodations: Museums, Omnimax theater, Reds and Bengals professional teams.

Location/Directions: I-75, exit 1E, G or H. Near I-71 junction.

Site Address: 1301 Western Avenue, Cincinnati Union Terminal Tower A, Cincinnati, OH
Mailing Address: PO Box 14157, Cincinnati, OH 45250-0157
Telephone: (513) 651-RAIL
Internet: www.rrhistorical.com/crrc

CONNEAUT RAILROAD MUSEUM
Museum
Standard gauge

DALE W. BROWN

Description: Displays antique exhibits of the Steam Era. The Conneaut station, built by the Lake Shore & Michigan Southern in 1900, is adjacent to Conrail (former New York Central) tracks. Inside are extensive displays of timetables, passes, lanterns, old photos, builder's plates, telegraph instruments, and models of locomotives, cars, and structures. An HO scale model railroad operates during regular hours. On display outside are a train, section cars, track equipment, and a ball signal. On the station platform are baggage trucks, hand carts, and old trunks. A steady parade of Conrail trains passes the station.

Schedule: Memorial Day through Labor Day: daily, 12 to 5 p.m.

Admission/Fare: Donations appreciated.

Locomotive/Rolling Stock: No. 755, 1944 Lima 2-8-4, former Nickel Plate. A 90-ton hopper car and a wooden caboose, both former Bessemer & Lake Erie.

Location/Directions: In the old New York Central station at Depot and Mill streets, north of U.S. 20 and I-90. Blue-and-white locomotive signs point the way to the museum.

      M

Site Address: Conneaut, OH
Mailing Address: PO Box 643, Conneaut, OH 44030
Telephone: (216) 599-7878
Internet: www.suite224.net/conneaut/rrmuseum.html

CARILLON HISTORICAL PARK
Museum
Steam, scheduled

CARILLON HISTORICAL PARK

Description: Outdoor history museum with transportation emphasis. Tour 20 buildings including an 1894 railroad station, a 1907 watchtower, canal lock and two bridges. Twice each month scheduled rides are given on the small scale live steam railroad.

Schedule: April through October: Tuesdays through Saturdays, 9:30 a.m. to 5 p.m. and Sundays 12 to 5 p.m.

Admission/Fare: Adults $2.00; children 6-17 $1.00; members are free.

Locomotive/Rolling Stock: 1835 B&O no. 1; 1912 Alco with tender; 1900 HK Porter; 1909 Lima fireless; 1903 railroad car; 1904 interurban; caboose.

Special Events: Annual Steam Festival Weekend, May.

Nearby Attractions/Accommodations: U.S. Air Force Museum, Sunwatch Indian Village, Wright Brothers Memorial, Dayton Aviation Heritage National Historical Park, Marriott, Holiday Inn.

Location/Directions: I-75 exit 51, east on Edwin C. Moses Blvd., right over bridge, right on Patterson Blvd., right on Carillon to entrance.

      M

Site Address: 2001 S. Patterson Blvd., Dayton, OH
Mailing Address: 2001 S. Patterson Blvd., Dayton, OH 45409
Telephone: (937) 293-2841
Fax: (937) 293-5798

Ohio, Dennison

THE DENNISON RAILROAD DEPOT MUSEUM
Train ride, museum, display, layout
N scale

RUSTY FOX

Description Restored 1873 Pennsylvania Railroad station, once the site of a World War II canteen that served more than one million GIs. The depot was part of a complex begun in the mid-1860s by the Pittsburgh, Cincinnati & St. Louis Railroad. Depot restaurant includes a "Canteen Restaurant" with a unique 1940s themed atmosphere and family dining; Exhibit includes a large N scale layout of Dennison during its heyday; original waiting rooms (men's and women's) filled with railroad displays; a ticket booth; a baggage room; a Railway Express building and office; a 1950 former Norfolk & Western caboose. This museum sponsors excursions ranging from 1-hour to all-day trips, through an arrangement with the Columbus & Ohio River Railroad in Coshocton.

Schedule: Year round: Tuesdays through Saturdays 11 a.m. to 5 p.m. Sundays 11 a.m. to 3 p.m. Tours by appointment.

Admission/Fare. Adults $3.00; seniors $2.50; children 7-18 $1.75; under age 7 are free.

Locomotive/Rolling Stock: 1946 Thermos Bottle engine; 1920s B&O flatcar; tank car; two passenger cars; 1940 Nickel Plate caboose; more.

Special Events: Train rides. Railroad Festival, third week of May.

Nearby Attractions/Accommodations: Amish country, Roscoe Village.

Location/Directions: At the junction of Routes 250, 36, and 800.

Site Address: 400 Center Street, Dennison, OH
Mailing Address: PO Box 11, Dennison, OH 44621
Telephone: (614) 922-6776
Fax: (614) 922-0105
Internet: web1.tusco.net/rail

Ohio, Hebron　　　　**BUCKEYE CENTRAL SCENIC RAILROAD**
Train ride
Standard gauge

BUCKEYE CENTRAL SCENIC RAILROAD

Description: We offer a scenic 1.5-hour round trip excursion through the rolling hills of central Ohio on historic Shawnee branch of the old B&O. Travel in vintage passenger coaches or in the open air gondola. On your journey pass over a steel bridge and two trestles.

Schedule: Memorial Day through mid-October: weekend departures at 1 and 3 p.m.

Admission/Fare: Adults $6.00; children 2-11 $5.00; under age 2 ride free. Charter trains available.

Locomotives/Rolling Stock: SW-1 no. 8599 EMD

Special Events: Haunted Halloween Trains, call for dates. Santa Specials, first two weekends in December, 2:30 and 4:30 p.m. Wild West/Train Robbery weekends, call for dates.

Nearby Attractions/Accommodations: Flint Ridge State Park, Dawes Arboretum, Heissy Museum, The Olde Mill, village of Granville.

Location/Directions: I-70, exit Route 13N to Route 40, turn left; or I-70, exit Route 79N to Route 40, turn right. Located on Route 40.

*Coupon available, see coupon section.

Site Address: 5501 National Road SE, Hebron, OH
Mailing Address: PO Box 242, Newark, OH 43058-0242
Telephone: (740) 366-2029
Fax: (614) 891-5847
Internet: www.infinet.com/~pcaravan

CUYAHOGA VALLEY SCENIC RAILROAD
Train ride
Standard gauge

Description: The CVSR in Northeastern Ohio runs through the heart of Cuyahoga Valley National Recreation Area. Each trip is a different adventure filled with fun, excitement, natural beauty, and historic sites. Ride comfortably in vintage climate-controlled coaches built between 1939 and 1940. The coaches originally saw passenger service on the NYC and Santa Fe Railroads. Destinations include Peninsula, Hale Farm and Village, Quaker Square, Inventure Place, Canal Visitor Center, and more.

Schedule: Call or write for information.

Admission/Fare: Call or write for information.

Locomotive/Rolling Stock: Alco FPA 4s nos. 15 and 6777; Alco FPA 4s nos. 4088 and 4099, former Delaware & Hudson.

Location/Directions: I-77 exit 155 (Rockside Road), travel east one mile. The train departs from the parking area on Old Rockside Road in Independence.

        Cleveland and Akron

Site Address: Independence, OH
Mailing Address: PO Box 158, Peninsula, OH 44264-0158
Telephone: (800) 468-4070
Internet: members.aol.com/cvsrail/index.html

AC&J SCENIC LINE RAILWAY
Train ride
Standard gauge

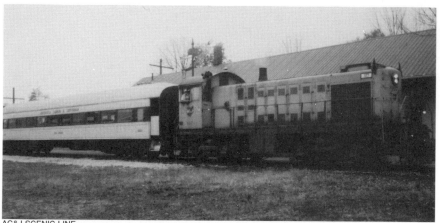

AC&J SCENIC LINE

Description: Enjoy a one-hour 12-mile round trip over the last remaining portion of the New York Central's Ashtabula to Pittsburgh "High Grade" passenger main line. Ride in vintage passenger cars pulled by a first-generation diesel. A family educational adventure.

Schedule: June 19 weekend through October: weekends, 12:30, 2, and 3:30 p.m.

Admission/Fare: Adults $7.00; seniors $6.00; children 3-12 $5.00; under age 3 are free when not occupying a seat.

Locomotive/Rolling Stock: No. 107, 1950 Alco S-2 diesel, former Nickel Plate and Fairport, Painesville & Eastern; no. 518, 1948 Alco S-2 diesel, former Erie and Centerior Energy plant switcher (Ashtabula); more.

Special Events: Spring and Fall Murder Mystery Trains.

Nearby Attractions/Accommodations: Ashtabula, Conneaut, Geneva-on-the-Lake, Pymatuning Resort area, Cleveland, Erie.

Location/Directions: I-90 from east/west exit Ohio 11 south, to Ohio 46 south to Jefferson, left at second light on E. Jefferson Street to tracks. Or north on Route 11, exit 307 west to Jefferson, right at second light to tracks.

Site Address: East Jefferson Street, Jefferson, OH
Mailing Address: PO Box 517, Jefferson, OH 44047-0517
Telephone: (440) 576-6346
Fax: (440) 576-8848

Ohio, Jefferson

JEFFERSON DEPOT, INC.
Museum

JEFFERSON DEPOT

Description: Historic restored 1872 Lake Shore & Michigan Southern Railroad Station and 1918 caboose.

Schedule: June through August: Guided tours Sundays 1 to 4 p.m. Other days by appointment. Available for group tours, meetings, reunions, weddings.

Admission/Fare: Adults $1.00 or more donation; children are free.

Special Events: Strawberry Festival and Craft Bazaar, third weekend in June. Antique car show, third Sunday in June. Annual Fall Foliage Train/Bus Trip, first Saturday in October. Holiday Open House, first Saturday in December. An Old Fashioned Williamsburg Christmas, second Sunday in December.

Nearby Attractions/Accommodations: AC&J Railroad scenic tours, Buccaneer Campsites, wineries, Pymatuning State Park.

Location/Directions: From I-90 go south on Route 11 to Route 46, south to Jefferson. Museum is located between E. Walnut and E. Jefferson Streets.

        M

Site Address: 147 E. Jefferson Street, Jefferson, OH
Mailing Address: PO Box 22, Jefferson, OH 44047
Telephone: (440) 293-5532 and (352) 343-8256

Ohio, Lebanon

TURTLE CREEK VALLEY RAILWAY
Train ride
Standard gauge

TURTLE CREEK VALLEY RAILWAY

Description: A one-hour train ride through the historic Turtle Creek Valley in southwestern Ohio. Two-hour rides on Sunday afternoons.

Schedule: April through December: weekends. May through October: weekends, Wednesdays, and Fridays. Closed November 22-23.

Admission/Fare: Adults $10.00; seniors $9.00; children 3-12 $6.00. Specialty trips are higher.

Locomotive/Rolling Stock: 1950 GM GP7 1500 horsepower; Pullman commuter coaches nos. 101, 102, 103, and 104; gondola no. 100.

Special Events: Mystery Ride-n-Dine events, summer ice cream socials, fall foliage rides, train rides with Santa.

Nearby Attractions/Accommodations: Kings Island Beach, Fort Ancient, The Golden Lamb Inn, Miami Valley Dinner Theater, Renaissance Festival, Blue Jacket Drama, golf, vineyards, canoeing, harness racing.

Location/Directions: I-75 exit 29; I-71 North exit 32; I-71 South exit 28.

Site Address: 198 South Broadway, Lebanon, OH
Mailing Address: 198 South Broadway, Lebanon, OH 45036
Telephone: (513) 398-8584
Fax: (513) 933-8219

MITCH CASEY

Description: A model railroad museum and operating layout featuring over 18 trains simultaneously in standard, O, and G gauge. Over 275 locomotives on display. Lionel, American Flyer, Ives, Williams and others.

Schedule: Year round: daily, 11 a.m. to 5 p.m.

Admission: Adults $5; seniors $4.00; children under 10 are free with paying adult; families $15.

Special Events: Sternwheel Festival, weekend after Labor Day.

Nearby Attractions/Accommodations: Butch's Cola Museum, Children's Toy and Doll Museum, Valley Gem Sternwheel, Showboat Becky Thatcher, Rossi Pasta Factory, Fenton Art Glass Company and Outlet, historic Lafayette Hotel, Ohio River Museum.

Location/Directions: I-77 and Ohio Route 7.

*Coupon available, see coupon section.

Site Address: 220 Gilman Street, Harmar Village, Marietta, OH
Mailing Address: 220 Gilman Street, Marietta, OH 45750
Telephone: (614) 374-9995 and (614) 373-5176
Fax: (614) 373-7808
E-mail: mttachamber@ee.net
Internet: www.eekman.com/harmarstation/

LUCAS COUNTY/MAUMEE VALLEY HISTORICAL SOCIETY

Museum, display

MAUMEE VALLEY HISTORICAL SOCIETY

Description: The depot is part of a five-building museum complex. Guided tours cover the entire complex. The depot and caboose are authentically furnished. Railroad memorabilia on display.

Schedule: Wednesdays through Sundays, 1 to 4 p.m.

Fare/Admission: Adults $3.50; children $1.50.

Locomotive/Rolling Stock: Caboose and baggage car.

Special Events: Model train exhibit in depot for Harvest Days, October 24.

Nearby Attractions/Accommodations: Toledo Zoo, Toledo Museum of Art, Toledo Mud Hens baseball, Tony Pacos Restaurant, Ft. Meigs.

Location/Directions: The museum is on River Road in downtown Maumee and can be reached easily from U.S. routes 20 and 24.

*Coupon available, see coupon section.

Site Address: 1031 River Road, Maumee, OH
Mailing Address: 1031 River Road, Maumee, OH 43537
Telephone: (419) 893-9602
Fax: (419) 893-3108

HOCKING VALLEY SCENIC RAILWAY
Train ride
Standard gauge

HOCKING VALLEY SCENIC RAILWAY

Description: Train rides on historic rail equipment over an historic right-of-way. Featuring a 12-mile round trip to Haydenville and a 25-mile round trip to East Logan with a visit to an 1850s village at Robbins Crossing.

Schedule: Memorial Day weekend through mid-November: weekends and holidays. Haydenville–12 p.m. departure. Logan–2:30 p.m. departure; Santa Train–11:15 a.m. and 2:15 p.m. departures.

Admission/Fare: Haydenville–adults $7.50, children 2-11 $4.75. Logan–adults $10.50, children 2-11 $7.25.

Locomotive/Rolling Stock: No. 33, 1916 Baldwin 2-8-0; no. 5833, 1952 EMD GP7, former Chesapeake & Ohio; no. 7318, 1942 General Electric; no. 4005 1953 Baldwin Lima Hamilton 500 hp switcher; more.

Special Events: Logan–Santa Trains, last weekend in November and first 3 weekends in December. Reservations recommended.

Nearby Attractions/Accommodations: Hocking Hills Area State Park, Robbins Crossing Museum, Stuarts Opera House ca. 1879, Historic Dew Hotel, Nelsonville Public Square.

Location/Directions: Southeastern Ohio on Route 33, 60 miles southeast of Columbus in Hocking Hills region.

*Coupon available, see coupon section.

        M

Site Address: US 33 and Hocking Parkway, Nelsonville, OH
Mailing Address: PO Box 427, Nelsonville, OH 45764
Telephone: (614) 470-1300 and (800) 967-7834
Fax: (740) 753-1152
Internet: www.hvsr.com

Ohio, Olmsted Township

TROLLEYVILLE, U.S.A.
Train ride, museum, display, layout
Standard gauge

DON SCOTT

Description: Streetcars and miscellaneous railroad equipment on display. Museum in the 1875 restored B&O Berea Depot. Ride on over 2.5 miles of track.

Schedule: May through November: weekends. June through September: Wednesdays and Fridays.

Admission/Fare: $5.00 adults; seniors $4.00; children $3.00; under age 2 are free.

Locomotive/Rolling Stock: Thirteen streetcars; 13 interurban; four work cars and locomotives; two boxcars; two cabooses; miscellaneous motorcars.

Special Events: Easter Egg Hunt, Murder Mysteries, Fourth of July, Train Shows, Moonlight Rides, Halloween, Christmas Festival of Lights.

Nearby Attractions/Accommodations: Cedar Point, Geauga Lake Amusement Park, Rock and Roll Hall of Fame, Museum of Science and Industry.

Location/Directions: I-480, exit 6A, 2 miles south, west side of road in shopping center

*Coupon available, see coupon section.

Radio frequency: 43.7

Site Address: 7100 Columbia Road, Olmsted Twp., OH
Mailing Address: 7100 Columbia Road, Olmsted Twp., OH 44138
Telephone: (440) 235-4725
Fax: (440) 235-6556
E-mail: cperry8599@aol.com

Ohio, Orrville

ORRVILLE RAILROAD
HERITAGE SOCIETY
Train ride
Standard gauge

RICHARD JACOBS

Description: This museum is a restored former Pennsylvania Railroad depot and an unrestored N5C caboose and switch block tower.

Schedule: Museum–May through September: Saturdays, 10 a.m. to 4 p.m. or by appointment.

Admission/Fare: Donations appreciated.

Locomotive/Rolling Stock: 1951 EMD F9 cab unit no. 82C; two B units; six Budd passenger coaches.

Special Events: Depot Days, June 12-13. Christmas Open House, November 26-27.

Nearby Attractions/Accommodations: Gateway to Amish Country of Wayne and Holmes Counties.

Location/Directions: On State Route 57, 3 miles north of U.S. 30 and 12 miles south of I-76.

         M

Site Address: 145 Depot Street, Orrville, OH
Mailing Address: PO Box 11, Orrville, OH 44667
Telephone: (330) 683-2426
Fax: (330) 682-2426

CEDAR POINT & LAKE ERIE RAILROAD
Train ride

DAN FEICHT

Description: Located in Cedar Point, the largest amusement ride park in the world, which has 6 steam-powered locomotives and is one of the largest operators of steam engines in the country. The 15-minute train excursion encompasses a 2-mile trip over bridges and through a land of "Old West" animation.

Schedule: Early-May through mid-October.

Admission/Fare: Call or write for information.

Locomotive/Rolling Stock: Maud L.–1902 Baldwin 0-4-4T rebuilt as 2-4-4T; Myron H.–1922 Vulcan 0-4-0 rebuilt as 2-4-0; Albert–1910 Davenport 2-6-0; George R.–1942 H.K. Porter Co. 0-4-0 rebuilt as 2-4-0; Jennie K.–1909 H. K. Porter Co. 0-4-0 rebuilt as 2-4-0; Judy K.–Vulcan 0-4-0 rebuilt as 2-4-0.

Site Address: Cedar Point, Sandusky, OH
Mailing Address: PO Box 5006, Sandusky, OH 44871-5006
Telephone: (419) 627-2223
Internet: www.cedarpoint.com

Ohio, Waterville and Grand Rapids

**TOLEDO, LAKE ERIE &
WESTERN RAILWAY**
Train ride
Standard gauge

GEORGE A. FORERO, JR.

Description: Each ride is a 20-mile round trip over the lines of the Nickel Plate between the historic towns of Waterville and Grand Rapids. Witness a spectacular view from our 900-foot-long bridge over the Maumee River, Providence Metropark, Ludwig Mill, and the Miami & Erie canal boat ride.

Schedule: May through October: Wednesdays through Sundays and holidays. Send SASE for hours or call.

Admission/Fare: Round trip–adults $8.00; seniors $7.00; children 3-12 $4.50. One-way trips and charters available.

Locomotive/Rolling Stock: 1946 no. 112 Alco S2; 1948 no. 5109 Alco S4; B&O chair cars nos. 401 and 403; New York Central nos. 405, 407, 408; more.

Special Events: Roch de Boeuf Festival, early September. Apple Butter Festival, October. Garage Sale Days. Call or write for details.

Nearby Attractions/Accommodations: Volmar's Amusement Park, Isaac Ludwig Grist/Saw Mill, Miami & Erie mule-pulled canal boat rides.

Location/Directions: Waterville–U.S. 23/I-475 to west on U.S. 24/Anthony Wayne Trail, north on Route 64, to Sixth Street, right turn. Grand Rapids–State Route 64, west on Route 578 over bridge, right on Route 65, left on Wapakoneta Road, right on Third Street. Follow signs for Warehouse Antique Mall.

*Coupon available, see coupon section.

          M

Site Address: 49 N. Sixth Street, Waterville, OH
Mailing Address: PO Box 168, Waterville, OH 43566
Telephone: (419) 878-2177
Internet: www.meettoledo.org (see Conventions/Visitor's page)

OHIO RAILWAY MUSEUM
Train ride, museum
Standard gauge

DAVE BUNGE

Description: Museum offers a 2-mile round trip on historic Trolley-Interurban cars.

Schedule: May through October: Sundays, 1 to 5 p.m.

Admission/Fare: Adults $3.00; seniors $2.00; children $1.00.

Locomotive/Rolling Stock: N&W no. 578 Pacific Steam; OPS no. 21 interurban; passenger cars, street cars, and interurbans.

Special Events: Ghost Trolley, Santa Trolley, State Fair, Twilight Trolleys.

Nearby Attractions/Accommodations: Columbus Zoo, Center of Science and Industry, hotels, and restaurants.

Location/Directions: I-71 exit Route 161, one mile west to Proprietors Road, turn north.

Site Address: 990 Proprietors Road, Worthington, OH
Mailing Address: Box 777, Worthington, OH
Telephone: (614) 885-7345
Internet: members.aol.com/orm578/page/ormhome.htm

Oklahoma, Bartlesville (Ramona)

THE TRAIN HOUSE
Train ride, display, layout

THE TRAIN HOUSE

Description: Trains, trains, and more trains running everywhere! Exhibits include an outdoor G scale garden railroad, a 28 x 48-foot Lionel layout, HO and N scale layouts, and a wagon-train ride through the park. Hobby shop features trains and accessories in all scales.

Schedule: Year round: Tuesdays through Saturdays 10 a.m. to 5:30 p.m., Sundays 1 to 5 p.m.

Admission/Fare: Donations appreciated.

Special Events: Main Line Train Show, first Saturday after July 4th. Christmas display, December.

Nearby Attractions/Accommodations: Osage Hills State Park, candle factory, restaurants, motels, Bartlesville, Oklahoma (15 miles).

Location/Directions: U.S. 75 to County Road 27, east 2 miles to stop sign, north 1.5 blocks to entrance.

Site Address: 26811 N. 3990 Road, Ramona, OK
Mailing Address: 26811 N. 3990 Road, Ramona, OK 74061
Telephone: (918) 336-5821 and (800) 845-5781

305

**CIMARRON VALLEY
RAILROAD MUSEUM**
Museum

CIMARRON VALLEY RAILROAD MUSEUM

Description: A 1916 Santa Fe depot filled with great variety of rail memorabilia, large railroad library, wooden Frisco caboose, 1917 tank cab, 1897 boxcar, 0-4-0 switcher locomotive.

Schedule: By appointment or chance.

Admission/Fare: Free.

Locomotive/Rolling Stock: 0-4-0 GE switcher; oil tank car 1917; wooden Frisco caboose; DL&C Co. 1897 boxcar.

Nearby Attractions/Accommodations: Jim Thorpe home, Oilfield Museum in former Santa Fe depot; Stillwater-Sheerar Museum, Oklahoma State University, athletic events, restaurants.

Location/Directions: 1.5 miles south of Highway 33 on S. Kings Highway. Extreme western edge of Cushing.

Site Address: Kings Highway and Eseco Road, Cushing, OK
Mailing Address: PO Box 844, Cushing, OK 74023
Telephone: (918) 225-1657/3936

RAILROAD MUSEUM OF OKLAHOMA
Museum, display, layout
Lionel, HO, N

JOE SMITH

Description: This museum, housed in a 1926-27 former Santa Fe freight house, has one of the largest collections of railroad artifacts in the midwest. Focused on preserving historically significant railroad equipment. Recapture the essence of railroad days as you climb aboard a 1925 steam locomotive, wander through cabooses from six different railroads, and view six different freight cars.

Schedule: Year round: Tuesday through Friday, 1 to 4 p.m. Saturdays, 10 a.m. to 1 p.m. Sundays, 2 to 5 p.m. Other times by appointment.

Admission/Fare: Donations appreciated.

Locomotive/Rolling Stock: 1965 GE 50-ton locomotive; 1925 Frisco Baldwin 4-8-2 no. 1519; Vulcan Chemicals 1965 GE 50-ton class BB switcher VMCX1; renovated BN, NP, SF, MK&T, UP and Frisco cabooses; 1928 automobile boxcar; 1937 3-dome tank car; 1953 single-dome tank car.

Special Events: Two model railroad swap meets and annual Christmas party each year.

Nearby Attractions/Accommodations: Water park, Science and Discovery Center, Cherokee Strip, Midgley, antique automobile museum.

Location/Directions: Enid is 30 miles west of I-35 in north central Oklahoma on Routes 60, 81, 64, 412. Museum is 6 block northwest of downtown.

          M

Site Address: 702 N. Washington, Enid, OK
Mailing Address: 702 N. Washington, Enid, OK 73701
Telephone: (580) 233-3051

Oklahoma, Hugo

HUGO HERITAGE RAILROAD
Train ride, museum
Standard gauge

CHOCTAW COUNTY HISTORICAL SOCIETY

Description: This operation offers a 2.5-hour round trip from Hugo (Circus City, U.S.A.) to points north and south, including Paris, Texas. A museum, located in the former 1915 Frisco depot, is the largest left on Frisco's southwest lines. Displays include an HO gauge model railroad on a mountain layout, railroad artifacts, turn-of-the-century memorabilia, rare photographs, and a working Harvey House restaurant.

Schedule: April through November: Call for dates and times.

Admission/Fare: Adults $20.00; children $13.00.

Locomotive/Rolling Stock: Commuter coaches; GP38 locomotive.

Special Events: Homecoming Events, first week in June. Fourth of July. Railroad Days, third week in October.

Nearby Attractions/Accommodations: Old Johnson Inn bed and breakfast, Mt. Olive Cemetery, motels, restaurants.

Location/Directions: Indian Nation Turnpike, exit Hugo, left on Highway 70, on left side at railroad tracks.

*Coupon available, see coupon section.

Site Address: 309 N. "B" Street, Hugo, OK
Mailing Address: 309 N. "B" Street, Hugo, OK 74743
Telephone: (580) 326-2681 and (888) 773-3768
Fax: (580) 326-2427

SUNBELT RAILROAD MUSEUM
Museum

SUNBELT RAILROAD MUSEUM

Description: Displays include railroad mementos, an operating telegraph station, and a library.

Schedule: Year round: Saturdays 10 a.m. Closed holidays.

Admission/Fare: Donations appreciated.

Nearby Attractions/Accommodations: Food and lodging in downtown Tulsa.

Location/Directions: Near downtown Tulsa.

Site Address: 1323 E. 5th Street, Tulsa, OK
Mailing Address: PO Box 470311, Tulsa, OK 74147-0311
Telephone: (918) 584-3777
E-mail: slsf4500@aol.com
Internet: members.aol.com/slsf4500

WAYNOKA DEPOT MUSEUM
Museum

WAYNOKA HISTORICAL SOCIETY

Description: Restoration of Waynoka's Santa Fe Depot and Harvey House Restaurant is expected to be complete in 1999. History of rail and air transportation.

Schedule: To be announced. Call or write for information.

Admission/Fare: Donations appreciated.

Special Events: Grand re-opening of Harvey House in 1999. Call or write for information.

Nearby Attractions/Accommodations: Little Sahara State Park and Campgrounds, Alabaster Caverns State Park, Cimarron River Stampede Rodeo, Glass Mountains, Trails Inn, Little Sahara Motel.

Location/Directions: Two blocks west of Highway 281 on Waynoka Street.

         M

Site Address: Waynoka Street & Cleveland Street, Waynoka, OK
Mailing Address: PO Box 193, Waynoka, OK 73860
Telephone: (405) 824-1886
Fax: (405) 824-0921
Internet: www.pldi.net/~harpo

YUKON'S BEST RAILROAD MUSEUM
Museum

JACK B. AUSTERMAN

Description: The museum contains an extensive display of railroad antiques and artifacts of the Rock Island Line and other railroads.

Schedule: Year round by chance or appointment. Call or write for information.

Admission/Fare: Free.

Locomotive/Rolling Stock: Rock Island boxcar no. 5542; caboose no. 17039; Mo Pac caboose no. 13724; UP caboose no. 25865.

Location/Directions: On historic Route 66. Main Street, across from "Yukon's Best Flour" wheat elevator.

Site Address: Third and Main Streets, Yukon, OK
Mailing Address: 1020 W. Oak Street, Yukon, OK 73099
Telephone: (405) 354-5079

CANBY DEPOT MUSEUM
Museum

CANBY HISTORICAL SOCIETY

Description: Museum with pioneer and railroad artifacts.

Schedule: March through December: Thursdays through Sundays. January through February: by appointment.

Admission/Fare: Donation.

Special Events: Holiday Open House. Antique and Artifacts Appraisal Days.

Nearby Attractions/Accommodations: Clackamas County Fair, August. Canby Ferry. Swan Island, parks, river parks.

Location/Directions: Off Highway 99E, east at fairgrounds crossing over north/south UP Railroad. I-5, exit Canby/Aurora at Wilsonville.

🔲 P 🚌 ✳ M

Site Address: 888 NE 4th Avenue, Canby, OR
Mailing Address: PO Box 160, Canby, OR 97013
Telephone: (503) 266-6712

PHOENIX & HOLLY RAILROAD
Train ride
15" gauge

PHOENIX & HOLLY RAILROAD

Description: Visitors can ride through acres of flowers at the Flower Farmer and enjoy a 1¾-mile ride with a stopover at the petting zoo (July through September).

Schedule: May through September: weekends 11 a.m. to 6 p.m. October: open daily, pumpkin patch.

Admission/Fare: Adults $2.50; children age 12 and under $2.00. Groups, weekdays by appointment.

Locomotive/Rolling Stock: Diesel locomotive purpose-built; diesel locomotive 5.5" scale; DRG&W side rod diesel; gondolas; flatcar; caboose.

Special Events: Swan Island Dahlia Festival, last 2 weeks in August. Pumpkin Run (to pumpkin patch), month of October.

Nearby Attractions/Accommodations: Swan Island, Canby Ferry, state park, golf.

Location/Directions: I-5 to Canby, north on Holly to site.

Site Address: 2512 N. Holly, Canby, OR
Mailing Address: 2512 N. Holly, Canby, OR 92013
Telephone: (503) 266-3581
Fax: (503) 263-4027
E-mail: lgarre@falconpc.com
Internet: www.rentaguardianangel.com/flowerfarmer

MOUNT HOOD RAILROAD
AND DINNER TRAIN
Train ride
Standard gauge

MOUNT HOOD RAILROAD

Description: Built in 1906, the train is a link between two of Oregon's most spectacular natural wonders–the awe-inspiring Columbia River Gorge and the foothills of dramatic, snowcapped Mt. Hood, the state's highest peak. For special occasions, take the dinner train, "The Four Course Dinner with a Thousand Views."

Schedule: April through December: Excursion train–10 a.m. and 3 p.m. Brunch train–11 a.m. Dinner train–5:30 p.m.

Admission/Fare: Excursion train–adults $22.95; seniors $19.95; children $14.95. Brunch train–$55.00. Dinner train–$67.50.

Locomotive/Rolling Stock: Two 1950 GP9s; historic Pullmans from 1920 to 1930.

Special Events: Train Robberies, Festivals, Halloween Spook Trains, Christmas Tree Train, Murder Mystery Dinner Trains.

Nearby Attractions/Accommodations: Mt. Hood, Columbia River National Scenic Area, biking, hiking, wind surfing, golf, historic hotels.

Location/Directions: Sixty miles east of Portland on I-84, exit 63 right to Cascade Street, left to parking lot.

Site Address: 110 Railroad Avenue, Hood River, OR
Mailing Address: 110 Railroad Avenue, Hood River, OR 97031
Telephone: (800) TRAIN-61 and (541) 386-3556
Fax: (541) 386-2140
E-mail: mthoodrr@linkport.com
Internet: www.mthoodrr.com

**OREGON ELECTRIC RAILWAY
HISTORICAL SOCIETY**
Train ride
Standard

BOB SPARKES

Description: Scenic trip on a trolley along the Willamette River from Lake Oswego to Portland.

Schedule: June through August: Wednesdays through Sundays 10 a.m. to 6 p.m. September through May: weekends and holidays.

Admission/Fare: Adults $6.00; seniors $5.00; children $3.00.

Locomotive/Rolling Stock: Blackpool no. 48; Broadway no. 813.

Nearby Attractions/Accommodations: Tillamook Ice Creamery Restaurant, Sharky's Restaurant.

*Coupon available, see coupon section.

Site Address: Lake Oswego, OR
Mailing Address: PO Box 308, Lake Oswego, OR 97034
Telephone: (503) 222-2226
E-mail: r.sparkes@ieee.org
Internet: home.sprynet.com/sprynet/subwayma/oerhs.htm

SAMTRAK
Train ride, museum
Standard gauge

SAMTRAK

Description: Climb aboard the open-air car or caboose pulled by "Big Red" for a one-hour round trip scenic ride along the Willamette River over former Portland Traction Electric Line.

Schedule: May through September: 11 a.m. to 3:30 p.m. Hours vary, call for schedule.

Admission/Fare: Adults $5.00; seniors $4.00; children 7-10 $3.00; children 2-6 $2.00; under age 2 are free.

Locomotive/Rolling Stock: GE 45-ton diesel no. 450; GE 25-ton diesel no. 2501; open-air passenger car; restored former Simpson Timber Logging caboose no. 900.

Nearby Attractions/Accommodations: Oregon Museum of Science and Industry. Oak Amusement Park.

Site Address: 8825 SE 11th Street, Portland, OR
Mailing Address: PO Box 22548, Portland, OR 97269
Telephone: (503) 653-2380
Fax: (503) 659-6546

WASHINGTON PARK & ZOO RAILWAY
Train ride
30" gauge

GEORGE BAETJER/WASHINGTON PARK & ZOO RAILWAY

Description: A 4-mile round trip around the zoo and through forested hills to Washington Park, passing the elephant enclosure for a close-up view of the zoo's world-famous pachyderm herd and overlooking the Alaska Tundra exhibit. The stop at Washington Park station offers a panoramic view of Mount Hood, the city of Portland, and Mount St. Helens.

Schedule: May 29 through September 6: daily. Trains depart at frequent intervals.

Admission/Fare: Round trip–adults $2.75; seniors and children 3-11 $2.00; under age 3 are free. Zoo admission required.

Locomotive/Rolling Stock: 4-4-0 No. 1, replica of Virginia & Truckee "Reno"; *Zooliner,* replica of General Motors *Aerotrain;* diesel-powered *Oregon Express;* diesel-powered switcher and fire train; streamlined cars and open coaches; two trains are wheelchair-accessible. The train is one of the last registered Postal Railway Stations in the United States.

Nearby Attractions/Accommodations: Portland Rose Test Gardens, Japanese Gardens.

Location/Directions: Zoo is located two miles west of Portland City Center, on U.S. Highway 26.

Radio frequency: 151.655

Site Address: 4001 SW Canyon Road, Portland, OR
Mailing Address: 4001 SW Canyon Road, Portland, OR 97221
Telephone: (503) 226-1561
Fax: (503) 226-6836
E-mail: hartlinej@metro.dst.or.us
Internet: www.zooregon.org/AboutVis/train.htm

Oregon, Redmond

CROOKED RIVER DINNER TRAIN
Dinner train
Standard gauge

CROOKED RIVER DINNER TRAIN

Description: Take a ride back to the 1800s and the Wild West with the James Gang. Join us for our Murder Mystery on Saturday night or our live action train robbery on Sunday afternoons.

Schedule: Year round: Saturdays, 6 to 9 p.m. Sundays, 1 to 4 p.m. or 11 a.m. to 2 p.m. Schedule varies, special train rides on select dates.

Admission/Fare: Saturdays–adults $69.00; children 4-12 $35.00; children 3 and under $16.00.

Locomotive/Rolling Stock: Two Milwaukee Road coaches; Burlington baggage car.

Special Events: Halloween, Thanksgiving, Santa Claus trains, New Year's Eve.

Nearby Attractions/Accommodations: Smith Rock State Park, golfing, biking, resorts.

Location/Directions: Three miles north of Redmond or at O'Neil Junction, turn east at flashing yellow light, train is ahead.

Site Address: 4075 NE O'Neil Way, Redmond, OR
Mailing Address: PO Box 387, Redmond, OR 97756
Telephone: (541) 541-8702
E-mail: dintrain@coinet.com
Internet: www.crookedriverrailroad.com

SUMPTER VALLEY RAILROAD
Train ride
36" gauge

SUMPTER VALLEY RAILROAD

Description: A ten-mile round trip from McEwen Station to the historic mining town of Sumpter.

Schedule: Memorial Day through September: McEwen–weekends and holidays, 10 a.m., 12:30, and 3 p.m. Sumpter–weekends and holidays, 11:30 a.m., 2, and 4:40 p.m.

Admission/Fare: Adults–round trip $9.00, one-way $6.00; children 6-16 6.50/4.50; families $22.00/$15.00.

Locomotive/Rolling Stock: 1920 Alco 2-8-2; 1915 Heisler; 18-ton Plymouth diesel.

Special Events: Moonlite rides, hobo stew, and music, July 4th weekend, Labor Day weekend.

Nearby Attractions/Accommodations: Sumpter Dredge State Heritage Area.

Location/Directions: Highway 7, 22 miles southwest of Baker City off I-84.

Site Address: Dredge Loop Road, Sumpter Valley, OR
Mailing Address: PO Box 389, Baker City, OR 97814
Telephone: (541) 894-2268

ALTOONA RAILROADERS MEMORIAL MUSEUM
Museum
Standard gauge

PETER D. BARTON

Description: Located in the former PRR Master Mechanics Building, the museum tells the stories of the people who laid track, built the locomotives, and guided trains across the Allegheny Ridge. Visitors experience what it was like to live and work in a community that was a company–the Pennsylvania Railroad.

Schedule: Open year round. Summer season–April: daily 10 a.m. to 6 p.m.; Winter season–November: daily, 10 a.m. to 5 p.m. Closed Mondays.

Admission/Fare: Adults $8.50; seniors $7.75; children 4-12 $5.00. Group rates and school packages available. Admission valid for 24 hours.

Locomotive/Rolling Stock: GG1 no. 4913; 1918 Vulcan 0-4-0 switcher; two diesel locomotives; the Loretto; other PRR equipment.

Special Events: Horn & Whistle Fair, June; Altoona Railfest, October. Call events line for more information.

Nearby Attractions/Accommodations: Horseshoe Curve National Historic Landmark. Call for free visitors guide (800) 84-ALTOONA.

Location/Directions: I-99 (formerly Route 220), 17th Street exit, Downtown Altoona.

*Coupon available, see coupon section.

Site Address: 1300 9th Avenue, Altoona, PA
Mailing Address: 1300 9th Avenue, Altoona, PA 16602
Telephone: (814) 946-0834 and (888) 425-8666
Fax: (814) 946-9457
Internet: http://www.railroadcity.com

RAILROADERS MEMORIAL MUSEUM

Description: The Curve's story is now told at the modern interpretive Visitor Center, located in a picturesque setting. A seven-minute film highlights the construction of this engineering landmark. Guests may ride to track elevation aboard a two-car funicular or walk the 194 stairs. It is located on Norfolk Southern's busy east-west main line with more than 60 trains passing each day. Trains climbing or descending the 1.8 percent grade can be viewed and photographed safely from the track-side park.

Schedule: Open year round. Summer season–April: daily 10 a.m. to 7 p.m.; Winter season–November: daily, 10 a.m. to 4 p.m. Closed Mondays.

Admission/Fare: Adults $3.50; seniors $3.00; children 4-12 $1.75. Group rates and school packages available. Admission valid for 24 hours.

Locomotive/Rolling Stock: Former Pennsylvania Railroad GP9, No. 7048 on display at track elevation.

Nearby Attractions/Accommodations: Altoona Railroaders Memorial Museum. Free visitors guides (800) 84-ALTOONA.

Location/Directions: Kittanning Point Road, State Route 4008. Follow Heritage Route signs.

Site Address: Altoona, PA
Mailing Address: 1300 9th Avenue, Altoona, PA 16602
Telephone: (814) 946-0834 and (888) 425-8666
Fax: (814) 946-9457
Internet: www.railroadcity.com

PIONEER TUNNEL COAL MINE AND STEAM TRAIN
Train ride
Narrow gauge

PIONEER TUNNEL COAL MINE & STEAM TRAIN

Description: Scenic ride along the Mahanoy Mountain behind a steam locomotive of the 0-4-0 type built in 1927 by the Vulcan Iron Works of Wilkes Barre, Pennsylvania. Guides tell the story of strip mining, bootlegging and the Centralia Mine Fire. Also available is a tour of a real anthracite coal mine in open mine cars pulled by a battery-operated mine motor. Mine guides tell the story of anthracite coal mining.

Schedule: April: weekday mine tours: 11 a.m., 12:30 and 2 p.m. Memorial Day through Labor Day: daily mine tours 10 a.m. to 6 p.m. Mine tours and steam train–May, September, October: weekday mine tours 11 a.m., 12:30 and 2 p.m. train tours for reserved groups only; weekend mine and train run continuously.

Admission/Fare: Steam train–adults $4.00; children under age 12 $2.50. Mine–adults $6.00; children under age 12 $3.50. Group discounts.

Locomotive/Rolling Stock: A spare "lokie" of the 0-4-0 type built by Vulcan Iron Work; two battery-powered mine motors.

Special Events: 7th Annual Pioneer Day, August 21.

Nearby Attractions/Accommodations: Pennsylvania Museum of Anthracite Mining.

Location/Directions: I-81, exit 36W (Frackville). Follow Route 61 north to Ashland.

Site Address: 19th and Oak Streets, Ashland, PA
Mailing Address: 19th and Oak Streets, Ashland, PA 17921
Telephone: (717) 875-3850
Fax: (717) 875-3301
Internet: www.easternpa.com/pioneertunnel

BELLEFONTE HISTORICAL RAILROAD
Train ride
Standard gauge

W.M. RUMBERGER

Description: Scheduled and special trips over the 60-mile Nittany & Bald Eagle Railroad to Lemont, Vail (Tyrone), and Mill Hall. Regular service includes stopovers at Lemont, Bellefonte, Curtin Village, and Julian Glider Port. Fall foliage and railfan runs cover up to 120 miles; all-inclusive restaurant runs to Tyrone are also offered. The Bellefonte Station, a restored former Pennsylvania Railroad structure built in 1888, houses an operating N-gauge layout of the Bellefonte-Curtin Village route, as well as historical photos and memorabilia of area railroading. A snowplow and caboose under restoration are displayed beside the station.

Schedule: May 30 through September 30: weekends and holidays. October: special runs. Call or write for information.

Admission/Fare: Adults $6.00 and up; children 3-11 $3.00 and up.

Locomotive/Rolling Stock: No. 9167, 1952 RDC-1, and 1962 No. 1953; air-conditioned passenger cars. Can be configured for meal service.

Special Events: Spring, Fall, Christmas trains.

Nearby Attractions/Accommodations: Curtin Village, Julian Glider Port, Penn State University, historic Bellefonte.

Location/Directions: Central Pennsylvania, a short distance from I-80.

Site Address: The Train Station, Bellefonte, PA
Mailing Address: The Train Station, Bellefonte, PA 16823
Telephone: (814) 355-0311 and (814) 355-2392

CATAWISSA RAILROAD COMPANY
Display
Standard gauge

CATAWISSA RAILROAD COMPANY

Description: A restored Reading railroad station, tunnel, two bridges, and 13 restored railroad cabooses on the Catawissa Branch.

Schedule: Year round: daily.

Admission/Fare: Free.

Locomotive/Rolling Stock: 13 cabooses.

Nearby Attractions/Accommodations: Campgrounds, golf, parks and state parks, antique shops.

Site Address: 119 Pine Street, Catawissa, PA
Mailing Address: 119 Pine Street, Catawissa, PA 17820
Telephone: (717) 356-2345
Fax: (717) 356-7876
E-mail: waltgosh@postoffice.ptd.net
Internet: www.trackman.com/cabphoto

**ALLEGHENY PORTAGE RAILROAD
NATIONAL HISTORIC SITE**
Museum
Standard gauge

NATIONAL PARK SERVICE

Description: This site preserves the remains of the incline railway used to portage canal boats over the Allegheny Mountains. It includes the first railroad tunnel in America, the Staple Bend Tunnel. The Visitor Center has film, models and special programs on the portage railroad and mainline canal system.

Schedule: Year round: daily 9 a.m. to 5 p.m. Extended hours possible in summer.

Admission/Fare: Adults 16 and older $2.00; national park passes honored.

Locomotive/Rolling Stock: 1893 Pangborn model of the Lafayette

Special Events: Summer: costumed demonstrations of stone cutting, log hewing, lifestyles of the past. Summer Saturdays: Evening on the Summit, concert lecture series. Summer Sundays: Heritage Hike series, hikes and bus tours of portage route.

Nearby Attractions/Accommodations: Gallitzin Tunnels, Johnstown Flood National Memorial, state parks.

Location/Directions: U.S. 22, Gallitzin exit.

Site Address: 110 Federal Park Road, Cresson, PA
Mailing Address: PO Box 189, Cresson, PA 16630
Telephone: (814) 886-6150
Fax: (814) 886-6117
Internet: www.nps.gov/alpo/

Pennsylvania, Cressona

MINE HILL & NORTHERN RAILROAD PRESERVATION SOCIETY
Display
Standard gauge

DAVID GAMBLE

Description: A collection of privately owned, full scale railroad equipment undergoing various stages of restoration. Members focus on anthracite railroads of northeastern Pennsylvania, but other railroads are also represented.

Schedule: By appointment only.

Admission/Fare: Donations appreciated.

Locomotive/Rolling Stock: LV 95116 caboose; CNJ 91516 caboose; RDG 94070 caboose; EL 319 caboose, NH 622 caboose; HRCX 5830 shop car; private car "Anthracite," former NYC coach.

Special Events: Rust-busters annual summer picnic.

Nearby Attractions/Accommodations: Pioneer Tunnel Coal Mine and Anthracite Technological Musuem at Ashland, Pennsylvania. Reading Company Technical and Historical Society at Leesport, Pennsylvania. Eckley Miner's Village at Hazelton, Pennsylvania.

Location/Directions: West Cressona yard is located in Cressona on routes 901 and 183, a short distance north of Schuylkill Haven and south of Pottsville, near the heart of the Southern Anthracite Field. The site is about 40 miles north of Reading and 45 miles east of Harrisburg.

     TRAIN

Site Address: Cressona, PA
Mailing Address: c/o Heritage Railcar, PO Box 334, Palmyra, PA 17078-0334
Telephone: (717) 838-3143

Pennsylvania, Gettysburg   **GETTYSBURG SCENIC RAIL TOURS**
Train ride
Standard gauge

AL SAUER

Description: Take a scenic ride along this beautiful former Reading Railroad line to Biglerville as you learn the crucial role of trains during the Civil War. You'll ride behind Vintage F-units through the Conewago Creek Valley and the First Day's Battlefield of Gettysburg National Military Park. Enjoy fine dining on the Cannonball Dinner Train, Saturday evenings.

Schedule: April through December: call or write for schedule. July and August: daily. Groups and charters welcome.

Admission/Fare: $9.00 to $34.99; varies by trip length, special events and dining.

Locomotive/Rolling Stock: Two F7s, nos. 81A and 81C, former Milwaukee Road; double-deck open air car; vintage open window and climate controlled cars available.

Special Events: Spring Blossom Excursion, Easter Bunny Train, Civil War Train Rides, Abe Lincoln Trains, Fall Foliage Excursions, Halloween Ghost Rides, Santa Claus Trains. Call or write for information.

Nearby Attractions/Accommodations: Gettysburg National Military Park, Eisenhower Farm, and numerous hotels and fine restaurants.

Location/Directions: From Harrisburg, Baltimore, or Washington D.C. take route 15 to U.S. 30 west to North Washington Street.

Site Address: 106 North Washington Street, Gettysburg, PA
Mailing Address: 106 North Washington Street, Gettysburg, PA 17325
Telephone: (888) 94-TRAIN
Fax: (717) 334-3562

BIG BEAR FARM
Train ride, museum
24" gauge

HOWARD J. WALTON

Description: A half-mile ride (eventually to be a one-mile loop) on a two-foot-gauge railroad through forest and pasture, where deer and other animals roam. Steam engines, gas engines, precision models, coal-mining equipment, an antique reciprocating-saw display, antique tractors, and other mechanical antiques, as well as a former Delaware & Hudson battery-powered coal-mine locomotive, a 1920 wooden Central Vermont caboose, and other railroad artifacts. Also located here is a performing-bear show, a game farm, and a museum.

Schedule: Call or write for information.

Admission/Fare: Adults $5.50; children $3.50.

Locomotive/Rolling Stock: 1922 Kraus steam engine; 1936 Whitcomb gas locomotive; gondolas.

Nearby Attractions/Accommodations: Ponderosa Pines Campground. Honesdale is the birthplace of the American railroad.

Location/Directions: Eight miles north of Honesdale. Take Route 6 west through Honesdale to Route 170 north, then follow signs for Big Bear Farm and the Ponderosa Pines Campground.

*Coupon available, see coupon section.

Site Address: RD 3, Honesdale, PA
Mailing Address: RD 3 Box 1352, Honesdale, PA 18431
Telephone: (717) 253-1794

Pennsylvania, Honesdale

STOURBRIDGE LINE RAIL EXCURSIONS
Train ride
Standard gauge

STOURBRIDGE LINE RAIL EXCURSIONS

Description: A 50-mile round trip from Honesdale to Hawley and Lackawaxen, through scenic Wayne and Pike counties along the Lackawaxen River, closely following the route of the old Delaware & Hudson Canal.

Schedule: Late March through mid-December: weekends.

Admission/Fare: Vary depending on excursion.

Locomotive/Rolling Stock: 1949 EMD BL2 no. 54, former Bangor & Aroostook.

Nearby Attractions/Accommodations: Claws and Paws Animal Farm, Wayne County Museum, glass museum.

Location/Directions: Northeastern Pennsylvania, 24 miles from Scranton.

*Coupon available, see coupon section.

Site Address: 303 Commercial Street, Honesdale, PA
Mailing Address: 303 Commercial Street, Honesdale, PA 18431
Telephone: (717) 253-1960 and (800) 433-9008
Fax: (717) 253-1517

Pennsylvania, Jim Thorpe

OLD MAUCH CHUNK MODEL
TRAIN DISPLAY
Layout
HO

OLD MAUCH CHUNK MODEL TRAIN DISPLAY

Description: This exciting HO scale model train display features 13 separate trains–some pulling as many as 50 railroad cars over nearly 1100 feet of track. The meticulously designed display also incorporates over 200 scale buildings, 100 bridges, 1000 street lights and moving automobiles into its scenery.

Schedule: Year round: call for current hours of operation.

Admission/Fare: Adults $3.00; seniors $2.00; children $1.00; age 4 and under are free.

Special Events: Many Jim Thorpe celebrations throughout the year.

Nearby Attractions/Accommodations: Many attractions and accommodations in the area.

Location/Directions: Located on the second floor of the Hooven Mercantile Company building on Route 209 next to the Railroad Station at Packer Park in historic Jim Thorpe.

*Coupon available, see coupon section.

Site Address: 41 Susquehanna Street (Route 209), Jim Thorpe, PA
Mailing Address: 68 White Pine Lane, Lehighton, PA 18235-9612
Telephone: (717) 325-4371

WANAMAKER, KEMPTON & SOUTHERN, INC.

Train ride
Standard gauge

WANAMAKER, KEMPTON & SOUTHERN, INC.

Description: A six-mile, 40-minute round trip through scenic Pennsylvania Dutch country over part of the former Reading Company's Schuylkill & Lehigh branch. Restored stations relocated from Joanna and Catasauqua, Pennsylvania; original circa 1874 Wanamaker station; operating HO-gauge model layout.

Schedule: May through October: Write for a detailed schedule.

Admission/Fare: Adults $5.00; children 3-11 $3.00; age 2 and under ride free.

Locomotive/Rolling Stock: No. 2, 1920 Porter 0-4-0T, former Colorado Fuel & Iron; no. 65, 1930 Porter 0-6-0T, former Safe Harbor Water Power; no. 7258 1942 GE diesel electric 45-ton, former Birdsboro Corp.; coaches nos. 1494 and 1474 and combine no. 408, all former Reading Company; coach no. 582, former Lackawanna; assorted freight cars and caboose, former Lehigh & New England; steel and wood cabooses, former Reading.

Special Events: Mother's Day Special, Father's Day Special, Sandman Special, Kids' Fun Weekend, Harvest Moon Special, Halloween Train, Santa Claus Special. Write for schedule.

Nearby Attractions/Accommodations: Hawk Mountain, Crystal Cave.

Location/Directions: Depot is located at Kempton on Routes 143 or 737, a short distance north of I-78. The site is 20 miles west of Allentown.

*Coupon available, see coupon section.

Site Address: 42 Community Center Road, Kempton, PA
Mailing Address: PO Box 24, Kempton, PA 19529
Telephone: (610) 756-6469

EAST PENN RAIL EXCURSIONS, INC.
Train ride
Standard gauge

WALTER M. MATUCH

Description: A one-hour train excursion through Amish and Mennonite farmlands of Berks County's East Penn Valley in the heart of the Pennsylvania Dutch country. Narrated 8-mile journey over former Reading Company branchline. Originally built in 1857 as Allentown and Auburn Railroad.

Schedule: Easter, June 5 through August 29: weekends and holidays only. October 2 through December 19: weekends only. Trains depart 12 and 2 p.m.

Admission/Fare: Adults: $8.00; seniors $7.00; children 2-12 $4.00; under age 2 are free.

Locomotive/Rolling Stock: GE 44-ton no. 57, former NY Dock; passenger cars nos. 838, 869, 834, former Reading; caboose no. 91545, former CRR-NJ.

Special Events: Easter Bunny, April 4-5, 12. Uncle Sam, July 4-5. Railroad Days, August 1-2. Santa Claus, November 29 through December 20.

Nearby Attractions/Accommodations: Crystal Cave, Hawk Mountain Bird Sanctuary, Mid-Atlantic Air Museum. WK&S Steam Train.

Location/Directions: Kutztown is located between Allentown and Reading off U.S. 222, Main Street.

*Coupon available, see coupon section.

Site Address: 110 Railroad Street, Kutztown, PA 19530
Mailing Address: PO Box 148, Kutztown, PA 19530-1048
Telephone: (610) 683-9202

KNOX & KANE RAILROAD
Train ride
Standard gauge

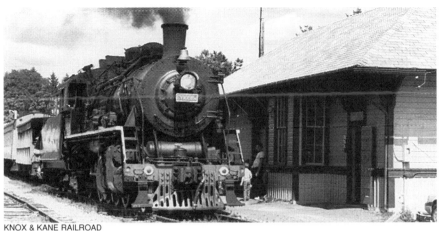

KNOX & KANE RAILROAD

Description: This line offers one round trip each operating day to Kane and the Kinzua Bridge over a former Baltimore & Ohio branch line. Passengers may board at Marienville for a 96-mile, 8-hour trip or at Kane for a 32-mile, 3½-hour trip. The 2,053-foot-long, 301-foot-high Kinzua Bridge, built in 1882 to span the Kinzua Creek Valley, was at the time the highest bridge in the world. It is on the National Register of Historic Places and is a National Historic Civil Engineering Landmark.

Schedule: June and September: Friday through Sunday. July and August: Tuesday through Sunday. Early October: Wednesday through Sunday. Depart Marienville 8:30 a.m.; depart Kane 10:45 a.m.

Admission/Fare: From Marienville: adults $21.00; children $13.50. From Kane: adults $15.00; children $8.50. Advance reservations suggested. Box lunches available by advance order, $4.70.

Locomotive/Rolling Stock: No. 38, 1927 Baldwin 2-8-0, former Huntington & Broad Top Mountain; no. 44, Alco diesel; no. 58, Chinese 2-8-2 built in 1989; Porter Switcher no. 1; steel coaches; open cars; two snack and souvenir cars.

Location/Directions: In northwestern Pennsylvania, about 20 miles north of I-80.

Site Address: Marienville, OH
Mailing Address: PO Box 422, Marienville, PA 16239
Telephone: (814) 927-6621
Fax: (814) 927-8750

Pennsylvania, New Freedom

NORTHERN CENTRAL RAILWAY
Train ride
Standard gauge

NORTHERN CENTRAL RAILWAY

Description: Enjoy entertainment, fine dining and dancing on a 3.5- to 4-hour ride through the scenic Codorus Creek Valley. See the historic Hanover Junction Station where Abraham Lincoln changed trains on his way to give the Gettysburg Address. Ride through the Howard Tunnel, the oldest railroad tunnel in service in the world. Pass by farms, forests and fields, as well as an emu farm.

Schedule: Year round: Saturday evenings and Sunday afternoons. Additional trips scheduled, call for details.

Admission/Fare: Dinner train $34.99 to $59.99.

Locomotive/Rolling Stock: 1959 FPA-4 no. 800, former CN and VIA; 1954 RSD-5 no. 1689, former CNW; vista dome; dance car; table cars; bar car; dining cars; private business cars available; more.

Special Events: Valentine's Day, Easter, Mother's Day, Father's Day, July 4th Firecracker Specials, Thanksgiving, Holiday Express, New Year's Eve.

Nearby Attractions/Accommodations: Stewartstown–Naylor Winery, Railroad; Jackson House Bed and Breakfast.

Location/Directions: New Freedom–I-83, exit 1, follow Route 851 west to New Freedom. Turn left on Penn Street, 1 block to the tracks. York–Business I-83 to Philadelphia Street, west to Pershing Avenue. Train departs from corner of Philadelphia and Pershing.

Site Address: 117 North Front Street, New Freedom, PA
Mailing Address: 117 North Front Street, New Freedom, PA 17349
Telephone: (800) 94-TRAIN and (717) 235-4000
Fax: (717) 235-5609
Internet: www.classicrail.com/ncry

NEW HOPE & IVYLAND RAILROAD
Train ride
Standard gauge

NEW HOPE & IVYLAND RAILROAD

Description: A 50-minute narrated round trip through the rolling hills and valleys of Bucks County. The train travels over the famous "Perils of Pauline" trestle and along the Delaware Canal.

Schedule: Year round: weekends. Mid-May through November: daily. Dinner train, Saturdays; brunch train, Sundays.

Admission/Fare: Adults $8.95; seniors $7.95; children 2-11 $4.95; under age 2, $1.95.

Locomotive/Rolling Stock: No. 40, 1925 Baldwin 2-8-0, former Lancaster & Chester; no. 3028, 1946 Alco 4-8-4, former National de Mexico; no. 614, 1948 Lima 4-8-4, former C&O; no. 2198, 1963 EMD GP-30, former Pennsy; no. 9423, EMD SW-1.

Special Events: Santa Express, Thanksgiving through Christmas.

Nearby Attractions/Accommodations: Mule barge rides, paddle boats, shopping, hotels.

Location/Directions: West Bridge Street, Route 179. Convenient access from I-95.

Site Address: 32 West Bridge Street, New Hope, PA
Mailing Address: 32 West Bridge Street, New Hope, PA 18938
Telephone: (215) 862-2332
Fax: (215) 862-2150

Pennsylvania, North East

LAKE SHORE RAILWAY
HISTORICAL SOCIETY, INC.
Museum, display
Standard gauge

RAY L. WAY

Description: A restored New York Central passenger station built in 1899 by Lake Shore & Michigan houses an extensive collection of displays. The museum is adjacent to Conrail and Norfolk Southern main lines. Passenger/freight station built in 1869 by LS&MS is also on the grounds.

Schedule: May 29 through September 6: Wednesdays through Sundays, holidays, 1 to 5 p.m. September 11 through October 30: weekends, 1 to 5 p.m.

Admission/Fare: Donations appreciated.

Locomotive/Rolling Stock: NYC U25B no. 2500; CSS&SB "Little Joe" electric locomotive no. 802; Heisler fireless 0-6-0; heavyweight Pullman sleeping cars; CB&Q heavyweight baggage no. 1530; GN lightweight diner no. 1251; passenger and freight cars.

Special Events: Wine Country Harvest Festival, September 25-26. Christmas-at-the-Station, December 4-5, 11-12. Call or write for additional special events.

Nearby Attractions/Accommodations: Peek 'n Peak Resort, Presque Isle State Park, Lake Erie nature walks, beaches and marinas.

Location/Directions: At Wall and Robinson Streets. Fifteen miles east of Erie, 2 miles north of I-90 exit 11, three blocks south of U.S. 20.

Site Address: 31 Wall and Robinson Streets, North East, PA
Mailing Address: PO Box 571, North East, PA 16428-0571
Telephone: (814) 825-2724
E-mail: lakeshorerwy@juno.com

Pennsylvania, Northbrook　　　**BRANDYWINE SCENIC RAILWAY**
Train ride
Standard gauge

BRANDYWINE SCENIC RAILWAY

Description: A 15-mile one-hour narrated round trip operating northbound and southbound from Northbrook Station through the Brandywine River Valley along the former Reading Wilmington & Northern Branch. A 20-mile 90-minute round trip is offered in the spring and fall. "Rails-to-the-River" combination train and canoe trips are available in the summer.

Schedule: Palm Sunday weekend through Christmas: weekends and holidays, 11 a.m., 1 and 3 p.m. Rails-to-the-River trips–Memorial Day weekend through Labor Day weekend: 9:30 a.m. and 1 p.m.

Admission/Fare: Adults $8.00; seniors $7.00; children 2-12 $6.00; under age 2 are free. Special events slightly higher. Group rates and caboose rental available.

Locomotive/Rolling Stock: 1924 Pullman-built steel open-window coaches, former Delaware, Lackawanna & Western; and more.

Special Events: Bunny Train Express, Spring Thaw, Fall Foliage, North Pole Express, Good Old Summertime, Murder Mysteries, Train Robberies.

Nearby Attractions/Accommodations: Brandywine River Museum, Brandywine Battlefield Park, Longwood Gardens, Valley Forge Park.

Location/Directions: On Northbrook Road, ½ mile north of Route 842, six miles west of West Chester, Pennsylvania. One hour west of Philadelphia.

*Coupon available, see coupon section.

Site Address: 1810 Beagle Road, Northbrook, West Chester, PA
Mailing Address: PO Box 403, Pocopson, PA 19366-0403
Telephone: (610) 793-4433
Fax: (610) 793-5144

THE FRANKLIN INSTITUTE
SCIENCE MUSEUM

Model railroad display, railroad display
Standard gauge

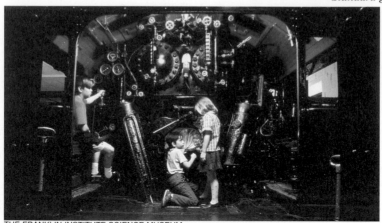

THE FRANKLIN INSTITUTE SCIENCE MUSEUM

Description: The centerpiece of Railroad Hall is a Baldwin Locomotive Works no. 60000, a 3-cylinder 4-10-2 built in 1926 and moved to the Franklin Institute in 1933. Two other locomotives share the room: Reading's Rocket of 1838 and a Reading 4-4-0 built in 1842. New to the exhibit is a G gauge model railroad that viewers can operate; it includes full-size signals actuated by the trains and a video hookup between the locomotive and a monitor in a half-size cab. The remainder of the museum collection covers the larger subject of U.S. industrial technology and science. There are models, films and quizzes on videodiscs, and a giant walk-through heart. The Franklin Institute is at 20th Street and The Parkway in downtown Philadelphia, within walking distance of Suburban Station.

Schedule: Year round: daily, 9:30 a.m. to 5 p.m.

Admission/Fare: Call or write for information.

Location/Directions: Center city Philadelphia.

       M 30th Street, ¼ mile away

Site Address: 222 N. 20th Street, Philadelphia, PA
Mailing Address: 222 N. 20th Street, Philadelphia, PA 19103
Telephone: (215) 448-1176
Fax: (215) 448-1235
E-mail: ewilner@fi.edu
Internet: sln.fi.edu/

EAST BROAD TOP RAILROAD
Train ride, museum
36" gauge

EBT COLLECTION

Description: The East Broad Top Railroad, chartered in 1856, is the last operating narrow-gauge railroad east of the Mississippi. The road hauled coal, freight, mail, express, and passengers for more than 80 years. Today the East Broad Top offers passengers a ten-mile, 50-minute ride through the beautiful Aughwick Valley with its own preserved locomotives; the ride takes passengers from the historic depot at Rockhill Furnace to the picnic grove, where the train is turned. On display are the railroad yard with shops, operating roundhouse, and turntable. Dates, times, and fares are subject to change. Call or write for latest information.

Schedule: June through October: weekends.

Admission/Fare: Adults $9.00; children $6.00.

Locomotive/Rolling Stock: 1911 Baldwin locomotive 2-8-2 no. 12; 1912 Baldwin locomotive 2-8-2 no. 14; 1914 Baldwin locomotive 2-8-2 no. 15; 1918 Baldwin locomotive 2-8-2 no. 17; all original East Broad Top RR.

Special Events: Fall Spectacular, Columbus Day Weekend.

Nearby Attractions/Accommodations: Raystown Lake.

Location/Directions: Pennsylvania Turnpike exit Willow Hill or Fort Littleton.

*Coupon available, see coupon section.

Site Address: Rockhill Furnace, PA
Mailing Address: PO Box 158, Rockhill Furnace, PA 17249
Telephone: (814) 447-3011
Fax: (814) 447-3256

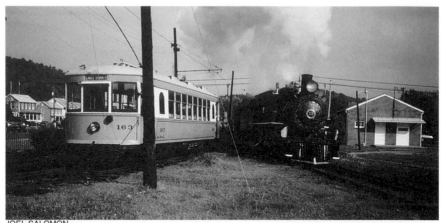

JOEL SALOMON

Description: A nonprofit, educational museum incorporated in 1962, the Rockhill Trolley Museum is composed of volunteers who preserve, restore, and maintain a collection of two dozen electric rail vehicles, about twelve of which are in operating condition. Trolleys operate over dual-gauge trackage on the former Shade Gap Branch of the East Broad Top Railroad for a 2-mile, 20-minute round trip. Standard-gauge street-cars meet narrow-gauge steam trains.

Schedule: Memorial Day weekend through third weekend of October: weekends and holidays, 11:30 a.m. to 4:30 p.m. Weekday bus groups by arrangement.

Admission/Fare: Adults $3.00; children 2-12 $1.00. Group rates available.

Locomotive/Rolling Stock: No. 163, 1924 Brill curveside car, former York Railways (Pennsylvania); no. 205 Brill "Bullet" former SEPTA; no. 1875 1912 open car from Brazil; 1899 snow sweeper former DC Transit.

Special Events: Fall Spectacular, Columbus Day weekend. Santa, December 12.

Nearby Attractions/Accommodations: Raystown Lake, Altoona Railroader Museum, East Broad Top Railroad.

Location/Directions: Twenty miles north of exit 13 of Pennsylvania Turnpike, adjacent to East Broad Top Railroad.

Site Address: Meadow Street, Rockhill Furnace, PA
Mailing Address: 1003 N. Chester Road, West Chester, PA 19380
Telephone: (610) 965-9028 and (814) 447-9576 weekends

KISKI JUNCTION RAILROAD
Train ride
Standard gauge

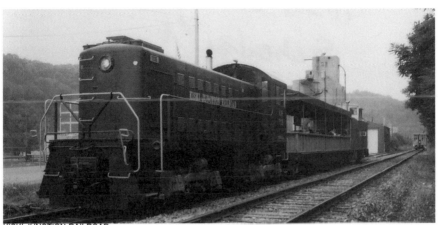

KISKI JUNCTION RAILROAD

Description: Ride along the Kiski River from Schenley to Bagdad on the former Pennsylvania Canal.

Schedule: Wednesdays 7 p.m. Weekends 2 and 4 p.m. Groups anytime by appointment.

Admission/Fare: Adults $7.00; seniors $6.00; children 4-12 $4.00.

Locomotive/Rolling Stock: Locomotive no. 7135.

Nearby Attractions/Accommodations: Tour Ed Mine.

Location/Directions: Thirty miles northeast of Pittsburgh on the Allegheny River. Route 66N out of Leechburg, two miles north to Schenley Road, turn west, travel 4 miles.

Site Address: 98 Railroad Street, Schenley, PA
Mailing Address: PO Box 48, Schenley, PA 15682-0048
Telephone: (724-) 295-5577
Fax: (724) 295-5588
E-mail: cebowyer@icubec.com

LAUREL HIGHLANDS RAILROAD
Train ride

LAUREL HIGHLANDS RAILROAD

Description: The Laurel Highlands Railroad offers a variety of rides along 62 miles of trackage from the former Pennsylvania and B&O Railroads. The Youngwood Historical Society maintains a railroad museum, also a hobby shop at both layovers.

Schedule: First weekend in May through Halloween: weekends and holidays. Call or write for schedule.

Admission/Fare: Adults $7/$8/$12; children 5-11 $5/$6/$9.

Locomotive/Rolling Stock: 1934 HK Porter 2-4-0; 1926 Jersey Central coaches.

Special Events: Scottdale Coal and Coke Festival, September. Civil War re-enactments, train robberies, Halloween Spook Nights, Santa Trains.

Nearby Attractions/Accommodations: Coal and Coke Museum, West Overton Museum, Seven Springs Mountain Resort, Zephyr Glen Bed and Breakfast, Pine Wood Acres Bed and Breakfast.

Location/Directions: Turnpike exit 8 (New Stanton) south on Route 119 south, to route 819 south, to Sheetz Convenience Store (next to parking lot).

Site Address: Scottdale, PA
Mailing Address: 25 South Broadway, Scottdale, PA 15683
Telephone: (724) 887-4568

Pennsylvania, Scranton

STEAMTOWN NATIONAL HISTORIC SITE
Train ride, museum, display
Standard gauge

KEN GANZ

Description: A 27-mile round-trip steam excursion will operate between Scranton and Moscow, Pennsylvania, beginning Memorial Day weekend through the first weekend of November. The site's visitor facilities include two museums, a theater, a visitor center, restored portions of the round-house, and a bookstore. Roundhouse tours, locomotive shop tours, preservation shop tours, and various additional programs will be offered. Many locomotives and cars are on display in the buildings and in the historic Delaware, Lackawanna & Western Railroad yards.

Schedule: Memorial Day through first weekend in November: daily 9 a.m. to 5 p.m. April through first weekend in January: shorter interpretive tours by train. Closed Thanksgiving, Christmas, New Year's.

Admission/Fare: Adults $7.00; seniors $6.00; children 6-12 $2.00; age 5 and under are free with paying adult. Separate fee for excursions. Combination rates and annual passes available.

Locomotive/Rolling Stock: Baldwin Locomotive Works 0-6-0 no. 26; Canadian Pacific 4-6-2 no. 2317; Canadian National 2-8-2 no. 3254.

Special Events: Memorial Day. Rail Expo, Labor Day weekend. Santa Train, Festival of Trees, The Polar Express, all in December.

Location/Directions: Downtown Scranton. Entrance is at intersection of Lackawanna and Cliff Avenues.

Site Address: Lackawanna and Cliff Avenues, Scranton, PA
Mailing Address: 150 S. Washington Avenue, Scranton, PA 18503
Telephone: (717) 340-5200 and (888) 693-9391
Internet: www.nps.gov/stea

ROADSIDE AMERICA

Description: Roadside America, an idea born in June 1903, is a childhood dream realized. From day to day and almost without interruption, this indoor miniature village has grown to be the largest and most beautiful of its type. More than 60 years in the making by Laurence Gieringer, it is housed in a new, modern, comfortable, air-conditioned building and covers more than 8,000 square feet of space. The display includes 2,570 feet of track for trains and trolleys and 250 railroad cars. O gauge trains and trolleys run among the villages.

Schedule: July 1 through Labor Day: weekdays, 9 a.m. to 6:30 p.m.; weekends, 9 a.m. to 7 p.m. September 6 through June 30: weekdays, 10 a.m. to 5 p.m.; weekends, 10 a.m. to 6 p.m.

Admission/Fare: Adults $4.00, senior citizens $3.75, children $1.50.

Location/Directions: I-78, exit 8, between Allentown and Harrisburg.

Site Address: Shartlesville, PA
Mailing Address: P.O. Box 2, Shartlesville, PA 19554
Telephone: (610) 488-6241

STEWARTSTOWN RAILROAD
Train ride
Standard gauge

RAY MCFADDEN

Description: A seven-mile, one-hour round trip between Stewartstown and the rural village of Tolna, in the Deer Creek Valley.

Schedule: May through September: Sundays and holidays. Call or write for schedule.

Admission/Fare: Adults $7.00; children 3-11 $4.00. Special trains slightly higher.

Locomotive/Rolling Stock: No. 9 35-ton Plymouth ML8 Plymouth 1943 Stewartstown Railroad; no. 10 44-ton diesel, FE 1946, former Coudensport and Port Allegany.

Special Events: Easter Bunny special, April. Country breakfast trains, June through November. Fall Foliage. Autumn Rail Rambles, November. Civil war re-enactments, October. North Pole Express/Santa Claus special, December.

Location/Directions: I-83 exit 1 (Shrewsbury) travel four miles east to Stewartstown.

*Coupon available, see coupon section.

Site Address: 21 W. Pennsylvania Avenue, Stewartstown, PA
Mailing Address: PO Box 155, Stewartstown, PA 17363
Telephone: (717) 993-2936

Pennsylvania, Strasburg

FRED M. DOLE

Description: This is a fantastic model railroad exhibit of Lancaster County with 18 operating O-gauge trains, 135 moving figures and vehicles, plus incredibly detailed hand-built scenery. See Lancaster County's Amish Country come to life on this 1700 square foot operating miniature village. Watch Amishmen at a barn raising. Stop by the 3-ring circus complete with aerial acts and operating amusement rides. The adjacent Strasburg Train Shop is filled with supplies for the hobbyist. The second floor has over 500 Thomas the Tank Engine & Friends items.

Schedule: March 27 through June 30: daily 10 a.m. to 5 p.m. July 1 through August 29: daily 10 a.m. to 6 p.m. August 30 through January 2: daily 10 a.m. to 5 p.m. Admission stops 30 minutes prior to closing.

Admission/Fare: Adults $4.00; children 5-12 $2.00; under age five are free.

Special Events: Canned Food Fridays, December 3, 10, 17. Admission is a can of food which benefits local church food banks.

Nearby Attractions/Accommodations: Strasburg Railroad, Railroad Museum of Pennsylvania, National Toy Train Museum, Pennsylvania Dutch Amish farmland.

Location/Directions: Located on Route 741 east of Strasburg, .25 mile west of the Strasburg Railroad. Strasburg is located three miles south of U.S. Route 30.

Site Address: Route 741 East, Strasburg, PA
Mailing Address: PO Box 130, Strasburg, PA 17579
Telephone: (717) 687-7911
Fax: (717) 687-6529
E-mail: choo2barn@aol.com
Internet: www.choochoobarn.com

NATIONAL TOY TRAIN MUSEUM

Description: Housed in a beautiful replica of a Victorian railroad station, this museum has one of the finest collections in the world of toy trains, dating from 1880 to the present. The collection includes items from such manufacturers as Ives, Lionel, American Flyer, LGB, and Marklin. Five operating layouts feature O, S, G, HO, and Standard gauge trains. A video on train subjects plays continuously. TCA national headquarters.

Schedule: May 1 through October 1: daily. April, November, and December: weekends and holidays. 10 a.m. to 5 p.m.

Admission/Fare: Adults $3.00; seniors $2.75; children 5-12 $1.50. Group discounts available.

Nearby Attractions/Accommodations: Strasburg Railroad, Railroad Museum of Pennsylvania, Choo Choo Barn

Location/Directions: From the Strasburg Station, travel east on route 741, turn north onto Paradise Lane past the Red Caboose Motel.

     M

Site Address: 300 Paradise Lane, Strasburg, PA
Mailing Address: PO Box 248, Strasburg, PA 17579
Telephone: (717) 687-8976
Fax: (717) 687-0742
E-mail: toytrain@traincollectors.org
Internet: www.traincollectors.org

**RAILROAD MUSEUM
OF PENNSYLVANIA**
Museum

RAILROAD MUSEUM OF PENNSYLVANIA

Description: The museum displays one of the world's finest collections of more than 90 steam, electric, and diesel-electric locomotives, passenger and freight cars, and related memorabilia. The 100,000-square-foot Rolling Stock Hall exhibits equipment dating from 1825 to 1992. Also hands-on activities and education center and Whistle Stop Shop.

Schedule: April through June, September and October: Mondays through Saturdays 9 a.m. to 5 p.m.; Sundays 12 to 5 p.m. July and August: Mondays through Thursdays 9 a.m. to 5 p.m.; Fridays and Saturdays, 9 a.m. to 7 p.m.; Sundays 11 a.m. to 5 p.m. November through March: Tuesdays through Saturdays, 9 a.m. to 5 p.m.; Sundays, noon to 5 p.m.

Admission/Fare: Adults 13-59 $6.00; seniors $5.50; students 6-12 $4.00; under age 6 are free; families $16.00. Group rates available.

Locomotive/Rolling Stock: See above.

Special Events: Charter Day, March 14. Pennsy Days, June 5-6. Reading Company Weekend, July 2-4. Railroad Circus Days, August 12-15. Halloween Lantern Tours, October 30. Home for the Holidays, December 11.

Nearby Attractions/Accommodations: Strasburg Railroad National Toy Train Museum, Choo Choo Barn, Pennsylvania Dutch attractions.

Location/Directions: Ten miles east of Lancaster on Route 741.

Site Address: 300 Gap Road, Route 741 East, Strasburg, PA
Mailing Address: PO Box 15, Strasburg, PA 17579
Telephone: (717) 687-8628
Fax: (717) 687-0876
E-mail: frm@redrose.net
Internet: www.rrhistorical.com/frm

STRASBURG RAILROAD
Train ride, dinner train
Standard gauge

G. FRED BARTELS

Description: A nine-mile, 45-minute round trip from Strasburg to Paradise. Train travels through lush farmlands and turns around adjacent to the Amtrak main line. The Strasburg Rail Road, one of the oldest and busiest steam tourist railroads in the country, displays a large collection of historic cars and locomotives.

Schedule: April through October: daily. Dinner Train Service–July through August: Thursdays through Sundays, 7 p.m.; September through October, May, and June: weekends. Call for reservations and information. Complete timetables are sent upon request.

Admission/Fare: Adults $8.00 and up; children $4.00 and up. Group rates available.

Locomotive/Rolling Stock: Open-platform wooden combine and coaches; "Hello Dolly" open observation car; first-class service including food and beverages aboard parlor "Marian." Lunch served on full-service diner "Lee Brenner" on hourly trains. No. 31, 1908 Baldwin 0-6-0 and no. 89, 1910 Canadian 2-6-0, former Canadian National; no. 90, 1924 Baldwin 2-10-0, former Great Western; more.

Special Events: Easter Bunny Trains, Halloween Ghost Trains, Santa Claus Trains, Thomas the Tank Engine Event.

Location/Directions: On Route 741 one mile east of the town of Strasburg.

Radio frequency: 161.235

Site Address: Route 741, Strasburg, PA
Mailing Address: PO Box 96, Strasburg, PA 17579
Telephone: (717) 687-7522
Fax: (717) 687-6194
E-mail: srrtrain@ptd.net
Internet: www.800padutch.com/srr.html

Pennsylvania, Washington

PENNSYLVANIA TROLLEY MUSEUM
Train ride, museum, display
5'2½" gauge, standard gauge

SCOTT R. BECKER

Description: A three-mile round trip trolley ride, guided carbarn tour, "Pennsylvania's Trolley Neighborhoods" exhibit, theater, gift shop and picnic area. Trolley ride is very scenic, following a creek and loop at one end.

Schedule: April through December: weekends, 11 a.m. to 5 p.m. Memorial Day through Labor Day and December 26-31: daily, 11 a.m. to 5 p.m.

Admission/Fare: Adults $6.00; seniors $5.00; children 2-15 $3.50. Group rates available with advance reservations.

Locomotive/Rolling Stock: New Orleans "Streetcar Named Desire"; trolleys from Pittsburgh, Johnstown, and Philadelphia. Trolley work equipment and rare 1930 Baldwin-Westinghouse diesel locomotive on display.

Special Events: Trolley Fair, June 26-27. Old Pittsburgh Days, July 24-25. Pumpkin Patch Trolley, October 9-10, 16-17. Santa Trolley, November 26-28, December 4-5, 11-12. Trolleys & Toy Trains, December 18-19, 26-31.

Nearby Attractions/Accommodations: Meadowcroft Museum of Rural Life, LeMoyne House, Ladbroke Meadows Racetrack.

Location/Directions: I-79 to exit 8 (Meadow Lands), follow signs. Thirty miles southwest of Pittsburgh.

*Coupon available, see coupon section.

Site Address: 1 Museum Road, Washington, PA
Mailing Address: 1 Museum Road, Washington, PA 15301-6133
Telephone: (724) 228-9256 and (877) PA-TROLLEY
Fax: (724) 228-9675
E-mail: ptm@pa-trolley.org
Internet: www.pa-trolley.org

Pennsylvania, Wellsboro

TIOGA CENTRAL RAILROAD
Train ride, dinner train
Standard gauge

RICH STOVING

Description: Tioga Central Railroad operates excursion and dinner trains on weekends. Enjoy a 24-mile round trip through beautiful country with excellent scenic views or a 42-mile round trip on our elegant dinner train. Dinner is prepared on the train.

Schedule: May 9 through October 17: weekends, departures at 11 a.m., 1, and 3 p.m. Dinner train–June 5 through October 23: Saturdays 5:30 p.m.

Admission/Fare: Adults $10.00; seniors $9.00; children 6-12 $5.00. Dinner train–$30.00 per person.

Locomotive/Rolling Stock: Alco S2 no. 14; Alco RS1 no. 62; Alco RS3 no. 506; PRR P70; CNR coaches, club car; diner car.

Special Events: Wellsboro Rail Days, October 23-24.

Nearby Attractions/Accommodations: Pennsylvania "Grand Canyon," Ives Run Recreation Area, covered wagon rides, hiking, hunting, fishing, rafting.

Location/Directions: Three miles north of Wellsboro at intersection of State 287 and U.S. 6.

*Coupon available, see coupon section.

Radio frequency: 160.725

Site Address: Muck Road, Wellsboro Junction, PA
Mailing Address: PO Box 269, Wellsboro, PA 16901
Telephone: (570) 724-0990
E-mail: infor@tiogacentral.com
Internet: www.tiogacentral.com

LYCOMING COUNTY HISTORICAL SOCIETY

Description: The Shempp toy-train collection is one of the finest in the country. More than 337 complete trains, 100 individual engines (12 are one-of-a-kind), and two working model layouts are on display. Exhibit includes items in L, TT, N, OO, HO, O, and 1 gauges; Lionel, American Flyer, Marx, Ives, and American Model Train Company pieces; an American Flyer Mayflower; a copper-and-gold-finished GG1; and American Flyer S-gauge displays.

Schedule: May 1 through October 31: Tuesdays through Fridays, 9:30 a.m. to 4 p.m.; Saturdays, 11 a.m. to 4 p.m.; Sundays, 1 to 4 p.m. November 1 through April 30: Tuesdays through Fridays, 9:30 a.m. to 4 p.m.; Saturdays, 11 a.m. to 4 p.m. Closed major holidays.

Admission/Fare: Adult $3.50; seniors, AARP/AAA $3.00; children $1.50.

Special Events: Toy Train Expo, December 12-13, noon to 4 p.m. Area collectors have displays and layouts throughout the museum.

Nearby Attractions/Accommodations: Little League Museum, Jenetti Hotel, amusement park, Reptile Land.

Site Address: 858 West Fourth Street, Williamsport, PA
Mailing Address: 858 West Fourth Street, Williamsport, PA 17701-5824
Telephone: (717) 326-3326

**Rhode Island, Newport
Connecticut, Essex**

DINNER TRAINS OF NEW ENGLAND
Dinner train

NEWPORT DINNER TRAIN

Description: Experience a scenic train ride while dining on fine cuisine, such as our award-winning baby back ribs.

Schedule: May through November/December: Fridays through Sundays, dinner.

Admission/Fare: $39.95 plus tax and gratuity. First class add $5.00. Entertainment add $10.00 per person.

Locomotive/Rolling Stock: Newport G.E. 1943 diesel.

Special Events: Murder Mystery, Comedy Wedding or Great Train Robbery.

Nearby Attractions/Accommodations: Newport–Historic downtown, mansions.

Location/Directions: Newport, Rhode Island–19 America's Cup Avenue.

*Coupon available, see coupon section.

Site Address: 19 America's Cup Avenue, Newport, RI
Mailing Address: PO Box 1081, Newport, RI 02840
Telephone: (800) 398-RIBS
Fax: (401) 841-8724
Internet: www.newportdinnertrain.com

South Carolina, Winnsboro

SOUTH CAROLINA RAILROAD MUSEUM
Train ride, museum
Standard gauge

MATT CONRAD

Description: This museum offers a 7-mile, 45-minute round trip between Rockton and Greenbrier on a portion of the museum's 12-mile long rail line, which was originally operated by the Rockton-Rion Railway. As track rebuilding progresses, the trip will be extended; please write for further details. Founded in 1973, the museum features exhibits in some of its pieces of rolling stock. Guided tours, which include the interior of the former Seaboard office car "Norfolk" dining car no. 3157 and Railway Post Office car no. 27 are also given.

Schedule: May through October: first and third Saturday of each month, 9:45 a.m. to 3:30 p.m. Charter trips available.

Admission/Fare: Adults $5.00; children 2-16 $3.00. Open-air car add $1.00. Infants not occupying seat ride free.

Locomotive/Rolling Stock: No. 44, 1927 Baldwin 4-6-0, former Hampton & Branchville; no. 76, 1949 45-ton Porter diesel, and no. 82, 1941 45-ton General Electric, both former U.S. Army Transportation Corps; more.

Special Events: Easter Bunny Train, April 3. Railfan Weekend, April 17-18. Caboose Day, July 3. Santa Train, November 27-28, December 4.

Nearby Attractions/Accommodations: Lake Wateree, River Banks Zoo, Days Inn, Ramada Inn.

Location/Directions: Junction of Highways 34 and U.S. 321.

Radio frequency: 151.865

Site Address: 110 Industrial Park Road, Winnsboro, SC
Mailing Address: PO Box 7246, Columbia, SC 29202
Telephone: (800) 968-5909
E-mail: imconrad@infoave.net
Internet: www.scrm.org

**BLACK HILLS
CENTRAL RAILROAD**
*Train ride
Standard gauge*

SOUTH DAKOTA DEPT. OF TOURISM

Description: Passengers can take a two-hour round trip journey between Hill City and Keystone Junction. Experience a ride from the past as you travel through the Black Hills, seeing the old mine sights and Harney Peak.

Schedule: Mid-May through early October: daily. Trains added during summer season. Call or write for information.

Admission/Fare: Adults $16.00; children 4-14 $10.00; age 3 and under are free. Group rates available for parties of 20 and up.

Locomotive/Rolling Stock: 1926 Baldwin 2-6-2 no. 104 saddle tank; 1919 Baldwin 2-6-2 no. 7; 1880s-1910 passenger cars.

Special Events: Railroad Days, last weekend of June.

Nearby Attractions/Accommodations: Mt. Rushmore and Crazy Horse Monuments.

Location/Directions: Highway 16/385, 24 miles south of Rapid City or Keystone, Highway 16A.

Site Address: 222 Railroad Avenue, Hill City, SD
Mailing Address: PO Box 1880, Hill City, SD 57745
Telephone: (605) 574-2222
Fax: (605) 574-4915
E-mail: office@1880train.com
Internet: www.1880train.com

PRAIRIE VILLAGE
Train ride, dinner train, museum, display
Standard gauge, 24" gauge

BILL NOLAN

Description: Prairie Village is a collection of turn-of-the-century buildings assembled from area towns. There are steam traction engines, gas tractors and displays of farm equipment. There is a two-mile loop of track used for passenger rides. Buildings include the Wentworth Depot and Junius Depot.

Schedule: Museum–May through September: daily, 9 a.m. to 6 p.m. Train–Sundays, Railroad Days, and Jamboree.

Admission/Fare: Museum–$5.00. Train–$3.00.

Locomotive/Rolling Stock: No. 29, 0-6-0, and no. 11, 0-4-0, former D&NE; GE 80-ton diesel; Russell snow plow; no. 7403 C&NW combination coach/baggage car; IC steel caboose.

Special Events: Railroad Days, June. Fall Jamboree, late August.

Nearby Attractions/Accommodations: Lake Herman State Park.

Location/Directions: Two miles west of Madison. From Sioux Falls, take I-29 north to the Madison/Coleman exit, then travel west on Highway 34 to Madison.

Site Address: West Highway 34, Madison, SD
Mailing Address: PO Box 256, Madison, SD 57042-0256
Telephone: (800) 693-3644 and (605) 256-3644
Fax: (605) 256-2798
Internet: www.prairievillage.org

356

WHETSTONE VALLEY EXPRESS

Train ride, dinner train, museum, layout
Standard gauge

WHETSTONE VALLEY EXPRESS

Description: A 20-mile round trip from Milbank to Corona over former Milwaukee Road branch. Dinner in the diner is available. The train is operated by the common carrier Sisseton Milbank Railroad in conjunction with the Whetstone Valley Railroad Historical Society.

Schedule: May 1 through October 15.

Admission/Fare: Adults $14.00; children $9.00. Dinner is additional.

Locomotive/Rolling Stock: 1954 EMD SW1200 no. 627; 1953 EMD SW1200 no. 561; GE 45-ton no. 992; caboose no. 992298; caboose no. 992299; dining car no. 756; coach no. 2111; coach no. 993; combination car no. 2705; caboose no. 991879; mail storage car no. 257.

Special Events: 15th Annual Train Festival, August 14-15.

Nearby Attractions/Accommodations: Hartford Beach State Park.

Location/Directions: Site is 126 miles north of Sioux Falls, 180 miles west of Minneapolis and 126 miles south of Fargo.

*Coupon available, see coupon section.

TRAIN   Fargo, ND   **Radio frequency:** 466.950

Site Address: Lake Farley Depot, Milbank, SD
Mailing Address: PO Box 631, Milbank, SD 57252
Telephone: (605) 432-5505 and (800) 675-6656
Fax: (605) 432-9463

CHATTANOOGA CHOO CHOO
Museum, display

CHATTANOOGA CHOO CHOO

Description: Opened in 1909 as the Southern Railway's Terminal Station, this depot welcomed thousands of travelers during the golden age of railroads. Today, the restored station is the heart of the Chattanooga Choo Choo Holiday Inn, a 30-acre complex with a full range of entertainment. Forty-eight passenger cars are part of the 360-room hotel; three passenger cars serve as a bar, formal restaurant, and meeting/banquet room.

Schedule: Season 1–Sundays through Saturdays, 10 a.m. to 8 p.m. Season 2–Mondays through Saturdays, 6 to 10 p.m. Call or write for current schedule.

Admission/Fare: Adults $2.00; children $1.00; under age 6 are free.

Locomotive/Rolling Stock: Five to eight trains running in museum.

Special Events: Victorian Holidays Open House, December.

Nearby Attractions/Accommodations: Tennessee Aquarium, IMAX Theater, Southern Belle Riverboat, Rock City, Ruby Falls.

Location/Directions: I-24 exit 178, take South Broad Street split and follow signs to Choo Choo.

Site Address: Chattanooga Choo Choo Holiday Inn
Mailing Address: 1400 Market Street, Chattanooga, TN 37402
Telephone: (423) 266-5000
Fax: (423) 265-4635
E-mail: choochoo.com
Internet: www.choochoo.com

TENNESSEE VALLEY RAILROAD
Train ride, museum, display
Standard gauge

STEVEN R. FREER

Description: A 6-mile, 45-minute round trip, much on original ET&G roadbed, across Chickamauga Creek and Tunnel Boulevard and through 986-foot-long Missionary Ridge Tunnel to East Chattanooga Depot, where a shop, turntable, displays, and active steam-locomotive repair shop are located. Tour of caboose, display car, theater car, diner, Pullmans, and various steam and diesel locomotives; Grand Junction Depot; large gift shop; audio-visual show; outside exhibits.

Schedule: April, May, September, and October: daily, 10 a.m. to 1:30 p.m. June through August: daily, 10 a.m. to 5 p.m. April through November: Saturdays 10 a.m. to 5 p.m.; Sundays 12 to 5 p.m.

Admission/Fare: Adults $8.75/$13.75; children 3-12 $4.75/$9.50. Group rates and charters available.

Locomotive/Rolling Stock: Nos. 1824 and 1829 EMD diesels, former U.S. Army; no. 610, 1952 Baldwin 2-8-0, and nos. 8669 and 8677, Alco RSD-1 diesels, former U.S. Army; no. 349, 1891 Baldwin 4-4-0, former Central of Georgia; no. 509, 1910 Baldwin 4-6-0, former Louisiana & Arkansas; no. 630, 1904 Alco 2-8-0, and no. 4501, 1911 Baldwin 2-8-2, both former Southern Railway; no. 913, Alco RS-1, former Hartford & Slocomb; no. 36, Baldwin VO1000, former U.S. Air Force; more.

Location/Directions: I-75 exit 4, Highway 153, 1.5 miles west.

M arm TRAIN MasterCard   **Radio frequency: 160.425**

Site Address: 4119 Cromwell Road, Chattanooga, TN
Mailing Address: 4119 Cromwell Road, Chattanooga, TN 37421-2119
Telephone: (423) 894-8028
Fax: (423) 894-8029
Internet: www.tvrail.com

COWAN RAILROAD MUSEUM

Description: The former station is now a museum housing a re-creation of a turn-of-the-century telegraph operator's office, various artifacts, and an HO scale model of the Cowan Pusher District. Nearby the CSX line from Nashville to Chattanooga (once Nashville, Chattanooga & St. Louis, later Louisville & Nashville) climbs over Cumberland Mountain south of Cowan. The grades are steep enough to require helpers in each direction; they are added to southbound trains at Cowan.

Schedule: May 1 through October 31: Thursdays through Saturdays, 10 a.m. to 4 p.m.; Sundays 1 to 4 p.m.

Admission/Fare: Donations appreciated.

Location/Directions: I-24 exit 135, travel west 12 miles on U.S. 41A/64.

  ♿ P M

Site Address: Cowan, Tennessee
Mailing Address: PO Box 53, Cowan, TN 37318
Telephone: (615) 967-7365

**CASEY JONES MUSEUM
AND TRAIN STORE**
Museum, layout
HO, O27

CASEY JONES MUSEUM AND TRAIN STORE

Description: Visit the home and railroad museum of Casey Jones. Casey
was living in this home at the time of his death in 1900. There are
three layouts on display in the 1800s baggage car and a replica of no.
382, Casey's engine, along with souvenirs and a hobby shop.

Schedule: Year round: daily, 8 a.m. to 9 p.m. Closed Easter, Thanksgiving,
and Christmas.

Admission/Fare: Adults $4.00; seniors $3.50; children 6-12 $3.00; children
age 5 and under are free. Lifetime passes available.

Locomotive/Rolling Stock: Rogers 4-6-0 locomotive; 1800s M&O baggage
car; IC caboose you can sleep in; 1890s sleeper car; HO and O27 model
train display.

Special Events: Casey Jones week, April 30 through May 6; Casey Jones
Hot Air Balloon Classic, October 16-18.

Nearby Attractions/Accommodations: State park, Shiloh National Military
Park, Home of Buford Pusser, Adamsville.

Location/Directions: I-40 exit 80A onto 45, 45 seconds off Highway 45,
look for caboose in the sky.

*Coupon available, see coupon section.

Site Address: 30 Casey Jones Lane, Jackson, TN
Mailing Address: 56 Casey Jones Lane, Jackson, TN 38305
Telephone: (901) 668-1222
Fax: (901) 664-7782

Tennessee, Jackson

NASHVILLE, CHATTANOOGA & ST. LOUIS DEPOT AND RAILROAD MUSEUM
Museum, display, layout
HO

MOORE STUDIOS, JACKSON, TENNESSEE

Description: The restored NC&StL Depot features a museum that reflects Jackson's history as West Tennessee's railroad hub. A working scale model depicts local railroad heritage. An Amtrak dining car, which seats up to 48 diners, can be rented for catered parties.

Schedule: Year round: Mondays through Saturdays 10 a.m. to 3 p.m.

Admission/Fare: Free.

Locomotive/Rolling Stock: Former FEC (Bunn 1947) dining car, Ft. Matanzas; Southern caboose X421; C&O caboose 2255.

Nearby Attractions/Accommodations: Brooks Shaw's Old Country Store, Historic Casey Jones Home and Railroad Museum, Pinson Mounds State Archaeological Area, Cypress Grove Nature Park, Chickasaw Rustic State Park, Pringles Park-Home of West Tennessee Diamond Jaxx baseball.

Location/Directions: Turn off Highway 45 bypass onto Martin Luther King Drive at the Jackson Main Post Office and go one block to South Royal Street. Turn right, proceed one block, depot is on the left.

Site Address: 582 South Royal Street, Jackson, TN
Mailing Address: PO Box 2508, Jackson, TN 38302
Telephone: (901) 425-8223
Fax: (901) 425-8589

Tennessee, Knoxville/Oak Ridge

**SOUTHERN APPALACHIA
RAILWAY MUSEUM**
Train ride, museum, display
Standard gauge

CHRIS WILLIAMS

Description: An 11-mile, 1.5-hour train ride aboard cabooses and air-conditioned coaches. Train travels former Southern Railway branch line through the U.S. Department of Energy K-25 site.

Schedule: Spring, summer, fall: trains run on select weekends. Call for schedule. Charters available. Reservations recommended. Viewing of equipment at other times by appointment.

Admission/Fare: Adults $10.00; children age 12 and under $7.50; toddlers and infants not occupying a seat are free.

Locomotive/Rolling Stock: 1949 Pullman sleeper car no. 2206 "Roanoke Valley"; 1926 Pullman dining car no. 3164; ACF coach no. 663, former Central of Georgia; baggage/commissary no. 543; 1928 RPO American Car and Foundry no. 34; caboose X261; 1947 Budd coach no. 664 "Fort Oglethorpe," former Central of Georgia; caboose no. 6487, former Louisville & Nashville; caboose no. 9990, former Oneida & Western; boxcar, former Boston & Maine.

Nearby Attractions/Accommodations: American Museum of Science and Industry, Museum of Appalachia, Great Smoky Mountains National Park.

Location/Directions: I-40, exit 356, turn north on Highway 58. Six miles to the East Tennessee Technology Park.

Radio frequency: 160.425

Site Address: Knoxville, TN
Mailing Address: PO Box 5870, Knoxville, TN 37928
Telephone: (423) 241-2140

BROADWAY DINNER TRAIN
Dinner train
Standard gauge

BROADWAY DINNER TRAIN

Description: Antique refurbished train that serves dinner on a 2.5-hour ride through Nashville suburbs and countryside every Friday and Saturday evening. A four-course meal is served with four entrees to choose from. Nashville singers/songwriters entertain in the two lounge cars.

Schedule: Fridays and Saturdays, 7 p.m. departure.

Admission/Fare: $59.95 plus tax.

Locomotive/Rolling Stock: E8A no. 5764, former PRR; "Hollywood Beach" sleeper coach no. 800129, former Seaboard; coach no. 4067, former PRR; dome lounge no. 504, former Santa Fe; diner Dixie Flyer no. 6507, former Seaboard; diner Southwind no. 245, former Seaboard; more.

Special Events: Murder Mysteries, children's excursions, receptions. Call or write for schedule. We cater to corporate and tour groups.

Nearby Attractions/Accommodations: Hotels, restaurants, dock for river taxi, carousel, Riverfront Park, Fort Nashboro.

Location/Directions: In Nashville. I-40 to exit 209B. Take Broadway to dead end at Riverfront Park. Train is to the right of park.

Site Address: 108 First Avenue South, Nashville, TN
Mailing Address: 108 First Avenue South, Nashville, TN 37201
Telephone: (615) 254-8000 and (800) 274-8010
Fax: (615) 254-5855
Internet: www.broadwaydinnertrain.com

Tennessee, Nashville

TENNESSEE CENTRAL
RAILWAY MUSEUM
Train ride, museum, display, layout
Standard gauge

BOB HULTMAN

Description: This is an operating museum sponsoring and operating up to a dozen excursion trains a year over the Nashville & Eastern Railroad. The museum also has a collection of 14 cabooses and several Budd stainless steel former ATSF coaches and former PRR buffet-diner car. The museum building is currently being renovated with museum displays, library/archives, audio-visual presentations and model railroad displays.

Schedule: Museum–Saturdays 9 a.m. to 3 p.m. except on those Saturdays the excursion train is operating. Train–periodic trips. Call or write for detailed information.

Admission/Fare: Museum–free. Excursions–$15.00 to $100.00.

Locomotive/Rolling Stock: Three locomotives; Pullman business car; coaches; slumber coach; buffet-diner car; baggage cars; boxcars; cabooses; maintenance of way cars; scale test car; motor cars; more.

Special Events: Excursions for Valentine's Day, Easter, Fall, Christmas, more.

Nearby Attractions/Accommodations: Broadway Dinner Train, downtown Nashville, Grand Ole Opry House, Opryland Hotel, Nashville Toy Museum, Music Row, 2nd Avenue North historic district, Nashville Arena.

Location/Directions: I-24/40 eastbound exit 212 Fesslers Lane. Left onto Fesslers, 0.5 miles to left on Lebanon Road, proceed 0.8 miles to right on Fairfield Avenue and follow signs to museum site.

       arm M

Radio frequency: 154.570

Site Address: 220 Willow Street, Nashville, TN
Mailing Address: 709 N. Lake Circle, Brentwood, TN 37027-7844
Telephone: (615) 781-0262
Internet: www.hsv.tis.net/~bgaddes/tcrm/tcrm.htm

DOLLYWOOD ENTERTAINMENT PARK
Train ride
Narrow gauge

RICHARDS & SOUTHERN

Description: The *Dollywood Express,* located in the Village area of Dollywood, takes visitors on a 5-mile journey through this scenic park, known as "the friendliest town in the Smokies." As passengers ride on the authentic, coal-fired steam train, they can catch a glimpse of the different areas of Dollywood: Daydream Ridge, Rivertown Junction, The Village, Craftsman's Valley, Country Fair, Showstreet, Jukebox Junction, and the Dollywood Boulevard. The *Dollywood Express* also takes visitors through replicas of a typical turn-of-the-century mountain village and logging community. During Christmas Festivals, the train is decorated with lights and features a special Christmas message for visitors.

Schedule: Thirty-minute rides every hour during park operating hours.

Admission/Fare: Adults $27.99; seniors $22.99; children 4-11 $19.99.

Locomotive/Rolling Stock: "Klondike Katie," a 1943 Baldwin 2-8-2, former U.S. Army no. 192; "Cinderella," a 1939 Baldwin 2-8-2, former U.S. Army no. 70; open-air passenger cars.

Special Events: Harvest Celebration, October. Smoky Mountain Christmas Festival, mid-November, December. School field trips.

Nearby Attractions/Accommodations: Numerous restaurants, lodging, shopping, and attractions in Pigeon Forge area.

Location/Directions: Call for directions.

Site Address: 1020 Dollywood Lane, Pigeon Forge, TN
Mailing Address: 1020 Dollywood Lane, Pigeon Forge, TN 37863-4101
Telephone: (423) 428-9488 and (800) DOLLYWOOD

LITTLE RIVER RAILROAD AND LUMBER CO. MUSEUM

Description: The museum is located on the original site of the Little River Lumber Company sawmill, housed in the original Walland Depot, which was moved to this site. The Little River Company logged huge tracts in what is now the Great Smoky Mountains National Park. Inside exhibits include over 200 vintage photos with text describing logging and railroad operations in detail, a history of train wrecks, and the full locomotive roster. The Little River was known for its innovative loco-motives, including the first 2-4-4-2 and the smallest Pacific ever built. Outside, Shay no. 2147 is displayed along with a vintage wood caboose and assorted logging and milling equipment.

Schedule: April, May, and September: weekends. June through August, and October: daily. November through March: by appointment only.

Admission/Fare: Donations appreciated.

Locomotive/Rolling Stock: Little River Shay no. 2147.

Location/Directions: Highway 321, near the western entrance to the Great Smoky Mountains National Park. Approximately 18 miles east of Maryville and 15 miles southwest of Pigeon Forge.

      M

Site Address: 7747 E. Lamar Alexander Parkway, U.S. 321, Townsend, TN
Mailing Address: PO Box 211, Townsend, TN 37882
Telephone: (423) 448-2211
Fax: (423) 448-2312

TEXAS PANHANDLE RAILROAD
HISTORICAL SOCIETY
Display
Standard gauge

TPRHS, JEFF FORD

Description: The TPRHS has cosmetically restored and maintains former Santa Fe Railway steam locomotive no. 5000. The 2-10-4, better known by its nickname "Madam Queen," was donated to the City of Amarillo, Texas, in 1957 and placed on display in front of the city's Santa Fe Depot.The TPRHS was formed in 1992 in part to preserve and interpret the locomotive as an important reminder of the Texas Panhandle's railroad heritage.

Schedule: Display–year round: outside, guided tours available by appointment or by chance when gate is open.

Admission/Fare: Free, donations appreciated.

Locomotive/Rolling Stock: 1930 Baldwin, Atchison, Topeka & Santa Fe Railway 2-10-4 no. 5000. The only locomotive of its class.

Special Events: Open House, Spring 1999 during annual Tri-State Train Show.

Nearby Attractions/Accommodations: Palo Duro Canyon State Park, Panhandle-Plains Historical Museum, 6th Street/Historic Route 66 Antique District, railfan hotspot where BNSF's transcontinental main line crosses BNSF Fort Worth-to-Denver main line.

Location/Directions: I-40, downtown exit north to 3rd Avenue, turn east. Located south of E. 3rd Avenue on Grant Street, downtown Amarillo.

    M

Site Address: E. 3rd and Grant Streets, Amarillo, TX
Mailing Address: PO Box 50422, Amarillo, TX 79159-0422
Telephone: (806) 352-8489
E-mail: info@tprhs.org
Internet: www.tprhs.org

SIX FLAGS OVER TEXAS RAILROAD
Train ride
Narrow gauge

SIX FLAGS OVER TEXAS RAILROAD

Description: This is a major theme park with trains running along the perimeter of the park.

Schedule: Summer months: daily. Spring and fall: weekends. Call for schedule.

Admission/Fare: $32.95 per person. Discounts for guests under 48 inches and seniors.

Locomotive/Rolling Stock: 1901 Dickson 0-4-0T converted 2-4-2 with tender, no. 1280; 1897 H.K. Porter 0-4-4T converted 2-4-2 with tender, no. 1754.

Special Events: Texas Heritage Crafts Festival, September. Holiday in the Park, November, December, January.

Nearby Attractions/Accommodations: Texas Rangers baseball, Six Flags Hurricane Harbor Water Park, Lone Star Park Race Track, Texas Motor Speedway, Dallas, Fort Worth.

Location/Directions: Located midway between Dallas and Ft. Worth in Arlington at the intersection of I-30 and Texas Highway 360.

Site Address: 2201 Road to Six Flags, Arlington, TX
Mailing Address: PO Box 90191, Arlington, TX 76004-0191
Telephone: (817) 530-6000
Fax: (817) 530-6044
Internet: www.sixflags.com

AUSTIN & TEXAS CENTRAL RAILROAD
Train ride
Standard gauge

AUSTIN & TEXAS CENTRAL RAILROAD

Description: Steam train ride through scenic Texas hill country. Downtown Austin boarding also available for historic ride through Austin.

Schedule: Hill Country Flyer–March through December: weekends, 10 a.m.; December: 2:30 p.m. Cedar Park departures–Saturdays 10 a.m. to 5:30 p.m. and Sundays 10 a.m. to 2 p.m. Downtown departures: 2 and 4 p.m.

Admission/Fare: Adults $17 to $38; children age 13 and under $9 to $19.

Locomotive/Rolling Stock: Southern Pacific 2-8-2 no. 786; six PRR P70 day coaches; three air-conditioned lounge cars.

Special Events: Twilight Flyers, selected weekends. Murder Mysteries, April and Halloween. Christmas.

Nearby Attractions/Accommodations: Highland Lakes, State Capitol, LBJ Library and Museum, wineries, Vanishing Texas River Cruise, Longhorn Caverns.

Location/Directions: Intersection of U.S. 183 and FM 1431 in Cedar Park, 19 miles northwest of downtown Austin. Downtown Austin train–intersection of 4th and Red River.

*Coupon available, see coupon section.

       M
 Radio frequency: 160.550

Site Address: Highway 183 and FM 1431 in Cedar Park, TX; 4th and Red River in downtown Austin, TX
Mailing Address: Box 1632, Austin, TX 78767
Telephone: (512) 477-8468 (reservations) and (512) 477-6377 (office)
Fax: (512) 477-8633
E-mail: ASTA786@juno.com
Internet: www.main.org/flyer

Texas, Dallas　　　　　**AGE OF STEAM RAILROAD MUSEUM**
Museum
Standard gauge

AGE OF STEAM RAILROAD MUSEUM

Description: One of the nation's finest collections of steam and early diesel era railway equipment. Complete heavyweight passenger train featuring restored MKT dining car and "Glengyle," the oldest all-steel, all-room Pullman.

Schedule: Wednesdays through Sundays, 10 a.m. to 5 p.m.

Locomotives/Rolling Stock: "Big Boy" no. 4018, 1942 Alco 4-8-8-4 and "Centennial" no. 6913, EMD DDA40X, both former Union Pacific; no. 1625, 1918 Alco 2-10-0, former Eagle-Picher Mining Co.; and more.

Admission/Fare: Adults $4.00; children age 12 and under $2.00.

Special Events: Whistle Fair, June 5-6. State Fair of Texas, September 24-October 17.

Nearby Attractions/Accommodations: The museum is located in Fair Park, a year-round collection of arts and cultural institutions housed in a restored art deco building originally constructed for the 1936 Texas centennial.

Location/Directions: Two miles east of downtown. I-30 westbound, exit 47A right onto Exposition Avenue, left on Party Avenue.

Site Address: 1105 Washington Street, Fair Park, Dallas, TX
Mailing Address: PO Box 153259, Dallas, TX 75315-3259
Telephone: (214) 428-0101
Fax: (214) 426-1937
E-mail: railroad@arlington.net
Internet: www.startext.net/homes/railroad

JIM CRUZ

Description: Largest railroad museum in the southwest with 46 cars, Renfert collection of fine railroad dining china, ghosts of travelers past, model railroad exhibits, mini train. The Union Pacific mini train holds 25 passengers and will operate from the museum through the Strand Historic District Model Train Shop.

Schedule: Daily 10 a.m. to 5 p.m. Seasonal schedule, call or write for information.

Admission/Fare: Adults $5.00; seniors $4.50; children 4-12 $2.50; under age 4 are free.

Locomotive/Rolling Stock: Forty-two pieces of equipment including steam locomotives; diesel-electric locomotives; passenger cars; cabooses; freight cars; maintenance of way cars.

Location/Directions: I-45 south, stay on Broadway, turn left on 24th Street. Turn left on Santa Fe Place, turn right into museum parking lot.

Site Address: 123 Rosenberg, Galveston, TX
Mailing Address: 123 Rosenberg, Galveston, TX 77550
Telephone: (409) 765-5700
Fax: (409) 763-0936
E-mail: railroad@tamag.tamu.edu
Internet: www.tamug.tamu.edu/rrmuseum

TARANTULA TRAIN

Description: Travel over 21 miles of the Cotton Belt Railroad, linking Grapevine and Fort Worth's historic stockyards; or take a ten-mile trek over a real working freight railroad that runs alongside the famous Chisholm Trail.

Schedule: Year round: seasonal.

Admission/Fare: Grapevine to Stockyards–adults $19.95; children $9.95. Stockyards to 8th Avenue–adults $10.00; children $5.50. Senior discounts on Wednesdays. Group rates available.

Locomotive/Rolling Stock: Cooke Locomotive Works 4-6-0 1896 steam locomotive no. 2248; 1925 day coaches nos. 206, 207, 208, 209, former Strasburg Railroad; 1927 touring coaches nos. 1808, 1819, former Wabash.

Special Events: Grapevine Heritage Festival and Grapefest. Stockyards Chisholm Trail Days and Pioneer Days. Train–Sweetheart Express, July 4 and Murder on the Tarantula.

Nearby Attractions/Accommodations: Grapevine–Camping at Lake Grapevine, near DFW Airport, wineries, Heritage Center, restaurants, specialty shops. Stockyards–Cowtown Coliseum, Stockyards Hotel.

Location/Directions: Grapevine–Hwy 114 or 121, north on Main Street. Stockyards–I-35W to westbound Northeast 28th Street, south on N. Main, left on Exchange Avenue.

Radio frequency: 160.215

Site Address: Cotton Belt Depot, 707 S. Main Street, Grapevine, TX
Site Address: Stockyards Station, 140 E. Exchange Ave., Fort Worth, TX
Mailing Address: 140 E. Exchange Avenue, A350, Fort Worth, TX 76106
Telephone: (800) 952-5717 and (817) 625-RAIL
Fax: (817) 740-1119
E-mail: Ttrain@onramp.net
Internet: www.tarantulatrain.com

TEXAS STATE RAILROAD
Train ride
Standard gauge

BILL LANGFORD

Description: Established in 1896, the Texas State Railroad now carries visitors on a 4-hour, 50-mile round trip across 24 bridges as it travels through the heart of the east Texas rolling pine and hardwood forest. Victorian-style depots are located in Rusk and Palestine.

Schedule: March through November: weekends. June and July: Thursdays through Sundays.

Admission/Fare: Round trip–adults $15.00; children $9.00. One-way–adults $10.00; children $6.00.

Locomotive/Rolling Stock: No. 201, 1901 Cooke 4-6-0, former Texas & Pacific no. 316; no. 300, 1917 Baldwin 2-8-0, former Texas Southeastern no. 28; no. 400, 1917 Baldwin 2-8-2, former Magma Arizona no. 7; no. 500, 1911 Baldwin 4-6-2, former Santa Fe no. 1316; no. 610, 1927 Lima 2-10-4, former Texas & Pacific no. 610.

Special Events: Murder on the Dis-Oriented Express, Great Texas Train Race, Special Dogwood Excursion, Civil War and World War II reenactments.

Nearby Attractions/Accommodations: Rusk–nation's longest foot bridge. Palestine–National Scientific Balloon Base.

Location/Directions: Highway 84, 2 miles west of downtown Rusk, 3 miles east of downtown Palestine.

Site Address: 2503 W. 6th, Rusk, TX
Mailing Address: Box 39, Rusk, TX 78785
Telephone: (800) 442-8951 and (903) 683-2561
Fax: (903) 683-5634
Internet: www.tpwd.state.tx.us/park/railroad/railroad.html

HISTORIC ORIENT SANTA FE DEPOT
Museum

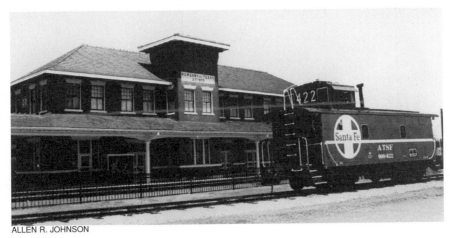

ALLEN R. JOHNSON

Description: This site educates and explains the history of railroads and its importance to the development of San Angelo and Concho Valley area of Texas.

Schedule: Summer–Thursdays through Saturdays 11 a.m. to 3 p.m.

Admission/Fare: Donations appreciated.

Locomotive/Rolling Stock: GE 44-ton center; ATSF caboose no. 999422.

Special Events: Cactus Jazz Series, January, March, May. Railfair, May. Fiesta del Concho, June. Fort Concho Frontier Day, June. Wild West Balloonfest, June and July 4th. Pops Concert and San Angelo State Park Gathering, September. Roping Fiesta, November. Santa's Santa Fe Christmas and Concho Christmas Celebration, December.

Nearby Attractions/Accommodations: San Angelo State Park, camping, Lake Nasworthy, Concho Park at Lake Ivie, Outlaws professional hockey, Angelo State Planetarium, restaurants, museums, specialty shops.

Location/Directions: East off Highway 87 south in downtown San Angelo.

♿ Ⓟ ✺ ☕ 📷 M

Site Address: 703 S. Chadbourne, San Angelo, TX
Mailing Address: 703 S. Chadbourne, San Angelo, TX 76903
Telephone: (915) 486-2140

TEXAS TRANSPORTATION MUSEUM

Description: Passengers enjoy a ⅓-mile caboose ride on the Longhorn & Western Railroad behind a 60-ton diesel. The track is being extended one mile. Santa Fe business car No. 404; heavyweight Pullman "McKeever"; Missouri Pacific transfer caboose; Union Pacific caboose; Southern Pacific station from Converse, Texas, with railroad displays and pictures; G gauge garden railroad; 5,000-square-foot display building with 100-foot-long HO model railroad; transportation toy display; fire trucks; antique automobiles and carriages; technology display.

Schedule: Train–Saturdays and Sundays, 12:30 to 3:30 p.m. departures every 45 minutes. Museum–Thursdays, Saturdays, and Sundays, 9 a.m. to 4 p.m.

Admission/Fare: Adults $3.00; children under age 12 $1.00.

Locomotive/Rolling Stock: Moscow Camden & St. Augustine no. 6; GE 44-ton no. 7071; Baldwin no. 4035 U.S. Army.

Nearby Attractions/Accommodations: San Antonio

Location/Directions: Site is located 2½ miles north of Loop 410, take Bwy or Wetmore exit, north of intersection of Starcrest and Wetmore.

Site Address: 11731 Wetmore Road, San Antonio, TX
Mailing Address: 11731 Wetmore Road, San Antonio, TX 78247
Telephone: (210) 490-3554

MARY IRVING

Description: Early Santa Fe and Missouri-Kansas-Texas station equipment and furniture, including a working telegraph for train orders. The depot museum houses a large collection of railroad artifacts and displays of early pioneer and railroading life. Research archives include a large collection of railroad timetables, passes, photographs and Santa Fe engineer's tracings for the Southern Division.

Schedule: Year round: Mondays through Saturdays, 10 a.m. to 4 p.m. and Sundays, 12 to 4 p.m.

Admission/Fare: Adults $2.00; seniors and children age 5 and older $1.00.

Locomotive/Rolling Stock: No. 3423, 1921 Baldwin 4-6-2, former Santa Fe; no. 2301, 1937 Alco, the oldest surviving Santa Fe diesel; steel caboose no. 1556, former Gulf, Colorado & Santa Fe; three section cars; steel caboose no. 140, former MKT; handcar, caboose, and boxcar, all former Missouri Pacific; World War II Pullman troop sleeper; an MKT (Glover Glade) Pullman sleeper (1917); former Santa Fe Chief Budd sleeper.

Special Events: Texas Train Festival, third weekend in September.

Nearby Attractions/Accommodations: Lake Belton, camping, bass fishing.

Location/Directions: I-35, exit Avenue H east to 31st Street.

*Coupon available, see coupon section.

        M arm 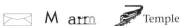Temple

Site Address: 710 Jack Baskin, Temple, TX
Mailing Address: PO Box 5126, Temple, TX 76505
Telephone: (254) 298-5172
Fax: (254) 298-5171
E-mail: mirving@ci.temple.tx.us
Internet: www.ci.temple.tx.us

WICHITA FALLS RAILROAD MUSEUM
Museum
Standard gauge

DAVID H. GAINES

Description: The museum is preserving the railroad history of Wichita Falls, Texas, and the surrounding area. Artifacts, displays, and the Wichita Falls Model Railroad Club HO gauge layout are housed in the historic Route Building. The museum's yard is located on the site of the Wichita Falls Union Passenger Station and is adjacent to the Burlington Northern Santa Fe's (former Fort Worth & Denver) Forth Worth to Amarillo main line.

Schedule: Year round: Saturdays, 12 to 4 p.m. and by appointment (unless temperature is below 32 degrees F or precipitation is falling).

Admission/Fare: Donations appreciated. Fee for special events.

Locomotive/Rolling Stock: FW&D 2-8-0 no. 304; MKT NW-2 no. 1029, FW&D RPO baggage no. 34; CB&Q power combine no. 7300; more.

Special Events: Zephyr Days Railroad Festival, last weekend in September. Depot Square Heritage Days, early October.

Nearby Attractions/Accommodations: Kell House Museum, Wichita Falls Police and Fire Museum, Texas Tourist Information Center, Econo Lodge, Holiday Inn Hotel & Suites, Radisson Inn at the Falls.

Location/Directions: Located on the east side of downtown Wichita Falls. From Holliday or Broad Streets, take 8th Street toward downtown. The museum's gate will be to the right at the end of the street.

 M

Site Address: 501 8th Street, Wichita Falls, TX
Mailing Address: PO Box 4242, Wichita Falls, TX 76308-0242
Telephone: (940) 723-2661 and (940) 692-6073

Utah, Heber City

HEBER VALLEY RAILROAD
Train ride
Standard gauge

STEVE BELMONT

Description: Experience history in motion aboard the Heber Valley Railroad. Visitors can choose between a 1-hour or 3.5-hour excursion across the farm land of the Heber Valley along the shore of Deer Creek and into the breathtaking Provo Canyon.

Schedule: May through October: daily. December through April: varies, call for schedule. Closed November.

Admission/Fare: 1-hour train–adults $9.00, children $6.00. 3.5-hour train–adults $17.00, children $10.00.

Locomotive/Rolling Stock: 1940 NW2 diesel; 1952 MRS1 diesel; 1953 Davenport 44-ton diesel; open-air cars; coaches; caboose.

Special Events: Blue Grass Express Train/Blue Grass music, summer. Murder Mysteries, summer. Thanksgiving trains, November. Christmas Trains, December.

Nearby Attractions/Accommodations: Park City Ski Resort, Alpine Forest, Cascade Springs, Provo River rafting, boating, fishing.

Location/Directions: U.S. 40 to Heber City, six blocks west of town.

Site Address: 450 South 600 West, Heber City, UT
Mailing Address: PO Box 609, Heber City, UT 84032
Telephone: (435) 654-5601 and (801) 581-9980
Fax: (435) 654-3709
E-mail: hebervalleyrr@shadowlink.net
Internet: www.hebervalleyrr.org

OGDEN UNION STATION

Description: Ogden Union Station is the home of the Spencer S. Eccles Railroad Center and the Utah State Railroad Museum. The newly remodeled and expanded museum houses a Union Pacific Northern no. 833, a Union Pacific Turbine X-26 and Centennial Locomotive 6916. The museum also includes the Wattis Dumke Model Railroad which features vignettes from many locations on the original transcontinental line and other displays.

Schedule: Mondays through Saturdays 10 a.m. to 5 p.m. Call for Sunday hours.

Admission/Fare: Adults $3.00; seniors $2.00; children under age 12 $1.00. Group discount available.

Locomotive/Rolling Stock: UP Turbine and Centennial locomotive; UP Northern locomotive no. 833.

Special Events: Hostlers Model Railroad Fair and Golden Spike Gem and Mineral Show, March. Railroad Festival, May. Handcar races, May and July.

       arm M

Site Address: 2501 Wall Avenue, Ogden, UT
Mailing Address: 2501 Wall Avenue, Ogden, UT 84401
Telephone: (801) 629-8446 and (801) 629-8583
Fax: (801) 629-8555

Utah, Promontory

GOLDEN SPIKE
NATIONAL HISTORIC SITE
Museum
Standard gauge

GOLDEN SPIKE NATIONAL HISTORIC SITE

Description: This is the spot where the famous Golden Spike ceremony was held on May 10, 1869, completing the nation's first transcontinental railroad. Exact operating replicas of the original locomotives are on display; these locomotives run to the Last Spike Site on their own power each morning (from April to the second weekend in October) and return to the enginehouse in late afternoon. In the Visitor Center are color movies and many exhibits. Park rangers are on hand to explain the importance of the railroad and the significance of the ceremony of 1869.

Schedule: May 25 through September 2: daily, 8 a.m. to 6 p.m. September 3 through May 24: 8 a.m. to 4:30 p.m. Closed Thanksgiving, Christmas, and New Year's Day.

Admission/Fare: Adults: $3.50; cars $7.00.

Locomotive/Rolling Stock: Full-sized operating replicas of Union Pacific 4-4-0 no. 119; and Central Pacific 4-4-0 no. 60, "The Jupiter."

Special Events: Annual Celebration, May 2. Annual Railroader's Festival, second Saturday in August. Annual Railroader's Film Festival and Winter Steam Demonstration, December 27-29.

Location/Directions: Thirty-two miles west of Brigham City, via Highways 13 and 83 through Corinne.

Site Address: Promontory, UT
Mailing Address: PO Box 897, Brigham City, UT 84302
Telephone: (801) 471-2209

381

TOOELE COUNTY RAILROAD MUSEUM
Train ride, museum
7.5" gauge

TOOELE COUNTY RAILROAD MUSEUM

Description: A mining and railroad museum.

Schedule: Memorial Day through Labor Day weekend: Tuesdays through Saturdays 1 to 4 p.m.

Admission/Fare: Free.

Locomotive/Rolling Stock: TVRR no. 11 Alco 2-8-0 consolidation; TVRR caboose no. 3; TVRR caboose no. 4; UP boxcar; military medical car; military dining car; TVRR snowplow.

Nearby Attractions/Accommodations: Benson Grist Mill at Stansburg Park, Donner Party Museum, Pony Express Station, Simpson Springs, hiking, mountain biking, motorcycling.

Location/Directions: From Salt Lake City–I-80 west to exit 99, take Highway 36 to Tooele, Vine Street east to Broadway.

Site Address: 35 N. Broadway, Tooele, UT
Mailing Address: 35 N. Broadway, Tooele, UT 84074
Telephone: (435) 843-2110 and (435) 882-2836

Vermont, Bellows Falls

GREEN MOUNTAIN RAILROAD
GREEN MOUNTAIN FLYER
Train ride
Standard gauge

GREEN MOUNTAIN RAILROAD

Description: Climb aboard and experience a journey into Vermont's rich history and scenic splendor. Ride the two-hour, 26-mile excursion in fully restored open-window coaches from the former Rutland and Jersey Central railroads.

Schedule: Call or write for information.

Admission/Fare: Call or write for information.

Locomotive/Rolling Stock: Alco RS 1 no. 405, former Rutland; EMD GP9 no. 1850, former Chesapeake & Ohio; EMD GP9 no. 1848, former Bangor & Aroostook; EMD GP9 no. 1851, former Norfolk Southern.

Special Events: Valentine's Day, February 14. Sugar on Snow, March 21. Easter Bunny, April 11. Mother's Day, May 10. Memorial weekend, May 23-25. Ludown Limited, July 4. Rutland Express, September 12. Santa Express, December 13, 19, 20.

Nearby Attractions/Accommodations: Basketville, Santa's Land, Vermont Country Store, Bellows Falls Fish Ladder.

Location/Directions: I-91 exit 5 to Bellows Falls route 5, north 3 miles.

Site Address: 8 Depot Street, Bellows Falls, VT
Mailing Address: PO Box 498, Bellows Falls, VT 05101
Telephone: (802) 463-3069 and (802) 463-9531
Fax: (802) 463-4084
E-mail: railroads@souer.net
Internet: www.virtualvermont.com/greenmountainrr

SHELBURNE MUSEUM
Museum, display
Standard gauge

SHELBURNE DEPOT

Description: This museum displays an extensive and internationally renowned collection of Americana housed in 37 historic buildings on a 45-acre site. The railroad exhibit features the restored 1890 Shelburne depot with a Central Vermont steam locomotive and the private car "Grand Isle." Nearby is former Woodstock Railroad steam inspection car "Gertie Buck." There is also a wooden replica of Baldwin's "Old Ironsides" of 1832 and a collection of railroad memorabilia. Other exhibits at the museum include a 220-foot sidewheel steamer, the *Ticonderoga*, which was moved overland from Lake Champlain, and collections of antiques, quilts, carriages, art, decoys, and tools.

Schedule: Late May through late October: daily, 10 a.m. to 5 p.m.

Admission/Fare: Adults $17.50; children 6-14 $7.00.

Locomotive/Rolling Stock: Locomotive no. 220; railcar Grand Isle.

Special Events: Lilac Festival, May. Apple Days, October. Celebrations of the Season, December.

Nearby Attractions/Accommodations: Vermont Teddy Bear Factory, Shelburne Farms.

Location/Directions: Site is located on Route 7, seven miles south of Burlington.

Site Address: Route 7, Shelburne, Vermont
Mailing Address: PO Box 10, Shelburne, VT 05482
Telephone: (802) 985-3346
Fax: (802) 985-2331
Internet: shelburnemuseum.org

EXMORE RAILROAD MUSEUM, INC.

Description: Museum and N&W caboose, display of PRR, B&O, NYP&N and many others.

Schedule: May 22: 10 a.m. to 5 p.m. September: 8 a.m. to 5 p.m. December 7: 8 a.m. to 5 p.m.

Admission/Fare: Free.

Locomotive/Rolling Stock: N&W caboose no. 557704.

Special Events: Town Yard Sale, 3rd Saturday in September. Santa Train, second Saturday in December.

Nearby Attractions/Accommodations: Eastern Shore Railway Museum, Kiptopeke State Park, Assateague State Park, Best Western.

Location/Directions: Turn off Route 13 bypass to Route 13 business Exmore, turn onto Willis Wharf Road, cross tracks, site on left.

  M

Site Address: Bank and Front Streets, Exmore, VA
Mailing Address: PO Box 1, Exmore, VA 213350
Telephone: (757) 442-4374

FAIRFAX STATION RAILROAD MUSEUM

Description: A restored Southern Railway depot rich in Civil War and local history. Clara Barton was a nurse here after the Second Battle of Manassas.

Schedule: Year round: Sundays, 1 to 4 p.m.

Admission/Fare: Adults $2.00; children $1.00; families $5.00.

Locomotive/Rolling Stock: Caboose N&W 518606.

Special Events: Annual Model Train Display, first weekend in December. Annual Civil War Day, Quilt Show, Art Show.

Nearby Attractions/Accommodations: Washington D.C., museums, Manassas Museum, Fairfax City Museum.

Location/Directions: Three miles south of Fairfax. Located ¼ mile from corner of route 123 (Ox Road) and Fairfax Station Road.

Site Address: 11200 Fairfax Station Road, Fairfax Station, VA
Mailing Address: PO Box 7, Fairfax Station, VA 22039
Telephone: (703) 425-9225 and (703) 278-8833
E-mail: ox6525@aol.com
Internet: www.fairfax-station.org/

U.S. ARMY TRANSPORTATION MUSEUM

Description: This military-history museum displays items of transportation dating from 1776 to the present. Inside the 15,000-square-foot museum are dioramas and exhibits; on five acres outside are rail rolling stock, trucks, jeeps, amphibious marine craft, helicopters, aircraft, and an experimental hovercraft.

Schedule: Year round: Tuesdays through Sundays, 9 a.m. to 4:30 p.m. Closed Mondays and federal holidays.

Admission/Fare: Free.

Locomotive/Rolling Stock: Steam locomotive 2-8-0 no. 607; steam locomotive 0-6-0 no. V-1923; ambulance ward car no. 87568; steam wrecking crane; 40-T and 50T flatcars; caboose; Berlin duty train cars.

Nearby Attractions/Accommodations: Colonial Williamsburg, Virginia Beach, Jamestown, Yorktown, Busch Gardens Theme Park.

Location/Directions: I-64 exit 250A.

    TRAIN

Site Address: Building 300, Washington Blvd., Fort Eustis, VA
Mailing Address: Building 300, Washington Blvd., Fort Eustis, VA 23604
Telephone: (757) 878-1115
Fax: (757) 878-5656
E-mail: bowerb@eustis.army.mil
Internet: www.eustis.army.mil/DPTMSEC/museum.htm

Virginia, Manassas

HISTORIC MANASSAS, INC.
1999 RAILWAY FESTIVAL
Presented by the Washington Post
Display

MARK MILLIGAN

Description: Attend this once-a-year festival and see living history, railroadiana vendors, modular exhibits in G, O, HO, and N scales, live railroad-related music, and excursion rides. Call or write for free brochure.

Schedule: June 5, 1999 10 a.m. to 4 p.m.

Admission/Fare: Free.

Locomotive/Rolling Stock: Full-size rail cars on exhibit, modern and antique.

Nearby Attractions/Accommodations: Historic Old Town Manassas, The Manassas Museum, hotels, shops, and restaurants.

Location/Directions: I-66 to route 28, south to Old Town Manassas.

Site Address: Manassas, VA
Mailing Address: 9431 West Street, Manassas, VA 20110
Telephone: (703) 361-6599
Fax: (703) 361-6942

EASTERN SHORE RAILWAY MUSEUM
Museum

JOHN E. BATES

Description: Restored 1920s Pennsylvania Railroad Station; original crossing shanty, toolshed, artifacts, gift shop. Home of Delmarva Chapter NRHS. Antique auto museum is also located on grounds.

Schedule: Year round: Mondays through Saturdays 10 a.m. to 4 p.m. and Sundays 1 to 4 p.m. November through March: closed Wednesdays.

Admission/Fare: $2.00; children under age 12 are free.

Locomotive/Rolling Stock: 1920s RF&P post office car; 1962 NP caboose no. 473; 1949 Wabash caboose no. 2783; Seaboard Airline diner car no. 8011; 1950 RF&P Fairfax River; 1927 Pullman "Diplomat" parlor/observation car.

Special Events: Parksley Festival, first Saturday in June. Santa Train, first Saturday in December.

Nearby Attractions/Accommodations: Chincoteague Island, Kiptopeke State Park, Ocean City.

Location/Directions: Midway between Chesapeake Bay Bridge Tunnel and Salisbury, Maryland. Route 13, 2 miles west on State Route 176.

     M

Site Address: 18468 Dunne Avenue, Parksley, VA
Mailing Address: PO Box 135, Parksley, VA 23421
Telephone: (757) 665-RAIL

OLD DOMINION RAILWAY MUSEUM

Description: This museum's collection includes a caboose, freight equipment, and track-maintenance equipment; a Richmond, Fredericksburg & Potomac baggage car contains exhibits on telegraphy, passenger depots, the Railway Express Agency, and railroad workers. Located in proximity to the 1831 birthplace of rail operations in Virginia.

Schedule: Year round: Saturdays, 11 a.m. to 4 p.m. and Sundays, 1 to 4 p.m.

Admission/Fare: Donations appreciated.

Locomotive/Rolling Stock: RF&P express car 185; David M. Lea & Co. 0-4-0T no. 2; SCL caboose 21019; Seaboard System boxcar 111935; Fairmont motor car.

Special Events: Floodwall Guided Walking Tours, second Sunday of each month 2 p.m.

Nearby Attractions/Accommodations: Downtown Richmond tourist area, Richmond Floodwall Promenade, James River boating, fishing, nature walks.

Location/Directions: I-95 , exit 73 (Maury Street). Turn right onto Maury Street, go two blocks. Turn left onto West 2nd Street, to right on Hull Street, to museum on right.

Site Address: 102 House Street, Richmond, VA
Mailing Address: PO Box 8583, Richmond, VA 23226
Telephone: (804) 233-6237
Fax: (804) 745-4735
Internet: www.odcnrhs.org/

Virginia, Roanoke

VIRGINIA MUSEUM OF TRANSPORTATION, INC.

Description: A large diesel and steam collection, a 4-tier O gauge model layout, archives, vintage trolleys, buses, carriages and cars.

Schedule: Year round: Sundays, 12 to 5 p.m.; Mondays through Saturdays, 10 a.m. to 5 p.m. January and February: closed Mondays.

Admission/Fare: Adults $5.25; seniors $4.20; children $3.15; under age 3 free.

Locomotive/Rolling Stock: No. 611, J Class 4-8-4, former Norfolk & Western; no. 4, 1910 Baldwin class SA 0-8-0, former Virginian Railway; no. 6, 1897 Baldwin class G-1 2-8-0, former N&W; no. 763, 1944 Lima class S-2 2-8-4, former Nickel Plate; no. 1, Celanese 0400 fireless locomotive; many diesels, City of Roanoke trolley, and D.C. Transit trolley; IT Presidential Business car, N&W Safety Car No. 418, N&W Dynamometer Car, Southern "Glen Summit" sleeping car, Southern "Lake Pearl" sleeping car, N&W Class PG passenger car.

Special Events: Cool Wheels Festival, August. Call or visit website for more events and exhibits.

Nearby Attractions/Accommodations: Blue Ridge Parkway, two national forests, two state parks on lakes, museums, zoo, and hotels.

Location/Directions: I-81 to I-581, exit 5 to downtown Roanoke.

*Coupon available, see coupon section.

           M

Site Address: 303 Norfolk Avenue SW, Roanoke, VA
Mailing Address: 303 Norfolk Avenue SW, Roanoke, VA 24016
Telephone: (540) 342-5670
Fax: (540) 342-6898
E-mail: vmt@rbnet.com
Internet: www.vmt.org

DAVE FRARY

Description: Broadway-designed layouts with computer lighting, collectibles, animations, hands-on exhibits, and over 30 (multiple scale) simultaneously operating model trains.

Schedule: Year round: daily, 10 a.m. to 6 p.m.

Admission/Fare: Adults $5.00; seniors/college students $3.50; children 3-18 $2.50; under age 3 are free; families $12.00 maximum. All day re-entry.

Locomotive/Rolling Stock: All eras from 1830s to present day represented by over 2,000 rotating model trains in operation.

Special Events: Special trains, displays, and discounts on all holidays.

Nearby Attractions/Accommodations: Busch Gardens, Mike's Trainland, Colonial Williamsburg, Army Transportation Museum, Marriott (2), Best Western, Holiday Inn, Ramada Inn, Hampton Inn (2), Quality Inn.

Location/Directions: I-64 exit 242A to route 60 east, next to Busch Gardens in the village shops at Kingsmill.

Site Address: 1915 Pocahontas Trail, Suite A4, Williamsburg, VA
Mailing Address: 1915 Pocahontas Trail, Suite A4, Williamsburg, VA 23185
Telephone: (757) 220-8725
Internet: www.trains.ontheline.com

ANACORTES RAILWAY
Train ride
18" gauge

THOMAS THOMPSON JR.

Description: The railroad offers one-mile scenic train rides from the historic Great Northern Depot to downtown Anacortes along the city's waterfront and tree-lined parkways. In operation since 1986, this family owned tourist line is one of the world's smallest narrow gauge passenger railways (as distinguished from a miniature railway). Turntables at each end rotate the locomotive for its return trip. Limited cab rides are allowed.

Schedule: June 12 through September 4: Saturdays 11:30 a.m. to 4:30 p.m. Frequent departures.

Admission/Fare: $1.50

Locomotive/Rolling Stock: Forney-type steam locomotive, rebuilt from a 1909 H.K. Porter compressed-air 0-4-0 mining locomotive, fueled with fir bark; four passenger cars. This train won the 1997 Preservation Award from the Tourist Railway Association.

Special Events: Waterfront Festival, May 15-16. Anacortes Arts and Crafts Festival, August 7-8. Depot Market, every Saturday.

Nearby Attractions/Accommodations: Maritime Museum, an art gallery in depot. Restaurant and motel at railways downtown terminal. Ferry to San Juan Islands and Victoria, British Columbia.

Location/Directions: 7th Street and R Avenue. Take R Avenue exit to narrow gauge railway crossing, turn right.

     Seattle, Everett and
Mt. Vernon, Burlington

Site Address: 7th Street and R Avenue, Anacortes, WA
Mailing Address: 5899 Campbell Lake Road, Anacortes, WA 98221
Telephone: (360) 293-2634
E-mail: anarail@GTE.net

CHELAN COUNTY HISTORICAL SOCIETY
PIONEER VILLAGE AND MUSEUM
Museum, display

CHELAN COUNTY HISTORICAL SOCIETY

Description: Visitors can see a caboose, dining car, ticket office, and section house, plus a pioneer village with over 20 furnished buildings and a historical museum.

Schedule: March through October: daily, 9:30 a.m. to 5 p.m. Closed Mondays.

Admission/Fare: Adults $3.00; seniors and students $2.00; children 5-12 $1.00; families $5 maximum; members free.

Locomotive/Rolling Stock: Great Northern wooden caboose X494; 1926 Pullman diner.

Special Events: Family Days, first Saturday of each month (free admission). Founders Day, last weekend in June. Apple Days, first weekend in October.

Nearby Attractions/Accommodations: Aplets and Cotlets Candy Kitchen tour, Ohme Gardens, Leavenworth's Bavarian Village, Chelan County Fairgrounds, North Central Washington Museum, Pewter Pot Restaurant, Cashmere Village Inn.

Location/Directions: Cashmere is located between Leavenworth and Wenatchee on Highway 2. Take Cotlets Way exit.

*Coupon available, see coupon section.

             M

Site Address: 600 Cotlets Way, Cashmere, WA
Mailing Address: PO Box 22, Cashmere, WA 98815
Telephone: (509) 782-3230
Fax: (509) 782-8905
E-mail: cchspvm@aol.com

**CHEHALIS-CENTRALIA
RAILROAD ASSOCIATION**
Train ride
Standard gauge

HAROLD BOROVEC

Description: A 14-mile, 1.25-hour round trip or a 19-mile, 1.75-hour round trip over former Weyerhaeuser trackage (former Milwaukee Road) from South Chehalis to Millburn or Ruth. The train passes through scenic rural farmlands and river valley. Select Saturdays feature dinner train added to Ruth trip.

Schedule: May 22 through September 6: weekends and holidays. Depart Chehalis–1 and 3 p.m. Ruth trip–Saturdays, depart Chehalis 5 p.m. Ruth dinner train requires reservations. Call for information.

Admission/Fare: Round trip–adults $7.00; children 4-16 $5.00. Ruth trip–adults $11.00; children $9.00.

Locomotive/Rolling Stock: No. 15, 1916 Baldwin 90-ton 2-8-2, former Cowlitz, Chehalis & Cascade, former Puget Sound & Cascade no. 200. This engine had been displayed for 30 years in a local park; restoration was completed in 1989 by Mt. Rainier Scenic Railroad shop and volunteers from Lewis County; Z-frame 40-foot wood boxcar used as shop/supply car, and more.

Location/Directions: Midway between Seattle, Washington, and Portland, Oregon. I-5 to exit 77. Turn west to first street south (Riverside Road). Proceed ¼ mile to Sylvenus Street. Turn left one block to railroad tracks.

*Coupon available, see coupon section.

Radio frequency: 161.385 and 160.635

Site Address: 1100 Sylvenus Street, Chehalis, WA
Mailing Address: 1945 S. Market Blvd., Chehalis, WA 98532
Telephone: (360) 748-9593

DAYTON HISTORIC DEPOT
Museum

DAYTON HISTORIC DEPOT

Description: Museum in historic 1881 depot building. Artifacts and memorabilia on display. Extensive photograph collection with copy service available.

Schedule: Year round: Tuesdays through Saturdays 9 a.m. to 5 p.m.

Admission/Fare: $2.00.

Special Events: Homespun Christmas, November 27-28.

Nearby Attractions/Accommodations: County Courthouse Tour, Historic Home Walking Tour, Lewis & Clark State Park, Patit Creek french restaurant. Weinhard Hotel a vintage Victorian hotel.

Location/Directions: Southeastern Washington, 30 miles from Walla Walla and 70 miles east of Tri-Cities. Located one block off Main Street, down 2nd Street.

        M

Site Address: 222 Commercial Street, Dayton, WA
Mailing Address: PO Box 1881, Dayton, WA 99328
Telephone: (509) 382-2026

Washington, Elbe

MT. RAINIER SCENIC RAILROAD
Train ride
Standard gauge

J. S. DAVID WILKIE

Description: A 14-mile, 1.5-hour round trip over a secluded right-of-way, over former Milwaukee Road trackage, on the south slope of Mt. Rainier. The train goes through farms, forests, and tree farms, over rivers and creeks, up hills and down. There is a 20-minute layover at Mineral Lake. Passengers may stay there to visit or picnic and return on a later train. The *Cascadian Dinner Train* makes a 4-hour round trip to Eatonville (26-mile trip), and offers a five-course prime rib dinner, prepared and served aboard a restored Union Pacific dining car and lounge/observation car.

Schedule: June 15 through Labor Day: daily. Memorial Day through September: weekends. Departures at 11 a.m., 1:15, and 3:30 p.m. Dinner train: spring and fall, 1 p.m.; summer, 5:30 p.m.

Admission/Fare: Adults $9.50; seniors $8.50; juniors 12-17 $7.50; children under 12 $6.50. Dinner train: $55.00. Reservations required.

Locomotive/Rolling Stock: A 1924 Porter 2-8-2 no. 5, former Port of Grays Harbor; a 1928 Climax 3-truck no. 10, former Hillcrest Lumber Co.; two commuter coaches; dining car, former Union Pacific; and many more.

Special Events: Christmas Train, first three weekends in December, Railfan Photo Specials, spring or fall weddings, charters, movies, commercials.

Location/Directions: Forty-two miles southeast of Tacoma on Highway 7.

P 🚌 ✳ ☕ 🍽 👤 🌲 🚂 ✉ TRAIN

🚆 Tacoma   **Radio frequency: 161.385 and 160.635**

Site Address: Highway 7, Elbe, WA
Mailing Address: PO Box 921, Elbe, WA 98330
Telephone: (360) 569-2588
Fax: (360) 569-2438
Internet: www.mrsr.com

Washington, Snoqualmie

NORTHWEST RAILWAY MUSEUM
Train ride, museum, display
Standard gauge

NORTHWEST RAILWAY MUSEUM

Description: Railway museum in and around the Snoqualmie Depot and train excursions between North Bend and Snoqualmie Falls. Heavyweight coaches are pulled by first generation diesels.

Schedule: Train–April through October: Sundays. May through September: add Saturdays. Museum–year round: Thursdays through Mondays. Hours are 10 a.m. to 5 p.m.

Admission/Fare: Train–adults $7.00; seniors $6.00; children 3-12 $5.00. Museum–no charge.

Locomotive/Rolling Stock: No. 201, Alco RSD-4 former Kennecott Copper Corp.; no. 1 Fairbanks H12-44 former Weyerhaeuser Timber Co.; no. 272 Barney and Smith combine, former SP&S; no. 1590 Pullman observation, former OWRR&NCO; no. 10 Alco Cook Rotary, former NP.

Special Events: Popsonus Father's Day Weekend, June 19-20. Railroad Days, July 31 and August 1. Santa Train, November 27-28 and December 4-5, 11-12.

Nearby Attractions/Accommodations: Snoqualmie Falls, hiking, Seattle.

Location/Directions: I-90, westbound exit 27 or eastbound exit 32.

Site Address: 38625 SE King Street, Snoqualmie, WA
Site Address: 205 McLellan Street, North Bend, WA
Mailing Address: PO Box 459, Snoqualmie, WA 98065-0459
Telephone: (425) 746-4025 or (425) 888-3030
Fax: (425) 888-9311

**YAKIMA VALLEY RAIL AND
STEAM MUSEUM**
Train ride, museum
Standard gauge

HAROLD K. CHANDLER

Description: This museum operates a tourist train on the former Northern Pacific White Swan branch line. Passenger excursions are 20-mile round trips from Harrah to White Swan. The 1911 former NP railroad depot in Toppenish serves as the museum and gift shop. The freight house has been converted to an engine house and the former NP section foreman's house is also adjacent to the depot.

Schedule: Museum–May through December: weekends 10 a.m. to 5 p.m. Train–September through October: Saturdays 10:30 a.m. to 4 p.m.

Fare/Admission: Museum–adults $2.00; seniors and children $1.00; families $5.00. Train–adults $8.00; children $5.00.

Locomotive/Rolling Stock: 1902 NP Baldwin 4-6-0 no. 1364; 1953 150-ton Alco no. B-2070, former U.S. Army; two 1920s P70 heavyweights, former PRR; 1947 NP coach no. 588; NH combination coach; 1907 NP wooden caboose.

Special Events: Halloween Run. Christmas Run with Santa, first two Saturdays in December.

Nearby Attractions/Accommodations: Over 50 murals by noted artists.

Location/Directions: Twenty minutes south of Yakima, Washington.

*Coupon available, see coupon section.

      M

Site Address: 10 Asotin Avenue, Toppenish, WA
Mailing Address: PO Box 889, Toppenish, WA 98948
Telephone: (509) 865-1911

YAKIMA ELECTRIC RAILWAY MUSEUM
Train ride
Standard gauge

DENNIS L. DILLEY

Description: A 90-minute round trip though city streets, past orchards, and along the Naches River and the shoulder of Yakima Ridge through Selah Gap, over a route established by the former Yakima Valley Transportation Company in 1907.

Schedule: May through mid-October: weekends and holidays. Depart Yakima–10 a.m., 12, 2, and 4 p.m. Depart Selah–11 a.m., 1, and 3 p.m.

Admission/Fare: Train–adults $4.00; seniors $3.50; children 6-12 $2.50; families $12.00. Charters available. Museum–donations appreciated.

Locomotive/Rolling Stock: Line Car "A," 1909 Niles 26-ton boxcab converted to line-car use in 1922 (in continuous service since 1909); freight motor no. 298, General Electric 50-ton steeple-cab; nos. 21 and 22, 1930 double-truck Brill Master Units that originally operated in Yakima from 1930 to 1947; nos. 1776 and 1976, single-truck Brill cars from Oporto, Portugal (the same type that operated in Yakima from 1907-1929); others.

Location/Directions: Passengers board at the Yakima Electric Railway Museum Shop at South 3rd Avenue and West Pine or at the Selah Terminal.

    M arm

Site Address: 306 W. Pine, Yakima, WA
Mailing Address: PO Box 649, Yakima, WA 98907
Telephone: (509) 575-1700
Fax: (509) 453-5088

CASS SCENIC RAILROAD STATE PARK
Train ride, dinner train, museum
Standard gauge

CASS SCENIC RAILROAD

Description: Cass Scenic Railroad is a state park that offers excursions powered by a steam driven locomotive. We have overnight accommodations with camping nearby.

Schedule: Regular season–May 29 through September 5: daily, 10:50 a.m., 1 and 3 p.m. Bald Knob tours–daily except Mondays, 12 p.m. Fall season–September 10-12, 17-19, 24-26 and October 21-24, and 28-31.

Admission/Fare: Adults $10.00 and up; children 5-12 $6.00 and up; under age 5 are free. Prices vary with event. Group rates available. Reservations recommended.

Locomotive/Rolling Stock: No. 2 1928 Pacific Coast Shay; no. 4 1922 70-C Shay; no. 5 1905 80-C Shay; no. 6 1945 150C Shay.

Special Events: Spring Railfan Weekend, May 21-23. Special Fall Color trips–October 1 18.

Nearby Attractions/Accommodations: Last Run Restaurant offers box lunches and more. Restored houses in park to accommodate groups of 2 to 10.

Location/Directions: State Route 28/92 between Dunmore and Green Bank in Pocahontas County, eastern West Virginia.

*Coupon available, see coupon section.

Site Address: Main Street, Route 66, Cass, WV
Mailing Address: PO Box 107, Cass, WV 24927
Telephone: (304) 456-4300 and (800) 225-5982
Fax: (304) 456-4641
E-mail: cassrr@neumedia.net
Internet: www.neumedia.net/~cassrr/

DURBIN & GREENBRIER VALLEY RAILROAD
Train ride
Standard gauge

DURBIN & GREENBRIER VALLEY RAILROAD

Description: This two-hour trip crosses Shavers Fork. Ride passes through Spruce to 4066-foot-high dramatic Big Cut Pass. Endless mountain vistas.

Schedule: May 27 through September 6: daily, except Tuesdays and Wednesdays, 10 a.m. and 2 p.m. September 30 through October 17: Fall Foliage. Weekends except November through March.

Admission/Fare: Adults $12.00; seniors $11.00; children $10.00; under age 4 are free.

Locomotive/Rolling Stock: 1982 220 hp diesel Leyland National R3 raibus.

Nearby Attractions/Accommodations: Monongahela National Forest, Seneca Rocks National Recreation Area, National Radio Astronomy Observatory, Cheat Summit Fort Civil War site.

Location/Directions: U.S. route 250, 38 miles south of Elkins and 20 miles north of Cass.

Site Address: East Main Street, Durbin, WV
Mailing Address: PO Box 44, Durbin, WV 26264
Telephone: (304) 456-4935
Fax: (304) 456-5246

COLLIS P. HUNTINGTON RAILROAD HISTORICAL SOCIETY, INC.
Train ride, museum

JEAN CHAPMAN

Description: Museum and rail excursion.

Schedule: Memorial Day through Labor Day: Sundays, 1 to 4 p.m. By appointment year round.

Admission/Fare: Donations appreciated.

Locomotive/Rolling Stock: C&O no. 1308 steam locomotive; two C&O coaches; C&O caboose; operating hand car; dome car; boxcar; and baggage car.

Special Events: Annual New River Train Excursions, October. One-day 300-mile round trips.

Nearby Attractions/Accommodations: Pilgrim Glass, Blenko Glass, Huntington Museum of Art, Radio Museum, CSX, NS main lines, Kentucky Highlands Museum, Greenbo State Resort Park.

Location/Directions: Excursions–7th Avenue and 9th Street. Museum–14th Street West and Ritter Park

*Coupon available, see coupon section.

Site Address: Excursions, 7th Avenue and 9th Street, Huntington, WV
Site Address: Museum, 14th Street West and Ritter Park, Huntington, WV
Mailing Address: PO Box 1252, Ashland, KY 41105
Telephone: (606) 325-8800
Fax: (606) 324-3218
E-mail: railtwo@aol.com

MOUNTAIN STATE MYSTERY TOURS
Train ride
Standard gauge

DIANA BISHOP

Description: Excursions of varying lengths to destinations with interactive theater on selected dates. Mystery adventure daytrips, overnights and weekends. Groups welcome.

Schedule: Year round. Call or write for information.

Admission/Fare: $99.00 to $399.00. Special Washington D.C., Chicago, or Cincinnati weekends $399.00 to $1199.00.

Locomotive/Rolling Stock: Modern Amtrak Superliner equipment.

Special Events: Sweetheart Express, February. Throw Mama On the Train, March-November. Outfitting Trains, March-October. West Virginia State Fair Trains, August. New River Fall Foliage, October. Santa Trains, December. Ski Train, January-February. Professional Baseball Trains, May-September.

Nearby Attractions/Accommodations: Camden Amusement Park, Huntington Museum of Art, Museum of Radio and Technology, West Virginia Heritage and Farm Museum, Beech Fork State Park, handmade-glass factory tours, Ohio River boat excursions, hotels and motels.

Location/Directions: Downtown Huntington, 10th Street and 8th Avenue. Call or write for specific directions.

Site Address: 1050 8th Avenue, Huntington, WV and other points
Mailing Address: PO Box 8254, Huntington, WV 25705-8254
Telephone: (304) 529-6412
E-mail: wvmystrain@aol.com

WEST VIRGINIA NORTHERN RAILROAD
Train ride
Standard gauge

BOB ROBINSON

Description: A 3-hour, 21.4-mile narrated round trip from Kingwood to the CSX interchange at Tunnelton, West Virginia. The train travels over the coal shipping route of the more-than-century-old West Virginia Railroad. The train proceeds through a switchback and a double switchback to climb 401 feet through woods to reach the 2220-foot summit. Travel through open fields, historic coal mining towns and Marion Curve. Half-hour layover at Tunnelton, where food is usually served.

Schedule: May through October: weekends and holidays, 11 a.m. and 3 p.m. October add weekdays.

Admission/Fare: Adults $12.00; children 3-12 $6.00. Charters available.

Locomotive/Rolling Stock: WVN no. 501946 EMD NW2 with SW1200 modifications; WVN no. 52 rare 1960 EMD SW1200 with factory installed dynamic brake.

Special Events: Fall Foliage Tours, October. Buckwheat Festival, last weekend in September. Nightmare Express, Halloween. Santa Claus Runs and more. Call for information.

Nearby Attractions/Accommodations: Pre-Civil War B&O tunnel, rafting on Cheat River.

Location/Directions: I-68, south on Route 26 to Kingwood, turn on Sisler Street at west edge of town.

Radio frequency: 161.250

Site Address: 156 Sisler Street, Kingwood, WV
Mailing Address: PO Box 424, Kingwood, WV 26537
Telephone: (800) 253-1065 and (304) 329-3333
Fax: (304) 329-2572
Internet: www.wvnr.com

West Virginia, Romney

POTOMAC EAGLE
SCENIC RAIL EXCURSIONS
Train ride
Standard gauge

DAVID W. CORBITT

Description: Diesel-powered, open-window coach train takes passengers on a 3-hour round trip through the beautiful West Virginia wilderness. Passengers ride the rails along the clear and tranquil waters of the Potomac River's South Branch and watch for American bald eagles that have returned to this remote valley and made it their home.

Schedule: May 8 through July 31: Saturdays, 1 p.m. August 1 through September 26: weekends 1 p.m. October 2 through October 10: weekends 10 a.m. and 2 p.m.; Mondays through Fridays 1 p.m. October 11 through October 24: weekends and Tuesdays through Thursdays 10 a.m. and 2 p.m.; Mondays and Fridays 1 p.m.

Admission/Fare: Coach–adults $20.00; seniors $19.00; children 3-12 $12.00. First Class Club Car $48.00-$50.00.

Locomotive/Rolling Stock: GP9s, former Baltimore & Ohio; F units, former CSX; 1920s open-window coaches, former CN; 1950s era lounge car, former C&O.

Special Events: All-day round trips to Romney/Petersburg, Railfan Days. Call or write for information.

Location/Directions: Train departs Wappocomo Station, 1.5 miles north of Romney on Route 28.

Site Address: Route 28, Romney WV
Mailing Address: Ticket Agent, 2306 35th Street, Parkersburg, WV 26104
Telephone: (304) 424-0736
Fax: (304) 485-5901
Internet: wvweb.com/www/potomac_eagle/

Wisconsin, East Troy

EAST TROY ELECTRIC RAILROAD
WISCONSIN TROLLEY MUSEUM

Train ride, museum
Standard gauge

SCOTT PATRICK

Description: The museum offers 10-mile round trip trolley rides over their original 1907 trolley line. The museum also offers elegant dinner train excursions on America's only all-electric dinner train in regular service. Photos, videos, and historic exhibits are on display in the museum's depot. The carbarn and trolleys are open for viewing.

Schedule: Trolleys May 29 through October 31: weekends and holidays, 11:30 a.m. to 4 p.m. June 16 through August 13: Wednesdays through Fridays, 11 a.m. and 1 p.m. Dinner trains–May 9, June 20, August 7, September 25, October 2, 16, 23, 30.

Admission/Fare: Trolley–adults $8.00; children 3-11 $4.00. Dinner train–$49.50.

Locomotive/Rolling Stock: CSS&SB 9, 11, 24, 35, 111; CTA S105, 4420, 4453; Duluth-Superior Streetcar 253; P&W 64; ETER 21; TMER&L 200, D23, L6, L8 and L9; CNS&MRR 228; Septa Pccs 2120 and 2185; TTC PCC 4617; WP&L 26 and TE-1.

Nearby Attractions/Accommodations: Located 45 minutes from Milwaukee and 30 minutes from Lake Geneva resort area. Elegant Farmer, Wisconsin's largest farm market. Several historic attractions, restaurants, two hotels, and a campground in East Troy area.

Location/Directions: I-43 and Highway 20, 35 miles southwest of Milwaukee.

Site Address: 2002 Church Street, East Troy, WI
Mailing Address: PO Box 556, Waukesha, WI 53187-0556
Telephone: (414) 548-3837
Fax: (414) 548-0400
Internet: www.easttroyrr.org

NATIONAL RAILROAD MUSEUM
Train ride, museum
Standard gauge

NATIONAL RAILROAD MUSEUM

Description: The museum offers a 20-minute train ride during the summer season in vintage rail equipment. During the ride a uniformed conductor describes the museum's history and the "way of the rails" as viewed through the eyes of a hobo. Year round the museum offers an exhibit hall, 70 pieces of rolling stock, 1500-square-foot HO model display and theater show. The museum was established in 1958.

Schedule: May through mid-October: daily, 9 a.m. to 5 p.m. Mid-October through mid-December: Mondays through Saturdays. Mid-December through April: Mondays through Fridays.

Admission/Fare: Adults $6.00; seniors $5.00; children 6-15 $4.00; families $18.00.

Locomotive/Rolling Stock: No. 4017 "Big Boy" 4-8-8-4, former Union Pacific; Eisenhower's World War II Command Train; Churchill's personal cars; AeroTrain; 1910 LS&I no. 24 2-8-0; PRR GG-1; and more than 60 other pieces of rolling stock.

Special Events: Railfest, June 24-27. Civil War reenactment, August. Haunted House and Train, October.

Location/Directions: Highway 41 or 172, Ashland Avenue exit, travel north to Cormier Avenue and east three blocks.

*Coupon available, see coupon section.

Site Address: 2285 S. Broadway, Green Bay, WI
Mailing Address: 2285 S. Broadway, Green Bay, WI 54304
Telephone: (920) 437-7623
Fax: (920) 437-1291
E-mail: staff@nationalrrmuseum.org
Internet: www.nationalrrmuseum.org

Wisconsin, Laona

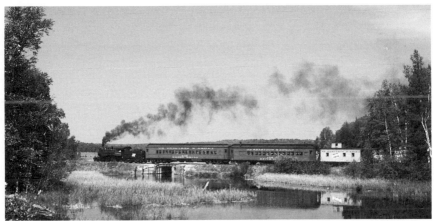

CAMP FIVE MUSEUM FOUNDATION, INC.

Description: Camp Five offers visitors a unique mix of history, steam railroading, and ecology. Visitors ride the *Lumberjack Special* steam train to the museum complex; once there, take a guided surrey tour through beautiful forests managed on a perpetual-cycle basis. A hayrack/pontoon ride on the Rat River is also an optional offer. Logging museum with an early-transportation wing and an active blacksmith shop; half-hour steam engine video; nature center with northern Wisconsin wildlife diorama; petting corral; large outdoor display of logging artifacts.

Schedule: Mid-June through August: Mondays through Saturdays: departures at 11 a.m., 12, 1, and 2 p.m.

Admission/Fare: Adults $14.00; students 13-17 $9.00; children 4-12 $4.75; families $38.00. Group discounts available.

Locomotive/Rolling Stock: 1916 Vulcan 2-6-2; cupola cabooses.

Special Events: Saturday Fall Color Tours, September 25 and October 2.

Location/Directions: West of Laona on Highway 8.

*Coupon available, see coupon section.

Site Address: Highway 8, Laona, WI
Mailing Address: RFD #1, Laona, WI 54541
Telephone: (715) 674-7400

ZOOFARI EXPRESS
MILWAUKEE COUNTY ZOO
Train ride
15" gauge

MIKE NEPPER

Description: This railroad has operated at the Milwaukee County Zoo since 1958, carrying over 13 million riders. The 1.25-mile trip across zoo property lasts about 8 minutes.

Schedule: May through September: daily 10 a.m. to 4 p.m. March, April, October: weekends 10 a.m. to 4 p.m.

Admission/Fare: Zoo admission required–adults $8.00; children 3-12 $6.00; parking $6.00. Train–adults $2.00; children $1.00.

Locomotive/Rolling Stock: Sandley light locomotive and rolling stock–coal-fired steam locomotive 4-6-2 no. 1924; coal-fired steam locomotive 4-4-2 no. 1916; diesel hydraulic switcher no. 1958; F2 diesel hydraulic no. 1996; 16 twelve-passenger day coaches nos. 1080-1096.

Nearby Attractions/Accommodations: Wisconsin State Fair Park, Summerfest Grounds, Milwaukee County Stadium, Milwaukee Public Museum, Mitchell Park Domes, Wehr Nature Center, Whitnall Boerner Botanical Gardens, Cool Waters Water Park, Best Western Midway, Holiday Inn Express, Sheraton Inn Mayfair, Excel Inn, many restaurants and area attractions.

Location/Directions: Zoo is located 8 miles west of downtown Milwaukee at the intersection of I-94, I-894, and Highway 45.

Site Address: 10001 W. Bluemound Road, Milwaukee, WI
Mailing Address: 10001 W. Bluemound Road, Milwaukee, WI 53226
Telephone: (414) 771-3040
Fax: (414) 256-5410
Internet: www.omnifest.uwm.edu/zoo/

NEW LONDON HISTORICAL SOCIETY

Description: Restored CNW depot complete with railroad artifacts.

Schedule: June through August: first and third Sundays, 1 to 4 p.m. or by appointment.

Admission/Fare: Donations appreciated.

Locomotive/Rolling Stock: Soo Line caboose no. 138; CNW caboose no. 11153.

Special Events: Rail Fest Days, second Sunday in August.

Nearby Attractions/Accommodations: Rainbow Restaurant, Mosquito Hill Nature Center, Memorial Park.

Location/Directions: Route 45 north to Business 45, High Street east to railroad tracks, north to the depot.

       M

Site Address: 900 Montgomery Street, New London, WI
Mailing Address: 612 W. Beacon Avenue, New London, WI 54961-1322
Telephone: (920) 982-5186 and (920) 982-8557

Wisconsin, North Freedom

MID-CONTINENT RAILWAY HISTORICAL SOCIETY
Train ride
Standard gauge

WILLIAM RAIA

Description: Mid-Continent, which has operated steam trains at North Freedom since 1963, is dedicated to preserving turn-of-the-century railroading. Its line and equipment are historic, all a part of the "golden age of railroading." The 7-mile, 50-minute "Experience 1900" round trip takes passengers on a former Chicago & North Western branch line built in 1903 to serve iron mines. Trains depart from a restored 1894 C&NW depot. The museum is nationally known for its wooden passenger and freight cars; restored equipment is displayed in the coach shed. The collection also includes locomotives, snow-plows (including a 1912 steam rotary), and steam wreckers. Artifact and photography exhibits are in the depot and the coach shed.

Schedule: Call or write for information.

Admission/Fare: Adult $9.00; seniors $8.00; children 3-12 $5.50; under age 3 are free. First class dinner train–fare $18.50; dinner $55.00.

Locomotive/Rolling Stock: No. 1385, 1907 Alco 4-6-0, former C&NW; no. 2, 1912 Baldwin 2-8-2, former Saginaw Timber; more.

Special Events: Snow Train, February 12-14. Autumn Color, October 1-3, 8-10. Santa Express, November 27-28.

Location/Directions: In Sauk County, seven miles west of Baraboo. Follow route 136 west to PF, then turn south to North Freedom. The depot is ½ mile west of the four-way stop in North Freedom.

Site Address: E8948 Diamond Hill Road, North Freedom, WI
Mailing Address: PO Box 358, North Freedom, WI 53951-0358
Telephone: (800) 930-1385
E-mail: midcon@baraboo.com
Internet: www.mcrwy.com

KETTLE MORAINE RAILWAY
Train ride
Standard gauge

R.M. HINEBAUGH

Description: The Kettle Moraine Railway offers a train ride back in time, when life was a little simpler. The train departs an 1889 refurbished depot making an 8-mile round trip, which takes approximately 50 minutes. This nostalgic ride behind a steam engine is both educational and recreational.

Schedule: June through September and Labor Day: Sundays, 12:30, 2:00, and 3:30 p.m. First four weekends in October: Saturdays, 12:30, 2:00, and 3:30 p.m. and Sundays, 11 a.m., 12:30, 2:00 p.m.

Admission/Fare: Adults $9.00; children 3-11 $5.00; under age three ride free unless occupying a seat.

Locomotive/Rolling Stock: 1917 65-ton Heisler no. 3, former Craig Mt. Railroad; 1943 Davenport gas powered 0-4-0 switcher no. 3.

Special Events: Goblin Express, first four Saturdays in October, 6:30 p.m. Call or write for information and dates.

Nearby Attractions/Accommodations: Holy Hill, Honey Acres, Hartford Car Museum, Old World Wisconsin.

Location/Directions: Nine miles north of I-94 on Highway 83 in North Lake.

*Coupon available, see coupon section.

         M

Site Address: Intersection of Highways 83 and VV
Mailing Address: Box 247, North Lake, WI 53064
Telephone: (414) 966-0516

OSCEOLA & ST. CROIX VALLEY RAILWAY
MINNESOTA TRANSPORTATION MUSEUM
Train ride
Standard gauge

MORT JORGENSON

Description: Enjoy the scenic St. Croix River Valley on a 90-minute round trip between Osceola, Wisconsin, and Marine-on-St. Croix, Minnesota, or a 45-minute round trip through rural Wisconsin between Osceola and Dresser. See the restored Osceola Historical Depot, featuring exhibits about railroading and the Osceola area. U.S. Railway Post Office exhibits aboard Northern Pacific triple combine no. 1102.

Schedule: Memorial Day through October: weekends. Charters available during the week.

Admission/Fare: Marine trip–$8.00 to $12.00; Dresser trip–$5.00 to $9.00.

Locomotive/Rolling Stock: Northern Pacific no. 328 4-6-0 steam locomotive; NP no. 105 LST&T switcher engine; nos. 2604 and 2608 cars, former Rock Island; NP triple combine car no. 1102; DL&W no. 2232 commuter coach.

Special Events: Romance on the Rails, June. Fireworks Express, July. Hi/Low Bridge Steam Trip, August. Fall Leaves Trip, September.

Nearby Attractions/Accommodations: Cascade Falls, St. Croix River Aveda Spa, St. Croix Center for the Arts, St. Croix Art Barn, Interstate Park, motels, and campgrounds.

Location/Directions: I-35W to Forest Lake, Highway 97 east to Highway 95, north to I-243 across the St. Croix River to Highway 35S, to Depot Road.

*Coupon available, see coupon section.

      M

Radio frequency: 161.355

Site Address: 114 Depot Road, Osceola, WI
Mailing Address: PO Box 176, Osceola, WI 54020
Telephone: (715) 755-3570
Fax: (715) 294-3330
E-mail: oscvrlwy@centuryinter.net
Internet: www.mtmuseum.org

**THE MINING MUSEUM AND
ROLLO JAMISON MUSEUM**

Train ride, museum

THE MINING MUSEUM AND ROLLO JAMISON MUSEUM

Description: The Mining Museum tells the story of lead and zinc mining in the Upper Mississippi Valley. Visitors tour an 1845 lead mine and ride (above ground) in converted ore cars pulled by a 1931 Whitcomb locomotive used in a local zinc mine.

Schedule: May through October: daily 9 a.m. to 5 p.m. November through April: Mondays through Fridays 9 a.m. to 4 p.m. Group tours available year round with appointment.

Admission/Fare: Adults $5.00; seniors $4.00; children 5-15 $2.00; under age five are free.

Locomotive/Rolling Stock: 1931 Whitcomb locomotive no. 13193.

Special Events: Heritage Day, July 4. Christmas exhibit including toy train layout.

Nearby Attractions/Accommodations: University of Wisconsin-Platteville. Chicago Bears training camp.

Location/Directions: Located at intersection of Main Street and Virgin Avenue, three blocks north of Highway 151.

Site Address: 405 E. Main Street, Platteville, WI
Mailing Address: PO Box 780, Platteville, WI 53818-0780
Telephone: (608) 348-3301
Fax: (608) 348-6098

RAILROAD MEMORIES MUSEUM
Museum, display, layout
G and HO

CARL SCHULT

Description: Historical, educational museum covering all aspects of rail-roading. Tools, equipment, track vehicles, memorabilia and history from the 1800s. Many station signs, books art and rare uniforms. Guided tours, videos, models. Eight large rooms full.

Schedule: Memorial weekend through Labor Day weekend: daily, 10 a.m. to 5 p.m. Groups by appointment.

Admission/Fare: Adults $3.00; children 6-12 $.50; under age 6 are free.

Special Events: Historical Railroad Days, June. Rodeo, July. Jack Pine Savage Days, August. Call 1-800-367-3306 for information.

Nearby Attractions/Accommodations: Namekagon Scenic River System, Bulik's Amusement Park, Museum of Wood Carving, Heart O' North Rodeo, State Fish Hatchery (largest musky hatchery in the world), lodging, restaurants.

Location/Directions: Easy access from Highways 53, 63 and 70. Downtown Spooner, corner of Walnut and Front Streets in CNW/CStPM&O Depot.

*Coupon available, see coupon section.

       arm

Site Address: Walnut & Front Streets, Spooner, WI
Mailing Address: N8425 Island Lake Road, Spooner, WI 54801
Telephone: (715) 635-2752 and (715) 635-3325

WYOMING TRANSPORTATION MUSEUM AND LEARNING CENTER
Museum, display

WYOMING STATE MUSEUM LIBRARY

Description: Transportation displays housed in the historic Union Pacific depot. Depot is under historical restoration.

Schedule: Year round: Tuesdays through Fridays, 10 a.m. to 3 p.m. and other times by appointment. Group tours available.

Admission/Fare: Free.

Special Events: Brewer's Festival, Father's Day weekend. Arts and Crafts Show, last full weekend in July.

Nearby Attractions/Accommodations: Capitol, Wyoming State Museum.

Location/Directions: I-80, Central Avenue exit to 16th Street.

Site Address: Capitol and 15th Street, Cheyenne, WY
Mailing Address: PO Box 704, Cheyenne, WY 82003-0704
Telephone: (307) 637-3376
Fax: (307) 634-9349

HERITAGE PARK HISTORICAL VILLAGE
Train ride
Standard gauge

HERITAGE PARK HISTORICAL VILLAGE

Description: Heritage Park is Canada's largest living historical village, where the past comes to life right in front of your eyes. We are a first-class summer tourist attraction and a year round catering and convention facility.

Schedule: May long weekend through Labor Day weekend: daily, 9 a.m. to 5 p.m. October through Canadian Thanksgiving: weekends and holidays only.

Admission/Fare: Call or write for information.

Locomotive/Rolling Stock: Two port steam 0-4-0T 1909 compressed air; 1902 no. 3 Vul Steam 0-4-0T; 1905 no. 4 CP CPR steam 0-6-0; 1942 no. 2023 USA ALCP steam 0-6-0; 1944 no. 2024 Lima Steam 0-6-0; 1949 no. 5931 CPR MLW steam 2-10-4; 1944 no. 7019 CPR 1 MLW S2 1000.

Special Events: Opening weekend in May. Festival of Quilts, May. Railway Days and Father's Day, June. Canada Day, July. Hayshaker Days and Heritage Family Festival, August. Old Time Fall Fair and Fall Harvest Sale, September. Call for information.

Nearby Attractions/Accommodations: Calgary Zoo, Olympic Park, Glenbow Museum, Fort Calgary, Alberta Science Centre.

Location/Directions: Follow Heritage Drive west.

Site Address: 1900 Heritage Drive SW, Calgary, AB
Mailing Address: 1900 Heritage Drive SW, Calgary, AB Canada T2V 2X3
Telephone: (403) 259-1900
Fax: (403) 252-3528
E-mail: heritage@heritagepark.org
Internet: www.heritagepark.ab.ca *or* www.heritagepark.org

FORT EDMONTON PARK
Train ride
Standard gauge

FORT EDMONTON PARK

Description: Nestled in Edmonton's river valley, Fort Edmonton Park is brought to life by costumed staff reenacting life as it was in Edmonton at the 1846 fur trading fort, and on the streets of 1885, 1905, and 1920. The train transports visitors through the Park.

Schedule: May 17 through September 7: daily, Sundays in September.

Admission/Fare: Adults $6.75; seniors and youth 13-17 $5.00; children 2-12 $3.25; families $20.00. Price includes train ride.

Locomotive/Rolling Stock: 1919 Baldwin 2-6-2 no. 107, former Oakdale & Gulf Railway (restored to its 1905 appearance).

Special Events: Call or write for information.

Nearby Attractions/Accommodations: Downtown Edmonton and West Edmonton Mall.

Location/Directions: Edmonton, Alberta.

Site Address: Fox Drive and Whitemud Drive, Edmonton, Alberta
Mailing Address: PO Box 2359, Edmonton, AB Canada T5J 2R7
Telephone: (403) 496-8787
Fax: (403) 496-8797
Internet: www.gov.edmonton.ab.ca/fort

ALBERTA PRAIRIE RAILWAY EXCURSIONS
Train ride, dinner train
Standard gauge

APST

Description: Round trip tours of several different types are featured from Stettler to a combination of rural lineside communities such as Big Valley, Castor, Halkirk and Coronation. Excursions are operated on a former Canadian National branch line through picturesque parkland and prairies in central Alberta and on a former Canadian Pacific branch line past Stettler to Coronation. All excursions include full-course roast beef dinner and on board entertainment and commentary. Fine dining excursions to Big Valley include a five-course meal and entertainment.

Schedule: Late-May through August: weekends and selected weekdays. September through mid-October: weekends. Fine dining–November through April, select dates.

Admission/Fare: Adults $59.00; seniors $55.00; youth $42.00; children $25.50. Fine dining–$75.00.

Locomotive/Rolling Stock: No. 41 1920 Baldwin 2-8-0, former Jonesboro Lake City & Eastern; no. 41, former Frisco; no. 77, former Mississippi; more.

Special Events: Murder Mysteries, Canada Day, Red Coat, Train Robberies.

Nearby Attractions/Accommodations: Ol' MacDonald's Resort, museum, golf, Rochon Sands Provincial Park.

Location/Directions: A two-hour drive from Edmonton or Calgary, one hour east of Red Deer in central Alberta.

Site Address: 4611 47 Avenue Stettler, AB
Mailing Address: PO Bay 800, Stettler, AB Canada T0C 2L0
Telephone: (403) 742-2811
Fax: (403) 742-2844
E-mail: apsteam@telusplanet.net
Internet: www.nucleus.com/heartland

CANADIAN MUSEUM
OF RAIL TRAVEL
Museum
Standard gauge

WALTER LANZ

Description: This static display portrays the elegant lifestyle aboard trains of the past. Plans call for five complete train sets, under cover. Several pieces for these future consists are now in storage. The centerpiece is an entire set of the Canadian Pacific Railway's 1929 "flag train," the *Trans-Canada Limited,* featuring restored inlaid woods, brass fixtures, plush upholstery, and wool carpets. The 1900-era Elko Station is the visitor center and gift shop. The dining car is often open for tea, coffee, and light refreshments.

Schedule: Summer: daily, 8 a.m. to 8 p.m. Winter: Tuesdays through Saturdays, 12 to 5 p.m.; shoulder seasons: daily 10 a.m. to 6 p.m.

Admission/Fare: Varies. Grand Tour tickets recommended.

Locomotive/Rolling Stock: "River Rouge" solarium lounge car; day parlor car no. 6751; sleepers "Rutherglen," "Glencassie," "Somerset"; dining car "Argyle"; baggage-sleeper car no. 4489; 1928 business car "British Columbia"; baggage car no. 4481, former CPR with HO train layout; more.

Special Events: School programs and Christmas Gala Dinners.

Nearby Attractions/Accommodations: Fort Steele Heritage Town, Bavarian City, Splash Zone Water Park, camping, lodging, restaurants.

Location/Directions: Downtown Cranbrook, Highway 3/95.

         arm

Site Address: 1 Van Horne Street, Cranbrook, BC
Mailing Address: Box 400, Cranbrook, BC Canada V1C 4H9
Telephone: (250) 489-3918
Fax: (250) 489-5744
E-mail: camal@cyberlink.bc.ca
Internet: www.cyberlink.bc.ca/~camal

BRITISH COLUMBIA FOREST MUSEUM
Train ride, museum
36" gauge

BRITISH COLUMBIA FOREST MUSEUM

Description: The British Columbia Forest Museum is located on 100 acres just north of Duncan. The train travels the circumference of the area, showing B.C. Forest heritage. There are also exhibits, demonstrations, and historical collections.

Schedule: May through September: daily, 9:30 a.m. to 6 p.m. First train departs at 10:30 a.m. and then every half hour.

Admission/Fare: Adults $8.00; seniors and students 13-18 $7.00; children 5-12 $4.50; under age 5 are free.

Locomotive/Rolling Stock: Shay locomotive no. 1.

Special Events: National Forestry Week, Mother's Day, Fords & Friends Picnic, Father's Day, Celebration of Steam Weekend, Labor Day Celebration.

Nearby Attractions/Accommodations: Duncan Totem Tours, Native Heritage Centre, Chemainus Murals.

Location/Directions: Located five minutes north of Duncan off Highway 1.

       M VIA

Site Address: 2892 Drinkwater Road, Duncan, BC
Mailing Address: RR4, 2892 Drinkwater Rd., Duncan, BC Canada V9L 6C2
Telephone: (250) 715-1113
Fax: (250) 715-1170
E-mail: bcfm@islandnet.com
Internet: www.bcforestmuseum.com

British Columbia, North Vancouver

BC RAIL, LTD.

Description: BC Rail offers a spectacular 80-mile, six-hour round trip to Squamish, including a two-hour stopover there. Heading the train is no. 2860, a stainless-steel-jacketed "Royal Hudson"; resplendent in polished maroon and black, it makes a fine sight at the head of its tuscan-red passenger train. The highly scenic route takes passengers along the coast of Howe Sound, where they view the island-dotted sea on one side and coastal mountains on the other. Passage available in standard class or parlor class (a restored vintage dining car). Train-boat option also available.

Schedule: May 30 through September 20: Wednesdays through Sundays, 10 a.m. departure.

Admission/Fare: Adults $47.50; seniors/youth $41.00; children $12.75; under age five are free. Parlor Class $85.00. Reservations required.

Locomotive/Rolling Stock: No. 2860, 1940 Montreal 4-6-4, former Canadian Pacific no. 3716, 1912 Montreal 2-8-0, former CP; power car, 11 coaches, two cafe lounge cars, two dining cars.

Location/Directions: Located at the foot of Pemberton Street, a 20-minute ride from downtown Vancouver.

*Coupon available, see coupon section.

 Vancouver

Site Address: 1311 West First Street, North Vancouver, BC
Mailing Address: PO Box 8770, Vancouver, BC Canada V6B 4X6
Telephone: (604) 631-3500 and (800) 663-8238
Fax: (604) 984-5505
E-mail: passinfo@bcrail.com
Internet: www.bcrail.com

British Columbia, Port Alberni

**WESTERN VANCOUVER ISLAND
INDUSTRIAL HERITAGE SOCIETY**
Train ride, museum, display
Standard gauge

BERT SIMPSON

Description: A 3-mile round trip along the industrial waterfront on MacMillan Bloedel Yard trackage and a historical display and gift shop in the restored 1912 Port Alberni Station.

Schedule: July 1 through Labor Day: weekends and statutory holidays, 11 a.m. to 4 p.m.

Admission/Fare: Adults $3.00; children $2.00.

Locomotive/Rolling Stock: No. 2, "Two Spot," 1912 Lima 42-ton 2-truck Shay; no. 7, 1928 Baldwin 90-ton 2-8-2 ST; no. 11, 1942 General Electric 45-ton diesel-electric; no. 1, 1928 Westminster Iron Works Buda gas switcher; no. 8427, Montreal Locomotive Works/Alco RS-3 diesel; no. 107 1927 Plymouth 8-ton gas switcher; more.

Rolling Stock/Equipment: Two modified cabooses, former Canadian National; early 1900s Victoria Lumber & Manufacturing Co. crew car.

Special Events: Grand Opening Parade of Locomotives and Vintage Trucks, July 1 weekend. Santa Claus Run, Sunday before Christmas.

Nearby Attractions/Accommodations: The station is the entrance to Harbour Quay, the departure point for the Lady Rose/Frances Barclay cruises down the Alberni Inlet to the Vancouver Island west coast.

Location/Directions: Harbour Quay in Port Alberni on Vancouver Island.

        M

Radio frequency: 160.305

Site Address: 3100 Kingsway Avenue, Port Alberni, BC Canada
Mailing Address: 3100 Kingsway Avenue, Port Alberni, BC Canada V9Y 3B1
Telephone: (250) 723-2118 station and (250) 724-0346 roundhouse

British Columbia, Prince George

FORT GEORGE RAILWAY
Train ride
2' gauge

FORT GEORGE RAILWAY

Description: One-half mile track.

Schedule: May 24 through Labor Day weekend: weekends and holidays, 12 to 4 p.m. Charters available.

Admission/Fare: $1.00; children under age 3 are free.

Locomotive/Rolling Stock: 1912 Steam engine built in Davenport, Iowa; two 25-seat coaches.

Nearby Attractions/Accommodations: City of Prince George.

Location/Directions: Fort George Park.

   VIA

Site Address: Fort George Park, Prince George, BC
Mailing Address: 101 Freeman Street, Prince George, BC Canada V2M 2P6
Telephone: (250) 564-4764

British Columbia, Prince Rupert

KWINITSA RAILWAY
STATION MUSEUM
Museum

KWINITSA RAILWAY STATION MUSEUM

Description: The Kwinitsa Railway Station Museum is housed in an authentic 1912 Grand Trunk Pacific Railway station. Several rooms are restored to their original state, including the telegrapher's office and living quarters, and the bunkroom for the section crew. This award-winning museum also features exhibits chronicling the early history of Prince Rupert and its role as the terminus of the Grand Trunk Railway. Videos depicting railway construction in 1911 and the operation of this and similar stations along the Skeena River complement the exhibits. In the old waiting room a small gift shop offers books on the railway and souvenirs. The scenic ocean-front location and the adjacent park make this an excellent place to visit.

Schedule: June through September 6: daily, 9 to 12 a.m. and 1 to 5 p.m.

Admission/Fare: Donations appreciated.

Nearby Attractions/Accommodations: Museum of Northern British Columbia.

Location/Directions: Located on the city of Prince Rupert's scenic waterfront at the western terminus of the CNR and Highway 16.

Site Address: Prince Rupert, BC
Mailing Address: PO Box 669, Prince Rupert, BC Canada V8J 3S1
Telephone: (250) 624-3207 and (250) 627-1915
Fax: (250) 627-8009

British Columbia, Squamish

**WEST COAST RAILWAY
HERITAGE PARK**
Train ride, museum
Standard gauge

WEST COAST RAILWAY ASSOCIATION

Description: See 65 cars and locomotives interpreting the history of railways in British Columbia. Miniature railway ride.

Schedule: May through October: daily, 10 a.m. to 5 p.m. Group tours year round and at other times by appointment.

Admission/Fare: Adults $4.50; seniors and students $3.50; families $12.00. Group rates available.

Locomotive/Rolling Stock: PGE no. 2 Baldwin 2-6-2 1910; CPR business car British Columbia 1890; Interurban sleeper Clinton 1923; BCE 960; BCE 941; CP 4069; locomotives; snow plows; cranes; cabooses.

Special Events: What's New Day, May 23. Canada Day, July 1. Mini Rail Day, August 29. Hobgoblin Express, October 31.

Nearby Attractions/Accommodations: Britannia Mines, Shannon Falls, windsurfing, rock climbing, Whistler Ski Resort.

Location/Directions: Highway 99, west on Industrial Way, follow signs to Government Road. One hour north of Vancouver.

Site Address: 39645 Government Road, Squamish, BC
Mailing Address: Box 2387, Squamish, BC Canada V0N 3G0
Telephone: (604) 898-9336 and (800) 722-1233
Fax: (604) 898-9349
Internet: www.wcra.org

British Columbia, Summerland

KETTLE VALLEY STEAM RAILWAY SOCIETY
Train ride
Standard gauge

DAVID WEST, WEST PHOTOGRAPHIC ARTS

Display: Take a 1.5-hour historic journey aboard the Kettle Valley Railway. Travel along cliffsides overlooking beautiful orchards and vineyards of the scenic Okanagan Valley while enjoying an historical narrative.

Schedule: May, June, September and October: weekends and Mondays 10:30 a.m. and 1:30 p.m. July and August: Thursdays through Mondays 10:30 a.m. and 1:30 p.m.

Admission/Fare: Adults $11.00; seniors/youth $10.00; children 4-12 $7.50; age 3 and under are free. Group rates available with reservation.

Locomotive/Rolling Stock: 1924 Shay no. 3 locomotive; two 1950 former BC Rail coaches; open air car; 1973 former CP Rail caboose.

Special Events: Great Train Robbery, BBQ, evening trains, Candy Express, Fall Color Tours, Sentimental Journey.

Nearby Attractions/Accommodations: Giants Head Mountain Park, Summerland Ornamental Gardens, Summerland Museum, Okanagan Lake Provincial Campground, Sunoka Beach. (Summerland is an old English theme with local festivals).

Location/Directions: Six km off Highway 97, 45 km south of Kelowna. Between Kelowna and Penticton.

*Coupon available, see coupon section.

         M

Site Address: 18404 Bathville Road, Summerland, BC
Mailing Address: PO Box 1288, Summerland, BC Canada V0H 1Z0
Telephone: (250) 494-8422
Fax: (250) 494-8452
E-mail: railway@summerland.com
Internet: www.railway.summerland.com

British Columbia, Surrey   **BEAR CREEK PARK TRAIN**
Train ride
15" gauge

DAVE PENN

Description: A ⅝-mile, 8-minute ride in Bear Creek Park's forest and gardens, through a tunnel and over a trestle.

Schedule: January through November: daily, 10 a.m. to dark. December: 10 a.m. to 10 p.m. for Christmas lights.

Admission/Fare: Adults $2.00; seniors and children $1.50. Group discounts available.

Locomotive/Rolling Stock: 1967 Dutch-built steam engine based on Welsh mining design; 1988 Alan Keef diesel locomotive; covered British antique coaches.

Special Events: Winterfest light display, December. Canada Day, July 1.

Nearby Attractions/Accommodations: Bear Creek Park is a 160-acre park with picnic facilities, art center, playground, water park, skate bowl, five-acre landscaped garden, walking trails, and sports fields.

Location/Directions: Twelve miles from U.S. border via King George Highway, 20 miles from downtown Vancouver.

Site Address: 13750 88th Avenue, Surrey, BC
Mailing Address: 13750 88th Avenue, Surrey, BC Canada V3W 3L1
Telephone: (604) 501-1232
Fax: (604) 507-2620

ROCKY MOUNTAINEER RAILTOURS
Train ride
Standard gauge

ROCKY MOUNTAINEER RAILTOUR

Description: Rocky Mountaineer Railtours is a two-day, all daylight train tour operating between May and October. Beginning in Vancouver, Calgary, Banff or Jasper, the train travels east- and westbound through the spectacular scenery of British Columbia, Alberta and the Canadian Rockies. All *GoldLeaf Dome* and *Signature Service* guests enjoy two days on board the Rocky Mountaineer, overnight accommodations in Kamloops, breakfast and lunch daily with exemplary service and magnificent views. This tour can be combined with a variety of independent package tours and customized group programs.

Schedule: Early May through mid-October: Sunday, Tuesday, Thursday departures.

Admission/Fare: Varies with trip and duration; call or write for rates.

Locomotive/Rolling Stock: Nos. 800, 804, 805, 806, and 807 General Motors GP40-2 locomotives. Passenger Cars–17 Dayniter 44-seat coaches, 1954 Canadian Car and Foundry, rebuilt 1972 and 1985-88; 20 cafe coaches; 48-seat no. 5749; 1949 Pullman, four 72-seat bi-level dome coaches; Rader Railcar.

Special Events: Winter Train 1999, December 14-15 and 22-23.

Site Address: 1150 Station Street, First Floor, Vancouver, BC Canada
Mailing Address: 1150 Station St., First Floor, Vancouver, BC Canada V6A 2X7
Telephone: (604) 606-7245 and (800) 665-7245
Fax: (604) 606-7250 reservations
E-mail: reservations@rkymtnrail.com
Internet: www.rkymtnrail.com

JOHN S. HIGH

Description: Static museum located on track 1 and 2 of VIA Rail Canada Station. Exhibits of CN and CP rolling stock, Greater Winnipeg Water District equipment, plus speeders and locomotives used in building Panama Canal, former Hudson Bay Smelting.

Schedule: June 1 through Labor Day: Fridays, Saturdays, Sundays, and holidays, 12 to 5 p.m. Winter hours: weekends and holidays, 12 to 4 p.m. weather permitting. Groups by appointment.

Admission/Fare: Free.

Locomotive/Rolling Stock: 1928 GE no. 93; 1909 Winnipeg Electric no. 356; 1911 Jordan spreader no. 51031; 1972 CN-PSC caboose no. 79553; more.

Special Events: Railroad Days, late September.

Nearby Attractions/Accommodations: The FORKS, downtown Winnipeg.

Location/Directions: VIA rail station, downtown Winnipeg.

      M VIA

Site Address: VIA Rail Station, Main and Broadway Streets, Winnipeg, MB
Mailing Address: RPO 48, VIA Rail Canada, Winnipeg, MB Canada R3C 1A3
Telephone: (204) 942-4632

SYDNEY & LOUISBOURG
RAILWAY MUSEUM
Museum

S&L RAILWAY HISTORICAL SOCIETY

Description: The S&L Railway Historical Society operates a three-building complex: the original 1895 station displaying railway artifacts; the original freight shed; and a new roundhouse. During the summer a Ceilidh (community party) is held with local musicians, singers and dancers, a mini-milling frolic, oatcakes, bannoch, and tea. A model railroad of the S&L line is being constructed in the freight shed.

Schedule: May, June, and September: daily, 9 a.m. to 5 p.m. July, August: daily, 8 a.m. to 8 p.m. Special tours by appointment.

Admission/Fare: Donations appreciated.

Locomotive/Rolling Stock: Two passengers cars, 1881 and 1914; boxcar; tankcar; caboose; small handcars.

Special Events: Heritage quilts on display in the roundhouse. Annual reunion, second Sunday of September. Ceilidhs at the roundhouse, July, August, September.

Nearby Attractions/Accommodations: Louisbourg Boardwalk at harbor, The Playhouse (designed after Shakespeare's Globe). Fortress Louisbourg, a 1744 reconstruction of French fortress. Motels, inns, motor home parks, campsites, restaurants, gift shops.

Location/Directions: On Main Street, which is a continuation of Route 22 as you come into town.

Site Address: Station Hill, Louisbourg, NS
Mailing Address: PO Box 225, Louisbourg, NS Canada B0A 1M0
Telephone: (902) 733-2720

CHATHAM RAILROAD MUSEUM SOCIETY
                                              Museum

GARY SHURGOLD

Description: This museum is located in a CN baggage car built in 1955. It was removed from active service in 1982 and was resurrected in its present form in 1989. This museum contains early railroad equipment such as switches, a caboose stove, several model trains, lanterns, and various other memorabilia used in Kent County by the men who made the trains roll.

Schedule: Summers: weekdays 9 a.m. to 5 p.m.; weekends 10 a.m. to 5 p.m. Group tours by appointment.

Admission/Fare: Donations appreciated.

Locomotives/Rolling Stock: CNR baggage car express no. 9626.

Special Events: Railroad Fun Days, call or write for information.

Nearby Attractions/Accommodations: Waterfront Weekends, all summer. Festival of Nations, July. Highland Games, July. Heritage Days, October. Chatham Cultural Centre, Chatham-Kent Museum, Thames Art Gallery, Wild Zone, Best Western Wheels Inn, Comfort Inn, Days Inn, Holiday Express Inn.

Location/Directions: The museum is located north of the 401 Highway on McLean Street, at the intersection of Queen and William Streets.

      M VIA

Site Address: 2 McLean Street, Chatham, ON
Mailing Address: PO Box 434, Chatham, ON Canada N7M 5K5
Telephone: (519) 352-3097

CNR SCHOOL ON WHEELS

Description: Allowing modern children and nostalgic seniors to visit one of the seven schools on wheels that taught children along the northern Ontario railways.

Schedule: May Victoria Day through Labor Day: Thursdays and Fridays 2 to 5 p.m.; weekends and holidays 1 to 5 p.m.

Admission/Fare: Free.

Locomotive/Rolling Stock: Canadian National 15089.

Nearby Attractions/Accommodations: Goderich Museum, Seaforta's Van Egmond original farmhouse, Stratford, Lake Huron and its attractions.

Location/Directions: Off Highway 4 near London, Ontario.

Site Address: Clinton, ON
Mailing Address: Box 488, Clinton, ON Canada N0M 1L0
Telephone: (519) 482-9583

Ontario, Cochrane

COCHRANE RAILWAY AND
PIONEER MUSEUM
Museum

COCHRANE RAILWAY AND PIONEER MUSEUM

Description: This museum preserves a 3-dimensional picture of the pioneer railway and homesteading days as a tribute to men and women who opened northern Ontario, an empire bigger than the territories of many United Nations members. A model train display aboard a former Canadian National coach introduces the main railway exhibits, which include a telegraph operator's corner, a ticket office, a document display, an insulator collection and uniforms. There is also a large varied display of photographs. Many of the pictures are from the large collection assembled by the Rev. W. L. Lawrence around 1912, for which the museum is now trustee. Also, in Train "Tim" Horton Memorial Museum is a display of hockey artifacts.

Schedule: June 29 through September 1: daily 11 a.m. to 7 p.m. Closed Thursdays.

Admission/Fare: Adults $2.00; seniors $1.00; students/children $1.50; families $4.00. Group rates available.

Locomotive/Rolling Stock: No. 137 2-8-0, former Temiskaming & Northern Ontario.

Special Events: Museum Days, August.

         M

Site Address: 210 Railway Street, Cochrane, ON
Mailing Address: PO Box 490, Cochrane, ON Canada P0L 1C0
Telephone: (705) 272-4361
Fax: (705) 272-6068
E-mail: 710029@can.net

KOMOKA RAILWAY MUSEUM
Museum
HO

KOMOKA RAILWAY MUSEUM

Description: Relive railroad history at this restored railroad station, letting your imagination run down the tracks as you examine early railway equipment. Take a few minutes to relax in air-conditioned comfort while watching multi-media presentations like "Workin on the Railroad."

Schedule: June through September: Saturdays 8 a.m. to 12 p.m. Sundays, Tuesdays through Fridays: 1 to 5 p.m.; Tuesday and Thursday evenings 7 to 9 p.m.

Admission/Fare: Adults $3.00; seniors and teens $2.00; youth $1.00. Group tours booked in advance $2.00 each.

Locomotive/Rolling Stock: 1913 Shay logging locomotive; 1939 CN baggage car no. 8731; 1972 GTW caboose no. 7919; collection of CN maintenance speeders.

Special Events: Museum Pancake Breakfast, April 17. Museum Toy and Hobby Show, October 17.

Nearby Attractions/Accommodations: Oriole Park Campground, Delaware Speedway, Little Beaver Restaurant, Cudney Homestead Bed and Breakfast, Komoka Provincial Park.

Location/Directions: Eight miles west of London on Glendon/ Commissioners Road. Follow highway signs on 402 Highway.

VIA

Site Address: 133 Queen Street, Komoka, ON
Mailing Address: PO Box 22, Komoka, ON Canada N0L 1R0
Telephone: (519) 657-1912
Fax: (519) 657-6791
E-mail: railmus@komokarail.ca
Internet: www.komokarail.ca

HALTON COUNTY RADIAL RAILWAY
Train ride
4'10⅞" gauge

J.D. KNOWLES

Description: Located on the right of way of the former Toronto Suburban Railway, Canada's first operating railway museum offers a 2-mile ride through scenic woodlands. More than 50 pieces of rolling stock from a variety of electric lines in Ontario. Visitors experience living history by touring our car houses and historically designated Rockwood Station.

Schedule: May, June, September, October, November: weekends and holidays. Last week of June through Labor Day: daily 10 a.m. to 5 p.m.

Admission/Fare: Adults $6.50; seniors $5.50; youth 3-18 $4.50. Discount rates available for groups of 4 or more.

Locomotive/Rolling Stock: No. 327, 1893 4-wheel open car (rebuilt 1933); no. 55, 1915 Preston single-truck closed car; no. 2894 1923 small Peter Witt Ottawa Car & Mfg. Co. Ltd.; London & Port Stanley no. 8 1915 interurban Jewett Car Co.; Montreal & Southern Counties no. 107 1912 interurban Ottawa; more.

Special Events: Special events held monthly; please call or write for more information.

Nearby Attractions/Accommodations: Niagara Falls, Toronto, Oakville.

Location/Directions: Highway 401 exit 312 (Guelph Line), travel north for 9 miles or Highway 7, south 3 miles via Wellington Road 44.

Site Address: 13629 Guelph Line, Milton, ON
Mailing Address: PO Box 578, Milton, ON Canada L9T 5A2
Telephone: (519) 856-9802
Fax: (519) 856-1399
E-mail: streetcar@hcry.org
Internet: www.hcry.org

Ontario, North Bay

HERITAGE RAILWAY COMPANY
Train ride
Narrow gauge

HERITAGE RAILWAY COMPANY

Description: This mini rail train ride is located in North Bay on the beautiful waterfront of Lake Nipissing. Also on site is an original CPR caboose.

Schedule: May through June and Labor Day through October 1: weekends. End of June through Labor Day: daily. Hours are 10 a.m. to dusk.

Admission/Fare: $1.00 per person.

Special Events: North Bay Heritage Festival and Air Show, first weekend in August.

Nearby Attractions/Accommodations: Chief Commander II Boat Cruise, North Bay Museum, Dionne Quints Museum, Model Railway Museum, Timber Train.

Location/Directions: Highway 11 to North Bay, then follow Lakeshore Drive to signs to waterfront. Highway 17 to North Bay, then follow signs to waterfront.

Site Address: 230 Memorial Drive, North Bay, ON
Mailing Address: 21 Cecelia Court, North Bay, ON Canada P1A 2S2
Telephone: (705) 495-8412 and (705) 497-1367
Internet: www.city.north-bay.on.ca/hrailco/htrain.htm

NATIONAL MUSEUM OF SCIENCE AND TECHNOLOGY
Museum, display

MALAK

Description: This museum features all types of transportation, from Canada's earliest days to the present time. On display in the Steam Locomotives Hall are four huge steam locomotives, a CNR narrow-gauge passenger car from Newfoundland, and a caboose. The visitors have access to two of the cabs, where sound effects give the feeling of live locomotives. The engines are meticulously restored, with polished rods and lighted number boards and class lights.

Schedule: Museum–May 1 to Labor Day: daily, 9 a.m. to 6 p.m. Fridays till 9 p.m. Labor Day through April: Tuesdays through Sundays, 9 a.m. to 5 p.m. Closed Mondays and Christmas Day. Train ride–July through August: Wednesdays and Saturdays.

Admission/Fare: Adults $6.00; seniors and students $5.00; children 6-15 $2.00; children under age 5 are free; family of 2 adults/2 children $12.00. Group rates available.

Locomotive/Rolling Stock: 1923 Shay steam locomotive; CN6400 4-8-4 Montreal 1936; CP926 4-6-0 1912; CP2858 4-6-4 Royal Hudson, Montreal 1938; CP3100 4-8-4 Montreal 1928; CNR business car Terra Nova; CNR 76109 caboose.

Location/Directions: Located ten minutes from downtown Ottawa. Queensway (Highway 417) exit St. Laurent south for 2.6 km, left at Lancaster Road (at the lighthouse).

Site Address: 1867 St. Laurent Blvd., Ottawa, ON
Mailing Address: PO Box 9724, Stn. T, Ottawa, ON Canada K1G 5A3
Telephone: (613) 991-3044
Fax: (613) 990-3654
E-mail: scitech@nmstc.ca
Internet: www.science-tech.nmstc.ca

PORT STANLEY TERMINAL RAIL
Train ride
Standard gauge

AL HOWLETT

Description: Three different rides, all from the station in Port Stanley, on the harbor next to the lift bridge. Trains pass over two bridges and northward for up to 7 miles through the Kettle Creek Valley. Port Stanley is a commercial fishing village on the north shore of Lake Erie. Equipment includes cabooses; heavyweight coaches; open coaches; baggage cars; boxcars; flatcars; hopper cars; a snowplow; tank cars; Burro cranes; and more. Ticket office and displays are in the former London & Port Stanley station. Open excursion cars; cabooses, former Canadian National, modified into enclosed coaches; standard coaches, former VIA. The "Little Red Caboose" can be chartered for birthday parties and other events with advance reservation.

Schedule: Year round: Sundays. May through November: add Saturdays. July through August: daily.

Admission/Fare: Adults $9.00/$11.00; children 2-12 $4.50/$5.50.

Locomotive/Rolling Stock: GE converted cabooses 25 and 44-ton.

Special Events: Easter, Teddy Bear, Santa, and Entertainment Trains.

Nearby Attractions/Accommodations: St. Thomas Elgin Railroad Museum.

Location/Directions: Located on the north side of Lake Erie, 25 miles (50 km) south of London, Ontario.

       Radio frequency: 160.575

Site Address: 309 Bridge Street, Port Stanley, ON
Mailing Address: 309 Bridge Street, Port Stanley, ON Canada N5L 1C5
Telephone: (519) 782-3730
Fax: (519) 782-4385
Internet: www.pstr.on.ca

FORT ERIE RAILROAD MUSEUM
Museum, display

FORT ERIE RAILROAD MUSEUM

Description: This museum displays railroad-related exhibits in two train stations, one built in 1910 and another built in 1873; also on display are maintenance-of-way equipment, a steam engine, a caboose, and a fireless engine.

Schedule: Victoria Day through Labor Day: daily 10 a.m. to 5 p.m. Labor Day through Thanksgiving (Oct. 11): weekends 10 a.m. to 5 p.m.

Admission/Fare: Adults $2.00; children under age 13 $.50.

Locomotive/Rolling Stock: No. 6218, former Canadian National 4-8-4; Porter fireless locomotive.

Nearby Attractions/Accommodations: Niagara Falls, Fort Erie Historical Museum, Battlefield Museum, Historic Fort Erie, Mahoney Dolls House, Willoughby Museum.

Location/Directions: On Central Avenue between Gilmore Road and Wintemute, northwest of the west end of the Peace Bridge.

Site Address: Central Avenue and Oakes Park, Ridgeway, ON
Mailing Address: PO Box 339, Ridgeway, ON Canada L0S 1N0
Telephone: (905) 894-5322
Fax: (905) 894-6851

Ontario, Sault Ste. Marie **ALGOMA CENTRAL RAILWAY INC.**
Train ride
Standard gauge

ELMER KARS

Description: We operate both tour trains and regular passenger service. Tour trains take you on a one-day wilderness excursion to Agawa Canyon Park. Regular passenger train provides service to Hearst, Ontario as well as access to a variety of wilderness lodges. Private car and camp car rentals available.

Schedule: Passenger service train–Year round. Agawa Canyon train–June through mid-October: daily. Snow train–January through mid-March: weekends. Group rentals available.

Admission/Fare: Varies, call for information.

Locomotive/Rolling Stock: Refurbished F9s; refurbished 1950s VIA coaches.

Nearby Attractions/Accommodations: Depot is located downtown close to hotels, restaurants, shopping.

Location/Directions: Located in downtown Sault Ste. Marie, minutes from International Bridge.

Site Address: 129 Bay Street, Sault Ste. Marie, ON
Mailing Address: PO Box 130, Sault Ste. Marie, ON Canada P6A 6Y2
Telephone: (705) 946-7300 and (800) 242-9287
Fax: (705) 541-2989
Internet: www.wclx.com

Ontario, St. Thomas

ELGIN COUNTY RAILWAY MUSEUM
Train ride
Standard gauge

GORD TAYLOR

Description: Walk through railway history when you visit this site. Several pieces of rolling stock inside 1913 MCRR shops. Also take in our "Railway Wall of Fame."

Schedule: Year round: Mondays, Wednesdays, Saturdays, mornings. May through September: add Sundays, 10 a.m. to 4 p.m.

Admission/Fare: Donations appreciated.

Locomotive/Rolling Stock: Hudson steam locomotive no. 5700; Wabash no. 51; CP no. 8921; L&PS L1 electric Pullman sleeper; more.

Special Events: Railway Nostalgia Weekend, first weekend in May. Railway Heritage Weekend, fourth weekend in August.

Nearby Attractions/Accommodations: Dalewood Conservation Area, Hawk Cliff, Super 8 Motel, New Elgin Motel.

Location/Directions: Exit 401 at Wellington Road South (London). Highway 3 bypass, exit bypass at First Avenue, then south to Wellington Street.

Site Address: Wellington Street, St. Thomas, ON
Mailing Address: RR #6, St. Thomas, ON Canada N5P 3T1
Telephone: (519) 631-0936
E-mail: sjbecrm@elgin.net
Internet: www.elgin.net/ecrm.shtml

SMITH FALLS RAILWAY MUSEUM
Museum
Standard gauge

SMITH FALLS RAILWAY MUSEUM

Description: Museum devoted to eastern Ontario railway, exhibits and equipment.

Schedule: July through August: daily 10 a.m. to 4 p.m. September through June: by appointment.

Admission/Fare: Adults $4.00; seniors/students $2.50; children age 12 and under are free.

Locomotive/Rolling Stock: CP S-3 no. 6591; CN 4-6-0 no. 112; CP M-260; CP M-297; CN combine no. 7195.

Special Events: Annual Jigger Festival, first weekend in August.

Nearby Attractions/Accommodations: Hershey Chocolate Factory, Heritage House Museum.

Location/Directions: Provincial Highway 15 from Kingston and Ottawa. Highway 29 from Brockville.

Site Address: 90 William Street W., Smith Falls, ON
Mailing Address: PO Box 962, Smith Falls, ON Canada K7A 5A5
Telephone: (613) 283-5696

Ontario, Toronto

POLAR BEAR EXPRESS
Train ride

POLAR BEAR EXPRESS

Description: One of the great rail excursions left in the world. The Polar Bear Express operates every summer between Cochrane and Moosonee on the James Bay Coast. Various 3, 4 or 5 day packages available.

Schedule: Late-June through Labor Day: depart Cochrane 0830, arrive Moosonee 1250. Depart Moosonee 1800, arrive Cochrane 2205.

Admission/Fare: Adults $46.00; seniors $35.00; children 5-11 $23.00; under age 5 are free; families $115.00.

Nearby Attractions/Accommodations: Cochrane Station Inn and Restaurant, Gold Mine tour, Timmins, Hunta Museum.

Location/Directions: Highway 11 north.

Site Address: Cochrane, ON
Mailing Address: 65 Front Street W., Toronto, ON Canada M5J 1E6
Telephone: (416) 314-3750 and (800) 268-9281
E-mail: busrail@ontc.on.ca
Internet: www.ontc.on.ca

SOUTH SIMCOE RAILWAY
Train ride, museum
Standard gauge

CHARLES BRYANT

Description: Travel back in time aboard South Simcoe Railway's historic turn-of-the-century steam train on a scenic journey through the Beeton Creek valley. Steam powered heritage railway. Operating railway museum.

Schedule: May 16 through October, Thanksgiving Day weekend (October 11 Canada) and December Santa Trains. May, June, November: weekends 10:30 and 11:30 a.m., 1, 2, 3, p.m. July, October: add Wednesdays-Fridays 10:30 and 11:30 a.m., 1, 2, 3, p.m. and weekends add 4 p.m. December: weekends 10, 11:30 a.m., 1:30 and 3 p.m.

Admission/Fare: Adults $10.00; seniors $9.00; children $6.50. Group rates for 20 or more.

Locomotive/Rolling Stock: Rogers no. 136 4-4-0 former CPR; CLC no. 1057 4-6-0 former CPR; vintages coaches and combine 1924-1929.

Special Events: Color Tour, fall. Santa Special, December weekends.

Nearby Attractions/Accommodations: Falconry Centre, Children's Petting Farm, conservation parks, convention centre, restaurants.

Location/Directions: Highway 400, exit 55 west 9 miles to Tottenham.

Site Address: Mill Street West, Tottenham, ON
Mailing Address: Box 186, Tottenham, ON Canada L0G 1W0
Telephone: (905) 936-5815
Fax: (905) 936-1057
E-mail: info@steamtrain.com
Internet: www.steamtrain.com

Ontario, Uxbridge/Stouffville

YORK DURHAM
HERITAGE RAILWAY
Train ride
Standard gauge

JOHN SKINNER, EAGLE VISION PHOTOGRAPHY

Description: See the newly restored 90-year-old Uxbridge Station with the unique "witch's hat" design. Inside the station is the railway's gift shop and museum. Displays include old photos and railway memorabilia.

Schedule: Victoria Day weekend through Canadian Thanksgiving. Uxbridge departures–10 a.m. and 2 p.m. Stouffville departures–11:30 a.m. and 3:30 p.m. Schedule subject to change.

Admission/Fare: Call or write for information.

Locomotive/Rolling Stock: RS18 3612; RS3 1310; Cafe car 3209; Cafe car 3232; baggage car 9636; former CN 4977; former CN 4960; wooden box car, former CN.

Special Events: Christmas in July, July 25. Father's Day. Halloween Special, week before Halloween Fall Color Trips.

Nearby Attractions/Accommodations: Stouffville–Strawberry Festival, Sales Barn. Uxbridge–Uxbridge Scott Museum, Foster Memorial, Lucy Maude Montgomery Interpretive Centre, Fall Fair.

Location/Directions: Uxbridge Station is located on Railway Lane off Brock Street in Uxbridge. From downtown Toronto take the Don Valley Parkway to 404, exit east on Stouffville side road. Stouffville Station is located on this road, which turns into Main Street in Stouffville. Approximately 35 minutes from Toronto.

Site Address: Uxbridge and Stouffville, ON
Mailing Address: PO Box 462, Stouffville, ON L4A 7Z7 Canada
Telephone: (905) 852-3696
Fax: (905) 852-5860
E-mail: kendra@ican.net
Internet: webhome.indirect.com/~gfergie

Quebec, Hull

**HULL-CHELSEA-WAKEFIELD
STEAM TRAIN**
Train ride
Standard gauge

MALAK

Description: Scenic rail tour on board a 1907 steam train from Hull to picturesque Wakefield, Quebec. Located only minutes from Ottawa's downtown and all other major attractions. On board bilingual tour guides and professional musical entertainers throughout the journey. Licensed concession and seat service in spacious, comfortable air-conditioned coaches. The exclusive Sunset Dinner Train offers a fine-dining experience with exceptional service. Enjoy spectacular fall foliage excursions.

Schedule: May 8 through October 17.

Admission/Fare: Adults $26.00; children $12.00; dinner train $59.00.

Locomotive/Rolling Stock: 1907 class 2-8-0 Swedish steam; 8-passenger coach; restaurant car; five diners.

Special Events: Sunset Dinner Train, featuring exquisite French cuisine and live entertainment.

Nearby Attractions/Accommodations: City of Ottawa, national museums, major hotels, Hull Casino.

Location/Directions: Highway 5 north exit Casino Blvd. One mile from Hull Casino.

Site Address: 165 Deveault Street, Hull, PQ
Mailing Address: 165 Deveault Street, Hull, PQ Canada J8Z 1S7
Telephone: (819) 778-7246 and (800) 871-7246
Fax: (819) 778-5007
Internet: www.steamtrain.ca

CANADIAN RAILWAY MUSEUM
Museum
Standard gauge

KEVIN ROBINSON

Description: Discover the golden era of railways, its brutish workhorses, its lightfooted fillies, and its fiery magnificent queens. Take a ride in the Museum's streetcar, one of the last to run in the streets of Montreal. A collections of more than 130 railway vehicles, one of North America's best, awaits you at the Canadian Railway Museum at Delson/St. Constant. Enjoy demonstrations of John Molson steam locomotive or the Sunday train rides.

Schedule: May 2 through September 6: daily, 9 a.m. to 5 p.m. Weekends and holidays to October 17.

Admission/Fare: Adults $6.00; seniors $5.00; students 13-17 $3.50; children 5-12 $3.00.

Special Events: Murder Mystery Evening, July. Model Train Show, August. Diesel Weekend, September. Please confirm.

Location/Directions: Highway 15 exit 42, Route 132 west to Chateauguay, left at fifth light, Route 209 south.

Site Address: 122A Saint-Pierre Street, Saint-Constant, PQ
Mailing Address: 120 rue Saint-Pierre, Saint-Constant, PQ Canada J5A 2G9
Telephone: (450) 632-2410 information and (514) 638-1522 administration
Fax: (450) 638-1563
E-mail: mfcd@globetrotter.gc.ca

BRENT HUME

Description: A museum depicting pioneer life in Saskatchewan includes a 1943 CPR caboose, a CN motor car, a CN tool shed, a 1905 one-room country school and a display of pioneer agriculture machinery.

Schedule: June 6 to Labor Day: daily 10 a.m. to 5 p.m.

Admission/Fare: Adults $2.00; students $1.00; preschoolers are free.

Special Events: Opening day, June 6.

Nearby Attractions/Accommodations: White Bear Lake, Skyline Motor Inn, Bear Claw Casino, Moose Mountain Provincial Park, waterslides, golf courses, swimming pool, tennis courts.

Location/Directions: At the junction of Highways 9 and 13, approximately 60 miles north of the U.S. border, and 40 miles west of the Manitoba border.

     M

Site Address: Railway Avenue, Carlyle, SK
Mailing Address: Box 840, Carlyle, SK Canada S0C 0R0
Telephone: (306) 453-2266

WESTERN DEVELOPMENT MUSEUM

Description: History of transportation museum with displays of artifacts from rail, land, air, and water transportation.

Schedule: April through December: daily 9 a.m. to 6 p.m. January through March: closed Mondays.

Admission/Fare: Adults $5.00; seniors/students 13-18 $4.00; children 6-12 $1.75; age 5 and under are free.

Locomotives/Rolling Stock: Vulcan 0-4-0 no. 2265; DS-6F no. 6555; G20 no. 2634; combination no. 3321; CPR coach no. 95; CPR caboose no. 6139; 1934 inspectors Buick M-499.

Special Events: May 20 through Labor Day: weekends and holidays, Shortline Railway 1914 Vulcan runs on museum grounds.

Nearby Attractions/Accommodations: Museum, historic sites, camping, motels, variety of cultural and sporting events.

Location/Directions: Junction of Highways 1 and 2.

Site Address: 50 Diefenbaker Drive, Moose Jaw, SK
Mailing Address: Box 185, Moose Jaw, SK Canada S6H 4N8
Telephone: (306) 693-5989
Fax: (306) 691-0511

Saskatchewan, Saskatoon   **SASKATCHEWAN RAILWAY MUSEUM**
Museum
Standard gauge

SASKATCHEWAN RAILWAY MUSEUM

Description: Seven acres of railway buildings and rolling stock. Museum houses small artifacts and a library.

Schedule: Mid-May through June 30 and September: weekends and holidays, 1 to 6 p.m. July through August: add Wednesdays, Thursdays and Fridays. Other times by appointment.

Admission/Fare: Adults $2.00; children under age 16 $1.00; under age 6 are free. Group rates available.

Locomotive/Rolling Stock: CP S-3 no. 6568; caboose no. 434044; no. 434102; sleeping car Kinkella; snow plow no. 400657; wash car no. 412718; CN caboose no. 78687; no. 79282; boxcar no. 428980; no. 524418; flatcar no. 57519; no. 59039; GE 23-ton 800-010; UTLX tank car no. 14532; Sask Power generator car; SMR streetcar no. 51; no. 203.

Nearby Attractions/Accommodations: City of Saskatoon, hotels, camping, Western Development Museum, Pike Lake Provincial Park.

Location/Directions: Approximately 4 km southwest of Saskatoon, on Highway 7, then 2 km south on Highway 60.

        M   VIA

Site Address: Highway 60, Pike Lake Road, Saskatoon, SK
Mailing Address: Box 19, Site 302, RR 3, Saskatoon, SK Canada S7K 3J6
Telephone: (306) 382-9855
E-mail: cal.sexsmith@crty.saskatoon.sk.ca

Other Tourist Railroads and Museums

These are additional sites that may be of interest to you. We are unable to provide complete information, so be sure to write or call for details.

Alabama, Calera
Heart of Dixie Railroad Museum
PO Box 727, Calera, AL 35040
(205) 668-3435

Arizona, Chandler
Arizona Railway Museum
PO Box 842, Chandler, AZ 85224
(602) 821-1108

California, Anaheim
Disneyland Railroad
PO Box 3232, Anaheim, CA 92803
(714) 999-4565

California, Point Richmond
Golden State Model Railroad Museum
900-A Dornan Dr., Point Richmond, CA 94801
(510) 234-4884

California, San Jose
Kelley Park Trolley
1600 Senter Rd., San Jose, CA 95112
(408) 277-3890

California, Yreka
Yreka Western Railroad
PO Box 660, Yreka, CA 96097
(916) 842-4148

Colorado, Denver
Forney Historic Trans. Museum
1416 Platte St., Denver, CO 80202
(303) 433-3643

Colorado, Grand Junction
Rio Grande Chapter NRHS
PO Box 3381, Grand Junction, CO 81504
(970) 434-9814

Connecticut, Essex
North Cove Express Dinner Train
176 Laning St., Southington, CT 06489
(860) 628-0803

Florida, Orlando
Florida Central Railroad Adventure Dinner Train
PO Box 967, Plymouth, FL 32768
(407) 889-7005

Idaho, Cascade
Idaho Historical Railroads, Inc.
PO Box 1039, Cascade, ID 83611
(208) 382-RAIL

Illinois, Rockford
Trolley Car 36
324 N. Madison St., Rockford, IL 61107
(815) 987-8894

Illinois, Waterman
Waterman & Western Railroad
PO Box 217, Waterman, IL 60556
(815) 264-7800

Maine, Fort Fairfield
Fort Fairfield Railroad Museum,
Box 269, Fort Fairfield, ME 04742
(207) 473-4045

Massachusetts, Holyoke
Holyoke Heritage Park Railroad, Inc.
221 Appleton St., Holyoke, MA 01040
(413) 534-1723

Massachusetts, Lowell
Lowell National Historical Park
67 Kirk St., Lowell, MA 01852
(978) 970-5000

Michigan, Chesaning
Chesaning Central & Owosso Railroad
PO Box 143, Chesaning, MI 48616
(517) 845-5448

Michigan, Clinton
Southern Michigan Railroad Society
PO Box K, Clinton, MI 49236-0009
(517) 456-7677

Michigan, Elberta
Soc. for the Preservation S.S. City of Milwaukee
PO Box 506, Beulah, MI 49617
(616) 882-4600

Minnesota, St. Paul
Twin City Model Railroad Museum
1021 Bandana Blvd. E., St. Paul, MN 55108
(612) 647-9628

Missouri, St. Louis
Holiday Crusin' Rails/Canadian Sunset Rails
3621 NW 43rd, Oklahoma City, OK 73112
(405) 942-2222

Nebraska, Goehner
Chippewa Northwestern Railway Co.
PO Box 6837, Lincoln, NE 68506
(402) 489-4458

Nebraska, Omaha
Union Pacfic Collection
1416 Dodge, Omaha, NE 68179
(402) 271-3305

New York, Greenport and Riverhead
Railroad Museum of Long Island
PO Box 726, Greenport, NY 11944
(516) 477-0439

New York, Manchester
Lehigh Valley Railroad and Historical Society
PO Box RR, Manchester, NY 14504

New York, Syracuse
New York, Susquehanna & Western Railway Corp.
PO Box 1245, Syracuse, NY 13201
(800) FOR TRAIN

North Carolina, Hamlet
National Railroad Museum and Hall of Fame
2 Main Street, Hamlet, NC 28345

Ohio, Bellevue
Mad River & NKP Railroad Society
233 York St., Bellevue, OH 44811
(419) 483-2222

Okalahoma, Choctaw
Choctaw Caboose Museum
2701 N. Triple XXX Rd, Choctaw, OK 73020
(405) 390-2771

Pennsylvania, Greenville
Greenville Railroad Park and Museum
314 Main St., Greenville, PA 16125
(412) 588-4009

Pennsylvania, Lehighton
Pocono Museum Unlimited
517 Ashtown Dr., Lehighton, PA 18235
(717) 386-3117

Pennsylvania, Middletown
Middletown & Hummelstown Railroad
136 Brown St., Middletown, PA 17057
(717) 944-4435

Pennsylvania, Reading
Reading Company Technical and Historical Society
PO Box 15143, Reading, PA 19612
(610) 372-5513

Pennsylvania, Titusville
Oil Creek & Titusville Railroad
PO Box 68, Oil City, PA 16301
(814) 676-1733

Tennessee, Chattanooga
Lookout Mountain Incline Railway
827 East Brow Rd., Lookout Mountain, TN 37350
(423) 821-4224

Texas, Dallas
McKinney Ave. Transit Authority
3153 Oak Grove Ave., Dallas, TX 75204
(214) 855-0006

Texas, Houston
Gulf Coast Railroad Museum
PO Box 457, Houston, TX 77001
(713) 631-6612

Vermont, Middlebury
Vermont Rail Excursions
PO Box 243, Middlebury, VT 05753
(800) 707-3530

Washington, Carnation
Remlinger Farms Railroad
PO Box 177, Carnation, WA 98014
(425) 333-4135

Washington, Friday Harbor
Model Train Museum
PO Box 4372, Friday Habor, WA 98250
(360) 378-3061

Washington, Renton
Spirit of Washington Dinner Train
PO Box 835, Renton, WA 98057
(206) 227-RAIL

West Virginia, Harpers Ferry
Harpers Ferry Toy Train Museum/Joy Line Railroad
Route 3, Box 315, Harpers Ferry, WV 25425
(304) 535-2521

Wisconsin, Eau Claire
Chippewa Valley Railroad Association
PO Box 925, Eau Claire, WI 54702
(715) 835-1411

Wisconsin, Spooner
Wisconsin Great Northern Railroad
PO Box 46, Spooner, WI 54801
(888) 390-0412

Wisconsin, Wisconsin Dells
Riverside & Great Northern Railway
N115 County Road N, Wisconsin Dells, WI 53965
(608) 254-6886

British Columbia, Fort Steele
East Kootenay Railway
Fort Steele Heritage Town, Ft. Steele, BC V0B 1N0
(250) 489-3351

British Columbia, Prince George
Prince George Railway & Forestry Museum
PO Box 2408, Prince George, BC V2N 2S6
(250) 563-7351

British Columbia, Revelstoke
Revelstoke Railway Museum
PO Box 3018, Revelstoke, BC V0E 2S0
(250) 837-3732

British Columbia, West Vancouver
Transit Museum Society, c/o BC Transit
949 W. 41st Ave., Vancouver, BC V5Z 2N5
(604) 325-9990

Ontario, Waterloo
Waterloo-St. Jacobs Railway
Box 40103, Waterloo Sq. PO, Waterloo, ON N2J 4V1
(800) 754-1054

Y

Z